AFRICAN WOMEN

AFRICAN WOMEN

A Historical Panorama

PATRICIA W. ROMERO

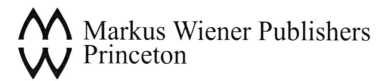

Markus Wiener Publishers
Princeton

Cover illustration: Women hawking fish on the Atlantic seafront, St. Louis,
Senegal (from the photo archives of Patricia W. Romero).

For information, write to:
Markus Wiener Publishers
231 Nassau Street, Princeton, NJ 08542
www.markuswiener.com

Library of Congress Cataloging-in-Publication Data

Romero, Patricia W., author.
  African women : a historical panorama / Patricia W. Romero.
  pages cm
  Includes bibliographical references.
  ISBN 978-1-55876-575-7 (hardcover : alk. paper)
  ISBN 978-1-55876-576-4 (pbk. : alk. paper)
  1. Women—Africa—History. 2. Women—South Africa—History.
3. Women—Africa—Social conditions. 4. Women—South Africa—Social
conditions. 5. Women and war—Africa—History. 6. Imperialism—Social
aspects—Africa. I. Title.
  HQ1787.R65 2014
  305.4096—dc23
  2014012276

Markus Wiener Publishers books are printed in the United States of America
on acid-free paper and meet the guidelines for permanence and durability of
the Committee on Production Guidelines for Book Longevity of the Council
on Library Resources.

For Tyler, Ryan, Julia, and Stephen (Toto)

Contents

Acknowledgments

My debts to friends and colleagues are many. The first person to single out is Franklin Knight, who invited me to join the Johns Hopkins Center for Africana Studies in the fall of 2011; knowing my publishing interests, he suggested I introduce a course on "Women in African History." My next debt is to the students in the first of these classes, in the spring 2012 semester. It was while teaching them that I comprehended the void in the pre-modern narrative history regarding African women.

A caveat is in order: several excellent studies on African women have been produced by major historians, and I have drawn on all of them with gratitude. But I wished to produce a different type of book—one that would involve case studies and personalize some of the leading women who have made contributions to African history. No single volume can do justice to the vast numbers of women or events that embraced them; thus, what is included here is representative rather than inclusive. Due to the magnitude of a project of this type, I turned to Barbara Callaway, then at Rutgers University, whose work has primarily centered on women in West Africa, with the proposition that we co-author what eventually developed into this book. Callaway's agreement was retracted soon thereafter when her husband's illness spiraled into a steep decline, sadly leading to his death in January 2013. She turned from co-author to caretaker, formally withdrawing from the project but nevertheless staying involved throughout. Callaway wrote the sections on the West African queens in Chapter One; and she has critically read and offered extended commentary on, as well as revisions to, all the chapters except Chapter 8. For that chapter, I turned to another dear friend, who also happens to be my son, Jeffrey. He experienced Africa first as a teacher in Kenya and later as a student of anthropology at Yale. Through the years, Jeff has served not only as stalwart supporter but also as critic and copyeditor for almost all of my books. In this case, he also put me in touch with his brother-in-law, Jean de Dieu Bizimana, who generously provided me with two useful studies, including the case studies detailing sexual violence in eastern Congo.

Of those accomplished scholars who have read and commented on various chapters, I am especially indebted to Jan Vansina. Jan not only helped appreciably with various segments of research on women in colonial Congo, but also referred me to many of the sources dealing with health and disease. John Lonsdale corrected some major bloopers in the text by critiquing several of the chapters; he also generously provided additional materials on the Mau Mau. David Anderson kindly sent me most useful data from his own Mau Mau publications, but he also put me in touch with Katherine Bruce-Lockhart, whose work on women in the Kamati and Gitamayu detention camps is the first to delve into the realm of Mau Mau women during their incarceration. Charles Van Onselen read the section dealing with Cas Maine and his family and has allowed me to draw rather heavily on his classic, *The Seed Is Mine.* Christine Obbo has provided considerable assistance during the course of my work on this book. She has read and critiqued several chapters, especially the material dealing with AIDS; and she has not only provided source material, but also sent me scurrying to sources that I otherwise would have missed. She also plays an unusual role in that Obbo and her work became subjects of the book as well.

The former Cape archivist and historian Con de Wet not only read the early material on the Cape of Good Hope but also rescued me from my copious errors in Chapter Two. Signe Arnfred read and sent suggestions relating to the section on Mozambique and the women's involvement with the freedom struggle. Last, but certainly not least, Randolph Vigne has been ever so helpful in many ways. He read and critiqued several chapters; provided me with a copy of William Gqoba's "Tales of Nongqawuse" from *Africa South*; sent me an unpublished memoir from the South African war; and graciously arranged permission for me to publish extracts of Bessie Head's letters—from his *A Gesture of Belonging: Letters from Bessie Head 1965-1979.*

William St. Clair kindly granted permission for use of the extracts from his *Door of No Return*, a history of Cape Coast Castle in today's Ghana. I am grateful to him for that and for his review of those materials I included. Juliet Barnes and her publisher (Melissa Smith) allowed me to quote a few lines pertaining to Mau Mau experiences from her history *The Ghosts of Happy Valley*. Likewise, Benjamin Kipkorir kindly gave me permission to quote from his memoir, *Descent from Cherang'any Hills*. In addition, I am indebted to Dan Moshenberg for permission to quote from his article "German Amnesia and Herero Women" (http://africasacountry.com/herero-women-challenge-german-amnesia/); to Stephanie Nolen for permission to include the excerpt "Alice Kadzanja" from her book *28 Stories of AIDS in Africa*; and to Eric Silla for permission to print an extract from his book *People Are Not the Same: Leprosy and Identity in Twentieth-Century Mali.*

Bettina Shell-Duncan and Nicole Petrowski were responsible for providing me with the then recently released 2013 UNICEF study dealing with Female Genital Mutilation/Cutting (FGM/C). Sharon Buchbinder, busy with her own fictional account of the Queen of Sheba, generously provided me with a copy of Bernard Leeman's unique study dealing with Sheba and biblical scholarship. My sincere thanks go to all of them.

I would also like to acknowledge that permissions were arranged by the Copyright Clearance Center to print excerpts from the following two articles: Edna Bay, "Belief Legitimacy and the Kpojito: An Institutional History of the Queen Mother in Precolonial Dahomey," *Journal of African History* 36 (1995), copyright Cambridge University Press, New York, 1995; and David Anderson, "Mau Mau and the High Court and the Lost British Empire Archives: Colonial Conspiracy and Bureaucratic Bungle," *Journal of Imperial and Commonwealth History* 39 (2011), copyright Francis & Taylor Publishers, London, 2011.

Permission was also kindly granted by Kassahun Checole, publisher of Red Sea Press/Africa World Press, to include an excerpt from Chris Prouty, *Empress Taytu and Menelik II: Ethiopia, 1883-1910*, Red Sea Press/Africa World Press, Trenton, 1986.

Two Johns Hopkins University undergraduates came to my aid in the form of Internet searches and creation of the maps. Zaire Julion worked unceasingly in January 2013 to garner stores of materials covering a wide range of topics on which I drew in Chapters Five through Nine. She has earned a place in the pantheon of the goddesses. Eliza Schultz undertook the challenging task of locating maps and providing keys to all of the people and places listed on the chapter maps. She handled with aplomb the frustration that marked her tenure as mapmaker. I congratulate her and thank both Zaire and Eliza for their significant input. Goucher College Library contains a copy of John Newton's 1795 *Narrative*, and it allowed me to photocopy segments of the text. Christine Ruggere at Johns Hopkins Institute for the History of Medicine put me on to S. P. Impey's *Handbook on Leprosy,* as well as brought to my attention related works. For several months I took serious advantage of the Towson University Interlibrary loan service. The efficiency with which the books were ordered and delivered deserves recognition. The Johns Hopkins University Eisenhower Library served as a resource beyond measure.

Susan Willis thought she was taking on a bit of part-time work when she agreed to check the manuscript for inconsistencies primarily in the notes and for typographical errors, as well as preparing the bibliography. The project grew and so, too, did Sue's involvement. She typed all of the extracts ranging from the old English in Chapter One to Bessie Head's letters—in which case Sue supplied a facsimile of Bessie's signature. She coped with an ever-growing bibliography, printed by hand on several legal pads, and produced a good rough draft. Alicia Burley came to the rescue with incredible technological skills and welded individual chapters with footnotes into a complete manuscript with the notes located where they should have been all along, had either Sue or I had the skills.

I wanted this book to be accessible to general readers—those who had not studied African history but who had an interest in the subject, especially regarding women. Thus, I turned to two friends: Marcia Harris and Jane Engel. They were most complimentary about my having achieved my goal, but, then, perhaps that is what friends are for? Mikita Green was my one and only consultant on the book cover—and her enthusiasm resonated with my own. In conclusion, Janet Stern, Peggy Roeske, Cheryl Mirkin, and Shanti Hossain, respectively, were the supervising editor, copyeditor, production manager, and assistant-in-chief at Markus Wiener Publishers.

While "thank you" seems trite and is certainly overly used herein, the expression conveys the heartfelt appreciation that I feel for each and every one of those who have so generously contributed to *African Women*. The errors and whatever weaknesses may exist are mine alone.

CHAPTER ONE

Pre-Colonial Queens and Powerful Women

Most African peoples have myths of origin (how a people or society came into being), and these often feature female protagonists. Some queens or women rulers, according to these myths, are most likely fictitious, but some can be historically documented as genuinely royal women, or at least women who were regarded as powerful due to their relationships with male rulers. Every society, including our own, has created national "stories" to explain their beginnings or how they got to where they are today. Most people, over time, recognized the place of gender as regards reproduction—the net natural growth of societies—and thus women occupy a role in their national stories. In Africa south of the Sahara, females are sometimes viewed as part of the occult (having supernatural powers) and sometimes as temporal co-equals with males. In the first section of this chapter, we are focusing on women rulers who were dominant in various parts of Africa and at different times in pre-colonial African history. The first of these is from the very distant past—the era of King David and his son, Solomon, or about one thousand BCE.

Sheba of Ethiopia

Sheba is one of the most widely recognized names among African queens. Her place of origin is claimed by Ethiopia. She was also called the "Queen of the South," and, while other regions around the Red Sea area claim her, Ethiopia has embodied in its own myth of origin Sheba and her visit to King Solomon in Jerusalem during Biblical times. This account is incorporated in the Kebra Nagast, the historical and legal document that was

The labels encircling the continent shown on the map of Africa in each chapter are the names of the people and places (and some key events) that are discussed in that chapter.

compiled over time by Jewish and then Christian religious authorities and, later still, by legal scholars. The Amhara (the ethnic group that long ruled over central Ethiopia and the later expanded kingdom) believe that Sheba converted to Judaism when she visited Solomon, and that it is their descendants who are responsible for the emergence of Judaism in this part of the world. In the fourth century CE, Judaism was supplanted by Christianity in Ethiopia, although a small group of Jews remained clustered near today's Gondar region.

Sheba's visit to Solomon is found in the Book of Kings, is mentioned in other books of the Old Testament, and is found again in Matthew 12:42 in the New Testament. It is also referred to in the Qur'an Sura 27:22-45. Thus we find her in the three holy books of the three major monotheistic religions whose adherents today are spread throughout the world and memorialize the Queen of Sheba.

As recorded in the Old Testament:
When the Queen of Sheba heard how wonderfully the Lord had blessed Solomon with wisdom, she decided to test him with some hard questions. She arrived in Jerusalem with a long train of camels carrying spices, gold, and jewels; and she told him all her problems. Solomon answered all her questions; nothing was too difficult for him, for the Lord gave him the right answers every time. She soon realized that everything she had ever heard about his great wisdom was true. She also saw the beautiful palace he had built, and when she saw the wonderful foods on his table, the great number of servants and aides who stood around in splendid uniforms, his cupbearers, and many offerings he sacrificed by fire to the Lord—well there was no more spirit in her!

She exclaimed to him, "Everything I heard in my own country about your wisdom and about the wonderful things going on here are all true. I didn't believe it until I came, but now I have seen it for myself! And really! The half had not been told me! Your wisdom and prosperity are far greater than anything I've ever heard of! Your people are happy and your palace aides are content—but how could it be otherwise, for they stand here day after day listening to your wisdom! Blessed be the Lord your

God who chose you and set you on the throne of Israel. How the Lord must love Israel—for he gave you to them as their king! And you give your people a just, good government!" Then, she gave the king a gift of one hundred and twenty-five talents of gold, along with a huge quantity of spices and precious gems; in fact, it was the largest single gift of spices King Solomon had ever received.[1]

According to some of the legends surrounding Sheba, her traditional religious beliefs centered on the sun—the Kebra Nagast ostensibly quotes her as saying that her people "worship the sun like our ancestors did. . . . There are some amongst us who acknowledge other deities from nature such as rocks and trees . . . [but] we worship the sun [because] she lightens our darkness and banishes fear . . ."[2] Thus, when Sheba made her pilgrimage to Jerusalem, her own belief system was intact. Most probably the reason for her visit was to extend trade between her kingdom and Solomon's (and in this case, we are following the Ethiopian version of her origin), although Sheba, it was claimed, was in search of his wisdom.

We include here the version of her visit and subsequent events from the works of a first-century Greek. This version closely parallels that recorded above from the Bible.

When this queen heard of the virtue and prudence of Solomon, she had a great mind to see him. . . . Accordingly she came to Jerusalem with great splendor and rich furniture; for she brought with her camels laden with gold, with several sorts of sweet spices, and with precious stones. Now, upon the king's kind reception of her, he showed a great desire to please; and easily comprehending in his mind the meaning of the curious questions she propounded to him [his wisdom] he resolved them sooner than anybody could have expected. So she was amazed at the wisdom of Solomon, and discovered that it was more excellent upon trial than what she had heard.[3]

In this version of Sheba's visit, when the queen presented her gifts she appeared to have accepted the Hebrew God. She not only had reverence for Solomon and his people but also noted that "one should therefore bless

God, who hath so loved this country" and its king. This version ends with her departure after having presented her gifts to Solomon. Yet other versions of the story contend that before Sheba left Jerusalem, Solomon had impregnated her and, at her departure, gave her a ring. The Kebra Nagast, for example, takes the same story and extends it to include Solomon's seduction. The queen spent "six months at . . . court, and when the time came for her to leave with her honor intact, he became quite distressed." Solomon staged a big banquet for her and, as part of the meal she was given spicy food that was drugged. Sheba went off to bed, with a servant sleeping nearby. Shortly thereafter, Solomon emerged in her quarters and announced that he too intended to sleep on the floor at her feet. During the night, the queen awoke to a great thirst and the only water vessel was near Solomon. When she reached the water jar, Solomon "grabbed her arm. . . . At last encountering the sordid dimensions of Solomon's ruthless character and with no hope of slaking her raging thirst . . . the queen had to endure Solomon's triumph. Next, according to the Ethiopians, Solomon bedded the handmaiden as well."[4]

Thus it was that not only did Solomon give Sheba the ring, he also sent her back to her home country pregnant. It is unclear exactly when and where she gave birth to their son, Menelik. The Ethiopians claim Menelik was born in what is today's Eritrea. When the boy reached the age of twelve, he began to inquire as to who and where his father was. The Ethiopian version of the story is that Sheba was angered by his inquisitiveness, stating she was both mother and father. That, however, did not satisfy the young Menelik. Reluctantly, Sheba described his father and noted that he lived a very long distance away. At her son's insistence, she finally agreed to allow him to go and establish contact with Solomon—giving Menelik Solomon's ring for purposes of establishing his identity.

When Menelik reached Jerusalem, he succeeded in using the ring to make contact with his father. Solomon was delighted to have his son at his court. After an extended visit, when the boy was preparing to return to Ethiopia and his mother, Solomon attempted to convince him to remain with him in Jerusalem, even offering him land over which to rule. But not only had the son vowed to go back to his mother, he also intended to take with him the Ark of the Covenant, that most sacred of Jewish treasures, from the High Temple where it was prominently featured. The Ark of the Covenant was at the time, and even now, believed to contain Moses' covenant with God. According to Ethiopian legend, Menelik nonetheless took it from the temple. There are several versions of how Menelik was able to deceive his father in removing the Ark. All accounts involve angels and a conspiracy among some in Solomon's court. Briefly, the Ark was replaced with a replica, and no one noticed the deception until Menelik was on his way south. When the high priest realized that the authentic Ark was gone, he notified Solomon, who sent troops after his son and his party. It was too late. Menelik reached his mother at her court near Axum in today's Ethiopia, and the Ark is said to have remained hidden there ever since (that is, about 965 CE).[5]

This account of Sheba, her son Menelik, and the Ark of the Covenant seems not to have been in circulation before the sixth century. At about that time, Cosmos Indicopleutstes, a monk living in Egypt, gained knowledge of Sheba's visit to Solomon (as the Queen of the South) from travelers to Ethiopia. If Cosmos' informants were correct, Sheba may indeed have ruled from the area of Axum.[6] Later scholars would try to place her in today's Yemen or somewhere else in Arabia. In fact, Christianity had been introduced to that central part of Ethiopia by the year 547 CE, when his *Christian Topography of Cosmos, an Egyptian Monk* was published.

The link between Solomon and Sheba provides us a global perspective: Sheba and her son Menelik brought Judaism to Ethiopia from Jerusalem and the Middle East. By the mid-fifth century, Christianity had been introduced, thereby reinforcing the legitimacy of Ethiopia as a player in the wider world over time. Although the link was not continuous (other, earlier Christian dynasties maintained a hold over parts of the country), in 1270 the Solomonic faction reemerged in Ethiopia, and they ruled (with some interruptions) until the death of the Emperor Haile Selassie in 1974.

Amina and the Hausa Queens of Northern Nigeria

Through the ages, myths have been spun around Sheba, but the historical record establishes her as a genuine ruler. Among the Hausa, in today's northern Nigeria and southern Niger, early oral traditions rest on what were probably fictive characters. The Hausa were a people of nomads and farmers who, during the ninth and tenth centuries, began to establish clusters of villages that they surrounded with mud (adobe) walls. Over time, the separate communities grew in size and independently developed stratified political systems. A Hausa state system developed. The Hausa believe that in the tenth century Bayajidda, a warrior from Baghdad who came across the Sahara into Katsina, one of the Hausa states, united them.

When he arrived in Katsina, Bayajidda encountered a powerful snake residing in the one well in the town. The snake would not allow the local people to draw water from the well—in the hot, dusty arid town—except on Fridays. Paralysis had kept the locals from striking at the snake, but Bayajidda courageously struck it dead. Then, as a hero, he married the ruler of the area, Queen Daura. They eventually had a son, Bawo. Bawo in turn produced six sons. The father and his six sons then each conquered a Hausa city-state, and these seven states became the seven Hausa emirates of northern Nigeria (Daura, Katsina, Zaria, Gobir, Rano, Hadeija, and Kano). Today, each of the original seven Hausa states claims a well named after a descendent of Queen Daura; indeed today the city of Daura still exists in Katsina State, and in one part of the city there is a statue of the snake symbolizing Bayajidda's daring deed.

Whether or not the legend of Daura is based on fact, it does establish the importance of the role of a founding queen in the Hausa stories of origin. Both oral traditions and the written word record a succession of queens in Hausaland. One of the most famous of these was Queen Amina, who built the capital of Zauzau; it endures today as Zaria, the capital of Katsina State.

Amina was the oldest of King Barka Tarunku's three daughters. Although she is the subject of many legends (and a movie, *Zena*), she is widely believed by historians to have been a real ruler, having reigned somewhere between the mid-fifteenth to late sixteenth century.[7]

As a teenager, Amina often rode into battle with her father and was known as a fierce warrior. When Amina was about thirty-five years old, her father died, leaving her to rule over his conquered lands. Amina had refused to marry, not wanting to be distracted by husband or children. Within three months of inheriting the throne, Amina embarked upon the first of the military campaigns that defined her rule. She personally led her cavalry into action. From their base in Zaria, Amina's armies conquered all the city states of Hausaland, including Rano, Kano, Daura and Gobir, thus connecting the western Sudan with Egypt on the east and Mali in the north.

In accordance with Hausa custom, Amina collected male slaves from all her subject cities. She slept with one after each battle and then had him put to death the next morning. Amina was formidable! She established the custom of building walls around the cities she conquered. Remnants of these walls remain to this day, and thus her legacy is concretely visible in the contemporary landscape of northern Nigeria. Distinctive mounds wind throughout the countryside in the vicinities of the old city-states of Hausaland. These remnants of walls have become known as Amina's walls. Amina is also credited with having introduced armor to the fighting armies of the area. Zaria's traders were well known far and wide for their metalworking, and they were soon producing iron helmets for Amina's troops. She continued to lead her armies throughout her reign. According to most accounts and the oral traditions of the area, Queen Amina ruled for thirty-four years. The kingdom she established survived into the colonial era of the nineteenth century.[8]

It is commonly believed that Amina was killed during a military battle and her body taken away by the winning army. Nonetheless, in the twentieth century, the memory of Amina, Queen of Zaria, has come to represent the spirit and strength of womanhood. In acknowledgement of her accomplishments, she has earned the epithet *"Amina, Yar Bakwa ta san rana,"* or "Amina, a woman as capable as a man."

Yennenga and Sogolon Kedjou of Ghana and Mali

During approximately the same time period that Queen Daura was said to have ruled in Katsina, oral traditions celebrate Yennenga as the founding mother of the Mossi Empire (in today's Burkina Faso). This story is especially interesting in that historically the Mossi were expert horsemen, and we will see the continuous role of the horse as we go on. As such, they raided their neighbors while also being able to fend off incorporation into the ancient kingdom of Mali. According to oral traditions (and many of them are still told), Yennenga was the daughter of Dagamba, the ruler of an ethnic group still found in northern Ghana. She was skilled in weaponry—the javelin, spear, and bow and arrow. Her father found her talents useful and thus refused to allow her to marry. Having failed over time to convince her father, the king, of her desire to lead a normal life, Yennenga dressed as one of her father's guardsmen and, with another, fled Dagamba. They were attacked, the other guardsman killed, and Yennenga, on her beautiful stallion, was left alone. Eventually she rode into a thick forest and there encountered a hunter who fell in love with her. The couple soon married and produced a son whom they called "Stallion." This son, in turn, led his people into battle, vanquishing all. He then founded the Mossi Kingdom. Hence we see horses being incorporated into the myths of origin, as well as the role of Yennenga—the young woman whose horse brought her love and marriage.

Yet another powerful female emerged in what was to become the great empire of Mali in the fourteenth century. This tale is also widely repeated and has several different versions. The essence is that rather than being a beautiful, beguiling woman, Sogolon Kedjou had some sort of deformity. She also experienced visions (i.e., had ties to the occult). At a young age, Sogolon Kedjou was captured by two hunters and brought before the king, who decided to marry her despite her unattractiveness. She gave birth to a son who, according to legend, was a favorite of his father. This may have been due to the little boy's lameness—the story goes that he was unable to walk for several years. This favoritism ignited the king's first wife to jealousy. Fearing for her son's life, Sogolon Kedjou, who had been told a prophecy that the boy was destined for great deeds, took him and ran away. This son, whose name was Sundiata, had his own griot (storyteller), who they took along into exile with the nearby Sosso people. There the griot in turn was abducted. Sundiata was aggrieved at this loss, raised a force, and went to war against the Sosso. After defeating them, he gradually extended his rule to conquer Bamako (the capital of Mali today) to form in 1325 the Kingdom of Mali. We do not know what happened to Sogolon Kedjou beyond the fact that she saved her ailing son, and he in turn conquered all around him and founded a kingdom which is indeed recorded in history.

Nzinga of Angola

In what is today's Angola another powerful queen emerged, this one in the seventeenth century. The Kingdom of Ndongo was situated on the Atlantic coast and ran a few hundred miles into the interior. The major ethnic group was Mbundu. The Mbundu were matrilineal (tracing descent through the

female line), but their rulers were generally bilateral in descent, meaning
that the progeny of women enslaved during war who became concubines
in the king's court were not eligible to rule. Neighbors included the Imbangala (also known as the Jaga), a group of kinless bandits who invaded just
as Nzinga was making her debut in 1621. Portugal annexed her provinces
with some of the Imbangala as allies. At this time, the Imbangala were also
opposing the neighboring Kingdom of Kongo from whom Nzinga was also
alienated. Alliances were made, broken, and restored between these factions, but many of the Imbangala played an important role in Nzinga's story
and her rule.

By this time, too, the Atlantic slave trade had spread from the Kongo
Kingdom into Angola, and the slave trade was the reason the Portuguese
were present in both Kongo and Angola. (As we will see, they were followed by the Dutch as competitors.) Nzinga's brother Ngola (king) Mbandi
had killed his own father so that he himself would rule. The Portuguese
were based in Luanda, on the coast, and had gained control over a considerable part of the interior. Then, by royal grant, the King of Portugal conveyed a large part of the Angola territory to a favored supplicant. Mbandi
was threatened by this acquisition and determined to do something about
it. In order to work out a peaceful settlement, Mbandi sent his sister,
Nzinga, as his emissary to negotiate on his behalf. Nzinga was entirely
aware of her rank, and when the Portuguese officials refused to offer her a
chair, she "seated herself on the back of one of her maids-in-waiting" to
press the issue of her status. Nzinga was also shrewd. She quickly figured
out that conversion to the religion of the Portuguese would be helpful to
her brother. Thus, Nzinga converted to Christianity and allowed herself to
be baptized as Ana de Sousa.[9]

Soon after her return to Ndongo, Nzinga's brother mysteriously died. It
is likely that she had him poisoned or did the deed herself. At any rate, she
stepped into the ruler- ship, now as a Christian, and immediately formed
alliances with both the Portuguese and the Imbangala. One problem for
her, however, was the fact that her brother had an eight- year-old son. Another was that, as noted above, children of slave concubines were partially
kinless, and hence ineligible to rule. Nzinga's mother had been a slave.
When another brother attempted to wrest the throne with complaints to the
Portuguese, Nzinga proclaimed that his ancestry was the same as hers, and,
in addition, that she was a Christian. In rapid succession Nzinga brought

the leader of the Imbangala into her camp, along with her nephew. If the Portuguese reports were correct, she murdered the lad, step by step solidifying her own claim. While her position was rickety, Queen Nzinga held on in Ndongo until the 1630s. When the situation became too perilous, Nzinga fled with her followers to Matamba, a deserted island, where she established her rule and remained for the rest of her life.

It is possible that in addition to the fratricide practiced within her family, Nzinga may have borrowed some of her more ruthless cultural practices from the Imbangala. Andrew Battell, an Englishman who had been held hostage by them, wrote that while the women gave birth to numerous babies, "as soon as the woman is delivered of her child, it is buried quick [alive] so that there is no one child brought up. . . . When they take any town they keep the boys and girls of thirteen or fourteen years of age as their own children."[10]

On her island, Queen Nzinga, possibly to maintain agency, and as a means of equating herself with her male peers, began dressing as a man. In the seventeenth century, European fashion prevailed among the elite in Angola; it is likely, however, that Nzinga chose a combination of traditional cloth and the skins common to the Imbangala. One historian of central Africa has suggested that there were precedents for gender change among powerful women in that era, as will be discussed below.[11] Nzinga also engaged in polyandry. She insisted that all of her husbands dress as women. In addition, she coerced her female attendants into male attire when they followed her into battle against the Portuguese in the 1640s. She had no children, and, if contemporary European accounts are accurate, Nzinga forced her husbands to sleep with her attendants but prohibited them to engage in sexual intercourse on the penalty of death.[12]

In Ndongo, Nzinga profited from the slave trade coming from the interior. After she relocated to Matamba, she was in a position to circumvent and evade the Kongolese hold on the trade, thus depriving Kongo of the taxes on slaves, which, instead, went to her. By opening and holding new routes, Nzinga not only extended her Matamba kingdom, she profited immensely from this human trade. One authority claimed that in the 1640s, 13,000 to 14,000 slaves passed through her lines each year.[13] In the late 1620s, the Protestant Dutch established a foothold north of Luanda. The Thirty Years' War in Europe had created hostility between the Dutch (Protestant) and the Portuguese (Catholic) rulers. This enmity carried over, too, into Brazil and central Africa. Soon after the Dutch built their fort on the Atlantic coast, Nzinga sent emissaries to create an alliance and to redirect the slave trade to them. Because relations with the Portuguese had been problematic over time, other local chiefs joined Nzinga, hoping to drive the Portuguese out of Luanda. But in 1641, hostilities between the Dutch, Nzinga, and her allies erupted. Before she could rally her allies against the Dutch, they signed an accord with the Portuguese in 1643 (ending the Thirty Years' War), leaving Nzinga in the lurch. But hostilities continued intermittently within Angola until 1648, with Nzinga leading her troops against the Portuguese. In 1648 Nzinga withdrew to Matamba.

During the war Nzinga had Dutch bodyguards. One of the officers described her as "a cunning and prudent virago." It was this prudence that led her to spare the lives of the captured Portuguese troops. The playing field was even—the African forces were armed with guns and ammunition, and Nzinga was recognized for her ability to wield these weapons, even in old age. Beyond her female warriors and her husbands, Nzinga's force was composed of Imbangala bands along with a large number of slaves. Ironically, considering how engaged she was in profiting from the trade, many who had escaped from the Portuguese sought refuge with her. Her valor was complemented by a trove of luxury goods that came as a result of the trade, providing her with largesse to dispense and adding to her legitimacy as ruler in Matamba.

Nzinga ruled for nearly four decades. She lost Ndongo. But in her retreat to Matamba, Nzinga created and extended a kingdom that lasted into the 1750s. A caveat, however, is that the Kingdom of Matamba came under the control of the Portuguese in the late 1680s and after she had died. While there is doubt that Nzinga was a true convert to Christianity, her sister Barbara was. As she faced death, Nzinga was able to secure her succession by this sister—via the Portuguese. Barbara ruled for a few years, and it was probably Barbara who saw to it that Dom Ana de Sousa received a proper Christian burial; the Capuchin missionary Giovanna Cavazzi, whose reports are included in this narrative, presided at her funeral.[14]

As suggested in Nzinga's saga, the practice of women's assuming male attire in the period and in the area was not peculiar to Nzinga. Actually, forms of this practice persisted in southern Africa at least into the early twentieth century. Initiation practices (*efundula*) among the Ovambo, an ethnic group located in northern Namibia, is a case in point. In the period following an initiation, girls were reported to practice "gender inversion" by moving into male roles whereby they assumed the names of great warriors "by whom they were said to be possessed." Armed with heavy sticks "they moved freely throughout the country." They were "entitled to whatever food they found during their wanderings, and could mock at, and beat every man they encountered . . . ; this included their (future) husbands, who received beatings as well, and were made to dance as 'women' before their wives." Covering their bodies with clay or white ash compounded power in their case. Because this was the colonial era in Namibia, they regarded themselves as being transformed into white people (Germany was the colonial power here) "because being powdered with white ashes—'nothing is prohibited.'"[15] We can draw an analogy earlier in time with Nzinga for whom being dressed in male attire and demeaning her husbands, meant that nothing was prohibited to her.

Hwanjile of Dahomey

One of the series of powerful women who assumed a unique role in the Kingdom of Dahomey in the eighteenth century was Hwanjile. She was a *kpijito* (a reign mate) to King Tegbesu (1740-1770). Hwanjlle was thought to have special powers over the occult and to be able to manipulate the gods *(vodun)* in her co-ruler's favor. The traditional religion of these rulers and their social status are complex. Thus we depend on the following extract from a scholarly article that begins with Tegbesu, providing some insights into eighteenth-century Dahomey customs and practices while illustrating Hwanjile's power in the period covered. It should be remembered that Hwanjile was an actual person, but the myths surrounding her were means of legitimizing power on the part of the ruling class of Dahomey. Note, too, that in this period of Dahomey's history, women occupied a range of positions within the palace that were not duplicated elsewhere in Africa south of the Sahara. They were there as slaves—all royals and most chiefs owned slaves. But here they served in a wide variety of roles: "guards, soldiers, messengers, spies, state-sponsored prostitutes, political advisors, ministers of state and government record keepers."[16] The following extract conveys the complexities of unraveling the history of these early, traditional, highly structured political entities.

Adonon, the first *kpijito*, is a crucial element in this story. Traditions vary about her relationship to Dakodonu [the ruler], but all point to her as a link between Dakodonu and Wegbaja [possibly the first king]. One account claims that she was a sister to Dakodonu, which would imply that her marriage to Wegbaja [created] alliance among the patrilineal Fon, linking the invading royal lineage through marriage with the lineage of the owners of the earth. Other traditions provide a more complex linking of the two lineages through Adonon. They claim that Adonon was not a sister of Dakodonu but rather a fiancée who was impregnated by Wegbaja. As such, her children would have been considered to be the children of Dakodonu. . . . [Wegbaja's act would have been regarded as incestuous.] As *kpijito* she was the symbolic progenitor of the Alladahonu. Dakodonu thus becomes father of the Alladahonu dynasty, and Adonon through marriage and incest links the Alladahonu to the previous owners of the land. Wife to one king, Adonon is simultaneously mother to another dynasty, which by patrilineal code is descended from her husband, Dakodonu. . . .

Alladahonu kings claimed descent directly from Agasu and each in his turn as head of the lineage embodied the strengths of the leopard. But Agasu's parent was Aligbonon, whose priest was Adonon. Adonon/Aligbonon becomes, then, the founding mother of the dynasty. Her title, *Kpijito*, underscores the symbolism of her office. *Kpijito* means literally the person who whelped the leopard. . . .

The myths, speaking through the idiom of kinship and marriage, legitimize the Alladahonu as rulers over the subjects of Dakodonu and, by extension, Dahomey. Yet the human players—Dakodonu, Adonon, Wegbaja—were not myths. . . .

The patterns of involvement in the monarchy that were to become typical of the *kpijito* can first be seen during the reign of Tegbesu, the successor of Agaja. Tegbesu gained power with the acknowledged assistance of Hwanjile, the first *kpijito* for whom we have documentation of direct involvement in a succession struggle. Not only is Hwanjile credited with assisting Tegbesu to gain power, but she was also involved in helping the monarchy to consolidate power through altering the religious life of the kingdom. Hwanjile is without question the most powerful female figure in eighteenth-century Dahomean history and arguably one of the most important individuals in the history of the kingdom. So widespread is her fame that there is a divinity in her name (Ouan-Guile) in the Antilles.

Hwanjile was an Aja woman from Ajahome, a town nearly due west of Abomey. Mother of two non-royal children born before she entered the palace, she was reputedly a power priest who perhaps was brought to the palace of Abomey because of her knowledge of the occult. . . . Like Adonon, Hwanjile as *kpijito* is said to have exacted revenge on enemies; the first recorded crucifixion in Dahomey was an Aja enemy of hers.

Traditions do not say how Hwanjile became an ally of . . . future king Tegbesu. However, they credit Hwanjile with helping him win a war of succession against his elder brother. . . . What emerges from this succession story is a pattern that would continue until the abolition of the kingdom by the French; powerful women within the palace would ally themselves with ambitious princes to build coalitions aimed at taking over the throne. The winning prince would rule as king; the king's ally would become *kpijito*. . . . Would-be kings saw control over the palace as key to control over the kingdom.

Tegbesu himself was said to have raced to the palace to take power as soon as he heard of his father's death. . . . Women within the palace could aid or oppose a would-be king with military, political or religious power. . . .

Different traditions credit Hwanjile with bringing nearly a dozen *vodun* to Abomey. However, her most important contribution to the efforts to legitimize and stabilize the monarchy was the establishment in Dahomey of Mawu and Lisa, who were brought from Aja country to preside at the head of the Fon pantheon of *vodun*. Installed just outside the central Abomey palace, they were (and are) "commanded" by Hwanjile herself. Mawu and Lisa theoretically controlled all of the other *vodun* of the realm and by extension all the living persons who served those deities. Their priest, Hwanjile, became the head of religious life in Dahomey.[17]

This supernatural power exceeded the temporal power that Hwanjile enjoyed as the reign mate of Tegbesu. As we noted, her legacy is embodied in bringing stability to Abomey within a generation after Tegbesu took power, and, even more important, in bringing *vodun* into the kingdom to supersede other gods in residence there.

In briefly examining the stories of these six queens, we can see that there were indeed powerful women rulers throughout African history. Some of these queens exist only in oral traditions or legends, others are documented in the historical record. All—in one way or another—clearly establish a role for women in guiding and indeed in controlling large kingdoms, leading armies, manipulating the occult, and transforming themselves into powerful leaders of their domains.

Women and the Formation of Societies

We now move to Tanzania. The Ikizu people are a small society located not too far from the Serengeti Plain, which will be familiar to some readers for the wildebeest and their migrations into and out of Masai Mara in Kenya.

This story is also one that features co-founders: a female and her male counterpart. It includes prophecies and the supernatural world. As is the case with the foundations of many pre-colonial African societies, we have no timeline for the Ikizu. Roughly, Nyakinywa was the granddaughter of a major chief who controlled a large area that, according to the legend, extended into parts of today's Uganda and Burundi. Her father was younger than the son who inherited the title from their father, and the family's wealth was centered on their cattle. According to the legend, when one of the cows swallowed the "emblem of authority," the chief called for the bovine to be killed. But Nyakinywa's father, who valued every cow, rebelled. When the chief prevailed and the cow was killed, the younger brother took his three daughters, his own herd, and some followers and departed from the clan.

As the leader now, Nyakinywa's father and his group settled in an area that was so agriculturally rich that their cows began to produce an over-abundance of milk, which the farmers threw into a nearby stream that carried it to where the Masai were encamped. Since the Masai are also cattle keepers and consume milk as a major part of their diet, they followed the stream to find the source of this milky water. Once they arrived where Nyakinywa's father and his people were located, the Masai attacked. They stole most of the cattle and left many of her father's people dead.

Then Nyakinywa's father became ill. He summoned all three of his daughters to his side and issued a prophecy that included a threat to the girls: one of his sons, at his father's death, planned to come and take the land he had left them. The father advised his daughters to leave the area and go to "a country with a tall mountain where their rule would be awaiting them."[18] Soon after this warning, their father died. The girls set off shortly thereafter seeking the mountain their father had mentioned in his prophecy. When they got to the Serengeti Plain, they encountered what appeared to be a cow, which, as it neared them, collapsed. Was this a sign? The girls then met up with a hunter to whom they addressed a series of requests. First: they asked that the hunter split open the beast's body, and if it contained "the emblems of their office" he was to hand them over; otherwise he could take the meat. Next: they asked the hunter to skin the cow to make them a container for carrying the contents that he had secured from the belly. These included (the very significant) rain stones, in addition to bits of beads and other jewelry worn by the chief, their father, thus indicating that they had recovered at least some of their father's emblems of office. Of course, these findings were signs from their father that he was protecting them.

After some time the three young women came to the mountain. They were taken in by locals who enabled them to stop for a brief period. But, alas, the rain stones began to multiply in such numbers that they were unable to carry all of them. One of the sisters—Wang'ombe— volunteered to stay behind and protect the stones. At the next stop, the other sister of Nyakinywa gave birth to a baby. She was unable to travel and Nyakinywa was unwilling to wait until the new mother and baby were able to move on. Thus Nyakinywa set off alone. After some distance, she discovered a cave. As she moved into the cave, she stepped on a rock that sent out beats like a drum. To Nyakinywa this was another sign; she realized she had reached the home her father had prophesied. Leaving behind her goods in the cave, Nyakinywa ventured across a nearby river and soon encountered Sombayo of the Muriho clan. The story continues: Nyakinywa had turned the cave into her home, into which she invited Sombayo. They fell in love, but Nyakinywa refused Sombayo's entreaties to marry. Still they lived together for some time—each with their own special powers. And from her home, Nyakinywa used the rain stones still in her possession to create the rain, while Sombayo possessed the ability to make fire. But they refused to share with each other their respective powers over rain and fire.

The narrative does not detail what transpired between the two until one day while Sombayo was out hunting; then Nyakinywa used her powers to summon rain and put out the fires Sombayo had left in their compound. When he returned, he set about in her presence to create fire, so Nyakinywa was able to learn his secret. Then he wanted to share her magic for making rain, but she refused, insisting instead that he go and get her sister Wang'ombe, who had been left behind watching over the other rain stones. Sombayo obeyed. Following the arrival of Wang'ombe, a power struggle developed between Sombayo and the two women. Sombayo lost, and after that relations between him and Nyakinywa began to deteriorate. First Sombayo was forced by Nyakinywa to marry his own daughter—incest to be sure, but that does not seem to figure as a problem in the legend, although it does indirectly assert Nyakinywa's power over her lover, since it was she who forced the marriage between father and daughter. The women then required that he build a house "for the drum of authority" at their compound. This he refused to do as it would symbolically transfer all power to the women. Instead, invoking his Muriho elders and extended family, Sombayo called for a council that would then divide the country between Nyakinywa and his people.

The outcome of the council was a division of the land into eight segments, and also certain conditions were leveled on Nyakinywa. Most important, she had to make rain "to show that she really had the power," and this she did. After proving her supernatural power, Nyakinywa agreed to accept four houses while Sombayo's people accepted the other four. "In this way," they "united to become one thing, the original Ikizu people."[19]

Another East African society for which no timeline (many hundreds of years) has been established is the Kikuyu.[20] They are today Kenya's largest ethnic group, and their myth of origin placed them below Mount Kenya.

In this story we initially encounter the matriarchal system of rule; then we move on to the patriarchy that characterizes the traditional Kikuyu contemporarily. According to the Kikuyu, the Lord of Nature (Mongai) dwelled on top of Mount Kenya. At some point in time, Mongai decided to send a man, Kikuyu, down to "a wonderful world," and when he reached the area Mongai had selected for him, he found a "beautiful wife" named Moombi (creator or molder). Moombi bore Kikuyu nine daughters but no sons. Kikuyu was troubled by this imbalance in his family and turned to Mongai on Mount Kenya to complain. As the Lord of Nature, Mongai sent down a plan, instructing Kikuyu to go to a sacred tree where he would find nine "handsome young men." Doing as Mongai advised, and finding the nine young men, Kikuyu promptly took them home. Following a brief repast there, the subject of marriage between his daughters and the nine young men came up. Kikuyu was delighted to wed his daughters, but only on the condition that the young men agreed to stay at his homestead and adhere to the matriarchy that they practiced—Moombi calling the shots at home and their daughters ruling their respective households. All accepted the conditions. They married and established families, calling themselves "*mbari ya Moombi*" (family of Moombi) to commemorate the wife of Kikuyu and mother of the nine daughters.[21] Eventually, as its numbers increased, the extended family divided into nine clans, each one taking of the name of one of Moombi's daughters.

But after several generations of matriarchy, things began to fall apart. According to Jomo Kenyatta:

> The women became domineering and ruthless fighters. They practiced polyandry. And through sexual jealousy, many men were put to death for committing adultery. . . . Men were indignant . . . and planned a revolt. But as the women were physically stronger than the men at the time, and also better fighters, it was decided that the best time for a successful revolution would be during the time when the majority of the women were in pregnancy.[22]

The men carried out their revolt. The women were defeated "without much resistance." That is when they decided to rid themselves of the matriarchal system and adopt the patriarchy. Furthermore, the men demanded that female clan names be abandoned, but this so angered the women that they announced their refusal to bear any further children. "And to start with, they would kill all of the male children who were born as a result of the treacherous plan of the revolt."[23] No doubt, previous experience with their strong-minded women, as well as the threat to their young boys and the prospect of no sex, prompted the men to quickly agree to restore the names of the nine daughters of Moombi as their major clan identity.

Thus in this Kikuyu myth of origin, we see a combination of several features that figure in previous legends and tales of legendary women. Here, too, is another founding story that incorporates both a woman and a man as equals, although without the occult power to make rain or manipulate the gods as we found among the Ikizu.

CHAPTER TWO

At the Cape of Good Hope:
European Interactions
with the Khoe/San

A t the southern tip of the continent, the Portuguese were the first Europeans to establish contact with the indigenous Africans. In 1479, Vasco da Gama anchored off the coast of Mossel Bay where he and his men encountered what were probably a group of Khoe livestock keepers. They were "tawny in color . . . [and] they wear sheaths over their virile members." In their group were some women who "wore decorated ivory bracelets" and rode on "fat oxen."[1] A succession of other Europeans—the British, Dutch and French—encountered the Khoe during the sixteenth through mid-seventeenth centuries, recording myriad accounts concerning those natives with whom they came to trade various pieces of iron, copper, bronze, or tobacco and liquor for cattle and sheep to replenish their vessels as they sailed further east.

Before we continue, it is necessary to differentiate between the various Khoisian people we shall be meeting at the Cape. The majority of them (referred to as Hottentots by the Dutch) were divided into clans whose livelihood was invested in their livestock. But a small group of Khoe, called "Strandlopers," dwelled at or near the Atlantic coast. These Strandlopers lost their cattle through conflict with neighboring clans or due to natural disasters. They tended to eat mollusks and forage for food. Other Khoisian people were referred to as "Bushmen," and they mainly lived in the interior beyond the coast, moving as their demands for meat (wild animals) and plants, herbs, and roots dictated. All are subsumed under the rubric

"Khoisian." The Bushmen and Khoe were both known for their click speech and shared common physical characteristics, and at times they could be interchangeable. If Khoe lost their livestock, they reverted to hunting and gathering or, like the Strandlopers, moved to the coast and foraged there. Their religious practices were similar, but their political systems differed by the time the Europeans established a firm foothold at the Cape in the mid-seventeenth century. The Khoe had a more interlinked political system of clans than the nomadic hunters and gatherers. The Bushmen were regarded by the early settlers as "savages" and "people of small stature, who own neither sheep nor cattle . . . relying for their subsistence on wild vegetables and game." They eat "ants, locusts, lizards and snakes while their weapons consisted of crude bows and poisoned arrows."[2] They shared with the Khoe a religion that centered on both the moon and the sun. In a trance, their holy men were transformed into part man and part beast.[3]

In 1620 the French captain Augustin de Beaulieu traveled inland to and around Table Mountain where he came upon what was probably a group of hunters and gatherers. In his account, he referred to "the most miserable savages," who did not engage in agriculture or, in the case of those he came across near the mountain, have cattle or sheep. "These people are of very low stature, especially the women, thin, and seem always to be dying of hunger. They eat certain roots, which are their chief food, about the size of small chestnuts and white, like the stalk of a leek . . . bearing a white flower."[4]

Khoe and European Imagery

Early Dutch seaman who engaged in trade with the Khoe at the Cape referred to them as *schepsels* (creatures). By 1508, the Khoe were depicted as "wild men" dressed in "broad leather sandals, a loose cloak of animal skin . . . and a loin cloth, with sheep intestines hung around their necks."[5] Almost all of the Europeans who encountered the Khoe initially made reference to their click speech, many writers comparing the sound they heard to that of turkeys clucking. The majority of seafarers repeatedly commented in their logs or diaries that the Khoe were thieves, stealing whatever items appealed to them—and this was not too difficult, since they came in groups. Other similar observations concerned the animal skins worn in the same manner by men and women, mainly around the upper parts of their bodies. The men—and this was remarked upon regularly—barely covered "their members" and usually with only the tuft of an animal tail or a bit of animal skin that hung in close proximity to their genitals.

As noted above, another facet of Khoe adornment was their habit of hanging dried or fresh intestines around their necks. In some cases, they were described as wearing both. Observers noted that the Khoe repeatedly sucked on the intestines, especially if fresh.[6] Their habit of smearing their bodies with a combination of animal fat and charcoal was consistently recorded, as was the fact that the smell was odious. The men were believed to have had one testicle removed, usually as children—accounts differed as to when this was done and why. (One seafarer claimed that mothers removed the "stone" soon after birth and, in addition, that they fed their babies tobacco.)[7]

Since no one spoke the language of the Khoekhoe, they were dependent on signs until one or two Khoe were taken away—one to England and another by a British ship to Bantam—and learned a modicum of English before they returned. This was in the 1620s and 1630s. Earlier, in 1612, a surgeon on a British vessel described the Khoe as "without Religion" or law. They went "naked saue onelie a pees of Sheepes Skyn to cover their Members. . . . Their persons are preporcionable butt ther Faces like an Appe or Babownne [naked save only for piece of sheepskin].[8] A Dane encountering a group of Khoe referred to them as "wretches," claiming that they were "man-eaters: they had killed and eaten seven men of these English on their outward journey."[9] As early as 1609, the stereotype developed among seafarers that they "were cannibals."[10] Another early traveler complained that the Khoe were "very stupid" as well as "brutish and savage." They "eat human flesh and entire raw animals, with the intestines and guts without washing them as do dogs."[11]

As for the intestines—all remarked on them—an early British seaman offered an explanation that may have had some merit in spite of his otherwise negative perceptions. They were "the most barbarous in the world . . . wearing the gutts of sheepe about their Necks for health, and rubbing their heads . . . with dung of beasts and durte [dirt]. . . . Theyre howses are but one matt [constructed] like an Ouen [oven] into which they Creepe."[12] While contemporary observers reported that they were a tasty snack, Richard Elphick, who has written extensively on the Khoe, suggests that

the sheep intestines were not decoration but were associated with their belief system.[13]

The French Huguenot theologian Isaac Le Peyrere categorized the Khoe
as "soulless men descended from Adam," or, back to the exotic interpretation, creatures that had emerged "spontaneously on earth."[14] Invoking the
curse of Ham, Thomas Hart regarded them as "being propagated" from
"Chem."[15] The theological implications under discussion were whether the
Khoe were men or beasts or, as Le Peyrere inferred, "soulless men." Nicolaus de Graaf observed in 1640 that they found at the Cape "nothing other
than wild heathen, dirty and stinking men who covered their nakedness
with skins, and knew nothing of God nor of his Law, and in their customs
were more like beasts than men."[16] Back in Europe, as these views were
disseminated, the concept of the exotic "other" emerged, as did the question
of where the Khoe should rank on the great chain of being.

Imagery and the Female Body

While we have generic impressions of the Khoe from the various seamen,
we now single out the women and how they were viewed. Of course, they,
too, strung sheep intestines around their necks, and they too smeared their
bodies with animal fat (and it made good sense in the windy, chilly Cape
winters to do that). One early Englishman conceded that some of their
women "are well featured" (and we shall see that this view was later shared
by the French traveler, Monsieur Vaillant).[17] Cornelis Matelief reported that
he had seen "a full two hundred" of the women who were "clothed in skins
and with a skin around their heads, an ugly rig-out."[18] What is interesting
here is the sheer numbers of women who sometimes accompanied the men
and cattle to trade.

The most detailed description of the Khoe, which included the women
present, was provided by a Dutchman in 1639:

> Their hair is stiff, wild and matted, their faces are full of wrin-
> kles and ugly. . . . The women ornament their arms with rings
> of iron, copper, brass, or pewter which they barter . . . for cattle.
> They are quite naked—men and women. . . . They cut their
> faces, arms and legs with many stupid signs, thinking them-

selves adorned thereby. . . . As an ornament, the women have in certain places short thongs hanging down, cut from the body for what reason . . . I have been unable to learn.[19]

What the writer was referring to was the extended labia characteristic of Khoe women. This was an aspect of Khoe female physiognomy that sparked widespread commentary among the Europeans.[20] This particular physiological issue was widely gossiped about among early travelers to the Cape, and it continued to incite the curious into the eighteenth century. One Cape informant, replying to a query from Europe (where curiosity was widespread among the men), wrote, "In many Hottentot-women the inner labia protrude. Some say this is caused by stretching, through daily pulling with the hands; others that this is an inborn characteristic."[21] In this quote we see not only the biological "other" but the lasciviousness visited on the female body.

The female breasts were subjects of much interest, too: the women "have large breasts and ugly, greasy black hair."[22] A French seaman noted "that their women have very long breasts" while they dress like their men.[23] But two British seamen provided, respectively, their own observations. The first of these, Edward Terry, noted in 1619 that the female Khoe "carry their sucking infants under their skins upon their backs, and their breasts, hanging down like bag-pipes, they put up with their hands to their children, that they may suck them over their shoulders."[24] Eleven years later, seaman Thomas Hardy added his observation (or was he merely repeating what he heard from Terry?). His journal contained this entry: "And here the Women gave suck, the Uberous Dugg [breast] being stretched over their naked shoulder" to reach the babe nestled on her back.[25] In fact, earlier, a 1596 Dutch drawing depicting the view described later by these sailors was widely circulated in Europe—the "body" being sexed both in print and in art for the titillation of and mockery by armchair travelers.

In the extract that follows, we find a traveler's 1673 impressionistic account of some of the Khoe customs that he either observed or was told about by residents at the Cape.

An Account of the Cape of Good Hope

C H A P. X.
Of the Shape and make of their Bodies.

AS all Mankind has a certain Instinct or Inclination (besides the Disposition depending on his native Country) so it is next to a Miracle, that during so many Ages, each Nation has retained certain Lineaments or Features, which, as they are infallible signs of their Dispositions, so they shew a vast difference betwixt several Nations.

The *Hottentotes* being very much Sunburn't, have general a tawny Skin, tho' some of them have a tolerable white Skin; but Blackness is the greatest beauty among them; for the rest they either strew a certain Earth, of various colours, upon their Heads, or mix the same with Suet, and so besmear their Hair and Faces, which they look upon as a singular Ornament; for there is a certain Mountain here, which furnishes them with Materials for divers Colours, which, if rightly manag'd, would turn to a good account.

As many as I ever had opportunity to see, appear'd to me slender and tall, shap'd with strong knotted Joints, and well set, with flat Noses (such as most Africans and Afraticks have) and bended Fore-heads; large thick Lips, curl'd Hair, woolly and cut or shav'd in different Figures. They appear for the most part naked, having only a piece of Leather, like an Apron, hanging down before from their Breasts.

C H A P. XI.
Of their Garments.

THE use of woollen Cloaths is not known among them, tho' they are now and then pinch'd with Cold, against which they preserve themselves with Ox and Sheep Skins, or of wild Beasts. This Garment, both of the Gentlemen and Plebeians, is nothing else but a Leather Vest, reaching down to their Knees (call'd by them *Karos*, and used instead of an under Bed) the only thing to defend themselves with against the Cold. These are made sometimes of Cows or Sheep Skins, sometimes of Panther or Goat Skins, with this difference only, that the common People cover their Privities with a piece of Ox Skin, the Gentlemen do it with the Skin of an Otter. In this point they seem to follow the Foot-steps of *Hercules*, who whilst he dwelt upon Earth, and convers'd among Nations, never made use but of one single Skin for his Garment, and one Club. During the rainy Season, they wear on their Heads a kind of Hat, or peaked Cap, of Leather, fitted close to their Foreheads, and reaching down below their Eyes. About their Necks they hang a Pouch, wherein they keep the Head of their Arrows, and sometimes their Tobacco. Their Arms, both above and below the Elbow, they adorn with Rings of Elephants Teeth, on which sometimes they fasten their Pouches. For the rest they appear naked, except that some few wear a kind of Bullocks-hide under their Feet, which in case of necessity are boil'd or broil'd, and serve them for Food.

The Women's Vests, as well as their Aprons (which cover their Privities) are made of Sheeps Skins, they being more sollicitous to cover the same in publick than the Men. On their Heads they wear such another peak'd Cap, like the Men; Shoes they never use, and instead of Stockens wrap about their Legs some dry Osier, or dry'd Guts, or perhaps the shreds of Bullocks-hide.

The chief Ornament they delight in most is, to shave the Hair of their Heads (like as we do our shagged Dogs) into several Figures of the fuller Half-moon or Stars. On their Fore-heads they wear Coral-beeds, notch'd Shells, Brass Money, the Bones of Cows, twisted Hair, etc. All, unless those that are very poor, have about their Necks Collars or Necklaces of Coral, Glass or Brass Beeds, which they exchange with the *Dutch* for their Cattle. About their Elbows they commonly wear Rings of Ivory, and about the Breasts Bracelets of Brass.

C H A P. XII.
Of their Dwellings.

THEIR Dwellings are only little Hutts (call'd *Krallen*) for as they are forc'd to change their dwelling places, for the better conveniency of feeding their Cattel, in a desert place, so they cannot have any fix'd Habitations. These Cabbins have but one entrance, arch'd on the top; The Coverings and Walls being made of the Leaves of the *African Sword Grass* (the Head whereof they make use of instead of Bread) twisted so closely together as to keep out the most severe rains and Cold. The largest Posts, Rafters and Lathes, are made of the boughs or Twigs of Trees. Every Man digs a hole in his Hutt, wherein he throws a Sheep Skin to wrap himself in, which serves instead of a Bed, wherein he is laid in the same posture as a Child in the Womb; the Wife lies in another hole next to his side. In these Hutts they now and then entertain fourteen or fifteen Persons at once; they commonly rank them on the Hills in the Fields, or near the Banks of the Rivers, among the Trees, in a kind of Circle or Enclosure, at five or six Paces distance from one another, wherein they preserve their Cattle, rather against the attempts of the wild Beasts than an Enemy.

When they are to change their Habitations, the Captain gives them the signal by a great Fire; the Women manage all the Houshold Stuff and other Utensils, which they put in Leathern Bags, and carry them upon their Shoulders; the Hutts they load upon the Backs of the Oxen, which serve for the same use when their Husbands go into the Wars to carry their Baggage.

C H A P. XIX.
Their manner of Dancing.

THEY delight so much in Dancing, or rather Skipping, that their chief Religious Ceremonies seem to consist in the activity of their Bodies; for, when they see the Moon rising, they meet together; and whilst the Men strike all at once, their Feet against the Ground, by turns, with a very grave Air, the Women clap their Hands, and sing certain Tunes to them. If they happen to look into a Looking–glass in one of our Houses, they are so delighted with their own shape (*Narcissus like*) that they fall dancing, and seldom leave off till they drop down (quite tired) upon the Floor; as I have often observed in a certain *Hottentot*, who was a Servant in our Lodgings.

C H A P. XX.
Of their Religion.

AS British and barbarous as this Nation is, yet are there among them some few Foot-steps of the Knowledge of a *Supream Being*; for whenever they see the Heavens Covered with Black Clouds, when it Thunders or Lightens, you shall hear them say, *The Great Captain is angry*; and if they have kill'd any of our People, and dread our Revenge, they will say in broken *Dutch, What shall we do? The Dutch-men* (say they) *will kill us: But if they kill me, I will go directly to our Great Captain, who will make me a Present of White Oxen.* Thus when it is a very serene Day, they say, Our Great Captain *will present us with White Oxen.* For the rest they seem to agree with the Ancient *Egyptians*, and other Pagans in this Point, That they look upon the *Sun* and *Moon* as Gods; *(a)* for they adore the *Sun* by gazing upon it stedfastly at Rising and Setting; sometimes they will sit down near the River side, and throw abundance of little Balls of Clay into the Water, which, they say, they do in Honour of the *Sun*; The *Moon* they worship with Dancing, as we told you before.

C H A P. XXIII.

Of their Marriages.

SUCH as have an Intention to marry together, having obtained their Parents Consent, apply themselves to their Captain, who giving his Consent, they marry at pleasure, tho sometimes all their Subsistence consists only in a Club, an ox to carry their Hut upon, a Milch Cow, and perhaps Ten or Twelve Sheep, some whereof certainly are kill'd for the Wedding Feast. The richer sort marry as many Wives as they think fit, and in case of dislike, divorce themselves. These commonly kill two or three Oxen, and a many Sheep for the Feast; the Flesh after it is parted from the Skin, they expose a little in the Air, and then boil it in its own Fat in their Earthen Pots, the Guts being roasted in the Ashes; they treat their Friends with these Dainties, and spend the Day merrily, according to their own way.[26]

Monsieur Vaillant, Rachel, Narina: Their Bodies

By 1790 any number of European men had traveled extensively around the Cape and parts of South Africa. Over time attitudes regarding the Khoe transitioned from fixation on the body to dependence on them as guides. Monsieur Vaillant was a big game hunter as well as explorer. Vaillant paints a somewhat romantic, if self-serving, portrait of his South African adventures. As he set out on his lengthy trip, Vaillant hired as head guide Klaas, a Khoe highly recommended for felicity who could also speak English. Month after month, Klaas was "ever faithful . . . he never quitted me in the hour of danger," such as when Vaillant was attacked by an elephant he failed to kill.

Vaillant indeed presented a more favorable view of the Khoe than did earlier travelers in their accounts. For instance on leaving the kraal of Khoe among whom he, Klaas, and the other Khoe in their party had been staying, Vaillant wrote: "Are these the savages who have been represented as thirsting for the blood of strangers—who are even mentioned with horror? Their goodness of heart and affability, as I was already [familiar] with their defects, where I saw nothing that could make me dread any dangers for the future."[27]

Vaillant prohibited women from joining the Khoe men on their travels, but several months out, while camping near the kraal of another Khoe clan, he enjoyed the domestic services provided by one of the local women who, during his time in residence, developed a relationship with Klaas. Vaillant relented to their entreaties to permit her to stay because of "a mutual and tender affection" between her and "the faithful Klaas. . . . I distinguished Klaas from his comrades" to allow her to remain. He named the woman "Rachel" and noted that "I had no reason to resent this step for . . . [she] served me with the greatest fidelity to the end of these travels."[28]

Unfortunately it was upon "Rachel" that Vaillant visited the gravest historical disservice. Did Vaillant, as quid pro quo for allowing her to remain

Rachel in skins (*left*) and Rachel depicted with sensationalized
and exaggerated genitalia (*right*).
Source: Monsieur Vaillant, *Travels from the Cape of Good Hope
into the Interior Parts of Africa, I*

Narina.
Source: Monsieur Vaillant, *Travels from
the Cape of Good Hope into the
Interior Parts of Africa, I*

with them, coerce Klaas or "Rachel" to remove the apron covering her lower extremities so that he could capture her body in ink and on paper? Or did he play on the naïve good will and innocence of the Khoe couple? Whatever means Vaillant employed, his grossly distorted image of her body can be described only as an anatomically incorrect caricature. This misrepresentation of Rachel's body was placed near another unflattering drawing of her—identified as "Rachel"—in both the French and English editions of the first volume of his *Travels from the Cape of Good Hope*, leaving no question as to the victim of his misrepresentation.

Yet Vaillant was paradoxical in his views of Khoe women. While he engaged in sensationalizing "Rachel's" body in print (thereby enhancing potential sales), he also developed an attachment to a young Khoe woman that may have gone beyond flirtation. By the time Vaillant met "Narina" (also named by him), he may have developed some facility with the Khoe click speech. Or perhaps Klaas served as interpreter in most of their encounters. Vaillant bestowed gifts on the young Khoe woman (whose likeness he also drew), but he was unable to deter Narina from the traditional Khoe practice of smearing sheep fat on their bodies—or as he wrote, "their filthy grease."

The following extract comes from Volume I of Vaillant's travels. We leave it up to the reader to ponder on the extent of his relationship with the beautiful Narina.

Vaillant's Travels

In the midst of these reciprocal offerings of friendship, I remarked a young girl of about sixteen, who shewed less eagerness to partake of the ornaments I bestowed on her companions,
than to consider my person; she examined me with such marked
attention, that I drew near, to satisfy her curiosity. Her figure
was charming, her teeth beautifully white, her height and shape,
elegant and easy, and might have served as a model for the pen-
cil of Albane; in short, she was the youngest sister of the graces,
under the figure of a female Hottentot.

The force of beauty is universal, 'tis a sovereign whose power
is unlimited. I felt by the prodigality of my presents, that I paid
some deference to its power. The young savage and myself were
soon acquainted. I gave her a girdle, bracelets, and a necklace
of small white beads, which appeared to delight her; I then took
a red handkerchief from my neck, with which she bound her
head, in this dress she was charming! I took pleasure in deco-
rating her, which finished, she asked me for ornaments for her
sister, who had remained at home; she pointed out to me her
mother, told me she had no father. Nothing could equal the
pleasure I took in seeing her, except it was in hearing her speak,
for I was so charmed with her answers, that I fatigued her with
interrogations. I asked her to stay with me, making her all sorts
of promises; but when I spoke of carrying her to my country,
where women I told her, were all queens, commanding Hoords
of slaves, she rejected my proposal, and even gave marks of im-
patience and ill-humour. A monarch could not have prevailed
on her to quit her Hoord and family, the bare idea inspired her
with melancholy, to banish which, I changed the subject, and
desired her to bring her sister, which she promised to do. Then
fixing her eyes on a chair, shewed me a knife that laid there: I
presented her with it; this she carried to her mother.

She was fully employed with her new decorations; examining
her arms, feet, necklace and girdle, twenty times feeling her
head, and adjusting her handkerchief, with which she appeared

much pleased. I set my glass before her, she viewed herself very attentively, and even with complacency, shewing by her gestures how much she was satisfied, not particularly with her person, but her ornaments.

On her departure from the Hoord in the morning, to visit me, her cheeks had been rubbed with grease and soot; I made her wash it off, but could never persuade her that these decorations diminished rather than increased her beauty, and whatever skill I used in my persuasions, she still remained as obstinately attached to her filthy grease, as in our climates, the ladies are to rouge and pastes, which though not less disgusting are more pernicious.

My charming pupil desired me to give her my looking-glass, I consented; she made good use of the empire her gentleness had acquired, to ask for all that gave her pleasure, notwithstanding I was obliged to deny her several things that were particularly useful to me, and might have been dangerous to her. My knee buckles had tempted her—the most sparkling gems were not so brilliant as her expensive eyes. I should have been delighted to have given them. How much did I wish at that moment for the most miserable fastenings to supply this useless luxury! unhappily they were the only pair I possessed—I made her comprehend that the buckles were absolutely necessary to me, from which moment she never named them.

I found her name difficult to pronounce, disagreeable to the ear, and inapplicable to my ideas, I therefore renamed her Narina, which in the Hottentot language signifies a flower, desiring her to retain this name for my sake. She promised to keep it as long as she lived, in remembrance of me, and in testimony of her love; a sentiment that was no longer a stranger to her heart; this was truly painted in her gentle unadorned language, which powerfully shewed how strong the first impressions of nature are, and that even in the deserts of Africa there is no happiness without an alloy.

I ordered a sheep to be killed, and a good quantity of the Hippopotamus to be dressed, to regale our visitors, who gave into the excess of gaiety; every one danced, my Hottentots not to be out-done in gallantry, entertained them with music, founding the Goura, the Foum-Foum, and the Rabouquin, nor was the Jews-Harp forgotten; this new instrument delighted our visitor. Narina, who thought (like all other pretty women) that she was capable of every thing, tried to play; to carry the likeness still farther, was soon tired of her lesson, and threw the instrument from her, calling it detestable.

The day passed in mirth and feasting; my men shared their brandy (besides what I had given myself) among our visitors. I saw with pleasure that Narina could not drink; her sobriety delighted me—I detest liquors myself, and am amazed how women (particularly) can accustom themselves to the most disgusting of all poisons. . . .

The reader no doubt supposed that Narina was not among those who were excluded [from] my camp. She had no idea of quitting her friend, 'til I pointed out her mother and companions who were about to depart, when I received the adieu of the gentle Narina.[29]

By the beginning of the nineteenth century, attitudes toward the Khoe were beginning to change. William Burchell, a traveler from England, provided a much more enlightened view than that presented by most of the early observers.

They were small in stature, all below five feet; and the women still shorter; their skin was of a sallow brown colour. . . . The women were young; their countenances had a cast of prettiness, and, I fancied, too, of innocence; their manners were modest, though unreserved. . . . One of them wore a high cap of leather, the edge of which protected her eyes from the sun; at her back, and entirely hid excepting the head, she carried an infant, whose exceedingly small features presented to me an amusing novelty.[30]

The Dutch East India Company and Krotoa

Soon after 1652, when Jan van Riebeeck and a small group of Vereenigde Ost-Indische Compagnie (VOC) employees were sent to the Cape in order to trade with the Khoe and to plant gardens of fresh vegetables and fruits to supply their ships, van Riebeeck and his wife, Maria de la Quellerie, took in a young Khoe girl whom they named "Eva." She was about ten years of age, and how she got to the van Riebeeck's is cloaked in mystery. With Eva we see that European attitudes had changed or at least modified. Perhaps van Riebeeck was influenced by Maria de la Quellerie, whose father was a French Huguenot pastor as was her brother, then in residence at the Cape. Eva ("Krotoa" to the Khoe) claimed that Autshumato, currently working for the VOC, was her uncle. Autshumato ("Harry" to the Dutch) may have been instrumental in arranging for Krotoa to join the family in domestic service.[31] Whereas Autshumato was a Strandloper, Krotoa's roots seemed to be in the livestock-keeping Khoe. She learned Dutch during her stay, which may have lasted as long as two years. She was also provided with religious instruction in the Dutch Reformed faith. In fact, Krotoa was the first of the Khoe to be baptized at the Cape.

Autshumato was unreliable—he stole company cattle and went off to unknown venues for lengthy periods of time. Krotoa began to fill in for him as interpreter before she, too, started to wander off on occasion and possibly at times with Autshumato. Their relations were sometimes friendly but often strained. In this period, another Khoe, who had been taken to Java and become fluent in Dutch, returned to the Cape. He was hired as translator for the VOC, joining Krotoa and Autshumato (when the latter was present). Doman (called "Anthony" by the Company employees) and Krotoa were never close. There must have been gender issues involved in Krotoa's relations with both Autshumato and Doman, along with competition among the three of them.[32] Doman came from yet another Khoe clan, and his allegiance to his people was closer than that of Autshumato and Krotoa to their respective clans.

Autshumato, no doubt with the aid of other Strandlopers, made off with a sizable number of the Company cattle, and in the process a herd boy was killed. Following this incident, he disappeared (with the cattle) for two years. Soon after he returned, Autshumato was banished to Robben Island. That left Krotoa and Doman as translators, with Doman increasingly hostile to her, especially because of Krotoa's close relationship with the van Riebeeck family. And Doman attempted to undermine her with the other Khoe with whom she negotiated, claiming that she was "the advocate of the Dutch; she will tell her people some stories and lies," betraying them all.[33]

By 1658, Krotoa had left the van Riebeeck compound and journeyed to the interior, where she reunited with an older sister who had not seen her since she was a small child. This sister was married to Oedasoa, a clan chief over the large kraal. At this time, if not during earlier unscheduled leaves, Krotoa abandoned her East Indian style dress for the animal skins that marked her reversion back to Khoe culture. But her new European religious beliefs seemed to prevail. During this first visit to her sister, and finding her ill, Krotoa taught her to pray (and prayed over her). Her sister recovered, which impressed Oedasoa, prompting in him not only an interest in what appeared to be the healing properties associated with Christianity but also a greater willingness to trade with the VOC. Thus Krotoa became a facilitator for the religion as well as a cultural broker between her extended family and the Dutch.

Relations, however, disintegrated between the Khoe and the VOC in 1659, and while Oedasoa was never actively at war with the Dutch, he faced conflict within his kraal caused by divisions among them as to whether they favored or opposed trade with the Company. Some were willing to deal with the Dutch, while others were in sympathy with the Khoe who were directly in conflict with the VOC at the Cape. Krotoa was suspected of being disloyal, and possibly she had ambiguous feelings—during this period she continued going in and out of the Cape and was always changing back to the animal skins. At this stage in her life, Krotoa was what Homi Bhabbha described as a "cultural hybrid."[34]

Tensions eventually resolved between the Khoe and the Dutch. But Doman and Krotoa remained in conflict until she dropped out of competition. In 1662, van Riebeeck was posted elsewhere, and she lost her sponsor. Earlier, in 1659 and during the period of conflict between the Khoe and the VOC, Pieter van Meerhoff, a Dane, arrived at the Cape. It is likely that he met Krotoa at the van Riebeecks' before he ventured off to explore the interior. He and Krotoa developed a relationship, and he signed on as an employee of the VOC before 1664 when they married. Rumors circulated that Krotoa engaged in prostitution and had given birth to two children before her marriage. They may have been van Meerhoff's; she had at least one child after they wed. Things began to spiral downward, however, for the year after their marriage, Meerhoff was posted to Robben Island. Krotoa failed to adjust well to that rather isolated environment, and soon there were rumors that she had taken to drink.

Krotoa's situation grew steadily more difficult when the Company sent her husband to Madagascar, leaving her alone with the children at the Cape in a small house the Company provided for her. Within eight months, Meerhoff was dead. Whatever adjustments Krotoa had made to the role of a European-type wife, they dissipated when she was left a widow. Many members of the European community disliked her, including the commander sent out to replace van Riebeeck. Zacharias Wagenaer resented her having given birth to the two illegitimate children, and no doubt to him, despite her adopting the Christian faith and her marriage, Krotoa was still the exotic "other." Nor at this time did she have recourse to the Khoe community. Soon she was drinking heavily and moved back into prostitution (if indeed she had done so earlier, as claimed).

In 1669, and at a dinner at Wagenaer's residence, Krotoa became quite drunk, shouting at the assembled guests vulgarities that were unbecoming—especially, as they saw it, from a woman. In this case, gender, exacerbated by her "otherness," caused the governor to threaten her with banishment. Instead, in panic, she ran away, leaving her children behind: "naked and destitute," she set out to return to her people.[35] Before she achieved her goal, Krotoa was caught by a search party as she was attempting to sell her children's clothes, arrested, and returned to the VOC headquarters. The Council voted that Krotoa be sent back to Robben Island. Although she made a few visits to the mainland, "she did not, in the government's view, show sufficient moral improvement" and was therefore confined to a lonely existence on the island.[36] Krotoa died in 1674 and was buried on the grounds of the Castle that had recently been completed as the new headquarters for the VOC. She was probably the first Khoe to be put to rest there—and she was provided with a Christian burial. But we have no way of knowing if she retained any religious beliefs—Khoe or Christian; her sad experiences, including her marginality, left her a broken woman.

Her epitaph, written in the Company journal, reflected the attitude of the Christian community among whom she dwelled and for whom she had worked during the van Riebeeck years:

With the dogs she returned to her own vomit, until finally, in death she put out the fire of her lust, affording a clear illustration that nature, no matter how tightly muzzled by imprinted moral principles . . . reverts to its inborn qualities.[37]

CHAPTER THREE

Women and Slavery

The Cape of Good Hope under the Dutch

In Chapter One, we found that an African woman played a role in the Atlantic slave trade, with Queen Nzinga of Angola selling slaves to the Portuguese and the Dutch in the seventeenth century. In Chapter Two, we came into contact with the Vereenigde Ost-Indische Compagnie (VOC) and its relationships with the Khoisian people, who were never legally enslaved. As the settlement at the Cape grew, demand for labor increased. This demand led the VOC to import slave labor, mainly to meet its needs. Released from their contracts, company employees stayed on to engage in agricultural pursuits, selling their produce to the VOC. The agriculturalists also required additional labor and found the Khoe unwilling or unreliable. Thus, two types of slavery developed at the Cape. The slave population there was unique: bondsmen and women shipped in from the East Indies and forced African labor that arrived mainly from Madagascar and East Africa. Originally the VOC assigned a small fleet of boats to deal in the trade, but, by the 1780s, the Company permitted French and British vessels to transport the bulk of the slaves.

Because manumission on conversion to Christianity was mandatory, few slaves were instructed in the Christian faith (most from the East were Muslims). Furthermore, Dutch law prohibited white men who fathered children by slave women from freeing those born to slaves. If, however, free women gave birth to a child by a bondsman, the progeny were automatically free. In the slave lodge, where the men and women were housed separately, and where births were all too common, if a woman managed by some means or other to secure baptism for her children, she had the expectation that they would be set free. But keep in mind, the Dutch Reformed Church did not seek to convert slaves.

The total numbers of slaves brought into the Cape during the period the VOC was in occupation is not known. As the Cape population grew, so did the requirement for slave labor, although the net natural increase provided a significant segment of slaves during the eighteenth century. Robert Shell argues that after 1770 more slaves were born at the Cape than were carried in. In the decades of 1780–1808 more females and children than men arrived from Africa as slaves at the Cape.[1]

The first major epidemic—smallpox—to hit the Cape arrived in 1713. Not only were the Khoe devastated—including those in the hinterlands where surviving town dwellers fled—but the slaves in both the lodge and in private households died in significant numbers as did their owners.[2] A measles epidemic struck in the 1730s, followed by two more epidemics of smallpox—in the 1750s and 1760s.[3] Each of these outbreaks took their toll on the slave population, but there is no record as to gender.

O. F. Mentzel, a German former employee of the Company, recorded his impressions of life at the Cape in the early 1700s. These insights included commentary on slavery:

> The first slaves were brought to the Cape from Madagascar, but the French afterwards [stopped] this traffic, and importations were made from India and the East Indies, from Bengal . . . Seurat and Malabar. . . . All of these races live indiscriminately together in the 'loots' [lodge]. . . . Some rebellious or recaptured slaves or some disaffected native subjects may be banished from Batavia to the Cape.[4]

Whereas it was true that the French diverted the VOC from securing slaves at Madagascar for a time, the first slaves actually came in from Angola on a Brazil-bound ship that the Dutch intercepted and brought to the Cape. But during the first slave trade with Madagascar (later reintroduced with the majority of slaves coming from there)—in 1695—a king of two Malagasy provinces insisted that a Dutch shipper take with him a woman of whom he was anxious to be rid. After three refusals, the king threatened to shoot the Dutch shipper and his companion. His urgency being obvious, they took her and a few extra women. Then a son of the king pressed on to the Dutch "his unwanted wife as well."[5] It would appear that discarded wives were victims of this trade with Madagascar. A sadder commentary on the VOC and early slave trade was the importation of children. According to Shell, the Dutch learned that children survived the journey better than adults. Hence "Many Malagasy children, even infants—were imported to the lodge."[6]

Mentzel refers to some East Indian slaves being banished to the Cape—but he does not tell us that many of them were imprisoned on Robben Island (which became notorious in the second half of the twentieth century with Nelson Mandela and other male members of the convicted African National Congress being housed there). From Mentzel's description of arrivals during his time at the Cape, we get an early view of how South Africa's history differs significantly from that of much the rest of the continent south of Sahara. Ethnic differences, or the "other," came to include not just the Khoe but peoples from today's Indonesia, India, and the Malagasy, who were themselves an amalgam of arrivals from the East intermingled with Africans from the mainland. These "other" were further identified by their status as slaves.

One small girl from Bengal was taken with her mother and father—all involuntarily—on a Dutch ship bound for The Netherlands in 1742. The ship stopped at the Cape, where the six- year-old was separated from her parents and left behind. She understood that they were to come back for her. Instead she was sold into slavery—probably by prearrangement. Sixty-four years later, the then seventy-year-old woman was brought before a local court of inquiry, where it was established that no actual document ever existed to verify her sale. She had only her memory on which to rely: and that was her mother's promise to "return to me in two years." In fact, her father died soon after reaching Europe; her mother followed him in death two years later. They were nominally free, but without doubt they were also helpless servants with no power to either send for or to retrieve the little girl. All she knew was that she received "two letters" from her mother, both read to her by the owner's wife. With no documentation attesting to her having been born free in Bengal, she was forced into "perpetual enslavement" along with "all of her descendants."[7]

The Company owned a sizable contingent of slaves—those who were housed in the lodge referred to by Mentzel. No colony was intended when Jan van Riebeeck was sent to open a fueling station at the Cape. By 1657 employees released from their contracts elected to stay on, starting their own farms, and began to constitute a settlement. Because the Khoe were judged to be undependable, the farmers purchased slaves from the Company or local agents. Mentzel advised that they "obtain their slaves on the local market," adding that VOC officials returning to Europe by way of the Cape often brought slaves with them to sell "privately" because they were not allowed into The Netherlands. [8]

The Company slaves were engaged in urban as well as rural tasks. The slave lodge was near the Company headquarters and was guarded by VOC employees. Separated by gender, the women housed there were systematically put at the disposal of local men (there were almost no free white women in the Cape from 1652 until the arrival of the French Huguenots in the 1680s). Seamen, when the ships were in port on their way to the East or returning to Europe, made use of the slave women in the lodge. Mentzel drew a misogynist picture, claiming that "Female slaves are always ready to offer their bodies for a trifle; and towards evening, one can see a string of soldiers and sailors entering the lodge . . . until the clock strikes nine."[9] Actually the women were victims of guards who were bribed to open the women's section for their exploitation—surely rape was often the result of these encounters.

Non-Company female slaves owned by individuals were primarily engaged in domestic service. As time went on and the wine industry grew at the Cape, they joined the men—and in fact owners as well—in picking and processing the grapes. The East Indian women were especially valued for their skills "in fine needlework, knitting and crocheting."[10] Their treatment, according to Mentzel, was good, compared with those owned by the Company. Not only were VOC slaves ill-treated, they were not well fed. Their punishment was harsh, with flogging routine for infraction of rules. "Female slaves who are condemned to death are usually strangled at the foot of the gallows"—a questionable concession to gender. By comparison, Mentzel noted that the men were often tortured before "a slow death by strangulation."[11]

The VOC continued to import and engage in exploiting slave labor until the end of its rule at the Cape. The end is generally regarded as coming at the conclusion of the eighteenth century. Some historians refer to the Cape as a colony during this span of nearly one hundred and fifty years of Company rule. Others recognized colonial status for the Cape (and ultimately for all of South Africa in time) as arriving with the English when they officially took possession (from an interim government) in 1815 at the conclusion of the Napoleonic wars. Still, it is important to note that slavery continued under British occupation until 1834, although the trade was officially halted in 1807.

East Africa: Slave Trade and Slavery

Ancient Egyptians imported slaves from Nubia (today's Sudan). The Greeks, followed by the Romans, continued the trade, as did the Muslims who conquered Egypt in 642 with the fall of Alexandria.[12] Non-Muslim women from Ethiopia were highly valued as concubines in the Middle East and in nineteenth-century Zanzibar. Thus black Africa, North Africa, and the Arab world had long connections to the slave trade.[13] Slavery existed within many of the African societies as well, and women were always an important component of this trade. The literature on this subject is extensive, with considerable coverage of women.[14]

In the second decade of the nineteenth century and continuing for the next fifty years, Zanzibar, which had been a minor point of departure for slaves being taken from the mainland to Arabia and the Persian Gulf, became a major player. In brief, Sultan Said bin Bu Said of Oman visited that Indian Ocean island in the 1820s, saw the possibilities of developing a plantation economy, especially as regards the production of cloves, and began encouraging Omanis to migrate there. They were followed by traders from primarily western India (and some Indians were there already; others came in from Oman). By 1840, when Said bin Bu Said transferred his capital to Zanzibar, the economy was booming, and much of it centered on the increased slave trade out of East and Central Africa. Many of the slaves were bought for use in Zanzibar. Others—thousands over time—were shipped to other Indian Ocean islands that were under British and French control, as well as on to Oman and other parts of the Middle East (and, for a time, to India). Arab-led caravans, often with Indians as financiers, delved further into mainland Africa in search of captives and also ivory, which was much in demand in many parts of the world and as far away as China.

Zanzibar became the major port of entry for the East African trade, with the sultan leveling a tax per slave. This tax produced a considerable source of his revenue—in addition to several large plantations that he (and other family members) owned. Over time other Africans on the mainland also became involved in the slave trade—some as bearers and supporters to the caravans, others in conducting raids to obtain slaves for the trade.

With this background, we now move to a case study from the late nineteenth century that features women as victims in this trade—of which very little has been recorded. This case concerns a young Yao girl by the name of Swema.[15] There are many variables to the story of Swema's amazing experiences. Whereas our interest rests in the empirical and not the theoretical aspects of Swema's narrative, it is important to note that her story was recorded by unknown sources and later translated into French by a Catholic priest—and there is no guarantee that the work was not used for polemical purposes. A leading scholar of the time and place, Edward Alpers, however, noted that the priest who made the translation, and for use in proselytizing the faith, "was a careful, intelligent observer of African life" who was not known for "falsifying or embellishing the evidence."[16]

Swema was born in Yao country in today's Mozambique in the mid-1850s. Her father was an agriculturalist who held a few livestock. He died as a result of an attack by a lion. Her mother, with the help of older sisters, managed to keep the family going, but within undefined time the older sisters and a small brother died. Swema may have been nine years old when she and her mother were forced to move on, settling in a village not too far from their original home. They built a small dwelling, sowed some seeds, having borrowed them from a neighbor to repay at harvest. Bad luck struck again, this time due to drought. Because the neighbor lost his crop as well, he sought repayment. Distraught and with no resources, Swema's mother pleaded for time. The neighbor obliged, while the mother threw herself into "making pots for sale." But she had not managed to scrape together enough to make the repayment when her neighbor came to collect. At just this time, the Arab caravan arrived nearby—in search of slaves.

> Who does not know how the passage of caravans is always dangerous for the weak? Evil subjects habitually steal children and poor people, whom they sell to the Arabs for salt, cottons, and beds. Creditors profit from circumstances to extract payment of debts. When the debtors are unable to pay, one seizes their slaves or their own children. Often it happens that they are reduced to selling themselves into slavery.[17]

In this instance, the neighbor/creditor sold Swema to the Arabs for some lengths of American cloth. It is hard to imagine the level of distress that Swema's mother suffered during this transaction. Knowing that she was helpless, she volunteered to join the caravan and to carry an elephant tusk.

They had no idea where their final destination was or how long it would take to get there. Even if Swema's mother had been in excellent health and well nourished, there was no way she could have carried a heavy tusk during the long hours they marched daily for a lengthy period of time. Swema, too, served as a pack animal of sorts, although she carried "some things belonging to the Arab" in charge of the caravan.[18] Her value rested on the profit the Arab expected to earn by selling her into slavery when they reached Zanzibar. Apparently he had little expectation for financial return from the mother, or he would not have allowed her to be bowed down with the tusk. After a few days, Swema's mother "was seriously weakened, and after she fell many times her load was taken over on orders of the caravan leader."[19]

At that point the Arab stopped feeding Swema's mother. Swema tried to share her food but was taken away; the Arab even had her forcibly fed to ensure that she would continue on. Despite the hardships she experienced, Swema's mother clung to life: she ate some grasshoppers and the red dirt that characterized the "dry step between the Ruvuma River and the Kilwa coast." It was from Kilwa that the party would transfer by dhow, or small sailing ship, to Zanzibar. In the meantime, Swema's mother continued to drag her body behind the caravan, before reaching an area where there was no sustenance including "red earth."

> When the caravan . . . stopped for its first night in this somber desert, the Arab leader ordered Swema's mother be chased out of the camp and threatened severe punishment to anyone who tried to give her anything to eat. She was all but dead. . . . [At dawn] the caravan was ready to continue its journey to the coast [and] Swema was forcibly wrenched from the arms of her mother, who had to be severely beaten to make her surrender her daughter.[20]

Swema attempted to free herself, was beaten repeatedly, and "lost the will to live." As a commodity, however, the Arab was determined to deliver her and be repaid his original investment. She (and the caravan) reached the coast, where they stayed a few days at Kilwa, and where Swema "remained listless and unaware of her surroundings. . . ." [They boarded the boat.] "Tight packing made it impossible for Swema and those with her to turn over, and even breathing was difficult."[21] The tropical heat was stifling. Swema and others were overtaken with thirst and sick from the rolling pitch of the sailing vessel. Their trip on water lasted six days—with little to eat or drink and again the heat of the burning sun day by day. On reaching Zanzibar, "Swema seems to have been suffering from extreme dehydration and her vision was impaired by 'a fog which obscured the view' of the city."[22]

Due to her poor condition and her inability to understand the Swahili language, when ordered to stand up by the caravan leader, Swema failed to respond. She was taken for dead or, more probably, nearly dead. "This slave is lost," commented one of the men involved in the trade. "It's too bad. It's annoying . . . place this cadaver in a straw mat and carry it to the cemetery. It's useless to nourish it any longer because one can't save it."[23] Thus Swema was summarily wrapped in the mat and carried to the cemetery, where she was buried in a shallow grave. She was frightened out of her wits. And she began to utter muffled sounds from beneath the mat and the dirt—both of which completely engulfed her little body. The child was miraculously rescued by a man from one of the Indian Ocean islands—no doubt a Catholic, since he carried her to their mission in Zanzibar town.[24] Malnutrition certainly was one of Swema's health problems, in addition to the hardships she suffered and the loss of her mother.[25]

In 1873 Sultan Bargash, a son of Said, under pressure from the British, formally ended the slave trade into and out of Zanzibar. Slavery continued, and the overland caravan trade flourished—although illegally—into the late nineteenth century.

West and Central Africa: Slave Trade and Slavery

From the eleventh century until the establishment of British rule in the beginning of the twentieth, the Hausa city states in today's northern Nigeria and southern Niger raided south for non-Muslim slaves. Keeping some for their own use, they sold others to areas in the north into the trans-Saharan trade. Female slaves were desirable internally as concubines, providing children who, in turn, added to a father's accrued wealth as well as providing additional labor. Eventually they could be married off, with fathers acquiring bride price for the girls. The concubine slaves were incorporated into the family, and most were freed at the birth of a child, who was absorbed into the father's lineage. This practice was often true of other slave-holding societies, especially among Muslims.

In 1804, the Fulani reformer, Usman Dan Fodio, led a jihad and formed a caliphate in Sokoto that encompassed the other Hausa city-states. His people, the Fulani, melded their culture with that of the Hausa, bringing with them the institution of government that joined religion and state together under the rule of the emirs. Women, as we noted earlier, had occupied powerful positions among the Hausa. Once the Fulani came in, women were relegated to the domestic sphere, although some women were important behind the scenes as wives of emirs.

Among the Hausa, wives of rulers were selected from the progeny of royal concubines. Slavery was abolished after the British established indirect rule through the emirs. This change occurred in 1901, or at the beginning of the colonial era. In time there were no acknowledged slave concubines and thus no daughters for royal marriage alliances. Mad'aki was one of the last to be born to a royal concubine of slave lineage, being married to the Emir of Katsina in about 1914. Or at least she was sent by her father, the Emir of Kano, to her husband's residence in Katsina when she was but seven years of age. She grew up in her husband's household, playing with royal children until she was old enough to be a sexual partner to him. Mad'aki remained childless, but, contrary to custom, she was not sent back home— probably because the emir had other wives and children, and also because she was deemed to be a favorite—she traveled with him to Europe and to Mecca, among other privileges unknown to wives at that time.

Mad'aki's grandparents were Hausa slaves. Captured and brought to the royal Kano household in the late nineteenth century, they married and had children, and one of their daughters was chosen as concubine to the then emir. She gave birth to Mad'aki in the palace. According to Mad'aki, abolishing slavery caused "the male slaves of the Emir [to marry] the children of men from out there, from the bush, and of the town, and they brought them here. So it was that we could not seclude very many because there were no second generation slaves."[26] This meant, in turn, that the old system of training daughters of concubines for the responsibilities of royal wives

came to an end—a loss of the old ways and perhaps not too great a gain
for the women of royal descent, who were still kept in purdah.

Moving back in time, to before Queen Nzinga traded with the Portuguese, Africans were being shipped as slaves from the Kingdom of
Kongo, located on the Atlantic coast, north of Angola. The following account by a Portuguese pilot provides some insights into how and why slaves
were made available in the 1530s.

> Great caravans of negroes [*sic*] come here [to the coast] bringing
> gold and slaves for sale. Some of the slaves have been captured
> in battle, others are sent by their parents, who think they are
> doing their children the best service in the world by sending
> them to be sold in this way to other lands where is an abundance
> of provisions. They are brought as naked as they are born, both
> males and females, except for a sheepskin cloth. . . . These
> [traders] give their merchandise in exchange and always wish
> to have the same number of male and female slaves, because
> otherwise they do not get good service from them. During the
> voyage they separate the men from the women, putting the men
> below the deck and the women above, where they cannot see
> when the men are given food; because otherwise the women
> would do nothing but look at them.[27]

These slaves were destined for the Spanish New World. Demands would
change over time, with major imbalances between the sexes, men far out-
numbering the women shipped in the trade. Here, too, women slaves were
often kept by their captors as concubines, with the progeny expanding male
lineages.

Land tenure was different in pre-colonial Africa than in Europe. Some
chiefs lay claim to all of the territory occupied by their clans or kingdoms.
In other areas, parcels of land were distributed based on what a man might
clear. Wealth was measured in other ways and especially as regards the
numbers of slaves that a chief or king possessed. In the 1670s, the French
sea captain John Barbot visited the kingdom of Benin (located in today's
Nigeria). The king at that time was an autocrat. He was young, and "his
mother was still living, to whom he pays the very respect and reverence,
and all of the people after his example honour her. She lives apart from her

son in her own palace."[28] But out of reverence or other prohibitions not specified, the king never visited his mother; he relied on her counsel through indirect communication via his officials.

The king's spacious household encompassed "slaves of both sexes, whose business is to furnish all the several apartments with all manner of necessaries for life and conveniency. . . . The women, for that which regards his wives and concubines, which all together makes the concourse of people so great at court" were segregated from the men.[29] On special feast days, the king traveled among the commoners, and, on these occasions, he distributed "men and women slaves among such persons as have the nation some service."[30] Benin was indeed a great and prosperous kingdom when Barbot was there to buy slaves (which he does not mention), and we see women in high position as well as serving the roles of progenitors, by contrast, being given away.

Many African societies employed scarification as a means of identifying their family and/or their ethnic group. When Captain Hugh Crow visited the Kingdom of Bonny (also in Nigeria), he described how some of the "Brechés distinguished rank among themselves: "every seventh child . . . about six or seven years of age, undergoes the operation . . . of having the skin of the forehead brought down from the hair, so as to form a ridge or line from temple to temple. This disfigurement gives them a very disagreeable appearance" and was done to only sons of "great men," although, Crow noted, he had seen "one female so marked."[31] We assume that she was the daughter of a chief. As to the slave trade, he estimated that no fewer than 16,000 of these people alone were annually exported from Bonny over the twenty years ending in 1820—thus Crow was speaking as a slave trader with long experience.[32]

Indirectly, and including women, was the internecine warfare that came increasingly to mark much of West and Central Africa, with millions being shipped away from her shores during approximately four centuries. During these wars, increasing numbers of European firms (and the Portuguese) posted employees at posts dotted along the coast of West and Central Africa. In 1700 one employee of the Dutch West Indies Company wrote home with mainly uncomplimentary accounts of the African nations he encountered from his post on the Gold Coast. Referring to their wars as "ridiculous," William Bosman had to confess that these conflicts were the result of competition for human cargo:

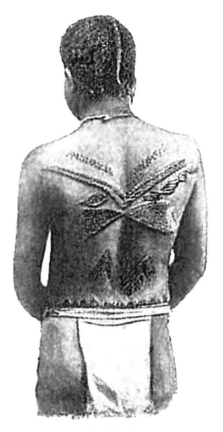

Scarification.
Source: Mary Kingsley's
Travels in West Africa[33]

Perhaps you wonder how the Negroes come to be furnished with fire-arms, but you will have no reason when you know we sell them incredible quantities, thereby obliging them with a knife to cut their own throats. But we are forced to do it; for if we would not, they might be sufficiently stored with that commodity by the English, Danes and Brandburghers.[34]

One slave trader, whose hymn "Amazing Grace" is well known to almost all readers, found himself, in the year 1748, as a virtual slave in Sierra Leone. John Newton was a troublesome seaman on the *Pegasus*. He was so difficult that the merchant seaman abandoned Newton to Amos Clowe when the ship was departing—with slaves—from Sierra Leone. Clowe was a slave trader of some rank and had an African wife—the Princess Peye. In later years Newton recalled the "hardships endured" during this period.[35] Clowe took him home to Princess Peye and set off on a slave-collecting voyage. The Princess Peye was, Newton recorded, "a person of some consequence in her own country," and it was due to her status that Clowe "owed his rise." Soon after his arrival at the homestead, Newton became quite ill with a fever. As his health improved, and his appetite returned, the woman provided Newton with very little to eat. Furthermore the woman often visited him, hurling insults such as "worthless" and "indolent." He was, he wrote, "rather pitied than scorned by the meanest of her slaves."[36]

John Newton on His Experience

My new master resided near Cape Mount, but now he settled at
the Plantanes, upon the largest of the three islands. It is a low
sandy island, about two miles in circumference, and almost covered with palm trees. We immediately began to build a house,
and to enter upon trade. I had now some desire to retrieve my
lost time, and to exert diligence in what was before me; and he
was a man with whom I might have lived tolerably well, if he
had not been soon influenced against me: but he was much under
the direction of a black woman, who lived with him as a wife.
She was a person of some consequence in her own country, and
he owed his first rise to her interest. This woman (I know not for
what reason) was strangely prejudiced against me from the first;
and what it made still worse for me, was a fevere out of illness,
which attached me very soon, before I had opportunity to shew
what I could or would do in his service. . . . When my fever left
me and my appetite returned, I would gladly have eaten, but there
was no one gave unto me. She lived in plenty herself, but hardly
allowed me sufficient to sustain life, except now and then, when
in the highest good humour, she would send me victuals in her
own plate after she had dined; and this (so greatly was my pride
humbled) I received with thanks and eagerness, as the most eager
beggar does an alms. Once I well remember, I was called to receive this bounty from her own hand; but being exceedingly
weak and feeble, I dropped the plate. Those who live in plenty
can hardly conceive how this loss touched me; but she had the
cruelty to laugh at my disappointment; and though the table was
covered with dishes, (for she lived much in the European manner,) she refused to give me any more.[37]

Clowe, to whom Newton referred as his "Master," returned from his
slave-gathering mission. Newton complained about the treatment he had
endured from the woman in his absence. The "Master" did not "believe"

him but decided to take Newton along on his next voyage. During the two months they were out, Clowe also mistreated Newton—implying that he was a thief—and continued to deprive him of adequate sustenance. When Clowe left the vessel, he locked Newton on the deck and left "a pint of rice for my day's allowance."[38] Rescue from this untenable circumstance came from a slave ship captained by a friend of Newton's father who, when he loaded up his complement of slaves, took Newton back to England.[39] Considering his experiences with Clowe and his African wife—similar in form to being a slave—it is surprising that Newton returned to Africa on at least three additional slaving voyages. Without doubt on these occasions, he avoided Princess Peye and Clowe.

In later years, Newton experienced a conversion, was ordained in the Anglican priesthood, and became an abolitionist. In his last years, he published *Thoughts on the African Slave Trade,* in which he addressed the plight of female slaves as they lay packed in the ships during the long hazardous voyage across the Atlantic. The women were ever so vulnerable to the lechery of ordinary seamen. Women, he wrote, may be restrained: "on some ships they are. That depended on the captains. Some were prudent, respectable men . . . but there were too many of different character. Moral turpitude was seldom considered . . . ; they who took care to do the ship's business, might in other respects, do what they pleased." Suggesting that raping women caused "fevers" or would "render the constitution less able," seamen engaged in "lewdness," which "too frequently, terminates in death."[40] We must assume that the fevers and death referred to the helpless women and rape.

Another, if minor, example of female actors as slaveholders was found among the patrilineal Yoruba of western Nigeria, where childless women could purchase slaves. Perhaps to rescue them from bondage, as Babatunde Agiri pointed out, these slaves "were often manumitted, and they enjoyed the status of freeborn as children of their owner."[41] In fact, among both Muslims and traditionalists, it was not uncommon for slaves to be manumitted for meritorious service or to pave the entry to paradise (Muslims). Treatment of slaves, on the whole, was generally benign among the Yoruba and among the other groups who were located on the Niger Delta.[42]

The eighteenth and nineteenth centuries witnessed an increase in not only the slave trade but the numbers of European factories. In the Senegambia area the French Senegal Company established two major shipping centers—one in St. Louis on the mainland and the other on Gorée Island. Employees were prohibited by company decree from bringing out their wives and from engaging in marriage with the local African women. The result was that cohabitation was widely practiced, as had been the case with the Portuguese who preceded them in the area. Eventually officials in France and administrators in Senegambia reached a compromise allowing employees to engage in traditional marriages to the mainly Wolof and Lebou women who dwelled near their factories. This move was practical. Local women could facilitate trade among their extended kin as well as benefit from luxuries from Europe.

The African climate proved to be a death knell to many of these Frenchmen and, as a result, some of the women buried one husband and soon married another. In this case their fortunes rose as did their increased knowledge regarding French language and culture. When those who survived malaria, yellow fever, or other tropical diseases returned to Europe, their African wives made another contract. A few relationships were consecrated in the Catholic Church, but mainly among the mixed-race progeny and their spouses. Whether by traditional or Christian marriage, their children assumed their father's surnames (in case of second marriage or more, each child kept the name of her or his own father). Due to their familiarity with the language, their sons often went to work for the Company. Daughters were culturally even more acceptable as spouses, and the cycle of marrying European men continued through the generations.[43]

Another perspective comes from a later period and provides testimony from European participants in these *Affaires de Coeur.* Cape Coast Castle was a major trading post for the British for 143 years (1664-1807).[44] As the headquarters for the British, many men were posted there as administrators and in lesser positions. The climate on the Gold Coast, like all of coastal Central and West Africa, was unhealthy for Europeans. The death rate for them was high, as for all of the Europeans, yet the potential prospects to a young man seemed sufficient to fill the quotas required. "One of the attractions," St. Clair tells us, "was the prospect of plentiful sex." Sex without benefit of marriage would not have been easily, or cheaply, obtained, at home. It was part of the welcome for a young officer arriving in the Castle to be supplied with a sexual partner, one of the ways in which the British embraced local law and customs without attempting to change them."[45] Note the irony.

The women were uniformly referred to as "wenches," and these relationships "were not informal sexual encounters, although these were available, too, but marriages conducted in accordance with local African
conventions that included polygamy."[46] These unions also called for the
British men to pay the mothers bride price to the families of the women.

> For a newly arriving writer or factor, the amount required was
> equivalent to about a third of his salary and taking a wench put
> him immediately in debt to the Company store. . . . The "wench
> notes" took the form of a standing order from the officer to the
> governor to make a monthly payment on presentation of the
> letter. . . . Wenches seem to have normally been free, not slaves,
> and are recorded . . . as owning their own house slaves, and hav-
> ing slaves bequeathed to them in officer's wills. In the   eigh-
> teenth century the local girls went entirely naked until they
> reached their menarche—which, according to European writers,
> they reached at around the age of ten—after which they covered
> the lower part of their body and were regarded as of marriage-
> able age. . . . And, as with tropical illnesses, the officers of the
> African Service suffered from errors about the effects of hot
> climate on their bodies, believing that heat stimulated sexual
> desire but also that those who succumbed to desire lost strength.
> . . . If an officer could afford to make payments, he might have
> more than one wench. Indeed, in accordance with local custom,
> the taking on more wives was an indication of rising status and
> wealth. Since by the later eighteenth century the Gold Coast had
> hosted a rapidly changing population of around forty young . . .
> [men] for more than a hundred years, many of the wenches were
> British Africans born in or near the Castle. . . . Gradations of
> skin color [developed and] many of the local unions were with
> women who were daughters of previous wench unions.[47]

Another account provides some insights into the acquired family of one
British man who died at the Castle in 1787. The estate paid the amount due
to "his mulatto wench" and "his black wench" and as "a gift" to another
"mulatto wench and child" plus "goods" to a second "black wench and
child." Four women and two children acquired payments, which, as St.

Clair noted, denied "that the property and inheritance of British marriage custom applied, and disowning any liability to make further payment."[48] This particular man was a governor at Cape Coast Castle, and St. Clair observed that if he survived "long enough to be able to afford [two] types of marriage, although 'he evidently preferred the African' having committed to paper his views on easy accessibility of sex without 'coquetry, platonism, inappetency and whim among the women.'"[49]

The following correspondence quoted in St. Clair's *The Door of No Return* is taken from the British National Archives and is reflective of relations with the African women on the part of officials posted in the Gold Coast in the 1770s.

Richard Miles at Anomabu fort to Thomas Westgate at Winneba fort, Sunday, December 13, (1770s).

My lady is in general pretty good Natur'd, but the loss of her son and Heir the other day has made me quite melancholy and has deprived her of her Days of Jollity; I suppose tho only for a little while—Apropos you're very secret in your amour with a certain Lady who I hear has the honor of napping in your room of late; though from the Branch she springs from I dare say she's useful in her way. Westgate to Miles (no date) I am sorry for your Lady's Loss—but she ought to be comforted when she considers That you can at any time cast a New Heir in the same Forge. Tis true I have taken a great Strong back'd W——e, rather surreptitiously, but it is only to tickle me when I happen to be in the humour—I find however it's impossible for an old fellow to do a foolish thing on *this here coast* without its flying (as Pope says) on poetic wings. Robert Collins, governor of Accra fort, kept in touch with his wench families in his previous fort Apollonia where the language and customs were different. The canoe journey was dangerous and expensive, and took many days in both directions: I expect my Appolonia Wenches & Children down [the coast] soon so beg you will give them a Canoe down if they arrive before you come away. If not, desire you'll order your Second [deputy] to give them a Canoe.

Most wenches remain nameless. However, occasionally, the

officers' wills specify legacies to named women and children: "I leave my slave boy . . . to my wench Eccoah." . . . Thomas Mitchell, who died on May 24, 1795 wrote in his will: "I give and bequeath to my wench Nance, in consideration of her strict attention and attendance on me during the three years we have lived together the sum of twenty pounds sterling to be paid her in gold dust . . . together with two gold rings which belong to me as a token of remembrance."[50]

While these women were taken care of through stipulated bequests and not through inheritances paid from the estates at home, they were free to spend the money as they chose. Even if they remarried, the African women had control over their personal finances. In England at that time women had no control over their personal assets—land, investment income, and cash—upon entering into the state of marriage. It must be recognized, too, that these men most often made provision for their African-born children through arrangements with their employers under the same terms: cash and goods.

While John Newton confessed to the vulnerability of female captives on the slave ships, St. Clair did not find sufficient archival evidence to make a case for exploitation of Castle-owned female slaves or those waiting to be exported. There were, however, cases where local women may have been slaves of others. Governor Miles "bought a girl identified as 'T[homas] T[rinder's] Shantee [Asante] Beauty,'" and later he purchased another that St. Clair judged to be "a young female slave."[51] Rather than actual slaves, some were regarded as "pawns" in that they were held as security for unpaid debts. Thus, in the letter that follows, St. Clair suggests that "the false delicacy that marks such writings [as follows] encourages us to decode what is implied":

Take as many good Women Girl Pawns as you can. By yr letter it would seem you expected to get more than the 17 indeed the whole 34; but mind at takg. the Girls for Pawns for to make a positive Agreement that there is to be no Palaver should any of these Ladys be—by any Body here—such a Law must be made or we will have Peace. Shall keep the 16 in Irons till the Palaver is settled then let them loose.[52]

St. Clair concluded that "the girls, like their pawns, could hope to be re-deemed by their families. But women and girls . . . like the Asante beauty came from the interior of Africa" and had no kin to aid them at the coast. These pawns traveled "through the forest paths [and in process] had lost their residual rights, including the names, and were perhaps already as available to their European masters in Africa as they would be on the slave ships and when they reached the new world across the ocean."[53]

We now move to the interior of Central Africa in what today is the Dem-ocratic Republic of the Congo, but in the late nineteenth century, the per-sonal property of King Leopold II of Belgium. The Kuba had developed a highly centralized political system and practiced matrilineal descent—meaning lineage was traced through the mother's line. This was more com-mon in early African history but rather rare by the nineteenth century due to corruption of traditional customs and the laws of inheritance under colo-nialism. Whereas slave-holding was widespread in many parts of Africa, the Kuba began to engage in the practice only as the colonial period dawned—or in the 1880s, around the time Leopold solidified his claim over this huge territory during the Berlin Congress, 1884-1885.

External disruptions had caused large numbers of migrants to flood into the Kuba Kingdom, including "a significant influx of Luba slaves." Of in-terest to us, as regards the Kuba, women and slavery, is that most of the slaves were initially purchased by the Kuba elite—men whose power over descendants was limited due to the system of inheritance. Later, because they were readily available, commoners, who could afford to, also became slaveholders. The royals, Jan Vansina observed, emphasized obtaining young female slaves, and by doing so they increased their families without having to pay bride price.[54] Beyond the economic issues were those of in-creasing power through increases in the male lineages. Because of matri-lineal descent, female slaves were especially valuable to men—both royals and commoners. The progeny of the slave women became part of their lin-eage system. Or as Vansina noted, the more people born as father's kin, the more the balance of power shifted, and this situation "encouraged all lead-ing men to acquire as many concubines as they could attain. As a result the demands for slaves never abated."[55]

Vansina and the Kuba provide another example of how slavery impacted on African societies. In the next chapter we will look at the transition from this dark blot on Africa's history to the interim period that leads to the colo-nial era and a different type of subjugation.

CHAPTER FOUR

Transitioning

W hereas the British legally halted the slave trade in the British Empire in 1807, the trade continued through much of the century from primarily Central and, to a lesser extent, Southern Africa. The East African trade, where in Chapter two we encountered Swema's story, was not officially ended until 1873. As we saw with Swema, Roman Catholic missionaries, the French Congregation of the Holy Spirit, were already in Zanzibar. The Universities Mission to Central Africa [UMCA] established its headquarters in Zanzibar in the 1850s, but only after setting up its first mission in today's Malawi.

Missionaries in South Africa

Protestant missionaries, however, began to practice conversion much earlier in southern Africa. The first of these was George Schmidt, a Moravian, who arrived in 1737 to work among the Khoe. Due to protests on the part of the Afrikaners, he was run out by 1744 but left behind at least thirty-two "New Christians," the first of them a woman.[1] The Moravians returned to the Cape in 1792, as the British made conversion more palatable and opposition from Afrikaners was less virulent. And the Moravians found one aged woman at Genandendal who had preserved her Christian faith.[2]

The plight of the Khoe and the Bushmen/San had been perilous in many parts of southern Africa before any missionaries came to work among them. The most egregious acts were visited on the hunter-gatherers by the early settlers. As the former VOC employees occupied land for farming, and later for livestock ranches far from the growing urban center of Cape Town, men often went on the hunt for Bushmen who, threatened by loss of their tradi-

tional hunting grounds, raided and at times destroyed property. These organized posses shot the men—ambushed them as they would wild animals—and brought their women and children back to their farms, where they were "kept in virtual, if not legal slavery."[3] The Khoe—many of whom had lost their stock and were vagrants or who, because of age and infirmities were no longer useful to their employers were abandoned—left uncared for and with no resources. Anders Sparrman, traveling in the Cape in the early 1770s, wrote sympathetically about "numbers of fugitive Hottentots of both sexes" who were forced to dig up "roots and bulbs out of the ground," competing with the ants for these "provisions." In close proximity he encountered a "Hottentot girl, who, though born . . . in service had got, as they said, even at that tender age, the Hottentot way of absconding." In this case, she encountered a wild beast, was frightened, and returned to her former place of residence, it being the lesser of the evils.[4] That says a lot about her treatment.

The first significant missionary activity launched in southern Africa was undertaken by the London Missionary Society [LMS] in the 1790s. They were followed by the Wesleyan Methodists, Presbyterians, the Church Missionary Society [Anglican], the Glasgow African Missionary Society, and even some American denominations. Over time these missionaries proliferated among the Khoekhoe, the Xhosa, and in the interior all the way to the Limpopo River spilling, across into what is today's Zimbabwe.[5] The first groups were sincere evangelicals bringing the "good news." While paternalistic, they were not racist. This would include the well-known David Livingstone, who became primarily an explorer and opponent of the slave trade while he carried the Word and, as a doctor, practiced healing among the people among whom he traveled from Southern to Central Africa.[6]

But in time, squabbles began to develop among various factions of the missionaries—inter- and intra-rivalries. One example of infighting involved a Xhosa woman in the Eastern Cape. An LMS missionary had appointed an African woman as "female Native teacher" over a school. The Glasgow (GLMS) missionary, who followed, refused to accept her. Apparently she had not been baptized. This good steward of Christianity refused to baptize her unless she was removed from the position. Here is an excellent example of how power struggles began to take precedence over the "very people they were charged with bringing to Christianity." As Elizabeth Elbourne pointed out, with more conversions, white missionaries "felt all the more insecure because people of African background . . . were carrying out evangelization in a way which threatened white control."[7] Still, many converts among Khoe, Xhosa, and later Zulu (and others) spread Christianity in Southern Africa during the late eighteenth and early nineteenth centuries, and the "majority of these were women."[8]

Perhaps the most relevant document regarding a descendant of these early female converts comes from Horst Kleinschmidt, the great-great-grandson of Zara Schmelen, a Khoe woman married to an LMS German missionary in the early decades of the nineteenth century.[9]Drawing on her husband's diary and letters to Dr. Phillip at the Cape, and others to the LMS in London, Kleinschmidt unraveled how a husband and wife worked together to create the "first formal grammar of the Namaqua [a Khoe clan] language," which in turn resulted in a translation of the "Gospels and hymns," which heretofore had been taught in English—a language that few Namaqua could understand.[10] Zara labored as they moved north, carrying their mission into what is today southern Namibia. The time frame involved is unclear, but the end result was the publication of their translated Bible in 1831 in Cape Town.[11]

The process they employed was, to say the least, innovative. Hinrich Schmelen, who was unable to master the clicks so dominant in the language, "endeavoured at first to find out how many different claps (clicks) and what part of the mouth was employed for pronouncation [sic]. . . . I therefore took a looking glass and I and my wife sat before it, that shee [sic] might proper show, and tell me afterwards, where and how the claps were made."[12] Due to the unusual symbols required to print the clicks, the printing process was lengthy. Zara was required to make the corrections to the proof sheets, and "when the last sheet was finished, she put down the quill and said, 'Now my work on earth is done.'"[13] In fact, the publication came very near the end of her life: that year, she died of "consumption . . . on an ox wagon journey home from Cape Town to the Northern Cape."[14]

Missionaries and Travelers

The late novelist Chinua Achebe provided us with some profound reasons why women in many African societies chose to desert traditional religion in favor of Christianity in his classic *Things Fall Apart.* In Achebe's story, the wife of Obrierika was forced to send her newborn twins for disposal in the Evil Forest because they were regarded as bad omens. This practice of killing twins was common among many ethnic groups in West and Central Africa. It caused irreparable pain to the mothers who bore them. They had to sacrifice their babies to traditional beliefs or, as they were taught, the ancestors would pour wrath on them or even on their villages. Women who were ill-treated by their fathers and their husbands also were early converts—again we see this occurring in *Things Fall Apart*. In fact, Achebe's novel was firmly rooted in his own Igbo traditions and written in such a way that, although we are sympathetic to the protagonist (Okonkwo), we are compelled to see the blemishes in Umuofia that left many of its inhabitants open to conversion.[15] These circumstances—superstitions—regarding twins and violence toward women were all too characteristic of many African societies in this period of time.

Mary Kingsley, an open-minded English traveler in Africa toward the end of the nineteenth century, reported that "There is always a sense of there being something uncanny regarding twins in West Africa. . . . The terror with which twins are regarded in the Niger Delta is exceedingly strange. . . . A [slave woman] and Eboe [probably Igbo] was the property of a big woman who always treated her—as indeed some slaves are treated in Calabar—with great kindness and consideration, but when her two children arrived all was changed; immediately she was subject to torrents of virulent abuse, her things were torn from her, her English china basis, possessions she valued most highly, were smashed, her clothes were torn, and she was driven out as an unclean thing. . . . As it was she was hounded from the village. No one would touch her, as they do not touch to kill. . . . By the time she had gone four miles, she met a procession, the women coming to her and all of the rest of the village yelling and howling behind her. On top of her head was the gin-case into which the children had been stuffed, on the top of them the woman's big brass skillet, and on top of that her two market calabashes. . . . [A missionary woman arrived and] took charge of affairs, relieving the unfortunate, weak staggering woman from her load.[16]

On another occasion, Kingsley cited an incident where punishment was visited on a woman who died in the late stages of pregnancy: everything she owned was burned, "blotting out her name and memory. . . . The body was thrown away into the bush, not near the path, where the bodies of little children are thrown in order that their souls may choose a new mother from the women who pass by."[17] Here again, we see the meaning of the Evil Forest in *Things Fall Apart.*

As coastal West Africa moved from slave trade to legitimate trade, many of the traders continued to hold concubines such as those we met at Cape Coast Castle in Chapter Three. The missionaries were critical of concubinage as they also were of polygamy. From the time of the early encounters between Portuguese Catholic missionaries in King Afonso's Kongo, and continuing (possibly until today in some remote areas of Africa), a policy developed whereby the missionaries pretended that the first wife was the only legitimate one. The others either were disregarded or efforts were made to induce the husband to free himself of the concubines. In the case of the coastal factors and their mistresses in the nineteenth century, the missionaries were dependent on the traders for their imports, and, hence, they could do nothing but complain.[18] This was true, too, in polygamous societies, as the new wave of missionaries swept in. They needed the support of chiefs in order to build their churches and to seek converts. Thus most of the missionaries kept their silence regarding these African leaders and their multiple wives.

Richard Burton, traveling in Somalia and eastern Ethiopia in the 1850s, noted that the women worked much harder than their men. Polygamy was, of course, institutionalized under Islamic law, and hence legitimate wives were limited to four. One man with four wives could prove quite dilatory, since the women had "care of the cattle, in travel the women lead and drive the camels . . . pitch the tent . . . bring water and firewood" and, of course, did the cooking and took care of the children. As in almost all African societies the marriages were arranged, with no choice over spouses available to the girls. Burton provided a short sketch of women he encountered in Zeila. The older women cover their heads "down to the neck," while the "virgins wear their hair long, parted in the middle with small braids that were, on occasion, littered with flowers and then enveloped in red ochre." Burton also wrote on female "Excision and Infibulation" with detail so precise, the query rises as to how he obtained it.[19]

Perhaps the most authentic, if indirect, voice we can hear comes from a woman who was in a polygamous marriage. The Swahili poetess, Mwana Kupona, was the third and last wife of Sheikh Bwana Mataka of Siu, a village located on Pate Island on the northern Kenya coast. Sheikh Bwana married Mwana Kupona sometime around 1841-43. We know little about them other than that he had two sons from the earlier marriages. He sired first a daughter and then a son by Mwana Kupona, who dictated this *utendi* [verse] to her daughter after her husband's death and following their move to Lamu. In this lengthy *utendi*, now known as "advice to her daughter," Mwana Kupona does not refer to the previous wives. Her admonitions, however, were surely meant to provide her daughter, Hashima Binta Sheikh, with the tools to monopolize her husband's attention, knowing that the daughter was bound to be in a polygamous marriage as well. Note in the poem that follows, Mwana Kupona directly addresses polygamy, invoking "the days that you are chosen." In fact, at the time she dictated this *utendi*, Hashima may have been facing the prospect of marriage and perhaps as an additional wife, although Mwana Kupona mentions her own critical illness as her rationale for imparting her wisdom in the opening stanzas. It is generally thought that she died within a year after composing the poem.[20]

Mwana Kupona's Poem

Let your husband be content with you
all of the days that you dwell together
on the days which ye are chosen may
he be happy and attribute it to you. . . .
When he goes out take leave of him
and when he returns pleasantly
greet him then ready for him
a place of ease-taking.
When he rests do not betake yourself
off draw near to him, caress him
and for cooling air let him not lack
someone to fan him.
When he sleeps do not arouse him and
don't speak with a loud voice
stay there, rise not from your
place so that if he wakes he has
to search for you.
When he awakes delay not prepare a

meal for him and take care of his
body perfuming and bathing him. . . .
Look after him like a child, who
knows not how to speak. One
thing you must look well to the
household expenses and income.
Be gay with him that he be amused
do not oppose his authority. If he
brings you will God defend you. . . .
When you need to go out be sure
to ask leave when you see that he
is vexed return and sit yourself at home.
Wait upon his permission that he may
be truly content do not loiter by
the way when the fourth hour has passed. . . .
Return quickly to your home that you
may sit with your lord make ready
cushions and rugs, so that you may
take your ease together.
And exalt your husband spread his
praises abroad but do not make
obligations for him which he
cannot fulfill. . . .
My child, be not sharp-tongued be
like me, your mother I was married
ten years yet we did not quarrel
one single day.
I was wed by your father with
happiness and laughter we did not
abase our mutual respect all the
days that we lived together.
Not one day did we quarrel he met with
no ill will from me and from him none
did I encounter until the time
when he was chosen.
And when death came he repeatedly
told me his content and resigned

himself in peace to God while my
heart was filled with grief. . . .
I pray to Thee, O Beneficent One
to grant me aid for the words that
are on my tongue and for all that
are in my heart.
All things of which I have spoken
O Lord, receive in trust for me
and to those which remain unsaid
I pray thee, grant me favour.[21]

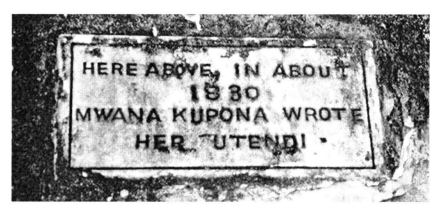

Plaque marking Lamu house where Mwana Kupona wrote her *utendi* (verse).
Source: Patrica W. Romero

Mary Kingsley had ambiguous feelings about the missionaries. On the
one hand, she praised them for attempting to stamp out inhumane practices
such as twin murder, and she was compassionate toward missionaries who
came to the rescue of the persecuted. On the other hand, Kingsley was
somewhat appreciative of the benefits of polygamy, believing that the missionaries failed to take into consideration some of its benefits. In the early
stages of contact between Africans and Europeans, "it is not to be eradicated." In fact, "it is perfectly impossible for one African woman to do the
work of the house, to prepare the food, to fetch water, cultivate the plantations, and look after the children attributive to one man." In addition, the
African women Kingsley encountered were satisfied sharing the husband

as long as "he does not go and give them more cloth than he gives to her."[22]

An early group of American missionaries went to Liberia, which had been founded by the American Colonization Society in the second decade of the nineteenth century. To their consternation, they discovered the practice of child marriage among members of their flock. Susan and John Savage arrived in Cape Palmas in late 1836. With little or no interest in the traditional customs that prevailed, they seemed to misunderstand bride wealth—exchanging a daughter's reproductive and productive powers for goods or stock. Dr. Savage wrote home that "It has been the custom . . . this people to betroth their daughters in infancy; in other words, *to sell them.*" The father "binds himself to hand over his daughter on demand. The age of the proposed husband never becomes a question." One of the students in "the female department [school they founded] . . . is victim to this horrible custom." The husband to be was an older man who lived in the interior—in other words not a Christian. The solution to this conundrum was almost amusing. The Savages learned that they could redeem the girl by paying her bride price directly to her parents. Soon, Dr. Savage reported, a number of fathers were happy to send their daughters to his school so that they might be "redeemed" for the sum of about twenty dollars. This was quite a large sum of money in the 1830s. In conclusion, Dr. Savage reported that "all girls now received into the mission are either secured by payment of the betrothment money to the parents or redeemed from a former purchaser."[23]

Until 1871, Germany was composed of a group of duchies, some of them Protestant and some Catholic. Beyond the Moravians and the Rhenish societies, there were no groups interested in missionary activities. Thus several Germans (pre-unification) went to England and joined the Church Missionary Society (CMS), and, once they undertook the requisite training, they were sent to various parts of Africa. In the 1840s, John Rebbman and Oliver Krapf ended up in East Africa and founded Rabai, a community for ex-slaves. In January 1849, David Hinderer arrived in today's Nigeria, setting up a station in Ibadan. On his first leave he returned to England, where he married a young British woman, Anna, who had been active in Anglican Church affairs. Together Hinderer and Anna established a school and continued his attempts to bring converts to the CMS.[24] The school was segregated by gender, with the girls' curriculum including domestic skills such as knitting, reading (English), and Bible study.

Mary Kingsley also reported a similar curriculum imposed by Protestant missionaries she encountered in Gabon. Here, too, it included the domestic "arts" such as washing, ironing, and sewing. Kingsley, however, was not optimistic regarding the end results of teaching European-style accomplishment; she believed, no doubt correctly at that time, that the women would not have the facilities to practice their skills after marriage to men who lived in the "bush," which was likely to be the case with the majority of them in both sets of circumstances.[25] Almost all of the early missionaries to Africa established schools. Some established schools for boys only, such as the Roman Catholic fathers in their respective missions, but many Protestants set up separate facilities for girls with the emphasis on European-style domestic education.

In the Niger Delta, the Opobo chief, Jaja, was a "remarkably enlightened man . . . [who] valued the educational aspect of missionary enterprise." But he opposed Christianity because, as he saw it, the foreign religion changed the culture. In fact, almost all of the missionaries insisted on instilling Western values, such as making girls and women don dresses covering, according to historian Jacob Ajayi, "nature's best kept secret."[26] Jaja worked out a compromise, allowing a school to be established but without "spiritual activities." He achieved this goal through the efforts of an African American woman who came to Opobo following some time in Liberia. This woman had been born to slave parents before the American Civil War, became a Christian while still in her native Kentucky, and, after the war, immigrated to Liberia and became a trader, traveling up and down the Atlantic coast. Opobo "struck her fancy," so she settled in, becoming an advisor to Jaja, and marrying a local man—a Mr. Johnson—who must have been a convert. As Jaja's "private secretary and prime minister" she exercised considerable influence in the kingdom, including starting the school, but her efforts to bring Jaja to Biblical study resulted in threats "to kill her."[27]

In the late 1880s Germany established a foothold in Tanganyika (Tanzania), blazing a "pioneering role" in establishing schools, but it left the education of girls to the missions.[28] A plethora of schools for girls in East Africa were opened by, first, the UMCA in the 1870s, followed by the CMS and LMS. The UMCA curriculum was less centered on domestic accomplishments but was hardly useful to the female students. They were taught "history and geography of England, Holland, France, Switzerland, and Athens [probably ancient Greece]." The inspector general in 1886 posed the obvious question as to what good these studies would be for African girls. One woman at a female boarding school in rural Tanganyika commented that "all of the girls will marry, and unless they marry Christians, half the work will undo for women in the real influence in the home."[29] It would have been unfortunate indeed for these girls to marry men who had no knowledge of European geography and history. Joining the White Fathers (boys only) near Lake Tanganyika was a group of Catholic sisters who catered to a few girls before the onset of colonialism in that area.

Missionaries opposed slavery, but most baptized slaveholders, believing that the institution would end in time and thinking it better to have them under their influence and that of the Christian church. In 1853 Anna Hinderer encountered a small boy on her way to Ibadan. He was "not yet three years old" and standing alongside the path calling out "Buy me, buy me; I want to go home with you." Inquiring about the boy, Anna learned that his mother had been taken away in the trans-Saharan slave trade "many months ago." The master of the house where he had been staying was away. An old slave fed him for a while but had little food for himself, "so the poor child was cast out into the street," until Anna came along and took him home and raised him until her return to England. Anna's husband spent some of their local currency "which had been for our comfort" to "rescue the daughter of the scripture reader from being sold" into the slave trade by the "Ibadan people" (Yoruba).[30] Witness the incongruity of Christian conversion and attitudes of fathers regarding their daughters.

David Hinderer encouraged his flock to grow cotton, which they sold to an African female trader, Madam Dinuba, who sent it to Abeokuta for ginning. Thus by 1850, women traders were already established in the area. When Kingsley was in the Niger Delta, forty years later, she encountered a wily, clever trader named Mrs. S., of whom she was in obvious admiration:

> "Mrs. S." who was a comely and large black lady . . . hailing from Opobo and frequently going up and down to Lagos, in connection with trading affairs of her own and another lady with whom Mrs. S. is in a sort of partnership. This trade usually consists of extensive operations in chickens. She goes up to Lagos and buys chickens, brings them on board in crates, takes them to Opobo and there sells them. [Of interest to readers is her return] to Lagos with those empty crates and the determination

. . . not to pay for them. Wise and experienced chief officers never see Mrs. S.'s crates, but young and truculent ones do, and determine . . . that she shall pay for them. . . . [The truculent African officer] says:

> "Here, Mrs. S. now you have to pay for those crates."
> "Lor mussy me, sar' . . . what you talk about?"
> "These here chicken crates of yours, Mrs. S."
> "Then," says the truculent one, "heave them over the side! We don't want that stuff lumbering up our deck."

Mrs. S. then expostulates and explains they are the property of a lone lorn lady in Lagos, to whom Mrs. S. is taken them from the highest of motives; motives "such a nice gentleman" as the first officer must understand. . . . She cites other chief officers . . . have felt a ray of sunlight come into their lives when they saw those chicken crates and it was in their power to share in the noble work of returning them to Lagos freight free. [Despite protestations to the contrary] my faith in the ultimate victory of Mrs. S. never wavers.[31]

The intrepid Mary Kingsley was more than a traveler. She was an avid observer of people and their customs—a forerunner of the anthropologists without a specific culture and with no formal degree. In fact, Kingsley got to Africa and roamed freely along the coast and traveled on several rivers on the pretext of studying various types of fish. She passed herself off as a trader and, indeed, engaged in trade with women as well as men. While in Lambarene (Gabon), Kingsley was fascinated by the Igalwa women with whom she came into contact. The Igalwa women sat in the sun on "their low, good country stools." The chairs nearby were for decoration and were "dandy"— not for use.

> Those among [the women] who may not be busy sewing are busy doing each other's hair. Hairdressing is quite an art among the Igalwa . . . and their hair is very beautiful, very crinkly, but fine. It is plaited up, close to the head, partings between the plaits making elaborate parterres. Into the beds of plaited hair

are stuck on river ivory [hippo], decorated with black tracery
and openwork, made by their good men. A lady will stick as
many of these into her hair as she can get, but the prevailing
mode is to have one stuck in behind each ear, showing their
broad, long heads above like two horns; they are exceedingly
becoming to these comely black ladies, very I think they are
comeliest ladies I have seen on the coast.[32]

As to dress, the women preferred paun (loin cloth), wrapping the cloth
under "their armpits" with "a graceful form of drapery." Around the upper
part of their body, they wrapped a shawl with "Chinese-looking patterns.
. . . When they wear anything on their heads, it is a handerkerchief folded
shawlwise. . . . Add to this costume a sober-coloured silk parasol . . . [and]
then a few strings of turquoise-blue beads or imitation gold ones worn
around the shapely throat."[33] These brief but descriptive passages from
Kingsley's book provide us with a snapshot of the ordinary African women
Kingsley encountered. The missionaries, well-intentioned but accompanied
by their Victorian values, were less forthcoming about the material cultures
of the many women among whom they lived. Still, as we have seen in this
section, to paraphrase an old hymn, they often "rescued the perishing"
while attempting to weld Christianity over traditional practices—some of
which were devastating in these mainly patriarchal societies.

Women: Royals and Ceremonial Roles

Before the onset of colonialism, many African societies were ruled by
women, as we saw with Queen Nzinga (Chapter One) in today's Angola.
Some of the smaller ethnic groups in many parts of Africa south of the Sahara were ruled by women, including a few Islamic societies. Before the
arrival of Europeans we mainly relied on oral traditions to convey data regarding women rulers. After Europeans began to trade and travel, some of
those who encountered women in high places recorded their experiences.
I have chosen two women whose stories have come down to us through a
combination of oral traditions and written documents.

The first encounter brings us to South Africa and the Zulu King Shaka
kaSenzangakhona, who ruled first over a small number of clans and, with

an increasingly large army, not only conquered other Zulu clans, but waged war against and dispersed other ethnic groups as his realm extended. Some have depicted Shaka as a ruthless tyrant whose reign left devastation in its wake, disrupting societies through military onslaughts from about 1818 until 1828, when his half brother (and another) killed him. More recently Shaka's career has undergone revision with other important factors, such as drought, being held responsible for the dislocation and dispersal of masses of people during this period.

Shaka established large military settlements as he conquered. In each of these settlements he placed a military leader and a royal woman in charge. Regimentation on all levels and for both genders was strictly adhered to. Although his households were dominated by senior women, he never married. Early scribes who wrote about Shaka ruled out sex altogether, due to what some armchair psychologists considered was his neurotic tie to his mother, Nandi. Whatever his problems, mother-related or not, revisionist opinions are that Shaka engaged in sexual relations with women, perhaps numbers of women, but if a woman became pregnant she was put to death. One could argue that Shaka may have been impotent. And thus any pregnancies that were attributed to him involved another man. But clearly he was troubled regarding the female gender. At one point Shaka even repeatedly referred to a woman that a European treated and cured as a dog.[34]

Henry Francis Fynn and his partner, Francis Farewell, arrived at one of Shaka's military establishments in the early 1820s after Shaka was firmly established as a major military presence in the area. They were there to open up trading relations with this now much expanded kingdom. The first sign that they were approaching Shaka's compound was "troops of cattle being driven," with troops "interspersed with regiments of girls, decorated in beads and brass with regimental uniformity, carrying on their heads large pitchers of native beer, milk and cooked food." Soon after they entered the camp, Fynn and Farewell were overwhelmed by the sheer numbers of Shaka's regiments. These included "girls, headed by officers of their own sex . . . to the number of 8,000 to 10,000, each holding a staff in her hand. They joined in the dance which continued for about two hours."[35]

Shaka appeared, greeted the British men, and advised that they should not be afraid of his troops—who were singing and dancing all the while. As the ceremony continued the women from the "seraglio" [harem] entered along with "about 150 others, who were called sisters." Why the harem?

Perhaps Fynn was misinformed? Or perhaps these were the senior women attached to his household?

One woman already possessed considerable power and had attained rank in at least one Zulu clan before Shaka emerged as a unifying and/or destructive force among the Zulu. Mkabayi was nothing if not formidable, in that she not only survived the military campaigns Shaka conducted against some of these clans, she also became "highly influential" and had charge of a regiment that was composed of only men—this was unusual, especially for Shaka.[36] In each of his military settlements Shaka installed one woman and one male military officer as leaders. The role of the female leader was usually to supervise the women who were part of the military regiments, their roles being to take part in ceremonies and to dance.

Mkabayi's attributes included the unique gifts of being able to climb the slippery slope of leadership while also enjoying the respect of the common people. Like Queen Nzinga, she cross-dressed as a military figure, carrying a "spear and shield." She must have viewed these symbols of male power as useful to her success with a man like Shaka, who had complicated issues regarding women. In addition, she was quoted as being "most happy when criticizing men."[37]

She outlasted Shaka and worked with his successor, King Dingane. Unfortunately, we do not know if Mkabayi was privy to Dingane's plan to assassinate his half brother, but, considering her high status under Shaka, it is likely that she did. In the last phase of her life, one of Dingane's officials reported that he saw Mkabayi "address the army. She was a great royal she-elephant, very large with rolls of fat . . . she was a kingmaker, too."[38]

When John Hanning Speke arrived at the court of Baganda King Mutesa in late February, 1862, he found a highly structured political system in place and soon learned that he was going to be dealing with two competitive courts. The first was that of the king himself, and the other was that of the Queen Mother Muganzirwaza, whose palace Masorisori was in a large separate enclosure containing officials, many of the king's wives, and her own ladies-in-waiting.[39] After a few days following on his encounters with the king at his residence, including the presentation of gifts, and treatment for a nondescribed illness from his medicine kit, Speke was taken to the "queen dowager's" large compound. He recorded his first encounter in his journal: "I took, besides the medicine chest, a present of eight bars of brass and copper wire, thirty blue-egg beads . . . and sixteen cubits of chintz [cloth]."

At her palace enclosure Speke found "huts [that] were full of women," along with drums and musical instruments that were "placed for amusement." In fact, most of Speke's successful visits to the Queen Mother centered on entertainment, although, on occasion, he was under duress and forced to remain in her quarters providing doses of medicines (mostly quinine).[40]

Muganzirwaza was "of a more affable disposition than her son. . . . Her Majesty was fat, fair and forty-five." She was on a "carpet spread on the ground," resting her elbow on a pillow made of cloth bark—the same sort of material that marked her initial costume. Her ornaments consisted of a necklace, the bark cloth tied around her head, and an emblem of her authority—a heavy copper and iron bracelet on one arm. Later, the dowager queen explained that the neck ring joined by wreaths of vine leaves "conferred on the bearer the power of seizure [and is] the great seal of this country. Whoever wears it catches little children."[41]

Beside her rested "an old or well used looking glass," while surrounding the Queen Mother were evidences of "magic powder and other magic wants" plus diviners ("devil drivers"), along with a "mass of other women." Soon after they exchanged pleasantries and he presented his gifts, Muganzirwaza "took up some sticks, selecting three, [she] told me she had three complaints": one stick represented her stomach, "which gives me so much uneasiness." The second was her liver, "which causes shouting pains all over my body." The third stick stood for her heart, which caused her dreams at night, "about Sunna [II] my late husband, and they are not very pleasant." Speke advised that she remarry to remove the disturbing dreams. He was unaware that she was prohibited from taking another husband or to engage in sexual intercourse due to her status as dowager queen. Regarding her more physical ailments, Speke discovered that he was unable to touch the royal person in order to examine her; thus all he could do was prescribe medication, which was first tasted by her advisers to ascertain that "there was no deviltry" involved. Furthermore, he advised that she limit her diet and her consumption of alcoholic beverages. The latter prescription "caused consternation as she imbibed heavily and often." Speke was presented with a "pombe [palm wine] drinking pipe," and he showed her his book of drawings ("picture book"), which fascinated her. The book was subsequently shared with all of the women in attendance upon the Queen Mother. [42]

He returned two days later to complaints that his "pills had done her no good." Muganzirwaza demanded "new and different medications," but to no avail. The following day Speke came back to "share a pipe with her" while allowing the Queen Mother to investigate the contents of his pockets, including his watch and, at the same time, sharing some of his travel adventures. On this occasion the dowager queen ordered that the pombe be brought out, with the queen and her "ministers" becoming "uproarious. . . . Small cups were not enough . . . so a large wooden trough was placed before the queen and filled with liquor. . . . The queen put her head in the trough and drank like a pig from it, and was followed by her ministers." All of the imbibing was accompanied by "music and dance performances." On this occasion, the queen disappeared to change from one comely outfit into another, still drinking, drifting into song: "All drank and drank and sang til in their heated excitement they turned the palace into pandemonium." Speke noted in his journal that, although he tired of the tedium, he was unable to retreat, and was instead forced to party into the night. The queen mother "hit the trough of pombe promising to take more medicines the next day."[43]

A careful reading of Speke's journal over the nearly two months he was in residence fails to produce much evidence that the Queen Mother engaged in affairs of state or, for that matter, that she evidenced interest in matters beyond her immediate health problems, and in requiring Speke's attendance. But we must keep in mind that Speke was arrogant, especially with regard to his rank in the British army (Lieutenant) and his quite Eurocentric sense of superiority. His concerns were inward directed, and he could not have been privy to Muganzirwaza's schedule when he was not present in her quarters. She was a flamboyant character. Oral traditions indicate that Muganzirwaza could be ruthless. It is claimed that she caused a chief to lose his standing by accusing him of "making amorous advances to her which she refused." She was said to be envious of other royal women. And in one incidence, Muganzirwaza "demanded the execution of a guilty king's maternal uncle who had been pardoned."[44] Thus we can see that she exercised power—including being able to appoint her own ministers who, in turn, presided over affairs regarding lands that she owned.

Mutese had forbidden his retinue any contact with Speke—and it is unclear if he was aware of that, since this fact does not come up in his journal. But Muganzirwaza's brother came to call on Speke and suffered no consequences—her brother, however, was one of her ministers.[45] In this case, we do see Muganzirwaza's power. One matter that plagued Speke, and which Muganzirwaza finally resolved, was the matter of his living quarters. Speke resented being placed in an area reserved for Arab traders and other outsiders, whom he deemed below him in status—and he made that point to the queen on several occasions, all jotted down in his journal. Muganzirwaza did not move immediately—it is possible she had to circumvent her son, the Kabaka. But, in due time he obtained more favorable quarters, continuing his visits to the queen (which were more infrequent due to additional time with the king, who became more approachable). When Speke introduced the quinine treatment, the queen forced him to stay in the hut where she slept. She refused to allow anyone else to medicate her.[46]

Near the end of the first month of his stay in Buganda, noting that efforts to pry information regarding certain customs from the king had gone nowhere, Speke confided to his journal that there was "jealousy" between the two palaces (located some distance apart); hence by sharing with the queen Mutesa's reluctance to discuss these customs, he "purposely" set her up. Among Speke's queries were: What specifically did "marriage" entail in their society? "There are no such things as marriage in Uganda. There are no ceremonies attached to it." If a man committed an "offense" against the king, and "had a pretty daughter . . . he might give her to the king as a peace offering; if any neighboring king had a pretty daughter, and the King of Uganda wanted her, she might be demanded in fitting tribute. . . . The women are regarded as property."[47] Muganzirwaza did not comment on her own marriage to King Sunna II, but she was one of his 148 wives. A great deal of credit must be given to her ingenuity and the unknown numbers of maneuvers she had been able to successfully navigate, to elevate her son to the kingship on the death of his father. Surely it was not the pombe and partying that characterized her during so much of Speke's visit to Uganda, although the journal is replete with incidents of both.[48]

Muganzirwaza developed concern for Speke's wellbeing—as she saw it. He was accompanied by forty some men, all of whom were housed in the Ganda king's compound. In addition, Speke had a cook and a servant in attendance. His fellow explorer James Grant had suffered an injury and was held back until early May. Thus Speke was alone with a large staff (which he was constantly trying to provide for through lobbying the queen and Mutesa) and no one of his rank for company. The queen mother, who seemed to develop a genuine fondness for Speke (referring to him in the last weeks as "my son") gave him two girls—the youngest twelve years of age and the second "a little older"—who were to serve as wives. Later, she added a third girl to his harem. Unknown to her, Speke accepted the girls with the intention of taking them to Zanzibar and freedom—"as a means of getting them out of this land of death."[49]

But Speke witnessed the imperious side of this queen mother as well. She frequently became piqued and even enraged when Speke failed to visit regularly—or when she was summoned and she failed to appear, and Speke would leave. On one such occasion, Speke told her that he had presented himself as directed but had been left for hours. Muganzirwaza's response was to deny having been notified and to then have her servant flogged. Following the gift of the first two "wives," the dowager queen inquired about them, and before Speke was able to respond she advised that he "chain them." Then, too, there were the allegations that, before she attained the high rank of queen mother, she had been responsible for the deaths of several of her husband's sons—helping to clear the way no doubt for her own.[50]

Finally, still only a few weeks into Speke's visit to Uganda (25 March), he recorded this entry in his journal:

> Nearly every day I have seen one, two or three of the wretched palace women led away to execution, tied by the hand and dragged along by the body-guard, crying out, as she went to premature death. . . . (O my lord) . . . (my King) in the most despair and lamentation; and yet there was not a soul who dared lift a hand to save any of them.[51]

Witchcraft, Spirit Possession, and Traditional Beliefs

The subject of the occult in Africa has been of interest to travelers, to missionaries, and, once serious academic research began, to a range of scholars across disciplines. One notable feature emerges from many of these academic studies, and that is the role of women. Women are recorded as witches, diviners, and practitioners of exorcism through spirit possession. The majority of women were deprived of power in mainly patriarchal societies, yet, through the vehicle of traditional beliefs, some women across the continent emerged to exercise authority because of their assumed ability to control supernatural phenomena. Returning to Achebe's *Things Fall Apart*, we find Chielo, the priestess, "possessed by the power of her god" where she "began to prophesy."[52] Certainly, Umuofia was cast as a most patriarchal village, yet Chielo enjoyed the respect of all her citizens due to her communion with supernatural forces.

What modern Western-leaning people refer to as superstitions were often based on circumstances (many long forgotten) that gave rise to prohibitions and practices that tend to bring approbation today. We have seen how twins in some societies were regarded as bad omens, threatening not just their parents but entire populations. The irregular—twins—threatened. Similar traditional beliefs enveloped other ethnic groups, and many of these were aimed toward or directly at women. For instance, Mary Kingsley encountered a form of witchcraft among the Okyon people that centered on the death of a mother of "a child over six months old." This babe was treated with "special care in the spirit of the mother who was bound to come back and fetch the child in order to pacify and prevent" its death. The small child, Kingsley wrote, is "brought in and held just in front of the dead body of the mother," and he or she is slowly moved away so that the deceased mother "cannot see it." The person holding the baby then advises the dead mother that she cannot have it, before the "child is smuggled out of the hut" and a "bunch of plantains is put in with the body of the woman and bound up with funeral binding clothes."[53] This bundle was to placate the mother as she went to her grave.

Being regarded as a witch was a mixed blessing. In some societies, such as the Barotse, women were vulnerable if accused of witchcraft. Frederick Stanley Arnot, a missionary in Central Africa, witnessed "a poor old woman, who had always been very kind to me . . . being burned as a witch." She was accused of trying to bewitch the king and was tried "by the boiling pot test" and condemned. The "boiling pot test" involved a boiling hot pot of water into which the condemned had to wash her hands and if, "after twenty-four hours, the skin came off, the victims were . . . burned alive." During his UMCA posting, Arnot noted that this form of judgment was an "almost daily occurrence."[54]

Among the Swahili on the East African coast, witchcraft and spirit possession were practiced rather widely in the pre-colonial era. G.S.P. Freeman-Grenville claimed that the major African contribution to the Swahili was witchcraft.[55] Indians, Arabs, and slaves brought their traditional beliefs with them when they migrated to the coast. In the 1890s German linguist Dr. Carl Velten asked a few "pure Swahili persons" (left undefined) to recall some of their old customs. Among these were those that pertained to spirit possession and sorcery. Grandmothers long dead, for instance, were capable of sending their "bad spirits" (*pepo mbaya)* to female descendants. Although Islam prohibits these practices, several of the recorded songs contained Islamic phraseology. For instance, the nineteenth century "Tambourine Spirit" called for a chorus to chant religious verses usually reserved to sing praises to the Prophet, but it was combined with non-Islamic behavior featuring a woman holding a sword while she chewed a betel nut and danced.[56] Here we see the outward symbols of power being manifested through the weapon.

Peter Lienhardt studied witchcraft among the Swahili in Bagamoyo in Tanzania and produced a series of poems with some interesting findings regarding the sexual organs. Women stowed various objects in their vaginas (which were also beneficial to nonwitches as storage for love potions). The male organ was useful to the witch who could, for instance, keep a knife sheathed in her husband's penis. When she returned to the coven from the kill, and while he slept, she inserted the knife which then prevented her husband from engaging in sex with her. After consultation with a medicine man, one husband caught his wife in the act of returning her knife into his limp organ and thereafter sought a divorce.[57]

Then there was also the "evil eye" phenomenon, which caused illnesses. In Lamu, Kenya, an old former slave confided that "a long time ago *kayambi* [a rattle filled with pieces of grain] was shaken while numbers of people danced after "the eye" attacked. "In those days a fire was built . . . big smoke from fire . . . to give healing a chance to chase the evil eye away." This woman's grandmother, who she believed was "a witch," used to perform, shaking the rattle and dancing. She no longer remembered the word, but she was convinced that the evil eye was another term for jinni (djinn), which were thought to come from the sea.[58] In this example we see a synchronic melding of Arab and Swahili culture—the jinn being Arabian in origin and frequently referred to in the Qur'an.

Illnesses in traditional societies required not only roots, herbs, and other natural substances, but also the intervention of the supernatural. Unnatural behavior, too, required extraordinary procedures, such as Salme binta Said remembered from her Zanzibar childhood in the 1830s. The healing processes she described were attributed to what historian Edward Alpers judged to be a spinoff from the Ethiopian *zaar* cult.[59] Where an adult illness was concerned, more severe measures were required to drive out the devil, including bringing in a medium. Salme referred to a "new-born child who might be restless" and cry more than warranted. The child was surely possessed and required treatment. In this case, Salme recalled that exorcism in the first instance required foodstuffs: "Little onions and bits of garlic are strung like pearls and suspended from the arms and neck"—while this remedy might appear "foolish" she pointed out that "for if the poor devil has any olfactory nerves, he could hardly withstand such an attack upon them."[60]

> Grown-up people are . . . frequently possessed—men but rarely, but many women, and of the Abyssinian [Ethiopian] women, nearly one-half. Convulsive attacks, want of appetite, and general apathy, the desire to remain shut up in dark rooms, and such propensities, are taken as sure signs. A person, thought to be possessed, is treated with a tremendous amount of respect, or rather—fear!
>
> The newly attacked woman sits down in a dark room, wrapped so completely in her *schele* [burka] that she cannot be touched by the slightest ray of light. She is then, in the true sense of the word, smoked out, a vase containing strong incense being held close to her nostrils. The company around her begin to sing a strange song, wagging their heads all the time to and fro. Some Abyssinian concoction, composed of corn and dates . . . is a beverage necessary for the occasion. I have been told that all of these combined influences put the victim in a state of second sight; she first talks incoherently, until at last she raves with foam at the mouth. Then is the time that the spirit has taken possession of her. The company present enter into conversation with this spirit, and request to be informed what it wants; for it must be understood that the sick are not plagued by evil spirits alone—there are also good spirits.
>
> Sometimes it occurs that two spirits, a good and a bad one, contest for the same person, and during this exorcism they are sure to manifest themselves.[61]

Moving to South Africa, we encounter a female prophet whose engagement with spirits from the dead had a profound effect on an entire Xhosa society in the Eastern Cape in the mid-1850s. This lengthy "tale of Nongqawuse" was written by William W. Gqoba, who actually witnessed the devastation that took place in the aftermath of Nongqawuse's prophetic visions. The story began in the year 1856, when two Xhosa "girls went out to the lands to keep the birds away from the corn."

What follows is the Tale of Nongqawuse from Gqoba's translation:

> One was named Nongqawuse [an orphan] . . . and the other daughter [her father's sister]. Near the river known as the Kamanga two men approached them and said "Convey our greetings to your people and tell them we are So-and-So and So-and-So." And the names by which they called themselves turned out to be names of people who were known to have died long ago. They went on to say: "You are to tell the people that the whole community is about to rise again from the dead. Then go on to say to them all the cattle living now must slaughtered, for they are reared by defiled hands, as the people handle witchcraft. Say to them that there must be no ploughing of land, rather must the people dig deep pits, erect new huts, set up wide, strong built cattlefolds, make milksacks. . . . The people must give up witchcraft on their own, not waiting until they are exposed by witchdoctors. You are to tell them that these are the words of their chiefs, —the words of Napakade ('Forever') the son of Sifubasibanzi ('the Broad-chested')."
>
> On reaching home the girls reported this, but no one would listen. Everybody ridiculed them instead. On the following day, they went again to keep the birds away from the corn, and after some time, these men appeared again and asked if the girls had told the people at home, and what people had said in reply. The girls reported that their message had simply been a thing of laughter, no one believing them. "The people simply said we were telling stories."
>
> The men then said "Say to the elders that they are to call all the chiefs together from [the wider area] and they must tell the news to them."

The following morning, Mhlakaza [Nongqawuse's father] and some other men went to the lands, but these strangers did not reveal themselves. They were heard without being seen. It was only Nongqawuse and the other girls who heard them, and Nongqawuse who interpreted what was being said by these spirits. They said, "Tell these men to go and call the chiefs and bring them here. Only then shall we reveal ourselves."

[Some of the men went to various kraals and to the royal palace carrying Nongqawuse's news. The king sent out others to the place but again no spirit came] . . . Maramnco, son of Fadana, accompanied by others attempted to check out the prophecy]. . . . All of these men made their way to the home of Mhlakaza. . . . On arriving there, they were told that Nongqawuse desired that the numbers to go to the Gxara be reduced, and that those who were to go must be mostly chiefs. This in truth was done.

As the people were rather fearful, it happened that as they drew near the River Kamanga, their throats went dry, and they felt thirsty. Meanwhile Nongqawuse, beautifully painted in red ochre, led the way. Then those who were thirsty were heard to say: "Is one who is thirsty allowed to drink?"

Nongqawuse replied: "He who does not practice witchcraft may drink without fear." Thereupon Dilima, here son of Pato, removed his kaross and stooped to drink. Then one by one the other men . . . followed suit.

The Vision

Just at this time, there was a tremendous crash of big boulders breaking loose from the cliffs overlooking the headwaters of the River Kamanga, whereupon, the men gazed at one another wondering, for they were seized with fear. It seemed that some unknown thing on the cliffs was going to burst into flames.

While they stood wondering, the girl was heard saying, "Just cast your eyes in the direction of the sea."

And they looked intently at the waters of the sea, it seemed as if there were people there in truth, and there sounds of bulls bellowing, and oxen too. There was a huge formless black object that came and went, and finally vanished over the crests of the waves of the sea.

Then it was that all of the people began to believe.[62]

[The tale continued with the reactions of chiefs and others among the Xhosa. Nongqawuse had not only convinced them that they must follow the spirits' directions—her vision became theirs—but] "truly the people were so deluded that they went so far as to claim that they had seen the horns of cattle, heard the lowing of milk-cows, the barking of dogs, and the songs of milk-men at milking time."[63]

On reaching their homes, the chiefs assembled their subjects and made known the news of the ancestors who were expected to return to life, and strong, of the promised coming-to-life again of the cattle they had slaughtered long ago.

Nongqawuse had said that anyone who, on slaughtering his ox, decided to dispose of its carcass by barter, should nevertheless engage its soul, in order that on its coming back to life it should be his property. And she had said that all those who did not slaughter their cattle would be carried by a fierce hurricane and thrown into the sea to drown and die.

The community was split in two. One section believed that the resurrection of the people would come some day, but not that of the cattle. Thereupon, father fell out with son, brother with brother, chief with subjects, relative with relative. . . . So some slaughtered their cattle and some did not.[64]

It will not surprise us to learn that "nothing happened." The people [who slaughtered] all of their cattle and burned their crops died of hunger and disease in large numbers. Thus it was whenever thereafter a person said an unbelievable thing, those who heard him said, "You are telling a Nongqawusa catastrophe."[65]

The outcome of Nongqawuse's vision resulted in economic disaster for many of the Xhosa. Because they had no cattle and no crops, some tried to force the Xhosa who had ignored the prophecy to feed and shelter them.

This caused upheaval in the larger community. Furthermore, a large number of displaced Xhosa flocked into Cape Colony, where they became low-level laborers for Europeans.

In this period of transition from the slave trade to colonialism, we have seen Europeans gradually encroaching into Africa's interior in the form of missionaries, explorers, traders, and settlers. In the case of the Xhosa, the Europeans were already present and colonialism was a fact of life, although, as we observed in Nongqawuse's case, traditional beliefs were responsible for the devastation visited on the Xhosa in the 1850s—the noose of colonialism had not yet tightened in many parts of South Africa in the nineteenth century. It had begun in Sierra Leone in the 1780s.

Liberia was never an American colony, but, as we saw, American missionaries arrived in the 1830s and began not only to implant Christianity but also to elevate the mainly African American refugees to what would become a ruling elite—black on black.

CHAPTER FIVE

The South African Body: Defiled, Diseased, Devastated, and Destroyed

In this chapter we again return to European imagery and the female body. As we begin, we transport that "body" to Europe at the turn of the nineteenth century, before progressing to the end of the 1890s and the encounter between British imperialists and the Boers (the Afrikaner rural folk that we met earlier). The end of the South African War leads us to a case study focusing on an African rural family which bridges the nineteenth and twentieth centuries. Finally we touch down next door in Namibia, which had been the German colony of South West Africa, and a major travesty affecting the Herero.

Sara Baartman, the Hottentot Venus

As we saw earlier, the extended genitalia of Khoe women had been a source of prurient interest to Europeans very soon after the Dutch arrived at the Cape. The question as to whether the Khoe (among others) were members of the human race or a subspecies continued to permeate "scientific" circles, especially following Linnaeus's classifications of people (and almost everything else) in 1735. While curiosity reigned, no Khoe had ever been to Europe until Sara Baartman arrived in June 1810. Her story began in 1790 at her birth in the Eastern Cape. Persistent Boer attacks on the Khoe were, they claimed, due to cattle raids. Their practice was to take away the surviving women and children and place them in their homes in a form of bondage (not legal slavery). This is what happened in Sara's case. Her village was wiped out, and she found herself bound to the Dutch farming family of Peter Cezar near Cape Town.

Sometime in late 1809 or early 1810, Peter Cezar's brother Hendrick and his companion, a British ship's doctor, paid a visit to the farm, where they encountered Sara. Like most Khoe women's, Sara's steatopygia (large protruding buttocks) attracted their attention. In brief, the two men schemed to take her to Europe and put her on display for a fee. They convinced Peter Cezar to let her go and then induced Sara to go with them—promising her that she could return in six years. Although he later regretted it, the British governor at the Cape, Lord Caledon, gave his permission for her to travel, surely having no idea what diabolical plans Cezar and his British companion had in mind for this now twenty-year-old Khoe woman.[1]

Three months after sailing from Cape Town to England, the two schemers took her to Piccadilly in London, where freak shows were a big attraction. Very soon after Sara went on display, the British doctor withdrew from the partnership, leaving her entirely in the hands of the unscrupulous Cezar. He placed an advertisement in one of the London papers announcing the "Hottentot Venus," who would be available for viewing from 1 to 5 p.m. daily at two shillings per head. Sara wore an apron cover over the front of her genitals, and two small cups covered her breasts. Her buttocks were bare. Cezar had added to her exotic "otherness" by painting "tribal marks" on her cheeks. She was placed in a cagelike enclosure, from which she was summoned for inspection by the paying public.[2]

Quite soon Sara became such a sensation that plays and songs were composed about her. One such song called attention to the steatopygia: "a rump she had, though strange it be . . . . and that is why people go to see the Venus Hottentot."[3] Cartoons ridiculed her body.[4] Vulgarity reigned. Although Sara was attracting the leering crowds, others in London took offense at the manner in which she was displayed and at the lurid publicity as well. Letters to the editor of various London papers began to appear, complaining about the exhibit and decrying her treatment, referring to threats from Cezar if she failed to exit the cage on command—much like a trained animal. One of the letter writers, signing himself as a "White Man," noted that Sara was the "victim of the lowest ribaldry."

Abolitionists—those who had successfully ended the slave trade only a few years earlier—were currently crusading to abolish slavery. Prominent members of the African Association, an abolitionist group, came forward to protest Sara's exploitation. They lodged a complaint with the courts, which, in turn, took up the case and called for a hearing to determine whether Sara was being coerced to perform. Cezar spoke first and argued that Sara was "getting a fair share of the profits" and was "treated with kindness." Then Sara was called on to testify. Questioned in Dutch, she stated that she "had agreed to come to England for a share of the profits." (She did not specifically state that she was given any of the profits.) Furthermore, she told the court, every Sunday she was allowed to take a carriage ride around the city of London, and she had "two black boys" to care for her—she had "everything that she wanted."[5] The case was dismissed.

No one knows what pressures Cezar may have placed on the poor young woman and, indeed, what terror she may have felt at the prospect of being turned loose alone and as an object of curiosity or even scorn. Sara and Cezar went underground for a period of time after the court hearing and later resurfaced in Manchester, where she was put on display, and, in 1811, she was baptized. She and Cezar went to Liverpool and other secondary places until, in 1814, he decided to take her to Paris.

There she was brought to the Palais Royale, which was similar to Piccadilly, with exotic exhibits that drew a large public. Then, Cezar, in September 1814, decided to transfer Sara to a French animal trainer as part of his entourage. We have no idea how much money changed hands, but surely Cezar did not step out of the picture without ample compensation. And the Frenchman no doubt saw profit in Sara's steatopygia. In addition to putting her on exhibit, he also rented her out to balls and banquets, as part of the "entertainment." On one such occasion, Sara's appearance drew the sympathy of a male guest, who later described the event: she wore "skin tight" clothes, and she jumped, sang, and played drums. Her arrival had so upset the sensibilities of some of the women present that they fled, hiding themselves and, in the process, upsetting Sara, who, as she performed, had "tears running down her cheeks."[6] A reporter offered Sara a lift home, whereupon she confessed that she was a "very unhappy Sara" and had concluded that she would never return to the land of her birth.[7] These are the only words (perhaps in paraphrase) that reveal the forlorn Sara's ongoing homesickness.

Soon Sara was moved for display at the Jardin des Plantes, on the outskirts of Paris. Beyond the curious gawkers, the gardens drew several French scientists who had become aware of her presence. Georges Cuvier was "France's greatest naturalist," who, with his colleagues, visited the Khoe woman over the course of three separate days to "observe." This included attempts to view her genitals. According to Stephen Jay Gould, Cuvier was unable to convince her to drop the apron.[8] Cuvier had requested that Sara be delivered to the National History Museum, where, of course, he planned to carry out the in-depth investigation he was denied at the Jardin des Plantes. But he never had the chance to examine her body before her early death, which occurred in January 1816.[9]

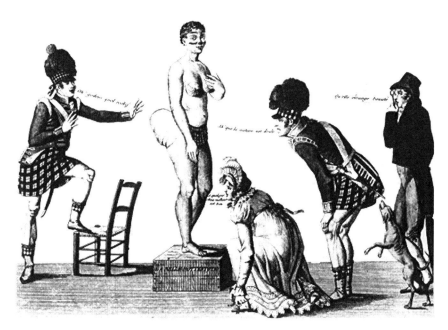

Sara Baartman depicted in a French cartoon.
Source: *Le Petit Journal*

Cuvier conducted a dissection of Sara's body, the results of which confirmed the general hypothesis of the time: "Saartjie herself emphasizes all points of superficial similarity with any ape or monkey." Cuvier wrote that her "movements had something brusque and capricious about them, which reveal those of monkeys. She had, above all, a way of pouting her lips in the same way we have observed in orangutans." This "Venus"—her sexual anatomy—was duly bottled and exhibited at a lecture by Cuvier to the French Academy: "I have the honor to present . . . the genital organs of this woman prepared in a manner that leaves no doubt about the nature of her tablier [genitals]."[10] This, according to Gould, left no doubt that the Khoekhoe (plus other aborigines) were relegated to "the lowest rung" on the ladder of "human progress."[11]

Sander L. Gilman also observed that, in the "fascination with Khoe women's figures," the body was "reduced to sexual parts. . . . Sara Baartman's sexual parts, her genitalia and her buttocks, serve as the central image of the black female throughout the nineteenth century." Indeed, not only Khoe but blacks in general "were a separate (and needless to say lower) race." But it was the "female body that attracted and repelled."[12] As further indication of cruel stereotypes visited on black women, Gilman quoted one South Carolinian writing in 1868 that the "hymen in black women was further up the vagina than white women." This, he proclaimed, "may be one of the anatomical marks of the non-unity of the races," supporting Cuvier and his colleagues in their racist misogyny.[13]

In the 1990s, negotiations began to return Sara Baartman's remains to her homeland. Her skeleton and a plaster cast of her body had been on display in the Musée de l'Homme. Apparently, the vessels holding her brain and her genitals—those dissected and examined by Cuvier—went missing from the shelves where Stephen Jay Gould had viewed them in the early 1980s. Thus in 2002, after negotiations had been completed, what remained of Sara was shipped to Cape Town; and on Women's Day in August of that year, she was buried in the Gamatoos River Valley, near her birthplace in the Eastern Cape.

Women and the South African War (1899-1902)

Very little documentation remains pertaining to women during the war.[14] But before we touch on the conflict itself and the atrocities against women, we need to sketch in some background. We left the British as colonizers at the Cape from (officially) 1814, noting, however, that slavery had been abolished there in 1834, as was the case elsewhere in the British Empire.

Dissatisfaction with British policies led to a stream of Boers moving from the Cape into Natal, which Britain annexed in 1842. That sent many Boers to what came to be the Orange Free State (OFS), and others settled across the Vaal River and spread out in the vast territory from the Kalahari

Desert to the Limpopo River in the north. Most of these Afrikaners or Boers (meaning farmers, which the vast majority were) who left the Cape in the 1830s and later were poor *bywoners* (those with no land who worked for others who did). This part of South Africa's history is dramatic in terms of encounters and conflict with African groups, in particular the Zulu; and it includes the experiences of those who trekked out and away. But, for our purposes, the result was the founding of two Afrikaner-dominated states that were recognized as independent by the British government in the 1850s: the Orange Free State, as noted above, and the Boer Republic of the Transvaal (Transvaal).[15]

Another facet of South Africa's history that began in the 1850s and continued into the early twentieth century was the importation of thousands of indentured laborers from India to work in the sugarcane fields for British landholders in coastal Natal. The Tamil indentured workers were followed by a number of "Cargo" Muslim Indians, mainly from Gujarat. They sold petty goods to the Hindu Tamils, who otherwise had no curries or familiar spices. When their indentures ended, the majority of the Tamils stayed on, and so, too, did the majority of the Muslim traders. The Indians experienced discrimination, especially from the Afrikaners, but their numbers swelled, and many of the generations following the indentured workers were upwardly mobile—going into business or earning professional degrees. While they were not welcome in the OFS or the Transvaal, during the war some of them were employed as medical personnel by the British.

Discovery of diamonds at Kimberley in the 1870s, and later the huge gold seams in the Transvaal in 1886, set in motion a series of events that led first to Britain annexing the Transvaal in 1877. By 1881, the Boer Republic had regained its independence following a surprise attack on British forces based in Natal. A consensus among British politicians in London and at the Cape favored ending the occupation. But this was only one minor retreat in a series of factors, not the least British imperialism, and the role played by European capitalists who controlled the gold mines in the Boer Republic. That led to war.

The Boers had spread out extensively in the Transvaal. Some lived in and operated out of their wagons. Others built substantial homes. They had no qualms about routing African livestock keepers from the land they occupied. As time passed, thirty or forty more years, in both the OFS and in the Transvaal almost all Boer farmers had African servants and laborers,

mostly sharecroppers, on their land. This is a very short and somewhat im-
precise summary, but it is important to note that African and Boer were unequal but often shared similar agricultural pursuits. African women and
their children were pressed into work—in the fields and in the domestic
sphere. Some Boer customs were those of the Africans around whom they
lived. But racial lines were tightly drawn.

It is important to note, too, that discrimination existed between the
British and other Europeans who moved into Natal and who came to farm
in the OFS, and the increasing numbers of outsiders who came into the
Transvaal, especially after the gold discoveries. In the nineteenth century,
many regarded the Boers as a "race" apart—ignorant, uncouth, isolated and
insular, relating only to each other. Some Dutch Reformed Churches were
established, but those living in far outposts might make a pilgrimage to the
nearest town to sell their goods once a year and, while close to a church,
marry and/or baptize their children. Today we would refer to these Boers
in class terms. But then class was not a trope; thus a form of racialism (as
it was called) existed between Brit and Boer. Attitudes toward many of the
Afrikaner farmers, again mainly in the Transvaal, were not much different
than they were toward blacks. (They did come together on occasion and
over time to fight the Africans, but that is another story). The British settlers' attitudes toward the various African populations echoed those of the
Boers.[16]

After the gold mines attracted masses of outsiders, the Boers levied
heavy taxes on equipment. As industrial development increased, the leaders
of the OFS and the Transvaal engaged in frequent communication as regards to what they saw as conflict being inevitable. In the Transvaal word
came that the British were sending troops from the United Kingdom. Fearing invasion, in October 1899, President Kruger decided to go on the offensive, believing that he and his commandos (militia) could take the
offensive as they had done at Majuba in Natal in 1881, and in a single attack
rout the troops posted at a British garrison. Their show of strength would,
he believed, ward off further conflict.

Initially the Boers were successful—they practiced a similar type of
guerrilla warfare that had been employed in parts of the American colonies
in their war with the British in the 1770s. Troop reinforcement, plus a
change in generals, turned into an absolutely ruthless policy directed toward
the Boers in Natal, the OFS, and the Transvaal. In 1899 the Boers attacked

Kimberley. There an early casualty was "an African woman, whose head was blown off" as she walked by "a club." Then a savage incident involved some African women, when several hundred Baralong (Africans) "attempted a mass exodus" from Boer troops. "Only ten got away; the rest returned. Many had been stripped naked and flogged by the Boers." A few days later, "a party of thirteen [Baralong] women were caught and nine were shot and killed. Only four returned, and two of them were wounded. They claimed that the Boers had deliberately finished off the rest of the women."[17]

In Mafeking, the black journalist Sol Plaatje wrote that the British were not welcome and among the reasons was their treatment of African women.[18] It was in Mafeking that the notorious British general Baden-Powell decided to "starve" the local Africans. (Baden-Powell later founded the Boy Scouts.) This decision had a profound impact on women and children as well as their men. A British journalist reported the outcome of this policy: "I saw them fall down on the veldt [fields] and lie where they had fallen, too weak to go on their own way. . . . Hunger had them in its grip. . . . Their ribs literally breaking through their shriveled skins—men, women and children." Some survived by digging up the "corpses of dogs buried outside the town."[19] Baden-Powell's policy of rationing could be generous: at one point he provided "ninety four unlicensed dogs" for the Africans to eat.[20] Ironically, these particular Africans were allies of the British.

By late 1899 the new commander of the British force, Lord Roberts, initiated the scorched-earth policy. This translated to burning the Boer homesteads, barns/outbuildings, fields, and at times even the livestock. Otherwise they slaughtered the stock for their own consumption. The result was that women, children, and the aged were homeless. As we noted earlier, records pertaining to blacks are nearly nonexistent. But when all of the buildings were destroyed and burned down and fields destroyed, that meant that African families, too, were displaced. Many of the blacks flocked to the British lines, bringing what they could of their livestock. By 1900 the British policy was to evacuate blacks living on Boer farms and to put them in locations near where they lived. (Locations were areas specifically designed for Africans only, the forerunners of the reserves and, later, the homelands). Later many were removed from the locations, their livestock was taken for British troops, and the Africans were put to work by the military.[21]

The scorched-earth policy and the subsequent store of "refugees" (as the British referred to the homeless women and children) led to the creation of concentration camps. These were begun while Lord Roberts was still in command in 1900 and increased in numbers—multiples—under General Kitchener, who took over in late 1900. Because very few data were collected or, if collected, not retained, it is difficult to try to reconstruct much about the black concentration camps, which, like everything else in South Africa, were separate. Elizabeth van Heyningen, who has written rather extensively on this period, suggests that parallels can be drawn from the white camps, on which considerable detail exists. "For women across the spectrum in the South African War, disempowerment, deprivation and disease were significant realities. . . . The working classes, black and white, starved most and lost the most children."[22]

What we do know about the blacks is that some African women, but probably not many, accompanied their madams to the camps as servants. In the African camps there were more men than in the white camps, but they were sent out to work, leaving the women and children behind. In fact, their camps were mainly located on Boer farms, where it was assumed that they could grow their own food, and most were also close to railroad tracks. Van Heyningen, however, pointed out that being located next to the rail lines could have deleterious effects. She quoted a report in which "British troops wantonly trampled over the mealie [corn] fields, destroying an entire crop" before taking the blacks' "pigs and fowls. At least 600 people were left destitute" as a result.[23]

When provisions were made available to those in the black camps, they were less than those given to the whites. Two women complained to camp military authorities regarding lack of food: "We have to work hard all day long but the only food we can get is mealies [corn] and mealie meal [ground corn] and this is not supplied free but we have to purchase same with our own money. Meat we are not able to get at any price, nor are we allowed to buy anything at the shops."[24] Van Heyningen speculated that, in general, adults received about a pound of meat per week, and children less.[25] In the camps on farmland Africans grew "corn and sorghum along with potatoes and pumpkins."[26] Some African women "were supplied to private employers near the camps," and others were sent to Johannesburg and placed in domestic service. Although the British opened schools for the white children in their camps, none were available to the Africans. But in some camps, the African Methodist Episcopal Church (begun by American missionaries) was active in spreading the gospel and providing comfort.

In April 1901 the population of the "Edenburg [black] camp had risen to over 2,000, half of them children," living in crude tents of big sticks stuck in the ground and covered by sacking material. Many children died during that winter [seasons are reversed in South Africa], and van Heyningen attributed their deaths to "bronchitis and pneumonia." Measles was a problem in all of the camps—black and white—with pneumonia often following.[27] The British believed that the high death rate among the children was due to neglect by their mothers. "Natives do not seem to care for their children till they reach a useful age," one of them reported.[28] In August 1901, one report stated that 24,457 blacks were held in the sixty camps that had been established for them. The problem is, we do not know how many of these were women and children. Liz Stanley suggests that more men than women were present in the black camps.[29]

Emelia Mahlodi Pooe on the South African War

Mrs. Pooe, a Sotho-speaking woman, was almost 100 years old when her story was recorded by a descendant. Her parents, the Molefes, of Ngwato-Kwena origin, had been unable to survive in Lesotho and had moved into the Orange Free State to become labour-tenants in the Heilbron district when she was born. By the time the South African War started, her family had become sharecroppers on the Zaaiplaas, just southwest of Heilbron. This region, later part of the "maize triangle," was thoroughly cleared and devastated by the British in the "scorched earth" clearings. The Molefe family did not escape. The men were conscripted into the British army and the women interned in the black camp at Vredefort Road. Their cattle, already devastated by the *rinderpest* (an infectious disease), were lost to them. To Mrs. Pooe the struggle for survival in this crowded environment was a foretaste of urban location life. Like the white camp inmates, rations were limited, firewood was in short supply and the ordinary institutions of daily social life were interrupted. The food was poor, the porridge made from the type of maize she knew as animal feed.

In September 1901 there were 1579 inmates at the Vredefort Road black camp, 163 men, 496 women and 920 children. Numbers stabilized at about 1500 in the months that followed. According to the official records mortality was low, averaging between three and four a month. The object of the black camps was to provide for the black inmates as cheaply as possible by making the people work the fields. Ms. Pooe's memory appears to have been somewhat vague by the time she was interviewed but she recalled the hard work of tilling the fields. "Although they were accustomed to eating green mealies, they were not allowed to do so in camp, as it was said that by so doing the projected harvest targets would not be achieved" (Keegan 1981: 348). Vredefort Road camp was slow to become completely independent, however. As late as March 1902, 742 inmates were still being rationed on reduced payment (they paid a reduced sum for bags of mealies) and 795 were maintained free. The cost of the camp for that month was £732, one of the most expensive camps in the ORC, of which about £32 was recovered from the men working for the British and £70 obtained through sales of "medical comforts".

The postwar era was hard. Blacks had lost as much or more than Boers in the war although, thanks to Lotbiniere's intervention, some received compensation. Before the war the Molefe family had owned a span of oxen, enabling them to sharecrop on a relatively equal basis. After the war, although they returned to Zaaiplaas, without oxen their position was far less favourable. Nevertheless, the family was more fortunate than some who had lost most members of their families and were left with no place to go except on the most difficult terms.[30]

In the white camps, and drawing comparisons to the black camps, diphtheria, typhoid, chickenpox, and whooping cough joined measles and pneumonia as major diagnosed illnesses. Dysentery was rampant. Stanley in

Mourning Becomes not only studied hospital and death records to establish the diagnoses leading to deaths, but also attempted to sift through racial identities. Her book contains innumerable tables and statistics; perhaps the most interesting factor was how racialized these were. "Coolies" (Indians); Coloureds (mixed race); and in some cases people of African ethnic identity such as Zulu or Sotho were placed in proximity to names. The total numbers of blacks who died in their camps was 19,000 and perhaps more, since records were haphazard if kept at all in some of them.

Concerning white women, they were in spiraling numbers of camps in Natal, OFS, and Transvaal. A large body of literature, much of it from diaries and memoirs, spells out in dramatic manner the experiences of those who were incarcerated. Sanitation was very poor. Large numbers of occupants were stuffed into the large white tents—the Boers had big families consisting of several children—and several families were often crowded into the tents together. We have seen that blacks received less in the way of rations than the whites, but these women and their children, too, were on limited diets and lacked fresh vegetables until at least 1901, following on a report issued to Parliament. At that time, too, the administration of the camps changed from military to civilian control. And at that time, too, Indian medical staff was brought in to minister to the health needs of the white women.

We have noted that the British attitudes toward the Boers were disdainful—and much criticism was leveled toward the women for lack of cleanliness. They also were reluctant to accept medicines prescribed by the medical staff (when they were present), preferring their own home remedies. (There were no medical personnel in the black camps, and thus the blacks were entirely dependent on traditional cures if they were able to obtain the roots/herbs and essential ingredients).[31] Word of terrible conditions in the camps and the increasing deaths in them seeped out and via news reports. They reached England, and brought an Englishwoman, Emily Hobhouse, in 1900 to inspect them. She did not visit any of the black camps.

Hobhouse returned to England and wrote a scathing report that was submitted to Parliament. It is, in part, reprinted here:

Partial Report of Emily Hobhouse
on Concentration Camps

Camp at Bloemfontein, 26th of January, 1901.

"There are nearly 2000 people in this one camp, among them only a few men and over 900 children. . . . The tents are like a furnace. On rainy nights the water pours through the linen and streams into the tents, as only rain in this country can stream, and the woolen blankets on which the people lie become wet through. . . . Mrs. P. expects her confinement in three weeks, but she must lie on the bare ground until she is stiff and sore. For two months she has had nothing to sit upon, and crouches upon a rolled-up blanket. . . . I call the whole camp system cruelty on a large scale. It will never, never be effaced from the memories of these people. The children are hit the hardest by it. They wither away in the frightful heat and in consequence of the insufficient and unsuitable food. Thousands, bodily weak, are faced with conditions of life, which, in their weakened condition, they are unable to endure. They are face to face with hopeless ruin. There are cases in which whole families have been parted and sent to various places, they do not know whither. . . . If the English people would only try to picture the whole hopeless state of things! The population of whole villages and districts torn from the soil to which they clung with all the roots and fibers of their being, and thrust into another barren spot! To keep up this kind of camp is nothing less than child-murder! . . .

"We have a good deal of typhoid and fear an epidemic. On this account I brought my whole energies to bear upon seeing that the water of the Modder River should be boiled. The doctors say one might as well swallow pure typhoid bacillus cultures as drink this water. And yet all of them cannot boil their water, because heating materials are so scarce. The quantity given out every week is not sufficient to cook *one* warm meal a day. . . .

In the next tent a girl of 21 lay dying on a stretcher. The father, a tall, mild-looking Boer, knelt beside her, while in the neighbouring tent his wife watched over a six-year old child which was also dying, and a five-year old which was pining away. This couple had already lost 3 children in the Hospital.

Camp at Norval's Point, 10th of February, 1901.

"The heat in the tents was very great. Even the large, cool, airy tents were often up to 104 degrees Fahrenheit, and in the small tents, made of ordinary sail-cloth, the temperature rose to 108° and 113°. The doctor said he could not use his fever thermometer in these tents, since it would not fall at all.

Camp Aliwal North, 12th of February, 1901.

"The scarcest of all is soap. Neither in this camp nor in Norval's Point has soap been given out, and those who have no money can neither wash themselves nor their clothes.

Camp at Bloemfontein, 17th of February, 1901.

"I am quite distressed by the lack of mattresses. If the military authorities will only give me hay or straw, I will soon have the people making their own. . . . The great majority are obliged to lie on the bare ground.

Camp of Bloemfontein, 18th of February, 1901.

"It is an absolutely false idea, rotten to the core, to create everywhere in these Boer states great, dismal settlements of these people who are officially called refugees, and are supposed to be under our protection, but loathe this protection, but who consider themselves prisoners of war, who are held by force and loathe this protection.

Camp of Bloemfontein, 27th of February, 1901.

"Five rows of corrugated iron huts (houses they could not be called) have been erected, 2 rows of single rooms back to back, 10 in a row. 20 in a building, and every one of these rooms shelters one or more families. About 100 families are sheltered thus. The iron dividing walls do not reach to the roof, so that noise, draughts and infection run riot through the whole building.

Camp at Springfontein, 4th of March, 1901.

"The people here are worse off for the merest necessities than I have previously experienced anywhere. Fortunately I had three chests full of clothes with me, but it is only a drop in this ocean of misery. I sat the whole day on the verandah of a farmhouse. One after another every family was brought out of its tent and ranged before me. I could give them just so many clothes as would suffice to cover their nakedness. . . . The worst necessity in this camp is the want of heating materials. There is no wood. A little coal was given out, but so little that on many days the people were unable to do any cooking at all. But the raw rations served out cannot be prepared without fire.

Camp at Kimberley, 13th of March, 1901.

"This is the smallest camp which I have seen as yet. The camps are too near together, and the whole enclosed by an eight-foot barbed wire fence . . . no matron. A large, unfurnished, empty tent, which is perhaps a hospital. Overfilled tents. Measles and whooping-cough are raging, the camp is dirty and smells foully. An army doctor, who naturally understands little about children's ailments. Firing, almost none. The wife of a commander is here with six children. Her youngest child suffered a tragic fate. An English general came with his company to her farm to order her removal. The child was only 17 days old when the troops arrived, and she herself was very weak. The child pined away from lack of milk and died when 3 months old. It seemed to me

like the realization of the words about the "slaughter of the in-
nocents."

Camp of Mafeking, 11th of April 1901.

"An old lady with whom I talked, was a real character. She was
completely broken down, something I had found in no other instance. She described to me the whole history of her being taken
prisoner, and the doings of the English general, how she threw
herself flat on the verandah and begged him to trample her un-
derfoot and kill her. She showed me the clothes she had brought
with her. The white bundle contained nothing but her shroud.
She evidently thought that was all she would need in the camp.

Camp at Kimberley, 13th to 15th of April, 1901.

"240 human beings have been brought here in one train, half of
them in open coal trucks. When I arrived, I saw the Comman-
dant who was to receive the arrivals. He told me that he had succeeded in begging, borrowing and buying about 25 tents for
these 240 people. So it will be worse yet. . . . 7 children died
during the few days while I was in Capetown, and 2 more since
my return. . . . Mrs. —— has been taken to the City Hospital,
she is very ill in consequences of a blow in the stomach given
her by a drunken soldier; something internal. . . . When it rains
at night, everything leaks through the tents and makes little
pools on the floor. No wonder the children fall ill and die.

Camp at Bloemfontein, 29th of April, 1901.

"There are now over 4,000 people here, that is twice as many
as there were 6 weeks ago. At Springfontein station I saw a train
with 600 more. It is miserable to see them, jammed together in
the train, many of them in open trucks. It was bitterly cold. It
had poured in torrents all night, and there were puddles everywhere. They tried to dry themselves and their clothes on the wet
ground. Some of the women attempted to mount the platform

in order to buy food for their children. The soldiers would not
allow it; I remonstrated. They said, they were very sorry, but
they had strict orders. . . . More and more women and children
arrived. A new razzia has begun, with the result that hundreds
and thousands of these unhappy people are either put into an already overfilled camp, or they are set out somewhere or other,
where it is intended to establish a new camp, but where nothing
is ready to receive them. . . . No wonder sickness increases.
Since I left, 6 weeks ago, there have been 62 deaths in the camp,
and the doctor himself is ill of a fever."[32]

This report moved Parliament to commission the Committee on Women
that was charged with sailing to South Africa to visit the camps. The British
Committee on Women was under the leadership of Millicent Fawcett, later
renowned for her role in the suffrage movement. The women arrived in
1901 and, like Hobhouse, toured only the white camps. Their findings resulted in significant changes, including that of military administration to
civilian control. Although measures were taken to improve the quality of
life, to increase food allowances including provision of fresh vegetables,
and to send more medical personnel, by the time the war ended more than
26,000 women and children had perished in those British concentration
camps.

Despite the toll that death and disease took on the Boer women, however,
it must be noted that they were almost uniformly stalwart in support of their
men and in defeating the British troops. The British plan had been to burn
them out, round up their women, and force the Boers to surrender. Instead,
the women who could took an active role in supplying the Boer commandos, served as spies, and at times even took part in the conflict. General De
Wet's wife gathered her family and servants into a covered wagon, took
along some of the livestock, and traveled to the distant part of the northern
Transvaal. She moved frequently but was able to send word to her husband
as to her whereabouts and was never captured. Other women formed a
laager (a group of wagons) and moved about to avoid the British troops.
On one occasion, in August 1901, a laager of women crossed the Vaal River
with their livestock, attempting to get into the OFS. Some of them were in

a carriage and others in their wagons. The axle on the carriage broke, so it was not with the laager when a party of British soldiers caught up with the occupants. But the Boer commandos were not too far away, and, when they learned that the women had been captured, they attacked. According to the oral testimony of one of these women, the British hid among the women. "The Boer women, who were naturally furious at the Tommies, pushed them out and enabled the Boers to shoot them."[33]

The women had no patience with other Boers who surrendered—the "joiners." One man who was found to have been a "joiner" was caught by some of the Heidelberger volunteers (Boers) and was taken to a group of women in hiding. He denied that he was a "joiner," but he was nevertheless "forced to run the gauntlet of sjamboks [whips]. . . . He raced [away] as the women rained blows at him with their whips."[34] At another time, a British soldier, under a white flag of truce, approached some of the Boer forces to advise them that "their women were dying in the camps and it was foolish for them to continue fighting," but it was the near universal stance of the women that the fight go on "to the bitter end."

The bitter end came in May 1902 with the surrender of the Boer forces. Both independent states were placed under British rule: the OFS became the Orange River Colony ORC), and the Boer Republic of the Transvaal was simply labeled the Transvaal. Thousands of blacks and whites had died. Homes—shacks or manor houses—were destroyed. Livestock was depleted or nonexistent. Devastation ruled. The British government offered compensation, but that is another story. Memories lingered. This was true for blacks as well as for whites.

Rural African Women, the Patriarchy and Hardships, and the Emergence of a Woman Leader

Soon after the war ended, word went out that sharecropping opportunities were available in the ORC and Transvaal. Boer farmers needed help, and they would provide land and seed to black labor. Although not involved in the immediate postwar reconstruction of the land, the Maines "and thousands like them were central to the building, feeding and shaping of this tortured country, as it struggled to brush aside the racial goblins that guarded entry into the modern world." These are the words of historian

Charles van Onselen, as he contextualized the long life of an African share-cropper and his extended family.[35]

Kas Maine, MoSotho in ethnicity, was a controlling patriarch who drove his family as hard as he drove himself. In the early 1920s, after his first marriage, when he began to establish himself as a family man, Kas was riveted to the rural environment that had marked him since birth. While the world around him changed over time, his views remained static and locked into an agricultural mentality. Kas single-handily coerced his wives and children—girls as well as boys—to pursue the goals of a traditionalist farmer, whose ties to the land were tenuous. (Keep in mind that the Land Act of 1913 had prohibited Africans from owning land except in the re-serves.) Over time Kas alienated them all, especially his children.

Kas married his senior wife, Leetwane, a MoSwana, between 1920 and 1921. Their first child, a son, died early. Leetwane became a convert to the African Methodist Episcopal Church (AME), which tolerated herbalists, diviners, and, of course, polygamists.[36] Then, a few years later, Kas reached back into the same family to obtain an older sister of Leetwane as his sec-ond wife. Lebitsa remained a traditionalist as did Kas, although he attended services with Leetwane on occasion. Lebitsa's only child, daughter Thak-ene, was born in 1925, while Leetwane continued to produce a steady stream of offspring over time.[37]

The family moved frequently from one sharecropping farm to another, despite the fact that this practice was illegal after 1913. Poor Afrikaners welcomed African farmers who, in turn, sought land not only to farm for income, but on which they could place their livestock. Their only form of property was their stock and, at harvest, their share of the crops. Some, like Kas, had oxen, which could supplement those of the landowner in plowing. Oxen, however, were replaced by the tractor on many more prosperous farms, and with the tractor a farmer needed less help. Thus Kas and his contemporaries were gradually supplanted by modern technology and eventually shuttled off to the reserves. One other factor that marked Kas—and all of the sharecroppers—was that their families were forced to work in the fields. When all hands were not required for the harvest, daughters were sent to the owner's house, where they performed the drudgery of do-mestic work for the farmer's wives and families.[38]

The Maine story is long and complex. I am extrapolating only a few de-tails that pertain to Kas's wives and three of his daughters. As a result, I

am presenting a somewhat skewed view of this man's life, although accurate in what it covers. Charles van Onselen, interpreting Kas's memories,
suggests that "perhaps Leetwane had been more concerned about the arrival
of the second wife than she cared to admit." (Keep in mind that Lebitsa
was Leetwane's sister.) Soon after the birth of daughter Morwesi (in 1925),
Leetwane went lame. Even though Kas was a well-regarded herbalist, he
brought in another to treat his wife. Her conditioned worsened; thus Kas
turned back to the maternal family and brought in yet a third sister, Tseleng,
to take on many of the burdens of the household and other duties that were
common to the rural wives of sharecroppers. Tseleng was "as attractive as
she was industrious."[39]

We cannot know whether Tseleng tempted Kas or, as a traditional polygamist, he seduced her. There is no body of literature on the sexual needs
of African women, and the stereotype we have is influenced by Victorian
and Western values. But whatever motivated them—him or her—they had
sex and Tseleng became pregnant. Kas observed that, when the pregnancy
became known, "a strong silence pervaded the households of Leetwane
and Lebitsa."[40] Tseleng presented Kas with another daughter, Matlakala;
he, in turn, went to the maternal household to make arrangements (pay the
bride price) for marriage to the third daughter. His offer was rejected, and
Tseleng remained unmarried.

We press on in time to the 1940s—keeping in mind that Kas and the
family were moving with some frequency from one farm to another, and
almost all of them under Afrikaner ownership. Tseleng and her daughter
lived mostly with the maternal grandparents. But Kas kept in touch with
his in-laws (as well as his own extended family, which play no role in this
short summary but were important to him over his lifetime). While Kas
and his family—through the hard work that marked them all—strove to
make ends meet and get a bit ahead financially, the world around them continued to change. Younger people flocked to the urban areas, seeking to
join the cash economy and a less demanding life—as they fantasized it.
This included men who went into the mines and industries, and young
women who entered domestic service. As the changes occurred, someone
in the hardscrabble rural areas knew someone who had escaped. It is difficult for us to appreciate the desire to go into the racist world of domestic
service and work for a white madam, as opposed to carrying on the onerous
farm chores but still living with the family.[41] In her teens, Matlakala (daugh-

ter of Tseleng) had experienced what she called visions. She came to believe that she had been possessed with supernatural powers. Morwesi (daughter of Leetwane) "was tough and independent," also a headstrong and difficult teenager whose parents were unaware that she had started slipping out of the house at night when she was sixteen to "visit male friends or distant neighbors." Thakane (daughter of Lebitsa) was "a quiet delicate and slightly withdrawn woman liable to overreact to criticism."[42] Kas thought that Thakene would make an ideal wife for one of his nephews and proceeded to begin arranging a marriage. Thakane refused. Not to be denied his patriarchal control, Kas then decided to make Morwesi the bride. She, too, refused. And Morwesi was backed in this decision by her paternal grandmother, whose strong Christian principles required consent on the part of both parties. Then, Kas decided to marry Thakane to another nephew with arrangements in process, when the family attended another wedding.

At that ceremony, both Morwesi and Thakane, who were having a good time, asked to stay on after their parents (both wives and Kas) departed. The girls arrived home after dark. Kas, no doubt fulminating on the wedding that had not taken place, greeted them with a sjambok.

> Thakane made the mistake of turning away from the shack doorway and running . . . screaming. . . . "Oh, you could hear Thakane crying bitterly, feeling the terrible pain penetrating her body, her heart. She sobbed and sobbed." [A] horse wheeled, leaving Thakane to stumble blindly . . . back toward the shacks and Morwesi.
>
> Morwesi met the horse and rider [Kas] head-on. "We are tired of running away every day. We are tired of being afraid of you. Do it! Do as you please!" And Kas did. He flogged her until he could no more; but she did not move an inch or utter a sound. . . . "Morwesi was very, very defiant. My God. Not so much as a tear ran down her cheek." . . . The next morning Kas found that Thakane had not returned home. He set off to find her as her wedding was just days away. She had run off to a family member, who protected the teenager from Kas's wrath. But when Thakane eventually reached home, her mother, also angered, attempted to assault her. "The return home signaled the end of Thakane's resistance." What is especially poignant in this

story is that Thakane had been given over to her maternal grandparents as a baby and had only returned to the Kas Maine home
recently as a teenager. She went off into marriage in exchange
for "sixteen cattle and ten sheep."[43]

Morwesi, at the age of 12, and another sister had been forced by Kas
into domestic work on the farm where they then lived. They had to walk a
long distance early in the morning and late in the evening after a long day
of domestic labor. In addition, and as noted earlier, in times of need they
were put to work in the fields. Then came another move, and again Morwesi was back in an Afrikaner kitchen. Eventually she left the family for
domestic employment of her own choosing. That did not work well, either,
and Morwesi took to the bottle. When she became pregnant, she brought
the baby home, stayed awhile, and then obtained a job in a liquor store.
Her life was defined more by alcohol than motherhood. Although intermittently she attempted to pay for schooling for Pakiso, her daughter whose
father was another farmhand driven by Kas, who was opposed to formal
education. Pakiso managed to accommodate herself to Kas and married
without incident. She remembered her mother moving in and out of her life
until, at the age of 44, Morwesi arrived at her home "a disheveled drunk."
Kas was present. He observed Morwesi's "gaping open mouth," which "revealed gaps in her yellowed teeth: her speech was halting and deliberate."
She came across "like thousands of other unskilled and uneducated women
pushed off the land of their birth and unable to secure a niche in the urban
economy."[44]

Matlakala, living with the Batswana family of her mother and including
an uncle on whose farm she worked, experienced the privation of rural life
but seemingly with more serenity. "When not much more than eight years
old she had fallen into such a deep and extended sleep that a traditional
doctor" had been called in, and it was "he who pronounced her to be in
possession of the ancestral spirit that had later pointed her in the direction
of 'faith healing.'"[45] At the age of fifteen, Matlakala's grandmother sent
her to "an initiation school," where she spent several weeks learning traditional practices. But when the end of the course featured a "mock genital
operation, the impressionable fifteen-year-old left the school feeling even
more vulnerable and insecure than when she had entered it." Back home
she was involved in "a sex scandal which resulted in her and several of her

cohorts being dragged before a tribal court . . . where they were flogged by
an elderly man until their clothing was 'covered in blood.'" After that Matlakala ran away to a nearby farm, where she must have found employment,
since she sent back food to her grandparents.[46]

In a year or so later, her dying grandmother sent for her. Within two
weeks Matlakala's grandfather died, too, leaving her a seventeen-year-old
"orphan" who went to join the Maines. Matlakala became estranged from
Kas, only really reuniting with him just before his death in 1985. He was
aware of the fact that she served as a "Prophetess" in several churches, including one not too far from one of his final residences. Van Onselen noted
that Thakane and Matlakala had a great deal in common other than sharing
the same father. "Both were only children, both had been relegated at a tender age to the physical, economic and psychological margins of the extended family and, perhaps as a consequence were frailer and less robust
than either Morwesi [and another sister]. . . . Thakane, like Matlakala, had
seen 'visions' while an adolescent and had left the Maine home after her
traditionally arranged marriage. . . . One day, while preparing a meal for
those working in the distant fields, she had fallen into a deep trance during
[which] the spirits" of grandmothers appeared. So, she too became a faith
healer, although she stayed with her husband and, eventually, at Kas' death,
took in the alcoholic Morwesi in the then homeland of Bophutswana. Kas
left Morwesi a house in the same reserve on condition that she could never
sell it; and, because he felt that Thakane had gotten short shrift in his lifetime, he left her half interest in his tractor (and he would have considered
that a great gift, keeping in mind a lifetime devoted to farming). Matlakala,
who had married, was left "in the care of her husband."[47]

Faith healing and divination were very common—and still are, especially among the traditionalists. Kas had been an able herbalist. He had also
been a well-recognized diviner—but he read bones while his daughters incorporated Christianity into their visions and prophesies.

Not all South African rural women were victims of the negative circumstances that marked the Maine daughters. Some had the benefit of missionary education and close affinity to their tribal societies. Charlotte Manye
was probably born in the Pietersburg area of the Boer Republic of the
Transvaal in 1874—or fifteen years before the South African War. It is
likely that she was raised in the Eastern Cape, and she may have been Pedi
or Sotho in ethnicity, although some speculate that she was Xhosa since

she wrote in that language.[48] Her family moved to Kimberley following the discovery of the diamonds, and she became a teacher. Keep in mind that so few educational opportunities existed for people of color, especially girls. After obtaining two or three years of primary education, those who desired could be put in the classroom to teach those just beginning to learn.[49]

As a Christian, Charlotte became involved first with a local choir, and that led to the formation of the African Jubilee Choir, a much larger group of singers. They toured the country and went to England in 1891. The most successful tour, however, was when they went to America in 1894, singing in what must have been before African American audiences. While in the United States, Charlotte enrolled at Wilberforce College in Ohio, which had been founded before the American Civil War for primarily mixed-race children of slave owners. When Charlotte arrived it had come under the auspices of the AME Church. She obtained financial support—probably a scholarship—and settled in to study, earning her degree in 1901. In the process, Charlotte Manye became the first African woman to graduate from college. Her time at Wilberforce also provided her with a husband, Marshall Maxeke, who was a fellow student and who returned home with her following the confirmation of their college degrees.[50]

The pair—husband and wife—worked together to sponsor various educational enterprises for Africans under the banner of the AME Church. While Kas Maine and his family were beginning to eke out a living on Afrikaner farms, Charlotte and her husband began a number of activities that put them in the forefront of the just-emerging South African civil rights movement. Before the Maine girls were born, the Maxekes were in Bloemfontein in 1912 when the South African Native Congress (later to change its name to African National Congress; ANC) was formed, with each partner participating. The next year, still in Bloemfontein, Charlotte took part in the first anti-pass movement; then she became a founder of the Women's League of the SANC, which continues to exist today under the auspices of the ANC.

Two different worlds marked South Africans in those decades. One was successful, rewarded, and remembered. The other was ignored and forgotten except for the remarkable work by Charles van Onselen and his team. The lives of Kas Maines's daughters mark the majority of African women, whether they were rural peasants or the down-and-out of the urban proletariat.

Germany in Southwest Africa and the Herero

Germany began to colonize parts of Africa in the 1880s, including moving into the area adjacent to South Africa on the Atlantic coast and south of Portuguese Angola. The Herero people with whom they established contact were livestock keepers, such as those we have met earlier in other chapters. They measured their wealth, power, and position in society based on the number of stock that they held—in fact, Herero culture was entirely built around livestock. Cattle required grazing lands. Women were measured against livestock. (Remember the marriage of Thakane Maine, whose bride price consisted of cattle and goats.) Southwest Africa was semiarid to arid in huge stretches of the territory, with a dry climate and little water, especially in the west. Thus the Herero (other ethnic groups also were present as livestock keepers but they are not part of our story) staked out the prime land.

Among the first of the Germans to move into this area were the Rhenish missionaries (United Evangelical Mission), who were moderately successful in converting the Herero to Christianity. In fact, because of their relationship to the missionaries, the Herero soon became aware of German ranchers' designs on their property. Initially, the Germans purchased land from the Herero. By 1913 they had bought more than 25 percent of what the Herero claimed to be their grazing lands.[51] But by 1913 the Herero had been defeated, massacred, and put into the desert to die.

In the decade between 1884 and 1904, land acquisition was significant, enough to trouble the Herero leadership. In this period, too, Germany decided to build a railroad line that would cut right through the Herero grazing lands. Because of the relationship the Christian Herero enjoyed with the missionaries, they became aware of these plans and were disconcerted. In addition, the missionaries began to involve themselves in selling houses and in mediating between German settlers and the Herero. This led the chief, Maharero, and his council to create a distance between themselves and the Rhenish missionaries—to the point of closing down some of the mission stations in their area.[52] Another source of antagonism revolved around the German traders. Because the Herero lacked cash, the traders took cattle in exchange for European goods and were accused of cheating and/or tricking those with whom they traded. In fact, some Herero cattle were stolen outright by the German stockmen—adding to the friction.

But the most important source of conflict was the treatment accorded to their women by the German men, and this was, at least in part, due to the heavy imbalance between the sexes among the Europeans. Rape and sexual abuse of the Herero women were "so common that German settlers had a name for it: *Verkafferung*, or going native, and *Schmutzwirtscharft*, or dirty trade."[53] The Germans were blatantly racist and held views toward the natives similar to those I discussed earlier in this chapter—they regarded the natives as subhuman or descendants of apes. Testosterone no doubt conquered negative stereotypes. In 1903 the son of one of the Herero chiefs and his wife picked up a German settler and took him home with them. While the chief's son was asleep, the settler forced himself on the son's wife—who refused him. The settler then "shot and killed her." This outrage, coming after many other instances involving rape and/or sexual misconduct, exploded when the German court acquitted the settler (although on appeal he was sentenced to three years in prison). The Herero "observed that the life of even a chief's daughter-in-law was worth little to the Germans." The issue of sexual abuse was joined by beatings of those employed by the Germans. One report noted that even a chief was "flogged until the blood ran."[54]

The Herero under Chief Maharero went to war against the Germans in January 1904. The Germans were outnumbered, and the Herero employed guerrilla warfare tactics—fighting from the bush— leading the Kaiser to send out reinforcements. Still the Herero held their own, until the arrival of German Lt. General von Trotha a few months after the armed conflict began. Von Trotha's policy, initiated by Kaiser Wilhelm was "No negotiations." In October 1904, some captured prisoners were "sentenced to death by a field court martial," and those who were hung included "women and children." As the war continued, the Herero retreated farther into the interior—the drier and more arid parts of the country. In August 1904, the Herero lost their last major battle at Waterberg. They then moved farther southeastward into the desert, with some fleeing to safety across the border into British territory (today's Botswana). As for those in the desert, however, von Trotha ordered his men to encircle them.[55] "Employing a 250-kilometer-long cordon sanitaire of troops . . . von Trotha annihilated the Herero." He also issued an order of extermination:

> All Hereros must leave the country. If they do not do so, I
> will force them with cannons to do so. With the German borders,
> every Herero, with or without weapons . . . will be shot. I shall
> no longer shelter women and children. They must either return
> to their people or I will shoot them. This is my message to the
> Herero nation.[56]

By late December 1904, the German Kaiser succumbed to public opinion and forced von Trotha to lift the order of extermination. Not all was
over, however, as the Germans then rounded up or enticed out of the desert
as many as survived and placed them in concentration camps. There many
thousands more died—including untold numbers of women and children.
Those who were able were put to work—in the camps, in various businesses, and for companies such as breweries. We do not know how many
women were forced to work, but no doubt the able-bodied were put into
domestic service if not more arduous labor. Rape and racism did not end
with the war; one camp was established for women to "service" German
troops.

A German missionary visited a camp in 1905 and reported on the devastating conditions that he witnessed. The people were, he wrote:

> housed in pathetic . . . structures constructed out of simple sack
> ing and planks, in such a manner that in one structure 30-50
> people were forced to stay without distinction as to age or sex.
> . . . The food was extremely scarce. . . . Like cattle hundreds
> were driven to their death and like cattle they were buried.[57]

Finally the camps were closed in 1908, four years after the war had
begun; the survivors were released. One caveat: all persons—male and
female— over seven years of age were forced to "carry metal discs around
their necks" as a way of keeping track of "free labor."[58]

More than 100,000 Herero died during this period—and as appalling as
the British-run concentration camps were during the South African War,
this particular carnage has been referred to by some as the first incidence
of German genocide in the twentieth century.

German Amnesia and Herero Women
by Dan Moshenberg

Over the weekend, Geoffrey York, the Africa correspondent for the *Canadian Globe and Mail* . . . wrote, from Namibia, about the current Herero struggle for land, dignity, and reparations. The 1904-1908 German genocide against the Herero is considered by many to have been the first genocide of the twentieth century; as such it serves as the gateway to the Modern Age.

As York accurately describes the situation, nothing much has changed:

> In the bush and scrub of central Namibia, the descendants of the surviving Herero live in squalid shacks and tiny plots of land. Next door, the descendants of German settlers still own vast properties of 20,000 hectares or more.

The Herero want their land back. They would prefer the State find a way, but if not, land invasions will do. The option is described as "a new kind of radicalism."

York ends his article with an old kind of European, and North American, representation, that of the tired old African woman:

> A Herero grandmother named Gendrede Kavari lives on a small dusty plot of land on the edge of Okakarara. Once she had a few animals, but she had no fence and they were stolen. Now she survives on a pension and a small income from collecting firewood. Some day, if she had a bit more land, she would like to have some goats. "We get our land back," she says.

Gendrede Kavari was never meant to survive. Neither were her grandmothers and great-grandmothers.

Germans butchered somewhere between 30 and 80% of the Herero population in a mere four years, and Herero women were special targets. Germany used a Herero uprising to justify the "streams of blood" program of annihilation. That uprising was partly inspired by the Herero resentment regarding German sexual violence against their women. . . . [The story of the chief's daughter-in-law that we covered above—women's lives with no value.]

That's the story of the genocide as well. Women and children were targeted. When the Herero were "allowed" to escape into the Kalahari Desert, it was assumed that most would die. It also was assumed that more women and children would die. That assumption was correct.

The German authorities explained that Herero women and children had to die because they carried dangerous diseases. Meanwhile, the German press shrieked that Herero women were "black amazons swinging clubs and castrating their foes."

And so good riddance.

When concentration camps were established for the few survivors, one female-only camp was set up to "service" the German troops. . . . A Herero leader Mburumba Kerina explained:

"Hey, that's my grandmother—a comfort woman." In the other camps, along with sexual violence at the hands of settlers and troops, Herero women were forced to boil heads, often of their own family members, and then scrape off the flesh with shards of glass. Those skulls were then shipped off to museums and universities, as well as anthropological and private collections in Germany, providing decades of "scientific" research as well as "entertainment."

To date, only a few Herero remains have been returned, while the overwhelming majority remains in Germany. Sexual violence was part of the colonization and subjugation process. From rape to murder to abduction and sex slavery to forced re-

moval of women, German settlers and the German Empire had
a special fate in store for Herero women. . . .[59]

I began this chapter with the sexual exploitation of Sara Baartman, and
I conclude with the devastation wrought on the Herero and their women—
through not only rape, sexual violence, and abuse, but also being subjected
to the torture of dying by thirst and starvation in the desert, and then, finally,
in the camps. We encountered the experiences of the Maine daughters and
their subjugation by the patriarch, as well as those of the Africans and Boers
in British concentration camps during the South African War. The black
female body attracted and repelled throughout the nineteenth century, as
Sander Gilman so correctly observed.

CHAPTER SIX

Women and Colonialism in Africa

B y the end of the nineteenth century, we witnessed the onset of colonialism with the British in South Africa and the Germans in Southwest Africa (Namibia). In what might be called "creeping colonialism" elsewhere, we find the French entrenched in parts of Senegal from the 1840s, and their traders located variously on parts of the West African coast. The Portuguese remained on the Guinea coast and were still to be found in Mozambique and Angola. The British too, were in parts of West Africa—in fact they had colonized Sierra Leone—and they had taken over Egypt and were spreading into Central Africa from the south. The United States had her toe in the door of the continent via the American Colonization Society in Liberia. King Leopold II of Belgium, on the pretext of wiping out the East African slave trade, had entered a claim to a considerable part of Central Africa.

Clearly much of Western Europe was on the march when the German Chancellor Bismarck summoned those with interests in Africa to a conference in Berlin in the fall of 1884. The conferees included those with connections to North Africa as well, but our emphasis is on the area south of the Sahara Desert. During the several months the Congress of Berlin was in session, and with some adjustments and treaties settling disputed areas coming later, most of Africa was carved up. The exception was Ethiopia, which was considered a "Christian country." Of note, not a single African—man or woman—was present at the Congress of Berlin. The factors behind Europe's scramble for Africa are largely irrelevant to African women, although their experiences changed, some radically as a result. A brief summary of the rationale behind the colonial impetus includes those missionaries that we covered earlier—the desire to "civilize" and carry Christianity to the benighted Africans. Under this rubric, too, was the desire to eliminate

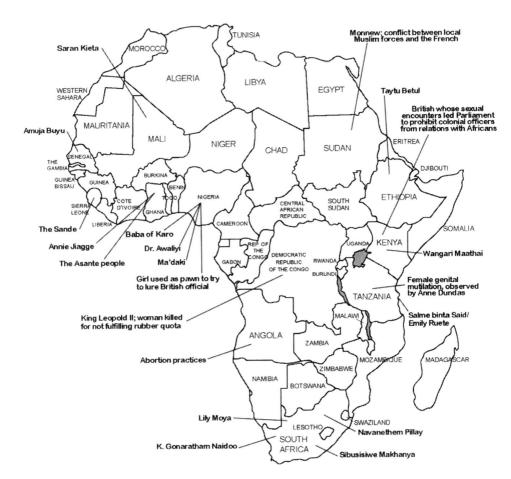

both the interior slave trade and slavery. Nationalism—carrying the flag—
was an important factor, and this was especially true in the competition between the French and the British, although all the countries wanted their
piece of the African pie. Business interests in Europe sought raw materials
for their growing industries and markets. Early in the century, after the Atlantic slave trade had mostly ended, expeditions and explorers had been
moving into the interior in many parts of Africa. Some were seeking to locate the sorts of raw materials that would be useful; others were interested
in geographical discoveries, such as Speke in his search for the source of
the Nile.[1]

Despite a series of acts passed in Lisbon regarding the Portuguese
African colonies, little was accomplished on the ground. Racist attitudes
co-existed with a great deal of miscegenation. Impoverished Portuguese,
convicts, and "vagabond women" went to the colonies in dribbles but did
little to develop them, including the introduction of social services such as
health care and education. One caveat, however, concerned the development of large cocoa-bearing plantations on the islands of São Tomé and
Principe. Most of the estate owners provided hospitals and, in a few cases,
a primary school.[2] In the 1930s the Portuguese Fascist government centralized control of the colonies in Lisbon, but, overall, this action did not provide for the well-being of the subjects.

In the case of Leopold II of Belgium, prestige was his motive for moving
into Congo. He personally underwrote the costs. He soon found that income
from gathering ivory and rubber exceeded his expectations, leading him to
farm out the rubber concessions on the basis of royalties paid to him. That
turned into a scandal of massive proportions. The natives were forced to
pick, collect, and deliver their allotted baskets of rubber or suffer the whip
or worse, including mutilation of hands and feet to those who failed to meet
their quota. Missionaries in nearby areas began to report home about the
atrocities they became aware of, and they were joined by a British journalist
whose stories regarding maltreatment hit the press at home. By 1908, and
in response to the negative publicity, the Belgian government stepped in
and took over Congo.

Not just the rubber workers but also women and children suffered from
the adverse effects of Leopold's misrule. Mercenaries were recruited from
the ex-slave population as overseers. If the laborers did not deliver their
quotas, the mercenaries maimed and shot villagers indiscriminately. A re-

vealing report came from an American missionary in the Congo who, in
1895, wrote of the outrages he witnessed in one district:

> Each town in the district is being forced to bring a certain quan-
> tity to the headquarters of the commissaire every Sunday. It is
> collected by force. The soldiers drive the people into the bush.
> . . . The soldiers do not care who they shoot down, and they
> more often shoot poor helpless women and harmless children.
> These hands, the hands of men, women and children, are placed
> in rows before the commissaire. . . . I have seen the ravages.
> . . . Meeting a poor woman whose husband was away fishing,
> [a soldier asked] "Where is your husband?" She answered by
> pointing to the river. "Where is his rubber?" She answered, "It
> is ready for you" whereupon he said, "You lie," and lifting his
> gun, shot her dead.[3]

Leopold II died in 1909, a year after ceding the colony to Belgium. The
Belgian government carried out reforms to the most blatant practices on
the part of the concessionaires. But it devoted little effort to provide education or health services to its African subjects until late in the colonial
period, and primarily in Katanga Province, where minerals were discovered
and mines established.

In some areas of Africa, women had held high positions as chiefs or ad-
judicators of their affairs, and, as we saw, were actively engaged as petty
traders. But with the onset of colonialism and the introduction of European
government officials, women's power and income were much diminished.
Like the missionaries, the colonial servants carried their own cultural attitudes with them. These precluded dealing with female leaders (with some
exceptions). Victoria might have been their queen, but in Africa her colonial
representatives had no intent or desire to deal with female leaders. In general, the French practiced direct rule, often appointing chiefs who had little
or no legitimacy among the people over whom they ruled. The overall phi-
losophy that best characterized the French was, the more like Frenchmen
their African subjects became, the more acceptable they were. The French
could be harsh tyrannical masters, but, after a rough start, many of the colonial servants settled down with an African woman in a fashion similar to
their predecessors, the traders. In fact, French policy encouraged "their

officers to take local mistresses."[4] The novelist Ahmadou Kourouma presents a biting critique of French colonial employees and their relations with local women in *Monnew*. This scene involves conquest in the Sudan between the local Muslim forces and the French, in which the local chief has collaborated—as was at times the case. The mixed-race men also have collaborated with the French, another facet of occasional reality. We begin with a griot sarcastically extolling the virtues of the whites after they have requisitioned (meaning rounded up) a group of men, women, and children:

> The Nazarene [Christian] is good, very good: the requisitioned men, young ladies, and the boys are not slaves. The Whites have abolished slavery.
>
> We were happy to know that our requisitioned sisters, brothers and children would not be carried away. . . .
>
> The lieutenant chose from among the Peul virgins the four girls who had the lightest skin and the straightest noses; they were reserved for the two White men. . . .
>
> That day, each of the conquerors assigned himself a woman. After the selection of virgins allotted to the Whites and mulattos, the interpreter and the Black rank and file shared out the virgins with black skin and flat noses. . . .
>
> The captain is satisfied, that's what he says. And so are all of the other guests, that's what we see. It's true as the palm of a frog's hand—once you've solved your guest's nocturnal problems, you've just about solved his day time ones. . . .
>
> Then the captain came up to them.
>
> The girls were extraordinary! You sent them for just fifteen days, but many of my tirailleurs [soldiers] have decided to keep them for wives. And I will too. It's an opportunity for Soba [the fictional locale]. We'll make many mulattoes for Soba, many half-breeds, so it will be a great city.[5]

In this extract we get the African view of not only the colonials but their myopia concerning the women being exploited for sex. The French officers also were willing to provide sexual outlets for their ex-slave soldiers in the early phase of conquest, but over time they altered their policies. Racial prejudice entered the picture by the 1880s, leading the French "to object to the presence of women" in the garrisons. The women exasperated "Soldiers over developed libido" and "negatively affected their performance of duties."[6] Still, this policy had its limitations. In this same period, and in the Sudan, the French incited their African soldiers "to kidnap or raid women on their own" so as to provide them with "wives."[7]

The British were more bound in their superiority and class attitudes, but many of them also followed the fashion of taking an African "wife." (Keep in mind that, other than the missionary wives, very few European women accompanied their husbands in the early colonial era.) A British administrator in Kenya engaged in multiple sexual adventures with the local women—so much so that his escapades provoked a serious discussion in Parliament.[8] As a result the British issued several directives forbidding their colonial officials from sexual encounters with African women. Nevertheless, one official based in Nigeria noted that "many bachelors used to have a local woman living with them."[9] But women also were used as pawns. A British official in another Nigerian province recalled that a local couple, seeking a favor, approached him with a "completely naked and shapely young girl as an offering." He said he refused.[10]

In the Muslim northern town of Maiduguri, a newly appointed colonial servant arrived, to be greeted by his interpreter: "If the master of the house wishes to have a Fulani or Shuwa virgin, it can be arranged." The interpreter equitably noted that they lived in "a man's world" and that it was natural to welcome a young virgin such as would be the case with any other chief.[11] Although it may be true that the British were more circumspect than their French counterparts, it should be noted that during this period many prominent mixed-race African families emerged with English surnames, including the Casely-Hayfords of Ghana and Sierra Leone.

In the Portuguese islands of São Tomé and Principe, contract workers from Angola were brought in to work on the cocoa plantations; "contract workers" however, was a misnomer. In fact, the Africans were rounded up in Angola's interior, marched to the coast, and signed for five-year contracts, and, until reforms were enacted, these contracts were automatically renewed. For more than a decade in the early nineteenth century, the Angolans were slaves in all but name.[12] In this period, the gender imbalance was about 55 percent men to 45 percent women. Females used their scarcity in numbers by serving as prostitutes for money and goods.[13] Although some of these women gave birth, others practiced abortion—the practice was known to them, and no doubt the knowledge was brought from Angola. Whereas the Portuguese government forbade sexual relations between white men and local, native women, cohabitation occurred. Some women worked as laundresses and in domestic capacities, while servicing the employees. If they bore children, the progeny were often claimed by their fathers, who, in some cases, provided a modicum of education.[14]

Taytu, Menelik of Ethiopia, and the Italians

Italy had united in 1871, and her leaders began to engage in the fantasy of re-creating the glories of the Roman Empire. Italy suffered from a growing population that could be resolved with colonies, plus expanded territories meant agricultural products to import. The Italians focused their eyes on the areas of the Red Sea and the Indian Ocean, and the only country that was not yet under the yoke of European imperialism.

In the 1880s, Ethiopia was actually an empire. To gain a rough picture of the political system in place, perhaps the best analogy is to look back to European feudalism with its many fiefs ruled by independent lords who, in turn, paid homage and tribute to a king or emperor. In time of war, these respective lords were responsible for bringing their own forces of men to support the kingdom or empire. Slavery still existed in Ethiopia, and so, too, did a form of serfdom. The rulers could and did award land to favorites and, just as easily, take it away. At any given time in the nineteenth century, antagonisms and/or ambition meant that conflict existed between one or more of the lords. Some supported whatever emperor was in power, while others conspired to take his place. The complexities in unraveling this period are enormous, and to single out one or two of the lords and their respective fiefdoms skews the actual historical picture. Thus, we turn to Menelik II, ruler of the central province of Shewa, and the woman who became his last wife, Taytu Betul.[15] In so doing, however, one factor requires stressing. Menelik was not satisfied with being merely King of Shewa. His ambition was to overthrow Johannes, the current King of Kings. At times Menelik worked with Johannes; but often he connived to establish alliances with other provincial rulers to win the title of emperor. This ambition meant war—and it also meant conquest in parts of the country that had not yet recognized Johannes as their overlord.

Menelik had been married a few times and had numbers of mistresses and several children before engaging in a long-time relationship with his common-law wife Bafena. He was forced to abandon her, or he would have lost Taytu, a strong-willed woman who suffered no competition. Taytu had hardly been idle—Menelik was her fifth husband, and she was still in her early thirties.[16] She claimed descent from Sheba in both the paternal and maternal line. This is problematic because, while her father was Amharic, the same ethnicity as Menelik and thus on the Solomonic line, her mother was thought to be Oromo. Some of the Oromo were animists, others Muslim; and, over time, those with ambition for power usually converted to Christianity. When, in later life, she had considerable power of her own, Taytu was accused of being Jewish, Arab, or Muslim.[17]

The details concerning Taytu's pre-Menelik life are sketchy. Chris Prouty, her biographer, drew on several sources, but none of them were totally accurate. One version claimed that, at age ten, Taytu realized she was being readied for marriage. Her marriage was to an officer in the forces of the then Emperor Tewodros (but we do not know whether it actually took place when she was ten years old). Her husband incurred the wrath of the emperor and was put in irons. Taytu followed the army on foot and was forced to ground corn like a peasant.[18] A later husband, in 1881 or early in 1882, was a brother of Menelik's mistress, Bafena. In this relationship Taytu suffered from domestic violence—her husband beat her—and she left, taking all movable property with her. Then, she met Menelik in August 1882.[19] They agreed to marriage, but, on his way to his headquarters, Menelik stopped for a rendezvous with Bafena. This angered Taytu, and, according to one source, she promptly married someone else. Menelik, however, was so taken with her, he was said to have paid off Taytu's current husband.[20] Taytu's intelligence and strong will, as well as her father's position in Semen (near Gondar) and family connections "in provinces beyond Shewa" prompted Menelik to pursue her.[21] Menelik aimed to please or deceive to realize his ambitions. Taytu was shrewd and forthcoming in her relationships with people, especially pertaining to the Italians.

Marriage in Ethiopia has its own complications. None of Menelik's or Taytu's earlier nuptials had been conducted in the Ethiopian Orthodox Church, the official religion prevailing among most of the nobility. Thus in 1883, when the couple was officially wed in a communion service by the patriarch (head of the church), they were considered permanently bound by the church. The wedding featured feasts and festivity and was held at Menelik's then *ghibbi* (residence). When Menelik queried his bride as to what she desired from him, she requested that she be allotted land and support to build a church in the Entotto Hills that stand majestically above the capital Addis Ababa (founded by Menelik in 1903). Taytu was a devout adherent to the church and so remained throughout her life. Soon after the nuptials, she set about arranging for the construction of her church, Entotto Maryam, while her husband took off on a military campaign.[22]

Taytu built a house in Entotto, and then acquired her "own stockyards, dairy farms, grain storage facilities, beekeepers, beermakers, flour millers, cooks, water carriers," and she grew agricultural products to supply her domain under the supervision of an "administrative head for each activity." In addition to the self-sufficient estate, Taytu also derived income from crown grants from "the districts of Bulga and Geren, both richly fertile."[23] She was known for her copious feasts during the many religious celebrations in the Ethiopian calendar year, as well as for her compassion and generosity to the peasantry, especially during periods of famine.

Despite her many marriages, Taytu was barren, and it is not known if she had been circumcised as an infant (or small child). Her biographer speculates that she had been. In the mid-1850s, when Taytu was born, the Amhara practiced limited removal of the clitoris through surgery performed by a local woman using a rough stone, a piece of glass, or perhaps a crude knife. Infection may have occurred but not so severe as to debilitate her beyond affecting her reproductive organs. She was described when young as having a "slender figure, a clear, brown complexion, and fine features. Although possessed of an elegant profile, her most striking features were large, expressive, dark eyes," which drew attention away from a slight defect on her lower jaw.[24]

Certainly it was irony that the Italian, Count Pietro Antonelli, who would most complicate their lives in the first thirteen years of their marriage, arrived in Menelik's court a week after their marriage.[25] Count Antonelli was duplicitous as well as charismatic. Menelik tended to be easily influenced by Europeans—he was interested in modernization, but he also was obsessed with obtaining the best and most recent weapons available in Europe. Taytu was more cynical. Some thought her xenophobic. Antonelli tried to curry her favor through gifts of jewelry, perfumes, and other items that he assumed a woman of her station and in the outback would prefer.

What Taytu wanted, and wherein rested her weakness, were religious objects and reliquaries for her church.

What did Count Antonelli want? He represented the Italian government, which, although it had a king as titular head, was officially run by a prime minister and parliament. His desire was their command: to create a dependency on Italy from the ruler most likely to be able to provide it. Britain was in Egypt and Sudan. But she also claimed, through Egyptian-Sudan, the eastern trading town of Harar, which had been part of Ethiopia, and the coastal port of Massawa on the northern Red Sea coast. France had small territory on the eastern Red Sea (today's Djibouti). And then, of course, there was Johannes, who was then the King of Kings, and who had an on-again, off-again relationship with the British. All of these complexities were played out between Antonelli's arrival and the first major contretemps between Italy and Ethiopia. First, Johannes was killed in a battle with the Sudanese Mahdists (Muslims) in 1889. Menelik quickly declared himself King of Kings (despite some opposition).

In the interim between 1882 and 1889, Menelik steadily imported thousands of modern weapons and great stores of ammunition, not only through the offices of Antonelli, but also via the French and through their Red Sea port. Italy had, in the meantime, been encroaching along Ethiopia's northwestern territory until, by 1885, she was holding the port of Massawa. In May 1889, Menelik signed the Treaty of Wachela with Italy; one article of the treaty allowed the Italians to occupy new borders which, in time, would be Eritrea. This was before Menelik and Taytu were crowned, respectively emperor and empress. Their coronation took place in November.[26] (Taytu was crowned and named Itage, later translated as Queen of Queens.)[27]

It was the Treaty of Wachela that ultimately resulted in war between the two countries. Article XVII had been creatively deceptive. The Italian version stated that Italy would be responsible for Ethiopia's foreign relations with other countries. The Amharic version, which is the only one Menelik had seen, said that Ethiopia "may call" on Italy as regards foreign affairs. When, through press revelations in Europe, Menelik realized he had been duped, he flew into a rage—joined by Taytu who was always suspicious of Count Antonelli and the other Italian diplomats who paid court to her and to her husband. After a few skirmishes, including one where the Italians were routed and retreated, and following numerous arguments calling for Article XVII to be amended, in October 1895, Taytu and Menelik set off to the north from Addis Ababa for battle, each leading their respective forces.

"The empress traveled with a suite of about 100 women, including the Princess Zewditu (Menelik's daughter)." Taytu and her 5,000 men, plus their women, animals, and porters carrying supplies, moved steadily forward:

> Her soldiers kept perfect order. The women were mounted on mules, astride . . . and kept silent, which must have been hard for them, for the daughters of Eve are the same in all latitudes.
> Her Majesty . . . like all Ethiopian women is very brave. She has a strong character—sometimes haughty—and is of interesting appearance. Her features and coloring are like those of an Andalusian. Her look is commanding and at the same time has finesse. . . .[28]
> The final battle was fought at Adwa. Taytu was there with "shells falling like drops of rain." At this moment, the empress removed her veil, and under a black umbrella advanced on foot as did the other women, among whom was . . . Zewditu, daughter of the king of kings.
> Empress Taytu, seeing some soldiers hesitate, cried to them with all her strength. "Courage. Victory is ours! Strike!" The soldiers . . . could not run away when encouraged by a woman and [returned to the fray]. Taytu shed her femininity and became a valiant warrior.[29]

The outcome was a victory for the Ethiopians but with terrible loss of life on both sides—a combined total of 11,000 dead.[30] This triumph was remembered in Africa—and is still invoked as the only successful long-term defeat of a conquering European army. It was remembered in Italy, too, and the loss rankled, especially after Mussolini's rise in 1923. In 1935, Italy again invaded and drove the then Emperor Haile Selassie I into exile. But the fantasy of restoring the old Roman Empire did not materialize. In 1941, with the aid of the British and African forces invading from Sudan, Italy was again defeated.

Queen Taytu Betul.
Source: *Le Petit Journal*

In 1908, Menelik suffered the first of several strokes. By 1910 he was nearly bedridden and confined to his palace in Addis Ababa. Taytu, who had often provided the strong pole to his sometimes weak spine, not only stood by him, she undertook to issue orders in his name that quickly rankled the male nobles who were her subordinates in title, but who had the power. By the time Menelik died in 1913, Taytu had been reduced in status to caretaker and nurse, confined to the palace as a virtual prisoner. After a short interregnum with Menelik's grandson as nominal ruler, who was soon deposed, Menelik's daughter Zewditu was crowned Queen of Kings. But again, misogyny reigned. Ras Tafari (later Haile Selassie I) was made regent. Zewditu performed the rituals and he ruled.

Taytu took up residence in her Entotto home, spent considerable time daily at prayer in her church, resigning from all affairs. Her one request to go to Gondar was denied. Zewditu invited her step-mother to her coronation in early 1917. She declined but she welcomed Zewditu, who "paid respectful visits." At Taytu's death in February 1918, one of her former enemies praised her in an obituary in which he quoted two members of the nobility who were present at her death:

> The blood slowly withdrew from that face which was once a
> rose, and on those eyes which once looked like great, luminous
> diamonds, the lashes slowly fell. Our hearts trembled. That dear,

revered, glorious empress, who, at the side of the second Menelik, had reigned, aggrandized and made Ethiopia prosper, was
now wrapped in her winding sheet and enclosed in a box where
she would remain for eternity inside a tomb where no light
would ever shine. . . . Death is strong, cruel and determined.
What to do? Hearts can be overcome with sorrow, we saw we
could do nothing. So we called everyone to weep.[31]

Salme binta Said, Zanzibar, and the Germans

Salme binta Said, a daughter of the ruler of Zanzibar whom we met earlier,
also was involved in a colonial misadventure but of a far different nature.
By the early 1880s, Salme was known as Emily Ruete and had lived in
Germany for forty years.
She was widowed by her
German husband with
three small children, in-
cluding one boy. Salme's
troubled life included
exile, apostasy, and es-
trangement from her Zanz-
ibar brothers. One had
served as sultan of Zanz-
ibar following the death of
Said bin Sultan in 1856. It
was he who discovered
that she was pregnant and,
according to rumor in the
European community, he
planned to send her to
Mecca where en route she
would have met her death,
had the British in Zanzibar
not arranged for Salme's
departure by stealth. Following the death of Majid

Salme binta Said/Emily Ruete.
Source: Emily Ruete, *Memoirs of an Arabian
Princess from Zanzibar*

in 1870, brother Barghash succeeded to the throne. And he became Salme's
bête noir—another story that is too long and complicated, except as it concerns Salme and Germany.

In brief, Salme seemed to have alienated her husband's family and had
little in the way of financial resources (she claimed that she was cheated
by his partners; more likely she spent too much on servants and upkeep).[32]
Despite her pecuniary situation, Salme never lost sight of her status as a
"Princess of Zanzibar." Thus, in her widowhood, she was able to create
relationships with members of the German aristocracy, including the wife
of the emperor's son, who was a daughter of Queen Victoria.

As we saw, Germany not only joined in the scramble for Africa, but took
the lead in calling the Congress of Berlin in 1884-1885. Beginning in the
1830s, merchants in the Hanseatic League had been engaged in profitable
trade with Zanzibar. By the 1870s, these traders—based in Hamburg—controlled 25 percent of Zanzibar's trade.[33] These same merchants had been
pressuring Bismarck to seek colonies; and other German agents had staked
out territory on the mainland near the Swahili island of Lamu in today's
Kenya. Furthermore, Carl Peters, a German of questionable repute, desired
to start a plantation economy in Tanganyika, which was the land mass on
the mainland across from Zanzibar Island. In 1884, Peters left Germany,
traveled in the interior of Tanganyika, and returned with a handful of
treaties he had inveigled African chiefs into signing.

Complications abounded. A somewhat skewed shortcut in a longer story
brings us to Britain's hold over Zanzibar and the sultan; German and British
unresolved problems elsewhere; and territorial disputes between the sultan
(backed by Britain) and Germany on the northern coast of Kenya. Salme
was quite aware of these issues. She moved in the kaiser's circle. Furthermore, Salme was known to have developed severe animosity to the British,
despite owing her life to the small coterie of British officials who arranged
for her clandestine departure in 1842. Part of this anger concerned her
claims for inheritance money from the deaths of several siblings. Barghash
had refused to honor her claims and, during a trip to England where he was
visiting in 1874, Salme blamed the British government for preventing contact with her brother. Actually, Barghash refused to see her while she was
in England during his stay. Then, later, in 1883, Salme had written Barghash
pleading with him to turn away from his friendship with the British and,
instead, to favor relations with Germany. Her denunciations of the British

were scathing, and Salme's letter had been turned over to British authorities by her brother.[34]

In the fall of 1885, Bismarck decided to send a fleet of the German navy to Zanzibar. Among those on board the *Adler* were Emily Ruete (Salme) and her children. In other words, Bismarck was engaging in gunboat diplomacy with a threat to blockade Zanzibar harbor, with Salme and her children as his backup. Soon after her arrival, Salme disembarked and made the rounds of the town. British Foreign Office documents suggest that she was always accompanied by members of the German navy. In her memoir, Salme reported that she visited her father's palace in the town and was "deeply moved. . . . There was nothing but a fast decaying ruin."[35] According to Salme, she was greeted with warmth by many of the residents she encountered on the streets as she perambulated about the town. Any efforts she made to see Barghash came to naught. Admiral Knorr presented her demands for money during one of his visits to the sultan (but keep in mind that his mission was viewed as a threat to Zanzibar), and to the British, who were lurking in the background. The sultan flatly denied Salme's demands for compensation, telling Knorr that she "had disgraced the family and done acts punishable by death, and having abandoned her Muslim faith was dead at law."[36]

Bismarck's rationale for sending Salme and the children was that if bombardment was decided on, a prince-in-waiting was there to usurp the throne—in the form of Salme's son—if the sultan was deposed or killed. On the other hand, the wily chancellor reasoned that "an accident might possibly occur to the lady—her brother might have her strangled."[37] An incident of that sort would give Germany license to attack. Salme's life was, as we can see, incidental to the larger picture—Bismarck regarded her as a pawn. After a few weeks that included still unresolved meetings between the factions, Admiral Knorr sailed the fleet out of Zanzibar's harbor and steamed back to Europe, with Salme on board and unrewarded. In the end, Barghash agreed to pay Salme less than one third of the amount she demanded but not to her directly—he would turn the funds over to the German emperor. Over her protestations, that small sum was eventually forwarded to the German Foreign Office and, after a series of negotiations, the sultan and Zanzibar reached an accord in 1886.[38] This treaty was largely supported by the British, whose representative in Germany worked out the details with the German Foreign Office while the British agent kept up pressure in Zanzibar on Sultan Barghash, who was otherwise entirely circumvented. Chancellor Bismarck's dismissive attitude toward Salme is perhaps the most egregious example of blatant misogyny in this period of African colonial expansion.

In Sickness and in Health

Most Western perceptions of Africa pertain to wildlife, issues regarding health, or, in recent years, war. What many people may not know is not only that traditional African treatments often were successful, but also that many of the roots and herbs employed by healers were taken to Europe, synthesized, and turned into prescription drugs. This was true, for instance, with some of the medications used to treat mental illness among the traditional healers and later by physicians in Europe and America.

Although mental illnesses were mainly thought to be the work of malevolent spirits, jealousy between co-wives could be provoked by potions and powders—another form of witchcraft. Baba of Karo recounted this episode from her area in northern Nigeria:

> There was a wife who went to a malam [teacher/healer]. She asked him to give her medicine so that her co-wife would go mad and leave her in the compound alone. He said, "Here it is. If you call her and she does not answer, you will go mad. If she answers, she will go mad. . . . She returned home and called her co-wife. Silence. Then she began to dance in the open space of the compound, then madness seized her. The co-wife's father was a malam also, and he had told her "Don't take anything she gives you, don't reply if she calls you." When she heard the other wife calling her name she remained quite quiet. When the jealous wife went mad she went off into the bush. . . . [N]owadays women get charms, but only to drive out their co-wives. They don't want to get caught and taken before the Christians and killed.[39]

A modern public health official noted, however, that "psychiatric diseases do not burden Africans."[40] This may be true insofar as Western treatment is concerned. In most traditional societies, the families of the mentally disturbed kept them at home—there was no institutionalization as was common in the West in this period. Anyone who has traveled extensively in Africa is likely to have noticed the mentally afflicted woman or man roaming about—sometimes raving and often covered in mud or a white powdered substance. Africans are tolerant of the mentally ill, whether their behavior reflected the intervention of negative spirits or, over time, was seen as mental illness.

Interestingly, illnesses of all types were known to Africans. The Ekpo in Nigeria carved masks representative of human faces, depicting members of their society afflicted with these diseases.[41] When Europeans began to apply diagnostic terms, these terms, they believed, agitated the various spirits. In the case of meningitis, Baba noted that "now you see there is illness, there is meningitis, there is trouble. This is the cause of it. They have been here since the creation of the world . . . but we can't see them." The spirits may have brought the illness, but the Europeans gave it a name.[42]

As for guinea worm, Smith wrote, "Oh dear, oh dear, there was a great deal of guinea worm, and it was trouble to get water."[43] Almost all of the Africans went barefoot or wore loose-fitting sandals. The worms are up to four feet in length. As they begin to mature, they cause a blister in the leg or on a foot—or, in the case of women, they can appear from their breasts. Extracting these worms from the body is laborious, and, if the worm is broken in the process, it retreats back in and dies. Then, infection is likely to develop, causing "severe arthritis" or death to the infested. The process of successful extraction is laborious and tedious. Traditionally someone— perhaps a healer—would begin to ease the worm out, slowly winding it on a stick. Guinea worms arrive in the body through water flies, in which they burrow, and which are found in ponds or polluted rivers. The good news is that, through the efforts of the Carter Center, the guinea worm has been almost eliminated in Africa.[44]

Smallpox had been present in Africa since about the twelfth century— coming in via the Indian Ocean trade.[45] We encountered it in South Africa in the seventeenth century; it arrived in Central Africa in 1893, when someone on Henry M. Stanley's steamer was stricken. Stanley ordered all of those who seemed to be affected put on shore with some supplies. Then he steamed away, leaving them but planning to pick up the survivors—if any—on his return. Unfortunately, some local Africans ventured by and picked up the supplies, taking them to their villages, carrying the disease along as well. A year later, according to Jan Vansina, smallpox "was still raging," and ten thousand Africans were said to have "to succumbed to it," including women and children.[46]

Back in northern Nigeria, Baba referred to having been vaccinated for smallpox as "a two year old." She had been taken by one of the family's slaves to family members for weaning. The type of vaccination was crude. Baba's took place in about 1904: "They used to scratch our arm until the blood came, then they got the fluid from someone who had smallpox and rubbed it in. It all swelled up and you covered it until it healed. Some children used to die."[47] No wonder, as the practice must have been hit and miss—transfer too much and it was bound to misfire. Baba preferred the modern method.

Baba was barren. In her youth she tried various remedies to get pregnant. "I drank malams medicine. I drank *bori* [spirit possession cult] medicine. But I never had one [child]."[48] Among some women who did get pregnant, abortion was a known option. As a remedy they "drank henna. They vomit and they get diarrhea and then usually miscarry. If they take indigo, they get very ill indeed." And, Baba confided, there "is a medicine man to make a pregnancy go to sleep." But some practiced a rather unique type of birth control: they tied a kola nut "round their waist so that they can sleep with a man and not get pregnant."[49]

Barren women were often thought to be victims of witchcraft. Bearing children was an essential in African societies. In many cases a barren woman was sent back to her family in disgrace. No one in those traditional societies considered that the man might be impotent. Among the Asante in today's central Ghana, female infertility was treated in several ways. A barren woman might be given a fetish in the form of a carving from wood or terra-cotta that was "intended to represent the human form." If hollow, it was filled with traditional medicine. Then, the "open ends of the legs are placed in the nostrils, and the medicine is inhaled."[50] The more well-known way to ensure pregnancy that was advocated by the Asante priests was for a woman to wear a *akua'mma* [carved doll] "on her back in the position such as a child is carried—face forward. The doll was to be carried until the woman became pregnant or delivered a child."[51] This practice is still prevalent among traditional Asante.

In mission journals running from the 1890s into the 1940s, Megan

Vaughan found reports of fetishes and other forms of witchcraft present on bodies when people came to the clinics. European doctors regularly encountered women bringing in their children with various bits of wood or string attached to their bodies. Their comments ran along this line: "What are the curious bits of wood hanging on that baby's hair, or those dirty pockets on that woman's neck. . . . They are heathen charms worn to keep off various diseases."[52] Because of these germ-producing relics, plus the complications of dealing with difficult births, missionary doctors tended to be against traditional midwives. Midwives, they believed, "exercised a large degree of social and moral control," which prevented Christianity from taking hold.[53] Whereas these missionary medical personnel were motivated to introduce improvements in maternal care, they were equally intent on producing converts to their faith.

Infant and child mortality decreased significantly in the post-colonial era and especially in areas with modern clinics and Western-trained medical personnel. Most children died before the age of five. The percentages that follow are based on reports and thus are not representative of areas where there were no records. In Ghana, statistics revealed that the numbers of children who died in the decades from the late 1930s to late 1960, declined by half. In (today's) Republic of Congo, deaths decreased in children five and below between the late 1940s and the late 1960s.[54] Then came the deluge: with one upheaval after another intermittently from the early 1960s on, resulting in ongoing war and devastation, with the subsequent rise in deaths of children.

Fever was repeatedly referred to among the missionaries in their letters home. The obvious assumption is malaria, but yellow fever (also carried by mosquitoes) was present in parts of tropical Africa as were typhoid and sleeping sickness.[55] When the Portuguese took their "contract" Angolans to the small island of Principe, they learned that the tsetse fly was a serious presence. Sleeping sickness presented such a problem that it inhibited work on the plantations, with many of the laborers being too ill to work or in hospital. One can only assume that among the women imported workers were those who were incapacitated by "an island beset by tropical diseases," which would have included malaria and possibly typhoid or yellow fever.[56] Eventually, some of the more prosperous plantation owners began draining the swamps, which was problematic in eliminating the tsetse fly. Regularly the figures of morbidity and mortality topped those of Portuguese workers in São Tomé and Angola.

The controversial missionary Dr. Albert Schweitzer, working along the Ogowe River and environs in today's Gabon, listed a number of diseases that he encountered, beginning with, of course, malaria and including whooping cough, leprosy, sleeping sickness, swamp fever, elephantiasis, and oddly, "Nicotine poisoning," which was worse among the women.[57] To his list we can add schistosomiasis, a waterborne parasite, with women susceptible because they (and their children) collected water from streams and rivers for domestic use. Also, dysentery crops up frequently; it is "probably always a concern to African populations."[58] Yaws, frequently confused with syphilis, was "transmitted primarily non-sexually by direct . . . contact in unsanitary conditions."[59] In the colonial era, and, due to misdiagnosis as syphilis, women were singled out.[60] Cholera was an ever-present problem before and during the colonial era (and still is in some parts of Africa). It, too, is water-borne. Epilepsy: was "very common" and was attached to the occult, as most traditionalists believed it was a sign of witchcraft. Tick-borne relapsing fever was thought to have increased during the colonial era due to the steady migrations from rural to urban areas. This was especially hard on children, and, sadly, colonial authorities did not seriously begin to try to control the spread of the insects until after World War II. Dengue fever "shares the same urban mosquito vector" as yellow fever. Where the anopheles mosquito was present, historically, the death rate was "as high as 80%" of those afflicted.[61] Finally, eye diseases posed a significant medical problem for traditional healers as well as those with Western training. Malnutrition and lack of vitamin A were causes. Leprosy caused blindness, as did cataracts. No attempts were made to deal with cataracts until the arrival of the missionary doctors.[62]

The Spanish flu of 1918-1919 came first into Freetown, Sierra Leone, and then spread throughout the rest of Africa (south of the Sahara). Although morbidity was extremely high, the mortality rate was estimated to "range from 1.35 million to two million people.[63] Among the Kuba, in the Belgian Congo, two flu epidemics felled considerable numbers of the population.[64] Tuberculosis was unknown in sub-Saharan Africa until the nineteenth century, and it quickly became a scourge, especially among the poor.[65] Pertussis (whooping cough) was, interestingly, more common among girls than among boys.[66] Measles, which is a viral disease, was often complicated by pneumonia and/or malnutrition (during periods of famine, for instance). And poor children were most often its victims.[67]

We now turn our attention to leprosy. It is one of the oldest diseases known to humankind. In medieval Europe lepers were stigmatized and, in some places, forced to wear a bell to notify residents of their presence. In pre-colonial Africa, probably the greatest tribute that can be paid to the missionaries was the willingness of some to devote themselves to treating lepers. There was no cure. Catholic priests joined Protestants in establishing settlements for lepers—working among them and, in a few cases, becoming victims themselves. For Africans no other disease had a comparable stigma associated with it. Before the advent of human immunodeficiency virus (HIV), only lepers suffered a severe stigma—almost all were forced from their families. Some were sent away, others placed in special huts. Everyone avoided the leper. Many were wrapped in tatters and rags and begged on byways and in villages. They were sent away as often as they were provided with tidbits of food.

In South Africa, the supposition is that leprosy existed among the Khoe before the advent of the Europeans, but no one actually knows. Not until Europeans began to recognize the presence of lepers among themselves did they begin taking measures to deal with it.[68] By the 1840s, the government transferred 400 patients from a leper colony on the mainland to Robben Island. Between 1845 and the end of 1894, 1,771 lepers had been admitted to the Leper and Lunatic Asylum, and these were "only paupers" and voluntary patients before the mandatory Leprosy Repression Act was passed in 1892.[69]

If it is possible to find anything amusing regarding this dread disease, the findings of Dr. Jonathon Hutchinson, an otherwise respectable research physician in England, qualify. Dr. Hutchinson traveled extensively in parts of the Cape and Natal in 1890, and he concluded that leprosy was caused from "eating fish as food"—including both salted and fresh fish. These findings were published in 1892.[70] They were refuted, indeed ridiculed, and Dr. Impey, in his *Handbook*, carefully explained that leprosy was caused by a "bacterium, *mycobacterium leprae*," the bacteria being related to that which caused tuberculosis (common in Africa at the time).[71]

Impey was director of the asylum for a number of years. While there, he made copious studies of the disease and kept records by sex and age in the provinces of the Cape, all of which he published in his *Handbook*. He believed that the disease largely concentrated "among the natives who are living in a more or less savage state." Referring to today's Lesotho, he suggested that the people there lived largely to themselves until 1835 when "a number of Bushmen [San] . . . made homes there and introduced leprosy." He referred to leprosy as "as the Bushman's disease."[72]

In South Africa, Impey found that more men than women were diagnosed with leprosy. The reason, he suggested, was "arduous labor, with injuries leaving broken surfaces and open wounds." But the range in ages at the asylum indicates that even children were affected. The ages of inmates ran from children three years old to men and women in their mid-sixties. Symptoms did not immediately appear. Impey wrote that it was "not much marked" before it had been present in the body for "about three years." Of those admitted to the asylum, he found that they lived with leprosy an average of six years.[73] Because there was no cure, Impey does not address attempts to treat the patients. In 1895, leprosy was known to be a contagious disease, but "not infectious," and "heredity has little or nothing to do with the spread." However, leper colonies even today continue to exist in parts of Africa. In the early 1890s, the asylum on Robben Island held 266 patients "who had 951 children; of these children, twenty-three became lepers."[74]

Elsewhere, midway through the colonial era, in the 1930s and 1940s, governments became more involved, taking over to some extent from the missionaries, who continued to treat the majority of the lepers. The German government ran a colony on an offshore island of Tanganyika. But their emphasis was, like the missionaries, "on the life hereafter." While their bodies were failing them, their souls could be "saved or lost."[75] After

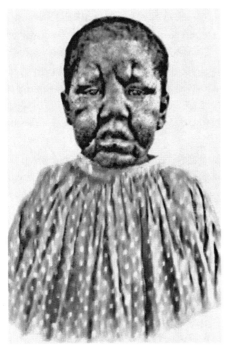

Child with leprosy at Robben Island.
Source: S. P. Impey, *A Handbook on Leprosy*

the Germans were defeated in World War I, another island community of lepers was established in Tanganyika by the British. According to Vaughan, the "sufferers" were apparently much cheered by weekly visits of the UMCA missionary and nurses, who not only brought bandages to wrap the affected limbs, but introduced a new, if ineffective, treatment "and a gramophone." The treatment consisted of injections of "hydnocarpus" oil, which even then most of the medical personnel regarded as a placebo, but it kept patients in the treatment center.[76] Only after World War II was a sulfa-based medication successfully introduced.[77]

Some officials and medical staff called for an end to the practice of isolating lepers, but their calls went unheeded. Even today there are leprosariums in a few countries, especially in West Africa. One of these leper villages was in Mali, where Eric Silla was conducting research on leprosy patients. He encountered the aged Saran Kieta, a victim of the disease, and recorded her life history. In 1992, Saran claimed she was eighty years of age. Silla was aware that most rural Africans had no strict accounting of their date of birth; time was usually calculated on events and seasons. He guessed that she was about seventy because her first child was born "around the time of Mali's independence" in 1960.[78] The story had an inauspicious beginning. Saran's older sister was betrothed. Her groom had paid the requisite bride price to the family, but, when he came to marry her, he found that the sister, Hawa, had developed red patches on her forehead. Recognizing the dread symptoms of leprosy, the groom rejected Hawa. Rather than requiring return of his bride price, he offered to marry Saran, then a child, when she was of age. By the time Saran reached puberty, her sister's former groom had married and no longer wanted her. Instead Janko, his younger brother agreed to take Saran as his wife; the bride price thus remained with the family, and Saran joined Janko in his village. This probably occurred in the late 1940s.

Her story includes the French who had colonized Mali and had been in the area since the 1890s. The French, however, rarely came to their village, and Saran had little experience with them, beyond the knowledge that they had conscripted her brother into the army during World War I. In time, Saran became aware that her sister, Hawa, had gone to a French government leper village in Bamako, which was a two-day walk from her village. After experiencing the ordeals that are detailed in the extract— Saran's own leprosy and her treatment by first her husband and then her own family—Saran followed her sister to Bamako and to the Institut Central de la Lepre. This she did on foot. Considering her lack of familiarity with an urban area or with the French, her desperation was matched by her fortitude.

Saran's Story

By the time Saran turned fifteen Masama was no longer the young and bold hunter-farmer whom everyone remembered. Having aged so, he had long since lost interest in Saran and allowed his younger brother, Janko, to take her. Janko was a strong and powerful man, head of the hunter's association. Saran's father agreed to the marriage and Sara moved to their village, Tigu. There she found people to be as friendly and welcoming as her own villagers.

At some point in the second year of her marriage, a reddish patch called a *bilen* (literally, "red") appeared on Saran's brown forehead. *Bilenw* (plural) ordinarily aroused little concern, since many villagers had them from time to time. Janko, however, summoned Tigu's most reputable healer, Bala Kamara, for a thorough diagnosis. Bala initially identified her condition as *kaba* (a fungal infection), but then she applied a medicine directly on the patch to make sure. Within a few hours her skin began blistering; a few days later it turned into a sore. Bala then informed Saran and her husband that it was not *kaba* after all but "the big disease," *banaba.*

Saran wept as Janko told her that she could not remain in his household. He insisted that the disease might spread to him. With no other refuge, she wandered out into the bush and constructed a small thatched shelter. Normally, only individuals with smallpox isolated themselves in this way. Most villages in this region shunned lepers but never banished them outside the village. The thought of returning to her family in Gwansolo did cross her mind, but she couldn't face the shame of divorce. Instead, she remained in the Tigu, spending nights alone on a goat skin beneath the shelter. During the day, when Janko was away in the fields, she would return to the compound. She did everything possible to avoid him, since, when he did see her, he often brought out his whip and beat her. In time, Janko married another woman.

When Saran first ran out into the bush, Janko's father had given her a small amount of millet. She subsisted on this supply until she was able to plant and harvest her own grain and peanuts. On a few occasions, Janko came and robbed her of even this food, claiming that he deserved it as compensation for the bride wealth. Janko's mother eventually took pity. She insisted that Saran sleep on a mat in her hut rather than alone in the bush. She also forbade her son from beating his leprous wife, instructing him to return her to Gwansolo if he really didn't want her.

Saran lived this way for two years, dividing her time between her mother-in-law's hut and her isolated shelter. Her condition progressively worsened. Janko had long since forbidden her from cooking, but now, with open sores, she could no longer even work for herself. People in Tigu didn't want a leper walking about in their village. They prohibited her from eating meat or fish, claiming that those foods would aggravate her condition. Saran became increasingly withdrawn and preferred the seclusion of the bush to the community of other sin, for which she felt so much shame (*maloya*).

One day, a madman (*fato*) appeared in front of Saran while she was sitting beneath her shelter. Having heard that he had killed and decapitated thirteen people, she tried to frighten him away by boasting that her husband was a reputable hunter. He quickly fled, only to reappear a few days later, this time while she was fetching water at a nearby creek. When he threatened to kill her if she dared cross over, Saran ran back to Tigu and told everyone about the encounter. They immediately sent out Bala Kamara, the man who first diagnosed Saran, to cut the madman's throat. Embarrassed by Saran's precarious life in semi-isolation, they also convinced Janko to divorce his wife for good and return her to Gwansolo.

When she was back in her mother's compound, Saran's life hardly improved. Other villagers in Gwansolo discouraged her from even trying to marry again. She and her older sister, Hawa, slept together in their mother's house apart from others. They took their meals alone and had their own utensils; it was said that leprosy spread through food and water. Ordinarily, women of her age prepared meals along with other adult women in the compound, but Saran and Hawa were excluded from this activity. They also cultivated rice alone with their mother. Visitors to their family's compound rarely greeted them, and old friends withdrew from their lives. Few people dared insult them directly, although they could scarcely sit down without driving others away. No other disease or condition provoked such treatment. Hawa eventually ran away to the "big town" (*duguba*, Bamako), where people said that lepers like herself could receive medicine and shelter from the *toubabs*. After she left, Gwansolo's gossips said that the *toubabs* in Bamako had killed her.

As a leper, Saran could not participate in women's social activities. This particular exclusion dispirited her more than any other. Every four years Siby's women held a festival, during which men danced with wooden mortars gripped between their teeth and women gathered in circles for their own rhythmic performances. A *jelimuso* (griot or praise singer) sang the women's praise, calling out one *jamu* (family name) at a time. A wrinkled and gray village matron meanwhile rightly rubbed the arms of each honored woman, whispering incantations up and down their length. As the drumbeats quickened and the *jelimuso's* singing grew louder and more shrill, the honored woman would break out into exuberant dance. In the center stood a cauldron of steaming hot sauce. If the woman was deemed strong enough, she dipped her arm into the pot, grabbed a piece of meat, and ate it immediately. Only those who achieved this without burning their skin or suffering pain were allowed to participate. The villagers restrained those whose hearts "pounded too much" or whose spirits "broke" too often. Once, when Saran herself was of very strong character, she participated without anyone's objection. Now, however, the "big disease" confined her to the periphery of the women's circle.

Even though Saran, "the leper," lived a life very different and separate from others, she continued to receive the basic support and sustenance due all members of the family, whether sick, old, or invalid. Nobody actually begged in Gwansolo. At worst, destitute villagers without any family discreetly received leftover rice from other families. Overt begging was considered an embarrassment to the entire village. True, members of Saran's family feared for their own health, yet they would never cast her out and leave her to beg for food.

Periodically, Saran's parents also sent her for prolonged treatment with Kalifa Keita, a hunter-healer living near Gwansolo in the village of Konkani. For three years he treated her with medicines which eased vomiting but scarcely improved her health. Claiming to protect her from other villagers, he often locked her in a hut out in the bush when he went away. Saran couldn't tolerate such severe isolation and broke out one day, fleeing back to her village for good.

After that episode, her family sent her to Jomaga Keita, another healer who resided in Gwansolo itself. Jomaga began his remedy on one arm first. He applied a medicine which caused severe blistering. He also prepared a solution made from boiled leaves for Saran to drink. A day later, a scab formed. After two weeks, the leprosy patches disappeared with the scab. Jomaga then applied his medicines on the other arm and, in weeks following, treated each of her limbs and body parts in similar intervals. Though effective, Jomaga's medicine was very painful and tired Saran considerably.

Every dry season many villagers (including Jomaga) journeyed to the hills in Guinea where they prospected for gold. Wanting to continue treating his patient, Jomaga invited Saran to join him, his wife, brother, and sister-in-law on the journey. This was the first time she ventured to other *jamanaw* (countries). After walking for one week they reached a village just beyond Kourémalé. There they settled in a large compound with other prospectors and panned gold from streams emanating from the mouth of old mines, perhaps those which once belonged to the great Mali Empire. People said that many spirits lived at those mouths. Jomaga and his family took large rocks and pounded them into gravel from which they then washed the precious metal. Occasionally they found chunks as large as berries. Dyula traders stood ready at hand to trade grain for the gold, which they carried away to distant towns. In the evenings men drank beer but never allowed the women to touch a drop, insisting that they would quarrel and fight under its influence.

Unlike her family and the other villagers in Gwansolo, Jomaga put Saran to work both at the mines and in the compound. Her diligence so impressed him that he desired her as a second wife, making his first wife, Kaaba, bitterly jealous. One day, as Saran was pulling water from an old mine shaft, Kaaba pushed her from behind and fled. Those who had witnessed this act found Saran unconscious and bleeding at the bottom of the shaft. The chief of the mines chased down Kaaba and brought her and Jomaga to meet with Saran. Kaaba publicly chided her husband for wanting to marry a leper, claiming that the "big disease" could spread to her as well. Though Saran appeared nearly cured at the time, everyone counseled her to return to Gwansolo lest she fall victim again to Kaaba's jealousies. She accepted their advice. In subsequent years, Saran returned to mines in other places, but only with her brother Masiri. On such expeditions she found enough gold for a set of earrings which she had made by a smith in her village.

Throughout this time, Saran's life in Gwansolo remained bleak. Her family continued to forbid her from eating meat and fish, while other villagers always feared her disease. Saran never knew what caused her illness until the day an old woman named Nankan Koné fell ill and was visited by a conjurer of spirits. In the course of drumming and dancing, the conjurer informed Nankan that sickness fell upon those who did not confess to their acts of sorcery. Nankan then called in Saran's family and related her story of how, many years earlier, she had grown jealous of Hawa and Saran for being such hard workers. Nankan had waited for the hot season when the nights seemed to swelter more than the days. She knew that this was a time of year when rusty laterite rocks absorbed all the suns' ferocity only to release it as dusk. For this reason, everyone slept outside in spite of their increased vulnerability to the sorcerers who stalked them at night. Nankan had obtained the necessary ingredients from a sorcerer, and then cast the leprosy-inducing medicine upon Hawa, Saran, and their brother, Jogo who somehow eluded the fate of his sisters. Nankan's confession came too late; she died a few days later.

For Saran, however, knowing the cause of her disease hardly alleviated the daily pains which came with being a leper. It seemed that she would suffer these pains indefinitely. One day, however, Gwansolo's chief announced that the *toubabs* were coming to inspect the skin of all the villagers. Several people with skin diseases including leprosy hid in the bush, fearing that the *toubabs* would capture and kill them. Long weary of her social isolation, Saran thought it better to die at the hands of *toubabs* than continue to suffer as she did. She lined up and the *toubabs* recorded her name. Though Jomaga's medicine had originally yielded the desired result of removing the patches from her skin, Saran found that, over time, the blemishes reappeared; in her eyes, *farafin* [African] medicine could never cure the "big disease."

During their visit, the *toubabs* invited Gwansolo's lepers to a place in Bamako where they could receive medicine, food, and shelter. Skeptical villagers said that Africans would only die in such a place, but Saran had recently learned that her sister Hawa had been living there happily for several years. Her brother Jogo, who had settled in Bamako's Hamdallaye quarter after completing his forced military service, also assured Saran that this *toubab* leprosy center was safe.[79]

Saran was able to reunite with her sister, who had married a leper; both were undergoing treatment. Soon Saran started the painful injections of *gorli*, oil made from a seed imported from elsewhere in French West Africa. This was the only treatment available and, considering what we learned about the injections in Tanganyika, it is possible that the *gorli* oil may have been more successful—but, as in Tanganyika earlier, the treatment kept many of the lepers in the center. In Saran's case, the patches gradually disappeared "while her strength returned."[80] Then, World War II summoned her doctor, who was replaced by another—whose requirements on the patients were harsh. Still Saran endured. As she recovered she took on more duties—those of a domestic nature.

Near the end of World War II, Saran married Bakari Kamara, another leper, and moved to his compound. Still continuing the treatment, Saran and Bakari settled on a small piece of land and farmed. After her marriage, Saran reconstituted her relationship with her natal family, although she had no desire to resettle there. By 1960, when Mali became independent, the treatment had changed from the painful injections to antibiotics. This is also when her daughter, the first of Saran's two children, was born. In 1968 Saran was declared cured. The joy of that momentous event was offset by the deaths of her sister Hawa and her husband Bakari that same year.

By 1992, when Eric Silla met Saran, her daughter was married and had given birth to two healthy children. In her old age, Saran seemed to have moved from the shadow of the stigma of leprosy. She cared not only for her own grandchildren, but also those of young healthy women as well. At this time, too, Saran became a traditional healer. According to Silla, she refused payment for her services, believing that money interfered with healing.[81] Saran's reputation as a healer and as a good and compassionate friend and neighbor compensated, one hopes, for the pain—figurative and literal—she experienced in her first marriage, and the treatments at the leprosy center during those long years prior to 1968.[82]

Sexuality always lurked in the background in both pre-colonial and colonial Africa as elsewhere. We encountered the lewd concern with the African female body and the Khoe, especially in regard to Sara Baartman. During the nearly three centuries of the Atlantic slave trade, Europeans (mainly men) often posited negative comments on the size of the African male member. Fears for white women abounded in slaveholding societies in the New World, based on the stereotype that African men were oversexed and prone to rape. This fallacy has continued in the United States into the present day. Megan Vaugan picked up on the theme of sexuality in her coverage of venereal disease in Africa.[83]

Female sexuality in Uganda emerged as a major topic in 1908 when a British military doctor published articles in two leading journals regarding what he judged to be an epidemic of syphilis in the colony. He speculated that 80 percent of the population was infected and predicted that 50 to 60 percent of their babies would die as a result.[84] Interestingly, this medical authority placed the onus for the high incidence of venereal disease on Christianity—the adoption of Christian values, such as the reduction of polygamy, caused a breakdown in the traditional patriarchal authority. This, in turn, unleashed "an uncontrolled female sexuality."[85] Not only was Christianity at fault, but so also was the arrival of African newcomers in Buganda (later part of Uganda). These migrants gave women license to act out their passion and, then, make "female sexuality . . . responsible for the syphilis problem."[86]

While these controversial views preoccupied many in the colonial medical service, efforts were made in Buganda to educate the population on the "immoral" features of the society, especially regarding polygamy, which we know the missionaries abhorred. When treatments were offered, more men than women came to the clinics because an examination was required. "In 1921 an English woman doctor appointed to Uganda to examine and treat women with venereal disease caused something of a stir by resigning in protest" against the required penetration into their genital areas.[87] The colonial official in charge blamed the chiefs, although it is hard to believe that traditional chiefs would demand such an invasion into women's bodies.[88]

In other parts of East, Central, and South Africa where males migrated to cities or to the mining areas, male sexuality was taken as a given. The double standard was alive and well—men needed sex. Women who provided it (prostitutes for the most part) were blamed for transmitting venereal diseases. They were referred to as "health hazards."[89] Officials in West Africa claimed that there was less stigma associated with venereal diseases; their subjects were more willing to come into clinics for treatment. We have seen how the French openly advocated that their officials engage in sex with local women; hence it is likely they had the same benign attitude toward the African men who were diagnosed with these diseases. An interesting obituary was posted in a Sierra Leone newspaper for an African member of the clergy, illustrating that the British there had little concern with venereal disease among the locals: "In spite of being a martyr to gonorrhea for many years, he continued his missionary work to the end."[90]

Jan Vansina has argued that venereal disease became a problem among the Kuba, in today's Republic of the Congo, only in the colonial era. From

1915 to 1917 (World War I) venereal disease afflicted many of the women of childbearing age, some of them "Luba pawn women concubines." The problem with this disease, he wrote, persisted in the area even into the late 1950s.[91] In the mid-1920s, the Belgian government joined the missionary clinics in attempts to bring the diseases under control.

World War I has not garnered the attention of scholars to the extent that marks the Second World War. One textbook author gave it a single sentence: "In the First World War the colonial powers had used a considerable amount of force to coerce Africans into supporting their colonists' interests in the war."[92] Both sides conscripted African men to fight for them within Africa, and the French and British sent Africans to the front lines in Europe, resulting in loss of lives and limbs. As for the women and the impact of the war on them, we know very little. We do know that the vast majority of Africans—male and female—were unaware that Europe was at war. The exceptions, of course, were people in those African colonies where actual conflict, and thus death and dismemberment, occurred.

During interviews with Margaret Strobel, a Swahili woman in Mombasa recalled bits and pieces regarding the First World War. The Germans, she said, "ran away to their place, Tanga." Dar es Salaam "was also their camp, full of Germans." The Germans "ran away and they were conquered." Her brother was conscripted into the Carrier Corps, encountering many who were killed. He was, he told Kaje wa Myene Matano, "sick to death, to walk on them. The dead that is."[93]

In her memoir, Wangari Matthai provided the following bit of family history regarding World War I:

Unbowed

Every family has a secret, and ours is no exception. In my family, there was a missing member, someone I did not find out about until I was well into adulthood. During the First World War, Africans in the colonies were conscripted to fight or serve as porters. In Kenya, if parents had an able-bodied son old enough to go to war, they were supposed to encourage him to join military training and then fight with the British army in East

Africa (most of the battles against the Germans . . . [were] fought in Somalia and Tanganyika). If he would not go on his own, the parents were expected to surrender him to the authorities.

My grandparents had such a son, Thumbi. My grandmother did not want her son, who was no more than twenty at the time, to join the war. She was in despair. So she advised him to hide in the dense vegetation near a high waterfall in the Tucha River near Ihithe, and brought him food from her farm every day. However, the British had developed a system to deal with parents who were reluctant to give up their sons to the war effort. They would confiscate all of their livestock. For people at that time, especially men, livestock was everything, as important as land. The authorities confronted my grandfather and threatened to take all his cattle and goats. The pressure worked. He told them where his son was hiding and they went and seized him.

"Ah, he'll come back," my grandfather said to his wife and anyone else who would listen once his son had gone to war. "He'll never come back," my grandmother replied, crying. And he never did. He became one of the more than one hundred thousand Kikuyus who died on the battlefield or from starvation or influenza during the First World War. When the war ended in 1918, my grandparents waited for their son to return from Tanganyika. But he didn't and they received no news about him. Then one day a man who lived nearby and who had also gone to the war said to my grandparents, "Make beer and I will come and tell you what happened to your son."

So my grandfather made beer. That was typical: to make beer and have guests come and drink and talk. That afternoon, the man came. Perhaps the beer gave him the courage to tell my grandfather what he knew about his son's fate. "I saw him get shot. He fell, and he didn't get up," he said sadly. My grandmother cried for her son for the rest of her life, and she always blamed my grandfather for the loss. "I told you he wouldn't come back," she would say.

My mother told me this story because I asked her why my uncles and aunt were naming their children after my father. In

Kikuyu culture, traditionally the first son is named for his paternal grandfather, so I always thought my father was my grandparents' eldest son. Later, I learned that my father was named after my grandmother's father, so there must have been another son. In explaining this, my mother told me that my grandmother had been so distraught by what happened to her son that she decided that none of her grandchildren would be named for him, lest she be reminded of that loss. The name of that young man—my eldest uncle—was lost with him, wiped from the face of the earth.

My grandparents and other families like them who lost sons in the First World War never received any official word about what had happened to their children, or any compensation. This is still an open wound. I want to say to the British government, "My uncle went to war and never came back, and nobody ever bothered to come and tell my grandparents what had happened to their son."[94]

The mission stations, and there were many throughout tropical Africa, and later government hospitals and clinics, advanced maternal and child welfare appreciably. As to the missionaries, they never lost sight of souls they might save, while also saving lives. Yet, Dr. Albert Cook, in Uganda, wrote in 1904, "It is not our job, nor have we the power, to convert the souls of men. . . . Yet we do see again and again death beds irradiated by the smile of hope and peace given from on high."[95] His wife, also a doctor, worked to revolutionize maternity care, apparently with less Christian zeal.[96]

By the 1930s, many clinics had been opened, where personnel, along with teaching mothers how to care for their babies, also lobbied to get them to deliver in hospitals rather than through traditional midwives—as had been the case also with the staff of the early missionary clinics. The colonials, however, recognized that rural women depended on midwives, and thus efforts were undertaken to train not only traditional practitioners, but new midwives as well. The Massey Street Maternity Hospital in Lagos, Nigeria, trained midwives. A few of these hospitals and clinics also featured investigations into the nature of illnesses and tropical diseases. For instance, the clinic in Dar es Salaam (located in a majority Muslim population), undertook to learn about the incidences of "malnutrition, bilharzias, hookworm" and other diseases.[97]

There was the downside, too. In the 1930s, Nigeria had twelve modern hospitals available for 4,000 Europeans, while only 52 were opened for around 4 million native Nigerians.[98] By the 1950s, the first African female physician, Dr. (Mrs.) Awaliyi was employed. And, the University College Hospital in Ibadan opened in 1957 at the very end of the colonial era.[99]

Down in South Africa, K. Gonaratham Naidoo returned to Durban as the first Indian woman trained in medicine. Her relatively wealthy family sent her for medical training in Scotland in the mid-1930s. But this was possible only after Goonam completed the equivalent of high school education, having been sent abroad after finishing primary school. As a woman of color—she was a Tamil Indian—Dr. Goonam faced discrimination not only against her gender, but also against her race. She elected to specialize in obstetrics and gynecology because, as a general practitioner, she knew that "no one will come."[100] Her patients included numbers of Zulu women—for whom she reduced her fees or did not charge at all.

While we have repeatedly witnessed missionary opposition to polygamy in areas where this was practiced, female genital mutilation [FGM] was an anathema. It is likely that colonial officials found f.g.m. repugnant as well, but their job was to govern, not to meddle with established customs. Thus in the 1920s, when Anne Dundas wrote of her visit to an initiation ceremony that included FGM, she described the event without passing judgment.[101] Dundas's husband was district commissioner among the WaChagga in Tanganyika. This ceremony marked the passage of young girls into formal womanhood—as was the case in the majority of societies where FGM was practiced. Prior to the surgery, the girls were heavily adorned so that "the young throat and breast are fairly weighed down with great ropes of varicolored beads; a belt of same encircles her waist and thighs, and on the legs and arms are worn great iron bracelets. Everything possible is done to divert the child's thoughts from the ordeal in prospect."[102]

Dundas was not present for the actual surgery, and it seems likely that it was the milder form of FGM, probably clitoridectomy—still it was a major health hazard especially with an unsterilized knife, razor, or even a sharp stone. Dundas was told that the "operation by a skilled old woman of the clan is performed on the girls singly in their own huts, surrounded by their female relatives."[103] Soon after the surgery Dundas encountered the girls, joined by their fathers, who "anointed" them "with fat;" and more dancing followed, with "bells clanging . . . a rhythmic musical note [the girls] swinging to and fro the staffs given them by their fathers." Mothers, symbolically marking their daughter's readiness for marriage, presented them with "a hoe and a cooking pot."[104]

Although the colonial representatives took the high road, the missionaries among the Kikuyu in Kenya did not. John William Arthur, an ordained minister in the Presbyterian Church as well as a medical missionary, began in the late 1920s to excommunicate girls and the parents of those who underwent FGM. This set off a storm that resulted in many parishioners leaving the church and starting their independent offshoots where not only FGM but polygamy was acceptable. Furthermore, many of the mission schools, including those of other denominations—the American Baptists among them—found themselves replaced by independent schools run by indigenous administrators and teachers.[105] Some Protestant missions "lost ninety percent of their members," but within five years after the controversy erupted, other than the American Baptists, which closed down their schools, the churches recovered their students.[106]

Jomo Kenyatta was steeply embedded in the customs of his people. After he went to England to represent the Kikuyu Central Association, he studied anthropology at the London School of Economics, earning a certificate for the course and writing his thesis on Kikuyu customs. This was later published as *Facing Mount Kenya,* and it featured a lengthy section in which he explained the importance of FGM to his people.[107] His defense, indeed acceptance, of the practice was at variance with the Kenyan constitution, which, in 1964, with Kenyatta as president, vowed to uphold, at independence. In that document, FGM was declared "an illegal practice and an infringement on the rights of women and unacceptable under all circumstances."[108]

The meaning of FGM to the Kikuyu and other Kenyan ethnic groups that performed variations of the surgery has been notably covered by Tabitha Kanogo in her study of women in colonial Kenya.[109] Whether in accepting or rejecting colonial attitudes toward this cultural custom, Kanogo argues that the issue provided women the opportunity to exercise their options and opened "spaces to female agency."[110]

How the Girl Is Operated On

Early in the morning of the day of the physical operation the girl is called at cock-crow. She is fed with a special food (*kemere kia oomo*), eaten only on this occasion, after which she is undressed, leaving only one string of beads across her shoulder, known as *mogathe was mwenji* (present for the barber). This is given to her sponsor as a symbol of lasting friendship and as a bond of mutual help in all matters. It also signifies that henceforth the girl is supposed to hide nothing from her sponsor nor deny her guardian anything demanded from her, even if it be the last she possesses.

After all necessary arrangements have been made, the girl is escorted to a place appointed for the meeting of all the candidates. From there they are led to a special river where they bathe. The boys are assigned to a particular place while the girls bathe at a point below them, singing in unison: "*Togwe-thamba na munja wa ecanake,*" which means: "We have bathed with the cream of youth."

This is done before the sun rises, when the water is very cold. They go up to their waist in the river, dipping themselves to the breast, holding up the ceremonial leaves in their hands; then they begin shaking their wrists, dropping the leaves into the river as a sign of drowning their childhood behavior and forgetting about it forever. The initiates spend about half an hour in the river, in order to numb their limbs and to prevent pain or loss of blood at the time of operation. The sponsors superintend to see that the initiates bathe in the correct manner, while the mothers, relatives and friends are present, painted with red and white ochre (*therega na moony*), singing ritual and encouraging songs. The warriors keep guard to prevent the spectators or stranger from coming too near to the bank.

When the bathing is completed, all the initiates are lined up following their order of adoption. The ceremonial horn is blown to warn the passers-by that the initiates are about to march and that the road must be cleared. No one is allowed to pass across the appointed path, as this is regarded as bad luck (*motino*). A small boy and a girl are chosen, in accordance with what the Gikuyu believe to be a lucky omen (*nyoni-ya-monyaka,* "lucky bird"). Their duty is to carry branches of creepers, called *mo-kengeria* and *mwambaigoro,* which is believed to have certain antiseptic and healing powers. The boy and the girl, with their branches of creepers, stand at the entrance of the homestead, in order to be the first to meet the initiates on their arrival.

As the candidates approach, a special ceremonial horn is sounded rhythmically. The initiates advance slowly towards the homestead with both hands raised upwards, elbows bent, pressed against their ribs, with the fists closed and thumbs inserted between the first and second fingers, *kuuna thano.* This signifies that they are ready to stand the operation firmly and fearlessly.

Unlike the previous day the songs take on an entirely different form. There is no more dancing and jumping. The singing is of a mournful character, in slow and gentle voices. This is a moment of great excitement and anxiety, especially for the mother and father whose first-born is to be initiated, for not only is their boy or girl passing from childhood to adulthood, but the father and mother are to be promoted to a higher status in the society. They all join in singing songs of anxiety, "*Twahirwoko tondo twagucithio motongoro?*" which means: "Where are we led to in this tedious procession?" In the meanwhile the elders select a place near the homestead where the operation is to be performed. This place is called *iteeri.*

Here a clean cowhide, tanned and polished, is spread on the ground; the ceremonial leaves called *mathakwa* are spread on the hide. The girls sits down on the hide, while their female relatives and friends form a sort of circle, several rows thick, around the girls, silently awaiting the great moment. No male is allowed to go near or even to peep through this cordon. Any man caught doing so would be severely punished. . . .

Each of the girls sits down with her legs wide open on the hide. Her sponsor sits behind her with her legs interwoven with those of the girl, so as to keep the girl's legs in a steady, open position. The girl reclines gently against her sponsor or *motiiti*, who holds her slightly on the shoulders to prevent any bodily movement, the girl meanwhile staring skywards. After this an elderly woman, attached to the ceremonial council, comes in with very cold water, which has been preserved through the night with a steel axe in it. This water is call *mae maithanwa* (axe water). The water is thrown on the girl's sexual organ to make it numb and to arrest profuse bleeding as well as to shock the girl's nerves at the time, for she is not supposed to show any fear or make any audible sign of emotion or even to blink. To do so would be considered cowardice (*kerogi*) and make her the butt of ridicule among her companions. For this reason she is expected to keep her eyes fixed upwards until the operation is completed.

When this preparation is finished, a woman specialist, known as *moruithia*, who has studied this form of surgery from childhood, dashes out of the crowd, dressed in a very peculiar way, with her face painted with white and black ochre. This disguise tends to make her look rather terrifying, with her rhythmic movement accompanied by the rattles tied to her legs. She takes out from her pocket (*mondo*) the operating Gikuyu razor (*rwenji*), and in quick movements, and with the dexterity of a Harley Street surgeon, proceeds to operate upon the girls. With a stroke she cuts off the tip of the clitoris (*rong'otho*). As no other part of the girl's sexual organ is interfered with, this completes the girl's operation. Immediately the old woman who originally threw the water on the girls comes along with milk mixed with some herbs called *mokengeria* and *ndogamoki*, which she sprinkles on the fresh wound to reduce the pain and to check bleeding, and prevent festering or blood poisoning. In a moment each girl is covered with a new dress (cloak) by her sponsor. At this juncture the silence is broken and the crowd begins to sing joyously in these words: "*Ciana ciito ire kooma ee-ho, nea marerire-ee-ho,*" which means: "Our children are brave, ee-ho (hurrah). Did anyone cry? No one cried—hurrah!"

After this the sponsors hold the girls by the arms and slowly walk to a special hut which has been prepared for the girls. Here the girls are put to sleep on beds prepared on the ground with sweet-smelling leaves called *marerecwa, mataathi* and *maturanguru*. The two first mentioned are used for keeping flies away or any other insect, and also to purify the air and counteract any bad smell which may be caused by the wounds, while the last-named is purely a ceremonial herb. The leaves are changed almost daily by the sponsors who are assigned to look after the needs of the initiates (*irui*). For the first few days no visitors are allowed to see the girls, and the sponsors take great care to see that no unauthorized person approaches the hut. It is feared that if someone with evil eyes (*gethemengo*) sees the girls it will result in illness.

Healing of the Wound

At the time of the surgical operation the girl hardly feels any pain for the simple reason that her limbs have been numbed, and the operation is over before she is conscious of it. It is only when she awakes after three or four hours of rest that she begins to realize that something has been done to her genital organ. The writer has learned this fact from several girls (relatives and close friends) who have gone through the initiation and who belong to the same age-group with the writer.[111]

Women, Education, and Legal Issues

Gendered education had always existed in traditional African societies. Little girls were assigned tasks that included caring for the small mobile infants. Learning occurred by doing; and by observing their mother's activities, as well as those of co-wives in polygamous societies. Although matters such as who was responsible for whom may seem mundane, in matrilineal societies part of the early education consisted of knowing that it was to the mother's brothers, not the father, to whom they should turn. In most African societies, grandmothers, or older women, played a significant role in conveying the mores and customs. The folktales carried down through generations conveyed more than entertaining stories; they taught right from wrong as this was interpreted by different ethnic groups. And gender itself was learned early on: boys did this and girls did that. In most societies gender lines were drawn quite early. By age six or seven most boys spent time in the male sphere, while girls were segregated into units consisting of women. Some societies created age sets, whereby all girls were assigned to specific groups where they passed through similar experiences together. Some of these age sets were named, and many of their occupants remained members for life, irrespective of individual identities and experiences.[112]

The Sande Society in Sierra Leone was typical of many of the secret societies created for girls. The function of these societies was to prepare them for adulthood and lives as wives and mothers. They received education in domestic skills, in farming, and in matters pertaining to sex, including the practice of FGM as a societal norm.[113] Some societies, including Sande, taught the use of traditional medicines and rudimentary healing techniques. Their teachers were practitioners. One anthropologist suggested that girls learned "the art of poisoning food to keep their husbands in line." Caroline Bledsoe referred to the paradox between teaching girls to be good wives and also "how to poison troublesome husbands."[114] She believed that girls learned little in these societies that they did not already know, or they reverted to the gendered education that was already taught to traditional groups historically. What did occur were the metamorphoses into adulthood: "When the initiates come out of the bush, a midwife of high rank . . . often accompanies them, symbolizing the birth of new people." They also learned handicrafts, which added to the coffers of the senior women through their sale.[115] In many respects, the traditional societies taught the same basics introduced by the Christians missionaries—who were mainly myopic where traditional education was concerned. The female body was emphasized by members of the Sande Society, and their sowo mask was illustrative of their concepts of women's beauty.[116]

But in Sierra Leone, Westernization had been a factor when the colony was first settled by descendants of Africans: those brought from Canada after the American Revolution, and also from England. Later, after Britain had ended the slave trade, her navy captured ships carrying slaves in the Atlantic and took them to Sierra Leone. The position of women was subservient—they were property. In the legal system, women were generally not allowed to sue in court and were regarded as minors.[117] Still, Kenneth Little argued that in traditional society, "the role of women is complementary rather than subordinate." And, in the female secret societies, women held all of the high offices and positions of leadership" denied them in the protectorate at large.[118] This was one of the remaining positions of power for women during the colonial era.

"Husbandless women," as the Mende refer to those who were old enough to be married but were not, "travel up and down the railway as trade and other interests direct. . . . And [they] attract young men, and even boys, to follow the same roving life." While they learn to trade, "many of them combine petty trading with semi-commercial form of prostitution." This was another learning experience, otherwise viewed as the lesson of survival.[119] Trade was one of the only avenues open to women, and even that was impacted by the introduction by outsiders of small stores carrying mainly Western goods.

The introduction of Western-style literacy caused its own problems. According to Little in Sierra Leone, "Literate, or civilized women, as they sometimes refer to themselves, are as yet very few in number [in the 1940s]." At that time there were "some 2,000 girls present at school. Two-thirds of the . . . schools are run by the Missions" in urban areas, "so that the process . . . brings the country-bred girl into a more sophisticated environment." This, in turn, induces them to dress themselves as Europeans, to furnish their homes in Western style, and to adopt the same "social values."[120] Most girls "do not go farther than Standard IV, and few gain qualifications sufficient for the only careers, nursing and teaching, open to women" in Sierra Leone.[121] This is the litany that continued elsewhere—teachers and nurses were prescribed as women's work.

Legal complexities for the Western-educated women abounded. Some missionaries opposed paying bride wealth. If the couple was married in a Christian church without bride wealth, and the husband died, the wife's claim would not be considered in a traditional court. If, however, she was wed in the traditional manner, she would inherit as she could and, for instance, claim compensation for "ill treatment." Then, there were the difficult legal problems in mixed marriages: "the intermingling of Christian and Muslim social controls" produced inconsistencies. "The consequences for the wife, being answerable for her conduct to far fewer people, are laid open readily to the charges of indiscipline. . . . Disputes are enhanced by the fact that their social training has equipped neither spouse with the necessary pattern of marital behavior which would enable them to make the series of personal adjustments" required.[122] What laws governed matters between husband and wife? In fact, whether literate or in a mixed marriage, women were still in an inferior position in Sierra Leone and elsewhere during the colonial era.

We encountered Hajiya Ma'daki earlier in our discussion on slavery. Although she was instructed in the Qur'an by private tutors in her father's Kano palace, Ma'daki's interests were not centered on the classroom, and she soon dropped away. After being sent to Katsina as a child bride and, upon reaching puberty, followed by her marriage to the emir, Ma'daki came into contact with a steady progression of European colonial administrators. She traveled extensively with her husband—to England and twice to Mecca. And although Western education had been rejected by the Muslim emirs in northern Nigeria, Ma'daki slowly came to see the benefits once her husband decided that the royal sons should learn English. When her husband decided to establish a school in Katsina, Ma'daki was skeptical, but she lent her support. Then, among her contributions in Katsina was overseeing "the appointment of a British woman" in the first school for girls in the north. The British referred to it "as a miracle of progress."[123] Following the death of her husband, Ma'daki returned to Kano, where her brother was then the emir. He, too, had decided to foster Western education and opened a school for girls. Ma'daki moved in as matron. In this capacity her day began with morning prayer and ended with the "final bed check" at night. Although she was not directly involved in teaching, Ma'daki had responsibility for all of the domestic chores assigned to the boarders as well, of course, their religious duties.[124] (Keep in mind, however, that these schools were for the elite.)

The Belgians were slow in introducing education in the Congo, but missionaries established schools in lower Congo as early as 1880-1895. Presbyterian and Catholic missionaries opened some schools in Kasai in 1891.[125] The curriculum was similar to that of other missionary groups elsewhere: it centered on religious instruction and the basics such as reading, writing, and arithmetic, with "emphasis on vocational training for the girls. The Protestant school even prepared some girls for stenographic services. Attendance was sporadic, and the Catholics failed to produce the same

"Teacher" sculpture depicted by
an African carver.
Source: African Society of Missions,
Musée africain SMA, Lyon, France

quality of education for girls that was available for boys." That lasted, according to Vansina, almost until the end of the colonial period.[126]

Elsewhere in the Congo, the colonial education system began to develop, and it "distanced women from salaried work at the same time it prepared men for it." The goal, with a few exceptions, was to turn girls into good housewives and mothers.[127] After reforms were introduced in 1948, some girls were trained as teachers, midwives and nurses— and, of course, were taught Christian moral values. Before then most girls attended schools run by nuns, beginning in the 1890s in the lower Congo. In the early 1950s, girls joined classes taught by priests and were brought up to the standards enjoyed by the boys.[128] Higher education was introduced only in the last few years of Belgian colonialism, leaving a major vacuum when it came to the transition of leadership.

Adams College (high school) was founded in Natal, South Africa, by the American Board of Missions in 1853, and it became co-educational in the early 1900s. In time Adams fell under the influence of what was called the Tuskegee Model, and featured vocational training for blacks, drawing on the educational theories of Booker T. Washington's Tuskegee Institute and Hampton Institute in Virginia. A strong proponent of this model was Davison Loram, born in South Africa in 1879. He traveled extensively in the American South, visiting Tuskegee and other black schools before enrolling in Teachers College, Columbia University, early in the twentieth century. On his return, Loram, a white supremacist, served in several education posts in Natal, and was influential in promoting vocational and agricultural training, although he did advocate that all Africans receive elementary education. This was an innovation but certainly not meant to create future leaders. The emphasis for the younger students should be on "character" and "health and hygiene."[129] Loram viewed Africans as "immature" in their stage of civilization, although, in fact, they actually "suffered from genuine social and economic disabilities."[130]

In 1949, Mabel Palmer, a semi-retired university administrator in Natal, began to receive correspondence from a fifteen-year-old Xhosa girl who lived in Umtata, Transkei. Lily Moya turned to Mabel for help in enrolling in a school there, and for financial support. Over a period of several months, Lily pursued Mabel, who, in turn, wrestled with the conundrum the girl presented. While Mabel pondered, without warning, Lily ran away from Umtata and arrived in Natal. The reason for this action was that Lily's uncle, and guardian, had arranged for an undesired marriage to an older man. Later, in a letter to Mabel, Lily confided that her uncle had acted upon personal greed: "He only wanted the dowary [sic]."[131] Shula Marks, who had studied numerous mission records, confirmed this conundrum: in the nineteenth and early twentieth centuries the mission files were "replete with stories of women fleeing to the stations to escape unwelcome marriage."[132] We saw this earlier in Liberia. In cases such as these, the missionaries provided a welcome sanctuary.

Eventually, Mabel arranged for Lily to enroll in Adams College and became responsible for most of Lilly's expenses.[133] While she was at Adams, the list of Lily's courses indicated that by 1950 the curriculum had mostly shifted away from the Tuskegee Model. "These" she wrote to Mabel, "are the subjects I take: English, Maths, Zulu B (keep in mind Lily was a Xhosa speaker), Geography, Botany, Zoology, and, the remnants of the old model, Agriculture.[134] The two years plus that marked their relationship were traumatic for Lily's elderly sponsor, who was troubled by Lily's problems. She disappeared from Mabel's life in 1951. Shula Marks has covered this remarkable cross-cultural adventure through the letters the two women exchanged in this period in *Not Either an Experimental Doll*.

In writing and editing Lily's story, Marks introduced a Zulu woman who served as a go-between during some of the difficulties Mabel experienced with her protégée. Sibusisiwe Makhanya was born in Natal in 1879. Her family was Christian and was affiliated with the Congregationalists. Sibusisiwe attended the American-run Congregationalist school before successfully completing the teacher training course at Adams College. She taught school for a brief period of time before engaging in "community affairs" and founding the Bantu Purity League. The title conveys its purpose: "To keep the girls pure in the right way" and to avoid premarital sex.[135]

Still Sibusisiwe did not entirely neglect teaching. She ran a night school from her home. The combination of her activities made an impression on officials with the American Phelps-Stokes Commission who visited Natal in the early 1920s. As a result, she was offered a scholarship to study in the United States at a segregated school in South Carolina. After a few months at what must have been a program based on the Tuskegee Model, Sibusisiwe left. She then spent a summer studying at Tuskegee. This experience reinforced her disdain for the Tuskegee approach to educating people of color.[136]

Sibusisiwe broke with Phelps-Stokes and went to Cleveland, where she studied at a school that later became part of Oberlin College—a much more liberal institution. This was followed by Teachers College, Columbia University. In 1930, she returned to South Africa and threw herself into community organization, founding "a new youth group," among whose stated goals were "appreciation of the culture of other races and to encourage interracial co-operation."[137] But Marks observed that the time she spent in America sewed "the seeds of race consciousness" in the "moisture" of the United States, which enabled Sibusisiwe to instill racial pride in her young charges—another and important aspect of teaching.[138]

Among the Swahili, female education began on the Kenya coast in the 1950s, but not without staunch opposition from some members of Swahili Muslim community. On the other hand, a more enlightened Muslim figure emerged to argue the following: "The Prophet says that women and men should be educated. In fact educating one woman is worth educating ten men, because she passes on her good character to her children. . . . Also a man should take pleasure in his wife's betterment. The Prophet says that better than worldly comfort is a good wife."[139] Farther up the coast, Sheikh Ahmed Jahadhmy donated land and was joined by a few other leading men in establishing a girl's school in Lamu in the late 1950s. This, too, was controversial, and drew only a few girls from among the elite.[140] The curriculum at these private schools featured the 3 Rs and, of course, religion as well as the standard course in domestic science. In Mombasa Swahili and Arabic were added. This was true also in Zanzibar, where the school opened, earlier, in the 1930s. When, in 1954, a small number of girls passed entry into high school, more opposition developed in Mombasa. Girls who had attained puberty were required to go into purdah. Gradually accommodations were worked out—and some girls took instruction at home.[141] District Commissioner H. E. Lambert, in his 1957 report, referred to the difficulties encountered by the principal—a Christian woman—who was "appalled by the lethargy of the majority of her charges." She had them "medically examined, when it was found that 85% of the girls . . . were suffering from ankylostomiasis [hookworm] and that malaria was present among them." The "vast majority of the Arab mothers are themselves uneducated." As a result, most Arab girls "who get any education at all get it from the Koran schools and accordingly suffer from . . . debilitating diseases caused by ignorance and lack of care."[142] Despite the prohibitions fostered by the Arab Muslim families, there are those who "see Indian and African girls earning good salaries in offices and think how pleasant it would be if their own girls could do likewise."[143]

Meanwhile the colonial government gradually began to open primary schools elsewhere in Kenya for girls. When the teacher training school in the late 1940s was established near Nairobi, girls were included. In the early 1950s a high school for girls opened in the Central Province. Only a handful of girls were considered eligible in the beginning, with the government exercising care to balance the selection based on ethnicity.[144]

Annie Jiagge was an early pioneer in women's rights. She was born in French Togoland following World War I and was heavily influenced by Christianity due to her father's occupation as a Presbyterian minister. Her parents were advocates of the British educational system, not the French, and they sent Annie to live with an aunt in British Togo so that she could attend a primary school there. As a result, Annie was accepted at the elite Achimota College (high school) in Accra, Ghana. During World War II she taught school, where her talents for organization were recognized, and soon she became the principal. But a career in education did not satisfy her. Annie made a rare and courageous move, by applying to the London School of Economics for advanced study in preparation for the law. At the time her female classmates were two British women and one Indian.[145] Whether she experienced both sexism and racism is not known. Annie's next, and out of character, move sent her to Paris to study fashion.

That career was just as unrealistic for an African woman as law—so she returned to London, passed her courses in 1950, and was admitted to Lincoln's Inn.[146] Annie went into private practice back in the Gold Coast, which was just on the throes of emerging from colonialism. She married, and, with her husband's support, Annie Jiagge—who was childless—became involved in myriad activities while maintaining her practice. Among the many organizations with which she was affiliated was the Gold Coast YWCA, where she became president in 1955. As the colony transitioned to Ghana, with final independence in 1957, Jiagge became a magistrate. By the time she retired in 1993, she had served on the Circuit Court, as a High Court judge, on the Court of Appeals and, finally as president of the Appeals Court.[147]

Annie Jiagge's greatest achievement may have been her selection to represent Ghana on the UN Commission on the Status of Women, where she was elected chair "of the 21st Session" in 1968—remaining on the Commission until 1972. In this role, Jiagge "exposed . . . the nature of violence against women worldwide." While serving on the Commission, she joined in writing the "basic draft on the Elimination of Discrimination against Women in 1967."[148] Once back in Ghana, Annie Jiagge continued to pursue women's rights—as an actor on the world stage and at home. Among her later accomplishments was raising money to help seed an international organization that educated women in banking in order for them to raise credit for beginning small businesses. In the mid-1990s this was a unique undertaking. Annie served on the Ghana section of the Women's World of Banking, where she was characterized as "a 'quiet heroine, a woman who understood the pain of women.'"[149]

Navanethem Pillay of Durban, South Africa, was another pioneer in the field of law. She became one of the first Indian women to join the bar after battling government officials for admittance to legal study. Pillay set up her own law firm in Durban and was active in the political arena. In 1972, Navi's husband, "Gaby," was arrested. While still a new and essentially inexperienced lawyer, Navi represented him (and others) in court. Some of Gaby's fellow prisoners had been tortured. Their crime was attending meetings. In addition, one hapless man contributed twenty-five cents at the meeting. He was sentenced to five years behind bars for such a petty "crime."[150] In representing various ANC and Communist Party men, Navi's work took her to Robben Island on a few occasions. She conferred with Nelson Mandela, with whom she disagreed in the matter of prisoner's rights. He "adopted the view that prisoners had no rights. That you are almost property. One should not bring a court case." Navi and her team "considered" Mandela's opinion but chose to proceed with their brief. The court agreed that, in this case, prisoners had rights—such as to work and to study, including obtaining books.[151]

Stress caused illness, and Pillay cut back on her civil rights activities. She received a fellowship to Harvard University, where she earned a doctorate in juridical science in 1988. This news was greeted in typical South African fashion—her race and gender duly noted by the press with no mention that Navi was the first South African of any race or gender to earn that

degree from Harvard. While at Harvard, Navi took a women's studies course. This awakened in her an interest in issues such as domestic violence. Back in Durban, she and another woman, an academic, established the first shelter for battered women in that city—with no discrimination with regard to race or class. As an outgrowth of her legal activism in South Africa and her interest in human rights at Harvard, Pillay was appointed "human rights lawyer for the World Wide Concerts in support of the UN Declaration of Human Rights in 1978. That appointment brought her two months of travel with the celebrated performers Bruce Springsteen and Sting. ("A gift from heaven" is how she referred to it, and few would disagree).[152]

Navanethem Pillay.
Source: Office of High Commission for Human Rights, United Nations

Navi continued her involvement on the larger stage: Amnesty International and then as a member of the Robert F. Kennedy Memorial Human Rights Award Committee. She reached the pinnacle of her career when, in July 2009, the director general of the UN selected Navi Pillay as commissioner for human rights, the position she occupied into 2014.[153]

The study of women's rights and law is increasingly attracting scholarly attention. Several studies have been made on the French colonies in West Africa, including the conflict between civil law and sacred law under Islam. The complexities of Islamic law and the evolution of an accommodation with the French legal system are beyond the realm of this discussion. Nevertheless, we draw on some particular circumstances from the Muslim Tribunal of Ndar, Senegal, from the 1880s to the 1920s.[154] Much of the "litigation . . . was brought by women" in this period, with their "most common grievances" centering on "abandonment and neglect by their husbands."[155] Not surprising, many of the complaints dealt with polygamy.

One case from Lydon's work concerned "Amuja Buyu, who first presented her complaint" to the French court before "being redirected to the Muslims' tribunal." Her husband, she testified, "exited her home, left her for 17 days. . . . Then he travelled without informing her or disbursing her maintenance. When he returned, he did not go to her," nor did he notify her of his presence in the area. This Lydon interpreted as "clearly a case where the husband favored one wife over another." A divorce was granted following on his claims that she refused him sexual intercourse and her refutation of the charges. In this case, "they agreed" to part without compensation.[156] Domestic grievances often included wifely disobedience, or, in one case, a husband who rid himself of his wife by claiming that she lacked cooking skills.[157]

We have very few data regarding women and the effects of World War I when, as we have noted earlier, the French and British wantonly conscripted African men. During this period, Lydon cited military conscription, noting that "abandonment cases were frequent." "On 3 December 1917 alone, the qadi [religious judge] of Ndar dispatched five letters to the qadi of Dakar" plus other letters to police commissioners "all inquiring about deserting husbands." Lydon points out that, during the war, the police department was sufficiently well organized that some would have had "intelligence on migrants such as traders, soldiers and other workers in the colonial economy."[158]

Beyond the inability to cook, other cases originated with men and appeared in the court records. Some wives refused to follow their husbands to a new locale. In one case of this type, the qadi ruled that if the husband took his wife "from country to country" he was obliged to pay her expenses. But if she chose to remain behind, she had to repay the bride price. The qadi gave her the option (which Lydon did not include).[159] What we can conclude is that women gained more access to file for litigation with the support of the French government, but in religious courts. In the nineteenth century, "women frequented the court with great ease, presenting their cases and claims. . . . At the same time, the qadis of Ndar invariably granted circumstantial divorces to women for reasons of spousal abandonment . . . neglect or physical abuse.[160] In the twentieth century, a major impediment—that of the language barrier—was mainly overcome; the results were what one academic "called 'a *rationalized* Islamic practice under colonial hegemony.'"[161]

The late Ghanaian historian Adu Boahen argued that "the impact of colonialism was deep and certainly destined to affect the future course of events" in Africa.[162] In terms of the women, colonialism reduced the status of many, especially those in tribal leadership positions. Their earning power decreased while, with their men migrating to cities and town, their labor was intensified. Western medicine improved their lives and those of their children, as did the introduction of Western-style education—although remarkably lacking in many parts of Africa, as we have seen. But during the colonial era, women were not entirely acted upon. As we will see, they were actors in their own behalf in the anti-colonial struggles.

CHAPTER SEVEN

Anti-Colonial Conflict and Health

In this chapter we are going to touch on a few of the anti-colonial conflicts in which women engaged. Beginning with the Women's War in Nigeria in 1929, we conclude with a brief survey of their many activities in South Africa's long march to equality.[1] Earlier, at the onset of colonialism, we celebrated Queen Taytu for her role in defending Ethiopia from Italian aggression in the late nineteenth century, when she was an anomaly. Mainly, the colonial era witnessed loss of economic power and changing social patterns for both urban and rural Africans, which augured negatively for the majority of African women. But first we require context regarding colonial administration as we move forward to concentrating primarily on the British colonies, to a lesser extent on the French and the Portuguese, and, finally, to South Africa, which was politically united after 1909 (although foreign policy remained under British dominion until 1961 when South Africa declared itself a republic).

Most of the colonized areas had been divided into political units—some quite large—and these were later subdivided, such as those in the French Sudan. These larger polities were eventually further divided into smaller administrative units. These smaller divisions remained largely in place at independence and became separate countries. Other colonial entities such as Nigeria, in British Africa, were very large, containing ethnic groups with indigenous political systems, customs, and languages that varied so widely that they had little or nothing in common, yet were linked together at independence.

In Chapter Six, we saw that the French had established Native Courts, which, in the example we provided, coexisted with Islamic sharia law. This same phenomenon occurred in northern Nigeria, which provides us with an example of British indirect rule. Although one governor was appointed

with total responsibility for colonial affairs in the colony of Nigeria, in the Hausa area of the north Britain ruled through the local emirs (such as Mad'aki's father, husband, and brother in Kano and Katsina). Elsewhere in Nigeria the colony also was divided into provinces, districts, and sub-districts. This political system was similar in most of the British colonies. (However, keep in mind that there were instances of indirect rule through chiefs in several colonies where the form of governance was mixed: direct rule through appointed officials and indirect rule through traditional or appointed chiefs).

In most cases each of the lower-level officials reported to the official above him, with the highest authority resting on the colonial governor, who, in turn, reported to the Colonial Office, which was responsible to the parliament. The British, like the French, recruited native soldiers in the non-officer ranks of their armies. In Nigeria, the majority of the soldiers came from the north. Western-style education was very late in coming to the north, so opportunities to join the cash economy or participate in colonial government service were limited, making the army attractive to many young men there. The Native Courts were established in all parts of the colony of Nigeria and the other colonies under British rule, and colonial officials paid little or no heed to local customs. They often placed people who spoke similar languages together, under the assumption that they had the same political systems and derived from a common line of descent. In fact, in southeast Nigeria individual villages originally may have been composed of residents with a common ancestor, but over time some villages developed separately, with traditional practices and laws that differed from those of their neighbors. Most of the Ibo/Igbo/Ibibo in the southeast followed patrilineal descent; but there were exceptions, and some few were matrilineal. In the Igbo villages leadership was primarily conducted by elders who were selected for a variety of reasons, mainly wisdom and maturity. (The exception was in Onitsha where the Obi had a hereditary ruler.) In conjunction with the spirits, in some cases judgments regarding interpersonal affairs, and even internal conflicts, were rendered by the elders. No Native Courts had ever existed until the Europeans superimposed them on the colonized. The Ibibo had a traditional council composed of worthy elders and members of specific societies, with wealth being a major determinant for higher grades and titles.

In the western part of Nigeria the largest ethnic group was the Yoruba.

We met missionaries among them earlier. The Yoruba kingdom was highly
stratified, with a king at the top, and local rule was conducted mainly by
the king's appointees. The Yoruba kingdom also was divided by religion:
a large majority of Yoruba were animists, although over time many had
converted to Islam or Christianity. Ibadan and Ife represented the old historical centers among the Yoruba, until the European intrusion at the coastal
juncture of the Niger River and the Atlantic Ocean promoted Lagos to
precedence. Despite the Yoruba's highly stratified political system, the
British installed the sort of divisions described above: there were provincial
commissioners, district commissioners, and district officers—these were
the most important. But again over time, layers of colonial officials were
added. And, of course, the Native Courts were distributed across Yoruba
land as well. Almost none of the traditional leaders selected members of
these courts—and, their appointments were based more on close association with the colonizers rather than authority within their respective communities. English speakers, for instance, and especially those who were
Christian—as were many of the Igbo-Ibibo ethnic groups in the east—were
favored.

The Yoruba women continued in settling local affairs during the colonial
era as had been the case in the pre-colonial period. The king's wives also
were his advisors. In some instances, depending on the king and his wives,
the women were instrumental in influencing foreign affairs. In Ibadan
Yoruba women were members of Oyo associations, which dealt with trade:
buying, selling and producing. One of their members served as a member
of the Council of State until World War I.[2] During the colonial era, however,
most women were reduced to subservience until a decade or so before
Nigerian independence: in the 1950s three women were appointed to the
"House of Chiefs."[3] One of the women was Funmilayo Ransome-Kuti, an
Egba from the east, whose long career has been documented by Johnson-
Odum and Mba.[4] The most intriguing woman of all, however, was Ahebi
Ugbabe, who had been appointed a warrant chief by the British in 1916.[5]
Among the Igbo and Ibibo peoples, women served in various consulting
capacities, especially regarding affairs peculiar to themselves and, in some
cases, in legal matters involving women. Some were, in certain villages,
involved in the local assemblies.[6]

A Yoruba woman—a Muslim trader in Lagos— had emerged as an important leader by 1910. She was illiterate but spunky, hiring others to aid

in dealing with market women's interests while pursuing militant action in a variety of forms over the years. Madam Alimotu Pelewura rose to positions of importance, first as a member of the traditional government in Lagos (and reporting to the king). Later, when Nigeria developed political parties, she served in the leadership of the Nigerian Union of Young Democrats. After World War II began, Pelewura led a fight against the government in its attempt to tax the women on their income—citing among other reasons, the wartime hardships they faced.[7]

The matter of taxes was briefly alluded to earlier. All of the colonizers levied taxes on their subjects, and these had to be paid in cash. The British and French required those who fell under their respective rule to help support the increasing layers of bureaucracy, arguing that they were doing so on behalf of those governed. The hut tax was generally the first of these, but other taxes followed, as the colonizers increased their local staffs. In time, some of these staff members included Africans—almost always in low-level and poorly paid positions. The burden of paying taxes, as we saw, meant that mainly men were thrown into the cash economy and into urban areas (or the mines where minerals were being exploited by European companies). Although men complained about being taxed, very few open rebellions occurred. In one southeastern province, a few men rioted in 1927 when the British introduced direct taxation. But no major eruptions occurred until, in 1929, word began to circulate that the women were going to be taxed on their small income and on their livestock.

The Women's War and Anti-Colonial Reactions

Profits from oil palm products had been relatively good, but in 1929 they declined—the worldwide depression reached even into the southeastern provinces of Nigeria. Women helped process the palm oil, but only the men handled sales and received the profits. Women also were allowed to process oil from the palm kernels, with smaller profits flowing to them. In addition they engaged in petty trades of one sort or another, such as basket weaving and selling their home-cooked foodstuffs. Their individual holdings of livestock must have been quite limited, but what they possessed were theirs to sell or keep.[8] Thus when the rumor began to circulate in November 1929 that women were about to be taxed, their meager profits were already low.

Reactions to the rumor were swift, and women in the market met to determine their response, should they be taxed. Some of them went to the homes of their chiefs and were told that the colonial authorities were indeed counting the "people." In an Ibibo province, an African chief warrant officer (of the Native Courts) was instructed to reassess the taxable holdings of his people. In so doing he ventured to the home of a married woman who "was pressing oil" and began to count her livestock. Angry and frustrated, the women lashed out at him, with physical interaction between the two following.[9]

At the end of November and soon after this incident, which was reported at a meeting by the woman who was directly involved, those present sent around a palm leaf to all of the women in the area—the palm leaf was a "symbol of trouble and a call for help."[10] Women from the countryside flocked to the village where the warrant officer, who had attempted the initial count, was based. Once there they demanded his cap, his emblem of office, and proceeded to "sit on" him. This "involved gathering at his compound . . . dancing, singing scurrilous songs," in which they made plain their anger at his subservience to the colonial authorities.[11] They then went to his residence, where "his own people tried to defend him." Although his house was damaged, the women continued to protest, going next to the European district officer and charging the warrant officer with assault for having physically engaged in combat with the first woman he encountered at her compound.

The warrant officer was arrested, and the district officer was no doubt worried about his own safety, since the uprising then numbered "over ten thousand." The women renewed their demands for the warrant officer's cap of office, and the district officer testified that he "threw it at them." Still, they stayed "in the thousands" at the District Office until the warrant officer "was tried and sentenced to two years imprisonment for assault."[12] Even after the chiefs and the other members of the British government in the area repeatedly assured the women that they would not be taxed, once the seeds of anger were planted—and these were deeply embedded in both men and women regarding the taxes—the women fanned out in all directions from Oloko, the site of the first incident.

According to Margery Perham, "the trouble spread in the second week of December to Aba," which was a larger trading center on the railroad line. There "converged some ten thousand women, scantily clothed, girdled with green leaves and carrying sticks." As to whether they actually destroyed European shops and a bank as alleged is not known, but they did break into the jail and release some prisoners. Mayhem reigned, although eventually the police were "supported by a hastily raised force of European traders and some Africans" and by a troop of Boy Scouts, who "worked hard" to subdue the crowd. Perham makes the point that the women's goal was to destroy the Native Courts, not to loot or rob.[13]

Despite efforts to subdue the rioters, the movement continued to gather steam. In the second week of December it spread to other towns and divisions, reaching Calabar on the coast. The resident there had called for an accounting "of a similar kind," which only reinforced the perceived intentions of counting the women and their stock for purposes of taxation. Thus, a similar reaction occurred, with many—men and women—running into the bush with their livestock. In one village, crowds of women appeared who were described as "scantily dressed in sackcloth, their faces smeared with charcoal, sticks wreathed with young palms in their hands, while their heads were bound with young ferns." Perham noted that none of the Europeans "understood the exact significance" of those symbols of palm fronds and the ferns. They were, however, recognized by the locals to mean proclaiming war.[14]

Next, the women carried their campaign to neighboring Opobo: "Mobs of women passed shouting and singing about the town, 'What is the smell? Death is the smell.'" At one trader they shouted "'All right, Bottle, no fear morning time five o-clock we go come for you.'" Finally, the district officer summoned his courage and agreed to meet with the seven women who were considered the leaders. The following day "palm-leaves were sent round to all the neighboring clans, and when the time came, not seven but several hundred arrived at the Office, armed with stout cudgels and dressed only in loin-clothes and palm-leaves."[15] Some sort of order was restored for a time while the women made their demands, which included not paying for "licenses to hold plays and that the local chief be removed." Proper forms were required, with signatures witnessed by the interpreter, and a stamp placed on each form—six in all for each of the divisions represented at the meeting.

The acquiescence on the part of the government did not quell the resistance movement. The crowd continued to swell. At one point the women referred to the African troops as "sons of pigs" (as Susan Rogers referred to the Muslim Hausa).[16] Unfortunately, the women labored under the mis-apprehension that the troops would not fire on them, which, possibly, might have been the case had not some members of the crowd struck the European officer in charge. Part of the crowd had been backed up to a fence, which, at that point, began to collapse. Someone fired, shot the leader through the head, and set off a stream of bullets that left "thirty-two dead and dying, and thirty-one wounded." This was on December 17. Within a few days, however, the government reported that "the situation was completely in hand." In all, more than fifty women died in the Women's War.[17] The results were mixed. Some administrative changes were made, but few affected the women.[18]

In January 1930, a Commission of Enquiry was established to look into the "loss of life" where the firing took place. That Commission reported by the end of January. But the "serious nature of the disturbances" was such that a second Commission was put in place to study the factors behind the Women's War (or as the British called it, "The Aba Riots"). Perham's account has to be evaluated on the basis of her being British, or a member of the ruling class, also keeping in mind that she was a woman who had experienced gender discrimination in her academic life back in England.

Perham benefited from the death of men available for study at Oxford just as World War I began to draw them into the armed forces. On completing her degree, Perham was appointed as the first female member of the faculty at Sheffield University—just as the war was drawing to a close. Ignored by her male peers, and suffering from the loss of a brother during the war, Perham fell into depression. Her doctor advised rest. In 1919, one of Perham's sisters was in British Somaliland with her husband. Margery joined them, thus beginning her introduction to Africa when she was quite young. After Perham returned to Sheffield, she became the first woman to receive a Rhodes Trust Traveling Fellowship to study the "race problem." Among the several areas she visited, Perham traveled widely in South Africa, from where she had only just returned when the government sent her to Nigeria. Her charge was to investigate the factors surrounding the Women's War. Gender came into play: Perham showed sympathy for the women involved in the disturbances, and at the time—this was late 1929— probably no better person could have been selected for this mission. For instance, she reported that the Nigerian women had not attempted to protect themselves with any magic (referring to the Maji Maji rebellion in Tanganyika in 1905-1907 when it was under German rule). And she stated that the women "had certainly armed themselves psychologically with a sense of security." Perham noted that, in talking to some of the participants, they made it clear "that they were prepared to die" although they thought that "no harm" would befall them.[19] As we saw, more than fifty women died. Perham correctly noted that defects in administration—in England and in Nigeria—had created the environment in which the Aba Riots took place.

Women and World War II

In order to hear the African voice in West Africa during this time, we turn to two novels. The first novel is *The Joys of Motherhood* by Buchi Emecheta. Nnu Ego, the female protagonist, came to be married to a hapless barely literate man in Lagos after failing to produce a child in her first marriage back in her home village. She proved to be fertile in her second marriage but otherwise endured one hardship after another, especially after her husband—a washman for white colonials—lost his job. Nnu Ego took the initiative and began to engage in trade. For a time that was fairly lucrative; babies arrived one after another; then her husband took a younger second wife who bore two children—all of them crowded into a small flat in Lagos. Jobs for Nnaife, the husband, proved problematic until he found employment at a government installation as a grass cutter. Unknown to the family, World War II had begun, and the British were engaging in conscription in Lagos, as elsewhere in their colonies.

Nnaife was at his lawnmower one day when he and his fellow grass mowers sighted army trucks. The work day ended. Nnaife was in the process of departing when, suddenly he and others in his group were approached by African soldiers [called Korofos here] who shouted an order. These men were Hausa, with their English as limited as was Nnaife's. Furthermore, Nnaife did not understand a word of Hausa. "Up went the truncheons" and orders to "From 'ere to ere! Gwo, gwo into the lorry—gwo, gwo."[20] The upshot was that Nnaife and others had been conscripted into the army.

The experiences that follow were similar to those of the many who suddenly found themselves the victims of the European war.

The Joys of Motherhood

He was too stunned to think of his family; all that went through his mind was the unfairness of it. He was so preoccupied with this that he could not make out if they were going to Ikoyi barracks on the island or the ones in Apapa or even the ones he had seen so often at Igbobi in Yaba. He was hungry, he was shocked and he was angry. How could one resist against men armed with heavy sticks and guns?

They were ushered into an open field and their names were taken. They were told to have something to eat and that an officer was coming to talk to them. Nnaife was reluctant at first but seeing others eating he too ate, telling himself that at least the problem of hunger was solved, so that when they let them go he would have enough strength to walk home. He became really alarmed when, after the food, a medical doctor came to examine them one by one. Nnaife knew then that he was done for. It was at that moment that he looked around and saw that his fellow worker Ibekwe was there, looking as stunned as he was. They communicated with each other through looks; there was little they could do but wait and see. The doctor, an Indian, knocked at Nnaife's chest, peered into his throat and ears, before pronouncing him "all right," that much Nnaife heard. All right for what? He was about to turn around and ask, but a Korofo pushed him along to make room for another man who came in stripped to the waist like himself.

In the corridor where they were asked to wait, most of them had subsided into silence, their minds busy as clocks and their eyes watchful. Soon the medical was over. Some people were called, and Nnaife never saw them again. He and Ibekwe and about thirty others remained, whereas sixty or so of them had been packed into the lorry.

In another room they were eventually told why they had been so enlisted. They were to join the army.

"Army!"

A few men had the courage to shout abuse; others joined in, and an officer with a moustache allowed them to go as mad as they could. After a while, during which time some men wept with tears pouring shamelessly from their eyes, he demanded silence. Later they were told that their wives and relatives would be well cared for. When asked about this next of kin, Nnaife gave the name of his wife Nnu Ego. He was told that the large sum of twenty pounds would be paid to her, and that she would be sent similar amounts from time to time. After recovering from the initial shock of his wife and family getting rich through his going to fight for the white man, Nnaife wanted to know how often this payment would be made. He was informed that it would be about two to four times in the year. They were assured that they would not be serving any longer than one year, since the enemy was on the point of being annihilated. More importantly, they were told, when they returned they would all be promoted in their places of work. Nnaife, for example, would move into the workshop and be apprenticed to a trade, on a higher income.[21]

Back home, Nnu Ego had no inkling of her husband's plight until one of his friends woke her the following day to the shocking news that Nnaife had been forced into the army. Of course Nnu Ego's response was, what could they do to release him? The answer is telling: "There is nothing we can do. The Brits own us." She was advised of a meeting of the people from her home village, but Nnaife's friend failed to tell her that an allotment was to be forthcoming and that Nnaife had sent word as to how the funds were to be dispersed.

No word came from Nnaife, nor did the allotment reach Nnu Ego. Eventually a letter arrived, and Nnu Ego took it to a literate friend, who read it to her. Nnaife was in a place called India. He sent money, which would pay her boys' school fees that were overdue. (Nnaife was reliable in supporting the family even when he was present and employed.) With several children and the second wife to support, Nnu Ego's hardship only increased despite the arrival of the funds. Her father died, sending Nnu Ego back to her home village for a brief period. The second wife, already engaged in trade at the market, went into prostitution and eventually moved out of their cramped quarters. Nearly destitute, Nnu Ego managed to scrape together enough pay for her two sons' tuition for a term or two; and then they were forced to drop out of school. It was perseverance alone that kept her going during the months when no allotment arrived, Nnaife was away, and her co-wife's reputation was sullied, but she also prospered. In the meantime, Nnu Ego's daughters were forced into petty trade in front of their dwelling, collecting and selling firewood.

The emphasis in the novel, as in most of African societal values, was on the sons, not the daughters. Another year passed, then came a letter from Nnaife. He was then in Burma and had been bitten by snakes and was ill, but he included more money in the letter. It was in this communication, written by someone else due to Nnaife's illiteracy, that Nnu Ego discovered the sixty-pound allotment that should have come to her. At the army head-quarters, Nnu Ego and her literate female friend collected the past due funds with no apologies from the government. Then, one day, with no advance notice, Nnaife appeared. Friends, even from their home village, crowded in to celebrate his return from war. "They all trooped into the veranda, and of course the palm sellers in that area got busy. They had missed their 'Ibo' [Ibibo] customer all these years."[22]

Although it is true that Emecheta creates many hardships and disappointments for Nnu Ego, she also shows the resilience and courage of character as a prototype for the African woman. Of interest to us are the war, conscription, and the hardships endured by the female urban proletariat and rural peasants left behind to fend alone.

In *The Old Man and the Medal*, Ferdinand Oyono tells the story of a man who converted to Catholicism somewhere in French West Africa, and who sent his only two sons to fight and die for the French. In addition, the protagonist, Meka, had donated a significant amount of his land to the Christian church. He was, in other words, regarded as a good African, even though Meka was an illiterate peasant with no connection to the French community that dwelt in the town. Following the war, however, the French administration decided to single out Meka for a special medal that was to be presented to him at a July 14th celebration. The novel's narrative deals with preparation for receiving the medal, the ceremony itself, and its aftermath. This included a reception at a community center, where the Africans were feted with champagne followed by hard liquor. Meka became inebriated, fell asleep, and was abandoned by his male friends when the police were called in to clear the premises. Then he was arrested and taken to jail for mistakenly entering the whites-only compound after a severe storm sent him fleeing from the community center. At this juncture in his story, Oyono increases the satire: Meka underwent a metamorphosis following one rude shock after another: his treatment at the award ceremony, the fact that the priest to whom he had donated the land rejected him; the litany of remarks concerning French racism that flowed from his friends at the community center; and then his own rough treatment by the police.[23]

This is a male-dominated novel, authored by an African man. Still, Meka's wife, Kelera, who dwelt in the background, served as a foil, and she was allowed to show her pain regarding her sons lost to the Europeans in their war. At the ceremony someone remarked that the medal seemed insignificant indeed, for having sent two sons to die for the French. "That was the false note that quenched all Kelera's enthusiasm. It was then that she knew that her sorrow was still sharp and that nothing could ever make up for the loss of her two sons." A friend held Kelera as she sobbed "with all her heart."[24] As Meka began to realize that he had been a fool—made worse by his treatment on July 14th—Kelera was allowed to mourn.

As she waited for Meka to come home (unaware of his arrest and treatment by the African policemen), Kelera sat in her compound, again "weeping to break her heart." Someone heard her sobs and enquired, is that Kelera? It was, and she retorted: "Is any wife or mother more wretched than I am? I thought I had married a man, a real man. . . . Instead I married an arse-full of shit. My children, my poor children—sold like the Lord was sold by Judas. At least he did it for money. The man who lay with me so that I should bear you did not get a good price for the drops of his seed. Both of you together, my little ones, priced at one medal."[25] Although Kelera spoke only for herself, it is not hard to imagine the collective loss of so many African mothers seeping through her wounded heart.

Despite the losses of thousands in the war, the West African economy not only recovered in this period, but grew appreciably. The need for palm oil products increased (including the kernels processed by women), as did that for cocoa (a major agricultural product in Ghana, for instance). Rubber was essential for so many wartime needs aiding the economy in Congo as well as in parts of West Africa.[26] Rice was critical for feeding the armed forces. Production increased in Nigeria—as in Sierra Leone and other parts of West Africa where it was a staple crop.[27]

Very few of the indigenous peoples in Africa understood the war or the issues involved, although the educated—a minority—in the urban areas read the newspapers and listened to the BBC. They were aware, too, of increasing numbers of military troops—African, European, and even American—stationed in various parts of West Africa. Regarding the African troops, an interesting fact emerged: 75 percent of the men inducted (through conscription or as volunteers) failed the physical examination. That was due to health issues and malnutrition. In Emecheta's novel, Nnaife, Nnu Ego's husband, managed to pass his physical despite what appeared to be alcoholism. The high percentage of physical problems should have alerted British officialdom that colonialism had not served the African people to advantage. But then it was war, and interest was centered on defeat of their enemies.

Although General Charles De Gaulle established his Free French headquarters in Brazzaville, Congo, he spent little time there. Nevertheless, opportunities for jobs opened up for African men, as harbors were extended, airfields were constructed, and other forms of construction went on apace in both the French and British colonies. Skilled and unskilled found employment in war-related jobs that had never before existed. These were all earmarked for men—those conscripted and those recruited. Thus it appears that some of those deemed unfit for military service were found in satisfactory condition for employment. Their earnings contributed to the welfare of mothers, wives, and children. Women in the rural areas—often joining the older men left behind, and their children—labored extensively in the fields as increases not only in exports, but in income from the produce sold but to the growing numbers of military, black and white, posted in their countries.[28]

Judith Byfield argued that women's role was essential in the Yoruba provinces of Nigeria. They processed cassava and the palm products noted above, and they played an important role in the "bulking cocoa crop" that moved to market from Abeokuta. Price controls within the colony, however, also meant that profits for women traders were low. While some lost money on goods that were controlled (or banned such as palm oil was briefly), others benefited when the government decided to export cassava, due to shortages in Java and Brazil.[29]

Meyer Fortes noted, too, that "a better quality of African leadership emerged during the war." Trade unions began to be formed. And there was a "growing shift in the class basis of urban politics."[30] Of note was the relative calm and lack of political unrest in those years. Fortes stressed the gains that took place from 1939 until 1945, the period covered in his survey; and this stability in the colonies surely benefited women and children. All of this led to expectations that could not be met by the colonial governments as the war ended and demand decreased, with political discontent beginning to fester.

The Ethiopian emperor, Haile Selassie I, fled into exile after the Italians invaded in May 1935. His entourage included several members of his family. His youngest daughter, Princess Tsãhay, went into nurse's training at Guy's Hospital in London. The princess, who had lived a life of luxury until the Italian invasion, became the only one of his children to pursue a profession—perhaps she was the first Ethiopian to earn a degree in nursing. Sadly, before she could put her skills to work after the Italians were driven out in 1941 and she returned home, the princess died. Another of Haile Selassie's daughters stayed behind. She was detained and held in Italy until 1939.[31]

Among the African troops involved in defeating the Italians in the Horn of Africa were members of the King's African Rifles (KAR) 25 Brigade. They stayed on in Eritrea until February 1942, when it became known that, without home leave, they were being shipped out to Ceylon.[32] Their reaction to this news was, according to Timothy Parsons, the cause of "the largest and most openly defiant act of non-violent collective resistance" among the KAR *askaris* (ordinary African soldiers) in the Second World War.[33] Some of the men were disturbed by gossip that circulated claiming that their wives were engaging in adultery at home.[34] This takes us back to Emecheta's novel and Nnaife's second wife, who did indeed engage in adultery, which then merged into prostitution.

While the men fantasized over their wives' possible disloyalty, many of them had no trouble breaking their bonds of marriage: "soldiers broke out of camp to look for women and drink in nearby Eritrean towns."[35] In fact, Ethiopian women, too, suffered at the hands of alien troops who were posted in their country, not only during the war, but afterwards, as the British continued to occupy the country after the emperor was restored to his throne, if not actually to rule. The South African troops were especially unruly, with many allegations of rape leveled at them during the British occupation.[36]

But some women profited from the sale of their bodies during the war. Luise White's study of prostitutes in Nairobi, Kenya, is possibly suggestive of other African cities where urbanization during the war meant an influx of males as workers, as well as a rise in the numbers of troops stationed close by. In Kenya, she wrote, there were around "20,000 to 40,000" posted during the war years. Thousands came from England and from parts of West and Central Africa—with many based in or near Nairobi. About 30,000 Italian prisoners of war were "marched" into Kenya by members of the KAR. They were mainly placed in camps, where they were under guard. Later, many of them were put to work on projects in the Nairobi area. White was unsure how they were able to avail themselves of the services of the local prostitutes, but she found that they had made their way to the African area of Pumwani (in Eastlands). Interestingly, the Italians had condoms—where and how supplied is unknown. Prostitutes, according to White, tended to charge them less for their services than the African men. The Italians were not good guests—they fought and drank heavily.[37]

Not specific to war, but certainly continued into World War II, were the sexual activities of many single women elsewhere in colonial Kampala (Uganda). These women, like the prostitutes White covered in Nairobi, benefited financially and were able to live well without seeking other employment. The unmarried woman "knows how much money she has to spend on her household and how much control she has over it." Some of these men were actual lovers, others transients. There were variations in types of arrangements between the prostitutes and their customers and/or lovers. The one commonality was that the men paid and the women controlled.[38]

In South Africa, Jan Smuts, who headed the fusion government, took the country into the war in 1939. This caused a collision with the Afrikaner-dominated National Party (part of the coalition), which withdrew altogether. Although the scars lingered and anger toward the British had not entirely diminished, few Afrikaners were actively opposed to the war, although the far right supported the Nazis and became saboteurs.[39] Only whites were deemed fit for combat, with Africans in the support forces. We saw that South Africans were in Ethiopia and left behind loathsome memories on the part of many there, including women who were assaulted.

Altogether more than 200,000 white men and women, Coloureds and Africans, volunteered in the war effort—the women, too, in support capacities. The South African Defense Forces fought in North Africa and the Far East as well as in Europe. South Africa was already on the road to industrialization before the war and was in the early throes of recovery from the Depression by 1940. Then, during the war, the country underwent increased industrial development. The loss of white males (about 135,000) meant that skilled jobs opened for Africans and Coloureds at home, and the increase in industries—many tied to the war—meant new opportunities. Black and white women went to work in defense industries—the South African version of Rosie the Riveters. Nancy Charton, a white woman whose roots were in the Afrikaner community, decided that she would become a pilot in the Air Force division. She was quickly dissuaded and ended up employed by the government—where jobs also were available to white women due to the manpower shortage.[40]

South Africa took over the German Southwest by League of Nations mandate following World War I. Many Afrikaner farmers had large cattle ranches in the territory, but a significant number of Germans remained. The official census of 1938 listed more than 18,000 Afrikaners, over 9,500 Germans, and a couple thousand English, with a total of 33,000 blacks.[41] The Germans, however, controlled a significant part of trade and the professions. According to Robert Gordon, the Nazis enjoyed the "best organized support outside of Europe in the former German colony." An American observer noted that "to be 'Heil Hitlered!' and given the Nazi salute in the African bush was almost too much to bear."[42] The excuse was that the Germans had so many business relationships in Germany that they were "hostages to fortune."[43] What is ironic is that, despite the genocide practiced by the Germans over the Herero at the turn of the nineteenth century, many of the Herero were pro-German—but not all. Chief Hosea Kutako lent his enthusiastic support to the South African forces and encouraged fellow Herero to join up.[44]

The League mandate prohibited "recruitment of indigenes for military service." Hence the government developed unique methods of drawing blacks into the armed forces. First, they called for volunteers—but that was not productive. Then they developed a strategy that led them to the reserves in Ovamboland. There they were offered higher pay than they would otherwise have earned. With many Germans interred and the mines cutting back production, that was an incentive to some. In the northern part of the country there was drought, meaning that many were in need due to lack of crops. Those recruited were originally expected to be sent to South Africa, where they would be trained before being moved into battle. Only a small number of the Africans from Southwest Africa went beyond South Africa, where they were engaged primarily in menial capacities.[45]

Problems emerged, however, that ended recruitment in the north as 1942 drew to a close. A contingent of Africans—a "42 man recruiting detail consisting of some 15 Kavango soldiers and a military band under the command of a European lieutenant and two staff-sergeants—" were sent to the Kavango area for recruiting purposes.[46] While there they "assaulted two people on the station grounds." It was against policy to engage in disruptive behavior, oddly, only on station grounds. The station commissioner did not deem their behavior sufficiently serious to order any punishment. This lack of judgment on his part "made the soldiers even more arrogant." One of the officials then wrote to the commissioner about the assault of "old men" and troops engaging in gang rape of local women. The commissioner, however, retorted that it "was well known that the native women . . . are immoral," brushing the complaints aside.[47]

Failure to act increased the problems. "Their rhetoric was downright seditious: 'We are soldiers. We can kill people if we wish to. There is no Law for us. We are not afraid of the husband of any woman whom we may wish to sleep with.'"[48] Bragging continued, with the men (among themselves) discussing women they encountered "at every camp." They even claimed that they had raped European women, and if "any woman complained to the Major or any other officer the next morning, the native soldiers would be paraded in a line, but the women concerned would not be able to identify any particular soldier."[49]

While this was mostly just talk, it was alarming. Finally the government recognized that some action needed to be taken since European women—wives and missionaries—were often alone and unprotected. The need for resolution reached all the way to the prime minister, who agreed that they should be fined and discharged. Smuts also ordered the end of recruitment in Southwest.[50]

War not only produces death and destruction, it leaves women particularly vulnerable—either by deed, as in Ethiopia, or in fantasies and actions such as those characterized by the Kavango soldiers. Still, in their case, it is possible that they were exerting their manhood—that manhood they were symbolically deprived of before they put on the military uniforms.[51]

The Mau Mau and Kenya

In June 2013, the British government finally acknowledged the role their forces played in the conflict they termed "The Emergency, "which is generally known as the Mau Mau uprising. The Mau Mau began in the early 1950s and lasted into 1957 (although remnants of the war dragged on sporadically into 1960). Torture, abuse, rape, castration, and mass incarcerations marked this period in Kenya's colonial history—and were all admitted to by the British foreign secretary more than fifty years after the conclusion of hostilities.[52]

Back in 1975 a young graduate student, Kathy Santilli, was the first to focus a lens on Mau Mau and women. At that time her sources were limited as she drew mainly on published materials, and all of them were written by men. Still she produced an overview that makes some important points that were later followed up on by other academics in interviews with surviving victims and in archival research.[53] Caroline Elkins, for instance, in *Imperial Reckoning*, conducted numerous interviews with women in her Pulitzer Prize-winning study of the Mau Mau.[54] What emerged first from Santilli, followed by others, is that women did not occupy important positions in the political hierarchy of the Mau Mau. They were both supporters of the counterinsurgency and also of its victims.[55]

Women—black and white—died during this war. White women were betrayed by their servants. Black women suffered assaults from the fighters and from those who supported the British (loyalists). Their homes were set fire, by both sides, and they watched their children being massacred or even roasted. Some women, a minority of those who supported the fighters, went into the forests. Others, as we shall see, served as spies. Their major contribution was in finding ways to provide food to those on the run and those holed up in the forests—a dangerous activity as the war picked up momentum and the KAR were supplemented by troops from the United Kingdom.

As in any conflict with long antecedents, an overview is bound to be somewhat skewed and leave out much of the requisite detail. The roots of the war were in issues pertaining to land in the highlands that the Kikuyu claimed was traditionally theirs. We witnessed the role of the missionaries where polygamy and FGM were concerned and the spinning off of independent schools and churches in these areas. The resentments lingered, as did the segregation that separated black from whites—a form of apartheid—that marked Kenya, from reserved areas set aside for blacks, to the urban areas where blacks were forced into ghettos. Black farmers were prohibited from growing the profitable tea and coffee crops that were reserved for whites only. All of these issues existed and were sources of anger on the part of the Africans from the time they were put into effect. In fact, the Kikuyu organized a protest group, the Kikuyu Central Association (KCA), in the 1920s; and it was as a lobbyist for the KCA that Jomo Kenyatta went to London in 1929 and, while there, began his anthropological study at the London School of Economics. Following World War II, he returned to his country, but the tenor of dissent had changed. Younger, more militant men were no longer willing to submit petitions and pleas regarding untenable rules, land tenure, and discrimination. Some of these younger men were veterans, who had established contact with other colonial subjects and found they had similar grievances. A number of these men came home radicalized. Lack of jobs in peacetime—especially in urban areas where younger men congregated—contributed to the developing militancy on the part of many. The KCA was subsumed into a new political party, Kenyan African Union (KAU). While enjoying titular leadership in the KAU, Kenyatta was relegated to the sidelines by the militants.[56]

Kenyatta was arrested in October 1952. His trial was held in an up-country town and involved considerable machinations on the part of the government. Many people believe that Kenyatta was pre-destined for conviction before the trial began. John Lonsdale, however, argues that "to the extent the trial was rigged . . . I think it was rigged only by appointing a notoriously prejudiced and greedy judge."[57] Lonsdale makes the valid point that, although Kenyatta was innocent of provoking the Mau Mau atrocities, "one cannot forget Mau Mau's habit of murdering Crown witnesses."[58] In April 1953, the judge rendered his decision. Kenyatta was sentenced to hard labor and sent to a camp on the coast where "the British relied on distant isolation and desert heat to prevent escape."[59]

In October 1952, the first major incident occurred when the government senior chief, Warihiu Wa Kungu, was brutally killed. Kungu had been adamantly opposed to the oaths of loyalty the militants demanded, and to the claims put forward by them that land be redistributed from the whites to the Kikuyu landless.[60] He was what would be termed a loyalist, with many others falling in that camp as well. The sides began to be clearly drawn, with the whites, including the government and many African government employees on one side, and the growing numbers of mainly Kikuyu members of the Mau Mau.

On Christmas Eve, 1952, direct attacks took place on five homes, and African women were among those murdered.[61] Isolated incidents occurred as a result of refusals on the part of some farm workers and others being pressed to take the loyalty oaths. But on New Year's Eve, 1953, the attacks started on the white farmers in their relatively isolated homes. The first murder involved a man who was alone—he was hacked to death by a machete. In fact, most of the whites were killed in this fashion, and all were set up by their servants or people in their employ on their farms. Next, a few weeks later, there was an attack on a man and his wife. They were badly injured but survived.[62]

Two single women, who had been instructed to keep weapons on hand at all times, noticed that their house servant seemed nervous—thus they were alerted to possible assault. As a member of the Mau Mau entered the room where they were sitting, one of the women fired and killed her assailant. Then, others came into the house, and the second woman shot at them, driving them away. Fortunately, yet more Mau Mau who were in another room created a stir. The women shot through the walls, killing two more.[63] In this case, the dead were the intended perpetrators.

But the most egregious of the assaults on the white community took place in January 1953, following the first murder of the single man on New Year's Eve. The Rucks were a young couple with a small boy of six, and, again, they were farmers with a considerable number of farm workers and a household staff. Mr. Ruck would not have been regarded as a sympathetic figure by his staff due to his being a member of the Police Reserve and being thought to possess strong conservative views. But his wife ran a medical clinic and treated local Africans, including their employees. The little boy grew up among and played with the Kikuyu children on the farm. When they became aware of a possible attack, Ruck emerged from the house with his gun at the ready. But he was caught from behind and was hacked to death on the spot. His wife ran out of the house when she heard her husband crying out, and, although she also had a weapon, she was quickly dispatched—again by machete. For reasons that defy rational explanation, the Mau Mau intruders went up to the second floor, found the six-year-old boy on his bed, and with their machetes cut short his already young life.[64]

The brutal murders of the Ruck family were publicized all over the world via newspapers, radio, and a newsreel that the press filmed prior to, and following, the funeral at the Anglican Cathedral in Nairobi. In those days, before the advent of television, sensational events such as this were filmed and distributed to movie theaters in almost all major cities in the West. One local outcome of significance was that the government was granted Emergency Powers, which then led to the hostilities being characterized by the British as "The Emergency." The Emergency Powers gave license to arrest and incarcerate those suspected of being connected to the Mau Mau.[65] This meant that proof was no longer required to detain and/or question, especially anyone who was thought to be Kikuyu and male. Later women would also fall under suspicion, again if they were Kikuyu. Troops from the United Kingdom were sent out to join the KAR in quelling the disturbances—which grew with more either willingly joining the Mau Mau or being compelled to under increasing threats from the militants.

The next major assault came toward the end of March 1953. A loyalist patrol (called Home Guards) found a body that had been mutilated lying on a path. Soon thereafter they saw fires raging from their village of Lari. Rushing in, they discovered that "five or six separate gangs, each numbering one hundred or more persons," had wreaked havoc on their families. With torches lit, to burn the houses, the gangs had machetes, "swords, spears, knives and axes." With ropes they tied the huts closed so that the people in them could not escape:

> As the occupants struggled to clamber through the windows to escape, they were savagely cut down. Most of those caught in the attack were women and children, but they were shown no mercy by the attackers, who seemed intent on killing every person in the homesteads. . . . As the bodies were cut down and viciously hacked, the attackers threw them back into the blazing huts.[66]

The story, however, does not end with the massacre at Lari. The loyalists sought revenge—retaliation was especially important because the majority of those killed at Lari had been women and children. David Anderson, who left no stone unturned in his research, was unable to unravel exactly what happened at Lari, as no "official inquiry" took place. There was, he said, "no doubt that a second massacre took place at Lari," and it was perpetrated against those considered Mau Mau and believed to have been involved in the initial attack on the loyalist families. "There was anger, chaos and confusion; and there were beatings, shootings and brutal cold blood killings."[67] A company of British soldiers arrived to find "some two hundred bodies" plus others that were scattered in the bush—so widely dispersed that a few days elapsed before the final body count could be made.[68]

Other killings followed—the guerrillas were without mercy. But, the retaliation was equally ugly on the part of the Home Guard and backed up by the British government and the military. It was in the Nairobi ghetto of Eastlands (including Pumwani) that the government acted out its frustration. The majority of the Africans in the crowded slum were Kikuyu—meaning that they were susceptible in official eyes to being involved with the Mau Mau or at least with its supporters. Thousands were rounded up and sent to camps for "screening." Screening actually meant that they were presumed guilty, with various nefarious measures employed to extract confessions. The result was that, after threats of violence and actual torture, many confessed.

For example, a white settler in Nukuru District collected two of his farm employees after they had undergone screening at a nearby camp. Both had been tortured and were hobbling. They had been screened by a loyalist woman, "who beat them on the feet with a short whip." Despite complaints to the authorities regarding this particular woman, "she continued to be employed in a number of screening camps."[69] Here, then, was evidence that some women participated in torture at the camps, with the government casting a blind eye. Even more outrageous was the allegation on the part of this white farmer's laborers that a British officer had raped an eleven-year-old girl at a camp (where others from his farm had been taken). This despicable act was confirmed by the girl's family.[70]

As for the majority of Kikuyu women in the Eastlands ghetto, more than 2,000 of them, taking 4,000 children, were sent to the reserves. They were followed by a large group of women who fled of their own volition after the British began their roundup.[71] There were few innocent players in this conflict of black on black, and the government was purposely myopic with regard to the Home Guard.[72]

Unknown to many students of the Mau Mau was the recently discovered role played by a German medical doctor who had come to Kenya and set up practice in the 1950s. Dr. Anne Spoerry's role in torturing and murdering Jewish women during World War II had been revealed by John Heminway, who was writing her biography. These revelations included Spoerry having been sentenced to prison as a war criminal. All of this was kept secret during her lifetime. And in Kenya, Spoerry was revered by many as the pioneering flying doctor who, beginning in the 1960s, flew to remote areas of the country treating black and white.[73] By pure happenstance, while Juliet Barnes was conducting research on a well-known group of white settlers and visiting their old homesteads, she reached out to members of the Kikuyu families who lived on the land previously owned by the whites—who were the objects of her study. Among those Kikuyu to whom Barnes was introduced, and hoped to interview with the help of her interpreter, were "several maimed Kikuyu elders to whom Dr. Spoerry remained a hated name." These were mainly peasants who were unlikely to be aware of Spoerry's fame as the flying doctor. On being requested to meet with Barnes, one elderly woman "would not see me at all: she never wanted to set eyes on another white woman." Some of the older men recalled their experiences in screening: they "were victims of torture, which they claimed had been perpetrated in her clinic by Spoerry and her Kikuyu assistant."[74] One was missing an eye, another had bullet wounds, and a third had a badly scarred leg. They told worse stories of fates that had befallen others in Mau Mau fights, many of whom had not survived to tell their tales of castration and lethal injections.[75]

We began this section on the Mau Mau by referring to the settlement reached between Kikuyu claimants and the British government in 2013. Of the five Kikuyu who brought their case before the British High Court, two were women who had endured torture—government sanctioned or via government covering over the abuses. One of the two women, Susan Ngonde, died before the case came to trial. The claimants were all old and in poor health.[76]

Jane Mara's story leaves no doubt as to the extent of the violence visited on her and the many other women whose voices we will never hear.

"Former Mau Mau fighters who are now in their 70's and 80's."
Source: file/photo/date 6 June 2013. Allafrica.com/stories/201306070636

Jane Mara's Story

The fourth claimant is the only woman among our small group, Jane Muthoni Mara. She was only about 15 years of age, in 1954, when her village, Ngugini, was subjected to a "cordon and search" operation by African Home Guard. Suspected of supporting nearby Mau Mau forest fighters, the villagers were ordered to demolish their own houses and to move to a new village where they could be held under surveillance of the government. This new settlement, to be known by the name Kianjiru, was established as part of the government's villagisation programme. Mara joined the other villagers in being forced to construct a trench around the new village, protected by a barricade of bamboo spikes. One solitary bridge was constructed across the trench to allow access in and out of the village, and each household was given a regimented compound within the village. Kianjiru was placed under the protection of Home Guard, who policed the village perimeter and enforced a curfew on the inhabitants.

A few weeks after moving in to the new village, Mara was accused of being a Mau Mau sympathizer. Along with a number of other villagers she was taken to a screening camp at a place known as Gatithi. Here and at prisons at Embu and Kamiti, Mara would be subject to repeated assaults and beatings by prison officers, police, and Home Guard.

Mara's experience at Gatithi was horrific. On arrival at the camp she was made to bathe fully clothed in a nearby river. She and other detainees were then made to sit on the riverbank in groups of five or six, with their legs outstretched in front of them. Mara recalls that a white officer, whom they nicknamed Waikanja, then walked back and forth over their outstretched legs in his heavy boots. Other African camp officers then joined him in this assault.

On the following day, Mara's ordeal began with further beatings by Home Guard, using a truncheon. Following this she was taken with three other women to a tent where a brutal interrogation began. Mara was repeatedly asked when she had taken the Mau Mau oath and she was pressed to tell them the whereabouts of her brother and other local members of the Mau Mau forest gangs. Despite being repeatedly beaten and kicked, Mara denied that she had taken any Mau Mau oath. Four of the African guards then pinned her to the floor and pried her thighs apart, holding them open. The senior African officer, name Edward, then produced a glass bottle, which under Waikanja's orders was forced into Mara's vagina, using the sole of the

African officer's boot to direct the bottle deeply into her. The pain was excruciating and Mara realized the bottle had been heated. When this ordeal came to an end, Mara was compelled to sit and watch as the three other women were subjected to the same misery.

Over the following weeks Mara was subjected to further beatings, to food deprivation, and to general abuse. Despite having made no confession she was eventually brought before an African chief at Kerugoya camp, who sentenced her, along with around 300 other detainees, to three years imprisonment for membership of the Mau Mau organization. The following day she was taken to Embu prison, where she stayed for three months. Here beatings and assault were daily regime, as was forced labour for all prisoners. From Embu Mara was moved to Kamiti prison, where she served a further two years. Mara then spent seven months at Athi River detention camp before returning to Kamiti, and then to Embu, for the remaining months of her detention.[77]

Charity Waciuma was a young student during this period and not an actual participant. But later she wrote *Daughter of Mau Mau*, a problematic memoir, although she interviewed a number of women who were involved in the struggle.[78] Many years after the event, another woman wrote her autobiographical account. Wambui Waiyaki Otieno was, however, a member of the Mau Mau and an activist. Her story places Otieno in a position of leadership over a group of nubile young Kikuyu girls whose assignment was to ply British soldiers in Nairobi with drink and then steal their guns and ammunition.[79] This ploy proved so successful that the young women began to go directly to the barracks, where they engaged in prostitution, again to take away weapons and ammunition—plus to obtain whatever information that they could from the men with whom they were engaging.[80]

From this success in spying and scouting, Otieno was assigned to the countryside to collect whatever information that she could—where troops were posted, how buildings were guarded, and other important tidbits that would be useful to the guerilla fighters. Her bravery in acting as a scout in both urban areas and small towns up-country was indeed remarkable, as Otieno had three small children at home, sired by her fiancé. She kept her activities secret from her family members, who would have disapproved. In fact, her undoing came after she deserted active participation in the Mau Mau (but remained a member) and became involved in politics—in the KAU. Then the father of her children turned her in.[81]

She was arrested and sent with her children into detention on the island of Lamu.[82] Otieno's repeated interrogation by a British officer failed to produce any incriminating details. Her jailor, however, brutally raped her. The first time he assaulted her was at the nearby village of Shella, where he had kept her, alone, for several hours. After that, she was returned to Lamu, where she requested a visit with her children. That was refused. The questioning continued, and her resistance remained intact. A day or so later, she was again in the company of the officer who raped her, walking on one of Lamu's narrow streets past houses with tall steep steps. At one point, her captor suggested that they stop and rest. That is when he forced himself on her again and again—a total of three times.[83] During these ordeals, Otieno made repeated attempts to ascertain the name of her rapist. Finally, someone provided his name. After the passage of several decades, she was able to get her revenge—sweet, perhaps, but she was never able to hold him accountable for the rapes following her release in January 1961. When she published *Mau Mau's Daughter*, Otieno named him twice.[84]

During 1953, the government forces and the Home Guard continued to round up suspects, while many of the guerrillas shifted their bases to the forests—Kirinyaga, near Mt. Kenya, and Nyandarua, in the Abedare mountain range. Kiringyaga was close to Meru. In both cases the fighters were located far enough into the forests to avoid detection but close enough, too, so that they could be supplied. Males and females patrolled; mainly the women, in disguise, moved into and out of the reserves obtaining and carrying supplies. Some of women had medical training and treated the wounded with whatever supplies were available from those who were able to provide them from the outside.[85] Many of the women were schooled in the use of traditional medicines, which also were widely employed. The vast majority of the residents in the forests were male. Marshall Clough makes the point that no records exist as to the women's roles beyond nursing and healing, but it can be assumed that they carried out domestic functions insofar as life in camps allowed.[86]

There was, however, opposition on the part of many of the guerrilla fighters to having women present.[87] The Kikuyu regarded sex "in the bush to be taboo."[88] Most the insurgents were young and not married, plus there were only a few women. No one knows how many, but estimates run from 5 to 20 percent.[89] In Nyandarwa, General China allowed for "faithful cohabitation" and let "women leaders in the reserve introduce officers to young and unmarried women." But Dedan Kimathi, the supreme leader, also in Nyandarwa, set parameters for sexual relations for his commanders by "employing the women's escort service" (in the reserves). Kimathi, however, set no limits on his own sexual needs. One of his intimate subordinates wrote "of the serial polygyny . . . by which he changed partners every few months."[90]

Katherine Bruce-Lockhart has analyzed recently available data from the Hanslope Park Disclosure regarding two camps that were established for women only. The first, Kamiti, was meant to house women who were considered to be the most fervent supporters of the Mau Mau, including those in the "passive wing" supporting fighters in the forest. Actually, many of these women were actively engaged in various types of support. In 1953, the government realized that rather than passive they were the "eyes and ears of Mau Mau."[91] Soon after the camp was established, the authorities realized that some of the women were beyond what they deemed rehabilitation. By 1957, it was clear that 162 "very fanatical" women were resisting British rehabilitative efforts. Those regarded as the most difficult were characterized as "thugs and witches" (hard core) left to remain in Kamiti camp where, Bruce-Lockhart maintains, they "were locked away and ignored."[92] Then a new camp, Gitamayu, was created, and this was to contain the remaining women believed receptive to "intensive rehabilitation."[93]

Action on the part of Mau Mau fighters resulted in victories and triumphs, despite the ongoing dragnet and the continued roundups that resulted in brutal treatment of those captured. The war dragged on and punishments multiplied, as did those who survived the Home Guards' assaults on prisoners in the holding pens. Whereas this brief summary has singled out the Kikuyu, others were sympathetic to the main body of fighters—including other ethnic groups whose languages were closely related and who lived in proximity to the Kikuyu. Despite not being actively involved in the hostilities, many others lent support in one way or another. General China surrendered in early 1954. He was sent into detention for nine years. But like the chameleon he was, China later emerged to serve in Jomo Kenyatta's government.[94] Dedan Kimathi was wed to Kikuyu culture, including the religious beliefs—more so than the other major figures in Mau Mau history. It took an obsessive white man and Kikuyu traitors and trackers from another ethnic group to finally locate Kimathi in the forest. He managed to evade them; he ran from where he had been hiding and got to the edge of the Nyeri reserve before he was trapped and shot. This was in the early morning hours of October 21, 1956—or as David Anderson poignantly noted, "four years to the day since the state of The Emergency" and bringing an end to the forest war.[95] Kimathi was tried, convicted, and hanged in February 1957.[96]

The government turned its attention to trials and punishment—for the surviving Mau Mau who had not been rounded up or killed. But the government also began to implement political reforms, which, within a few years, led to independence—with Jomo Kenyatta elected as president. The loss of so many lives—sons, fathers, and brothers—left a permanent void in the lives of thousands of women. Dislocation by being forcibly moved and/or relocated in non-traditional areas was another outcome of the hostilities. Still, we have seen how women played a role of support, as fighters, scouts, and spies, and by providing food under perilous conditions. But as the country transitioned, not a single female was selected to serve in Kenyatta's cabinet, and not one was elected to Kenya's parliament.

The Portuguese Colonies

Earlier we touched on the Portuguese in Principe and São Tomé, where forced laborers from Angola were settled to work on the plantations. The Portuguese made no significant contributions to these, or any of their colonials, with the exception of some who were of mixed race. A few schools were established in Guinea-Bissau, Angola, and Mozambique and were run by Catholic or Protestant missionaries, but only a smattering of government schools were open to blacks. Over time, as the metropolitan economy failed to expand, a trickle of Portuguese settled in all of the colonies, most particularly in Angola. Those who came in "had few skills and no capital. They lived in extreme poverty, left the land to work as petty traders and run stores or joined the shiftless unemployed in the towns."[97]

The Portuguese who settled in Mozambique were poor and rural and came in "considerable numbers."[98] When the British and French colonies came to independence—from 1957 (Ghana) through the mid-1960s, Portugal refused to enter into negotiations with the emerging leaders in her African possessions. And it was the smallest, poorest of them all that led in the wars of liberation.

Amilcar Cabral, from Cape Verde Islands, started the opposition to Portuguese rule in Guinea- Bissau. In 1956, the Marxist Cabral founded *Partido Africano da Independência da Guiné a Cabo Verde* (PAIGC). By 1959, Cabral and his party were ready to move. He brought together dock workers and other urban laborers in a series of strikes and demonstrations, believing that these would be sufficient to motivate Portugal to withdraw. Instead the government sent more troops to back up General Spinola, the commander of forces there. Cabral cast a wider net, gaining more supporters; and by 1963 he launched the war for independence. This conflict endured until 1974, when, ironically, a military coup in Lisbon with General Spinola and a few other highly placed officers involved. The coup was closely linked to the colonial wars. These "soldiers in Africa had learned about popular mobilisation and guerrilla wars—principles they brought to bear in their home country."[99] They decided that Portugal could not win—wars were simultaneously being fought with Angola and Mozambique as well.

During the years Cabral was the central opposition figure in Guinea-Bissau—from the early strikes and through the war—he was committed to gender equality. Cabral saw the "armed struggle not as an end in itself but as part of a politic to establish a new society."[100] He was that rare visionary among leading members of the African opposition. He "defended women's rights, respected women," and called for them to be respected as well. Stephanie Urdang interviewed numbers of women in Guinea- Bissau in the wake of the revolution. Uniformly, they commended Cabral and his political party for having been made aware of their struggle for equal rights.[101] In this patriarchal society, under the yoke of colonialism, men had only their women and children to dominate. One woman confided that:

> I first heard about women's rights at the beginning of mobilization. . . . I understood what was being said immediately, that equality is necessary and possible. . . . I understand that I have to fight together with other women against the domination of

men. But we have to fight *twice,* once to convince women and
the second time to convince men that women have the same
rights as men.[102]

Another woman cogently referred to fighting on two fronts: against the
Portuguese and against men.[103] They supported the fight against the Portuguese in a number of ways. When the men fought, the women produced
the crops—mainly rice—and became the major suppliers of food to the
troops. Women also served in important positions of leadership within the
party, and they were elected to offices in local village councils. In fact, the
party required that "at least two of the five" council members in each community had to be women.[104]

Another important innovation was the introduction of a People's Court
that upheld new regulations, adding to "increased freedom of women."
These included allowing women to seek divorce, abandoning forced
(arranged) marriages, and the most utopian of all: eradication of polygamy.
Realizing that multiple wives were regarded as essential in the rural areas,
according to Urdang, the intent was to move slowly toward implementing
the decree against polygamy.[105] Even during the war social services were
gradually introduced, and, when it ended, emphasis was placed on expanding health clinics and education.[106]

Unfortunately, gender equality, along with the other achievements, were
subsumed and negated when one coup after another followed the overthrow
of Cabral in 1980.

Contract labor continued to mark the Portuguese policy in Angola.
Newitt found that, in the 1930s, 15 percent of the adult males were contract
laborers; and by "the late 1950s [it was] up to 80 per cent." Some historians
referred to a "democratic haemorrhage" that resulted from blacks' departure
in the 1940-1950s.[107] Problems existed, too, between the north and the south
in Angola. These came to haunt the people during the civil war.

Angola's war against Portugal began in March 1961. Members of the
Movimento Popular de Libertação de Angola (MPLA), which was organized in the mid-1950s, were mostly in jail when an uprising began in the
hinterland, organized by peasants protesting against Portuguese forced
labor practices. This revolt spread to Luanda (the capital) and resulted in
mass murders on the part of the government forces. The die had been cast,
and very soon another guerilla force, from another competing political

party, FNLA (*Fronte Nacional de Libertação de Angola*), founded by Holden Roberto and his uncle, invaded from the north.[108] Brutalities marked all sides—and after the Portuguese withdrew in 1975, the MPLA and the FNLA joined by UNITA (*União Nacional para a Indenpendência Total de Angola*) all fought among each other until, finally in 2002, hostilities ceased, with the MPLA triumphant. Possibly, the fact that many readers will know about this war was that land mines were planted indiscriminately in the rural areas. Indeed, some of them still remain. Women suffered tremendously during the Angolan civil war—they were displaced, raped, or pushed into forced marriages with commanders and other members of the armed forces. But the war with which we are concerned is that of liberation from Portugal.[109]

In the early throes of the conflict with Portugal the MPLA included an auxiliary women's group, *Organização da Mulher Angolana* (OMA). One female figure who emerged early on as a leader was Deolinda Rodrigues de Almeida, who was a founder of OMA and who is remembered as "Mother of the Revolution" for having taken part in storming the jail in which the MPLA members were held in February 1961.[110] During the long years of the struggle women served as leaders, as activists, and even as combatants. They had the advantage of their own organization by which they provided support to the MPLA, as did a similar group of young people in their own auxiliary to MPLA. The women not only served in military capacities, but many of the OMA engaged in educating those peasants in areas where they were being liberated.[111] The outcome might have been women's emancipation, but, due to the onset of civil war, women found themselves transitioned from leadership to nonentities.[112]

In Mozambique the war against Portugal started in 1964 and came to an end in 1975, when the Portuguese military leaders decided to end all conflicts in their African possessions.[113] There women were active in armed conflict (*Frente de Libertação de Moçambique* or Frelimo's Women's Detachment). In fact, it was the women who requested that they be allowed to serve. In addition to serving in active combat, women grew food and transported goods and weapons over long distances and by foot. According to Signe Arnfred, husbands tended to "lose authority over militant wives." If husbands forbade them to "carry out tasks of mobilization or transport," the women went straight to Frelimo, which in turn, provided them with support.[114]

One of the women involved was Américo Magaia, who spent five years in jail under the Portuguese. Nevertheless, she maintained that women's involvement in the war was essential to their later emancipation: "In our traditional culture, women perform the household duties," she said. But Frelimo changed all of that. "In the beginning women did food preparation and nursing, etc. As a progression women participated militarily . . . as carriers of weapons. They have the ability to do what men were doing. . . . Because of traditions, women accepted their inferiority. But since they proved they could shoot and kill the enemy, then there was a difference."[115]

Fighting in the Women's Detachment, females trained in the same camps with men. Some of the men—as might be expected—opposed this initially, but for reasons that may surprise: the women wore military uniforms (i.e., pants). Older people and recruits were critical as women were seen as transitioning into men. There were concerns, too, about sexual relations, making recruitment into the Women's Detachment difficult in the beginning (1964).[116]

Graca Machel attended missionary school and, showing promise, was sent to Lisbon, where she obtained an undergraduate degree. She returned to Mozambique in 1973 and soon thereafter went into military training in Tanzania, although she never engaged in combat. Soon after independence she married Samora Machel, president of the country from May 1970 until his death in 1986.[117] He was killed in a plane crash during the civil war that followed the war of liberation.[118] When he assumed the presidency, Machel spoke out often in support of women's rights. In 1973, he elaborated on some of Frelimo's objectives for the future:

> The emancipation of women is not an act of charity. . . . The liberation of women is a fundamental necessity of the revolution, the guarantee of its continuity. . . . The main objective of the revolution is to destroy the system of exploitation and build a new society which releases the potential of human beings. . . . This is the context within which the question of women's emancipation arises.[119]

In spite of her loss, Graca Machel threw herself into working for human rights and into government, serving as minister of education in Mozambique. Because of her significant contributions, the UN awarded Machel a medal marking her work on children's rights and with refugees. Then, in 1996 Graca Machel married Nelson Mandela (of South Africa), making her the only African woman to serve as first lady to two presidents and in two countries.

Among the female combatants during the war of liberation were members of the remote Makonde ethnic group. The Makonde were split between Tanzania and Mozambique by the Ruvuma River. They were mainly Muslim, having had long contact with Arab slave traders, and coming to the notice of Europeans in the early part of the twentieth century. Not only did they serve in the struggle against the Portuguese, but many fought in the civil war on the side of Frelimo. In this period—from 1964 to 1994—those Makonde who participated in the conflict adopted unusual personas: "they began to act like Makonde men."[120]

In 1975, at war's end and before the civil war began, Makonde women veterans formed a dance group with their own masks, modeling their dances on those performed by men. Touring the countryside, "they met with tremendous resistance" as they borrowed practices associated with male dances. This was a form of acting out their emancipation and was supported by the national government, if not the traditional leaders, who were Muslim men. Although attempts to stop the women dancers succeeded in one case, others "came under the protection of the state, and the dance form" continued.[121]

Gender relations changed during the war. After hostilities came to a halt, however, Frelimo abandoned the changes. Arnfeld learned from field interviews that some women believed that they lost more of their rights "than they had before" the war and their involvement.[122] Then came the civil war and dislocation and abduction, with women and girls "forced to act as sex slaves and laborers" for the opposition.

> They were kept by soldiers for extended periods of time before being abandoned in unfamiliar locations, making it difficult, if not impossible, to find their way home. . . . Another significantly brutal aspect of the civil war in Mozambique was the deliberate, large-scale mutilation of women, children, and the elderly in order to reduce their productivity.[123]

This very brief depiction of the civil war in Mozambique is replicated in the many intra-African conflicts that have characterized the post-colonial period.

Southern Africa and War

Southern Rhodesia was another white-settler colony, although dissimilar to Kenya in some respects. Many of the whites who went to Kenya in the early twentieth century were members of the aristocracy. It was they who formed the backbone of the leadership, followed to be sure by others from all walks of life and mainly from the United Kingdom. Rhodesia had been settled by John Cecil Rhodes in the 1890s, with a small group of men who staked out land, but who went there with the prospect of finding and mining the gold that had been known to exist during the time of the Mutapa Empire (fifteenth century). Over time, many from South Africa who were land poor moved across the Limpopo, bringing their attitudes toward people of color with them as part of their cultural baggage. Settlers from the United Kingdom tended to be people from the lower classes, and they quickly adapted to the racial mores in place—not to mention with the abundance of African labor. Staking out large land holdings and building spacious homes with swimming pools, they lived a life unimagined back home. The descendants of both groups maintained the strict racial barriers in towns and in the rural areas over the course of most of the twentieth century.

When the British started granting independence to their African colonies, beginning with Ghana in 1957 (with limited independence from 1954), Nigeria in 1960, and, more importantly, Kenya in 1963, the whites in Southern Rhodesia faced the prospect of majority rule with horror. Whites had political power over their internal affairs—to the exclusion of blacks. In 1965, after failure to work out an accord with Britain to maintain their power, the whites took it on themselves to declare a unilateral declaration of independence (UDI), calling their country Rhodesia. The British failed to recognize the independent government but sent no troops. In the meantime, disaffected blacks set up their own political organizations, with some of them creating armed wings. They also chose to refer to themselves as fighting for Zimbabwe, for the ancient kingdom whose ruins can still be visited today.

The two major parties were the Zimbabwe African National Union (ZANU) and Zimbabwe African Peoples Organization (ZAPO). The two groups emerged after a split between Joshua Nkomo (who came to lead ZAPO), and Robert Mugabe, who had first served as Nkomo's lieutenant before forming the rival ZANU. ZANU's armed wing was ZANLA (liberation army). There were, too, ethnic majorities in these groups, with ZANU drawing mainly from the Shona. ZAPO drew mainly from the areas inhabited by the Ndebele—although other smaller ethnic groups either had their own organization or joined ZANU. From 1966 until the end of 1979, conflict reigned in Rhodesia cum Zimbabwe. The government forces (called "the soldiers") were led by whites and were composed of white and black regiments. After the African-led freedom fighters went on the attack, "the soldiers" were ruthless in the pursuit of all they suspected to be in opposition to the government—brutally detaining and torturing ordinary citizens as well as actual freedom fighters.

Women clamored to be involved primarily in ZANU and insisted on their right to participate in the armed conflict (as members of ZANLU). Some have argued that women served in high levels of authority, with "thousands of women" serving as spies and smuggling goods and weapons—sometimes wrapping items in blankets to resemble babies.[124] Margaret Perez's extensive survey of the literature concluded that women were heavily and actively involved in the liberation struggle as armed combatants and in support roles. This, however, runs contrary to the earlier work of Norma Kriger, who concluded that women's roles were more limited. In joining the armed contingents, many women found themselves serving as babysitters, teachers, and cooks and also performing agricultural tasks. Kriger noted also that ZANU, most widely celebrated for its promotion of women, sent only men to represent it abroad (as was the case with the other armies of liberation, too).[125]

In 1990 Irene Staunton compiled a remarkable series of life histories of women from across the country, recorded in their own languages, and recounting their experiences during the war.[126] Thirty women agreed to participate, and the stories they tell reveal the hardships that almost all experienced from the loss of husbands and sons (and a daughter and one sister) to the guerilla forces; homes being burned; coercion to feed and supply the troops—and more often willingness to provide supplies and to cook. Much of what these women tell us could have been said by the women in

Guinea-Bissau, Angola, and Mozambique. Regardless of their support for the freedom fighters, the hardships were immeasurable for many women.

Coercion, for instance, was widespread, especially in the early phases when many of women had not yet been awakened to the conflict—intertribal as well as against the government.[127] On the other hand, fear of the "the soldiers" (government troops) increased as husbands were detained and severely beaten. But some of the women also were beaten. Margaret Viki received a visit from "the soldiers," inquiring about the presence of "freedom fighters." When she denied "seeing them" and the patrol discovered that, in fact, the guerillas had been at her home: "A white soldier called me into my house, picked up a small axe and swing it as if he were going to chop me down. Then, suddenly, he threw down the axe, and beat me thoroughly with the back of his rifle instead."[128] On another occasion, elsewhere, "the soldiers came to a home which was in the next village and found guerillas there. They just opened fire and a lot of innocent people died because all of the people gathered there had no choice." The soldiers, Elizabeth Ndebele recalled, "were very ruthless. They never warned that they were going to attack."[129]

Meggi Zingani's son went into Mozambique to fight with Frelimo without notifying his family. After a time, he was heard broadcasting by radio from there—she assumed to alert his family where he was. Soon the police came to her home. "From that time I was considered a terrorist mother." After hostilities increased in Zimbabwe, she and her husband ran a small shop. The freedom fighters visited them—this apparently was when she became aware of the war in her own country—and they needed supplies. She and her husband filled their requests and "kept secret" their presence. Later Meggi Zingani became an active supporter. She advanced from cooking for the troops to supervising food preparation. The women on the committee mended and laundered the men's clothing. On one occasion, the "soldiers" came to her area "and took people quite unawares and many died. Girls were brutally killed, having their breasts cut off. One of these girls is still alive (late 1980s) but she is crippled."[130]

Josephine Ndiweni's sister told her she was going to the garden. Instead she "had left for the struggle." Reporting to their father, Ndiweni said that his reaction was to do nothing: "We wondered why she had gone so suddenly but we knew a lot of people were leaving . . . and she only did what other young people were doing."[131] Ida Mtongana, looking back, recalled that, in 1978, "two of my children went to join the struggle. My daughter was twenty years old when she left and the boy was eighteen."[132]

The refrain that ran through most of their memories was support for the guerillas and for those with loved ones in the fight. Everywhere people were distressed—"I cannot say where I got my courage from: the war was with us and there was no going back. We wanted to be free, so we simply had to press on."[133]

One of the women interviewed was the wife of Joshua Nkomo. After Nkomo had been detained twice, and "for a long time," she was destitute. Christian Care came to her aid with financial support. But when Nkomo was in the field leading his troops, mapping out strategies and moving from place to place, Jonnah carried on, no doubt with support from their followers. Then, the security forces arrived in search of her husband. They looked in every corner and under every bed, but to no avail. Two days later, Jonnah Nkomo was advised that the security forces were looking for her daughter, who had been sent out of the country. Knowing that they might decide to come for her, she reached out to her husband, who decided that she should go into exile in Zambia. She provided no date, but it must have been in about 1977, because soon thereafter Jonnah joined her husband in England, and, after a brief trip to America (to visit children), she was sent to the GDR (East Germany) for three years, with Nkomo visiting her on occasion. Significantly, she was with Joshua Nkomo for the celebrations of Zimbabwe's independence in February 1980—Nkomo having competed against and lost the election to Robert Mugabe. Jonnah recalled how joyous the occasion was, including meeting Robert Mugabe and his wife for the first time. Despite the hostilities between the men and their organizations, "we all met as one people and that was wonderful."[134]

However, the aftermath was not wonderful at all—the Ndebele were aggrieved at the results of the election. Troubles started in the Bulawayo area, with the consequences resulting in the deaths of around 20,000, and another several thousand wounded and or detained in prison camps. Civil war on the levels of those experienced in Angola and Mozambique was avoided, but the systematic and publicly suppressed campaign against the Ndebele continued even after Mugabe brought Nkomo into his cabinet in 1986. The ZANLA freedom fighters were manipulated by Mugabe to the disadvantage of the people he claimed he was freeing during the war of liberation—and to the disadvantage of the freedom fighters as well.

Down in South Africa, the Afrikaner-dominated National Party won the general election in 1948. Then the party embarked on a series of measures that legalized one form of discrimination after another. The parliament passed laws that regulated the movements of, and indeed, the residences of, people of color (including Indians and Coloureds) and more. But while the government acted to legalize segregation (and a lot of that already existed in the country), the African National Congress (ANC) came under the leadership of younger more militant leaders. The seeds for the new militancy on the part of the ANC had been sown in a number of organizations that were already protesting against hiring policies, unequal pay, and lack of civil rights. The body of literature on the liberation movement in South Africa is extensive. A growing body of material also is available on the roles played by women—some of which we will touch on here.

For instance, the so-called Coloured Cissie Cool, whose father was a politician but of the old school of more conservative bent, founded, or was involved with, several organizations at the Cape from the 1930s—all of a political nature. She also became affiliated with a group that brought together the Trotskyites and the Communists in advocating racial equality—even though the October Club was dominated by the Coloureds, many Africans from a nearby township also were members. In 1938 Cissie Cool won the local election for city council. She was the first woman to hold such a position in Cape Town. But that year, too, she was elected to the Politburo of the SACP—a fact she later denied when the Suppression of Communism Act was passed in 1950. She was detained in 1960 and held for three months, but by that time she was out of politics, although still active in the liberation struggle.[135] But she was undaunted by her loss of public power and continued her involvement in the party until she was felled by a stroke in 1963.[136]

Cool was one of the earliest of the so-called Coloured activists, but one of many professional women of color who protested against unjust laws and practices. Over in Durban, Dr. Goonam joined the Non-European Unity Movement in 1943 soon after she established her medical practice. During the Defiance Campaign and in 1951-1953, she joined other Indians in regular protests in which they invited the government to arrest them. After the Criminal Law Amendment Act was passed in 1953, Dr. Goonam was not only detained, but she was sentenced and sent to jail for six months in Ladysmith: "They treated us as criminals. Gave us a place where it was riddled with fleas and vermin. . . . [At Ladysmith] we had to wear gunny bags because it was so cold." Despite the hardships they experienced, Goonam became all the more committed to the struggle—"We are going to fight this government"— and she later affiliated with the ANC. In 1960, Goonam and a female member of the Communist Party were arrested in Alexandria Township (north of Johannesburg). Her companion called Nelson Mandela, who was still practicing law even though under a cloud himself. He obtained their release. Skipping ahead, in the 1960s Goonam was forced into exile. After a short time in London, she went to Lusaka, Zambia, where an increasing number of ANC members of the liberation struggle were based as part of the underground. She returned to South Africa only when political change loomed.[137]

Another female Indian activist, Phyllis Naidoo, went into exile in Zimbabwe. Her home in Harare "was a necessary stop for all leading and middle-ranking cadres of the organization, where meetings would take place . . . where activists from inside the country would meet with exiles." Jacob Zuma, then head of intelligence, who later would become president of South Africa, was one of her visitors: "He would always turn on the radio when talking to you about important matters." Foreigners from Europe and supporting African nations came to discuss funding and map out military moves.[138]

The Eastern European migrant parents of Ruth First were founding members of the South African Communist Party (SACP) in 1921. First grew up in opposition to the government and the myriad of policies that deprived people of color of equal pay and equal opportunities. By the early 1960s and after the founding of the armed wings of the ANC (MK) and the Pan African Congress (Poqo), and following the conviction of Mandela, Sisulu, and others, Ruth First was detained. She was kept in solitary confinement for ninety days (probably because she was a member of the SACP). After her release, First stepped out onto the street and was rearrested for nearly a month longer. As soon as they could, following her second release, First, her husband (Joe Slovo), and children went into exile—initially to England and then later to Mozambique, with Ruth taking a teaching job at Eduardo Mondlane University. There she published a book on African migrants: thousands of migrants from Mozambique worked in South Africa's mines, leaving families behind and being able to return once a year when the mines closed down for holiday. In August 1982, Ruth First received a letter containing a bomb; it went off and the subsequent explosion killed her.[139]

Another active member of the SACP was Ray Alexander, who had carved out a reputation at the Cape for organizing the Food and Canning Workers Union. She was relentless in working for better conditions for women and, of course, for the eradication of racism in all forms. Active in the Defiance Campaign, she also joined a few other women to organize the Federation of South African women, continuing to pour her energy into the trade union movement. But she and her husband, Simon, a university professor and also a stalwart member of the SCAP, were both under scrutiny by the government and had been since the 1930s when they were briefly detained. She had begun working in the SACP underground while her husband remained free of involvement—to better hold on to his university position. By the 1960s tensions were high and Alexander remembered that, from 1964 on, "police were standing outside our house all the time." In 1965, Alexander and Simon decided to leave (while they could). They went to Manchester, where he taught and she undertook studies in Russian and German (although she had read Russian as a child in Latvia). The couple began a new book together, but before it was ready for publication they decided to join other exiles in Lusaka. There they remained until 1992, when they received permission to return to South Africa.[140]

These short biographical sketches of women active in the liberation struggle are but small representations of the many who took part in organizational activities, as members of the underground and, as we shall see, as combatants. Many women were ANC supporters but played a secondary role when their husbands were members of the leadership. This characterized Albertina Sisulu, whose husband was one of the major players in the resurrected and increasingly militant ANC from the mid-1940s on. Walter Sisulu influenced and supported Mandela—standing trial with him and going to Robben Island with him in 1962. Albertina stayed in their Soweto home and kept a low profile while still remaining active with the ANC underground. Mandela's wife, however, did not follow Sisulu's example. She was fearless in her opposition. She was arrested, banned, and very quickly broke the bans by speaking publicly and critically with abandon.

Soon after the 1976 uprising in Soweto, Winnie Mandela was imprisoned for several months. Then in May 1977, she and her two daughters were taken by the security forces to a black township in the Orange Free

State, where they were under constant observance and where they lived for seven years. The tiny house in which they dwelled lacked running water and indoor plumbing, and Winnie was forbidden to establish contact with her neighbors, although in keeping with her practice of ignoring government directives she not only made some friends in the township, but was acquainted with sympathetic Afrikaners as well.[141] Perhaps this period of relative isolation, in combination with the stress of her earlier incarcerations, and the constancy of the police surveillance were too much for Winnie. On her return to Soweto, in 1987 she formed the Mandela United Football Club, which was alleged to be a group of bodyguards. Negative rumors began to fly concerning activities of this group of young men. And Winnie was moving under a cloud already when, in November 1988, and at a rented house in Diepkloof where she had taken temporary refuge, a fourteen-year-old boy was murdered. The ANC leadership began to distance itself from Mrs. Mandela.[142]

On Nelson Mandela's release from prison in 1990 the two reunited. Shortly following their reunion, Winnie was convicted of kidnapping and of assaulting the fourteen-year-old boy and was given a sentence of six years. Later the sentence was reduced to a fine only. Subsequently, Winnie developed other problems, which led to separation from her husband in 1992.[143] They were divorced in 1996. And while they did not live together from 1992 on, Winnie is officially listed as his first lady from his assuming office until the divorce.

In the conflict that marked South Africa's liberation struggles, white women were enlisted for duty in the South African Defense Force (SADF). First, the government opened a "military training college" in the Eastern Cape where women were to be trained for "civil defense" and to be a "citizen's force."[144] They were taught how to handle weapons, but they were excluded from combat. The prevailing rationale was to use "women not so much out of the need for women's labour as the need for women's identification with white supremacy . . . white political unity."[145]

In what Jacklyn Cock calls the "Mata Hari image," some of the women were engaged in intelligence gathering, using their sexuality "to get access" and to gather information regarding the ANC. Olivia Forsyth was an officer in SADF, first as a student spy at Rhodes University, reporting on white dissidents. She became known as a radical on campus before going into the underground "by posing as a defector." Then she was sent to "the front-

line states," including Rhodesia, where, in 1989, her ruse was detected and
she was detained in an ANC camp in Angola.[146] Another young white
woman was recruited by Forsyth and did "valuable work" for five years,
including infiltrating the rather innocuous Black Sash (white women pro-
testers regarding many civil rights). But she managed to penetrate into ANC
circles and even visited an ANC camp in Mozambique with a friend—
surely reporting back to the South African Police force (SAP).[147]

The ANC-MK began to recruit women in the 1970s, too, but very few.
In the 1980s, the conflict deepened, and the ANC instituted more training
camps in several frontline countries. The SADF carried out systematic attacks on these camps, while ANC forces penetrated into the country and
also recruited in the townships, where battles raged internally. And more
women joined MK. Men and women trained together. "We lived in the
same camps. The women did exactly the same training as the men. . . .
Drilling, handling weapons."[148] On the whole, the women claimed that their
actions earned them the respect of their male comrades, including positions
in the leadership.[149]

Due to the imbalance between the genders, problems cropped up.
Women forming "relationships with senior figures" created resentment because the men were able to offer them "more of the good things in life" in
outposts where conditions were rugged.[150] Then, the strains that developed
between husbands and wives—both serving together—caused friction. Sexual harassment—attendant to any military force with men and women sharing space together—presented difficulties, as did incidents of rape or
assault.[151]

But these issues did not deter the women from participating nor lessen
their loyalty to the ANC and the cause for which they all fought. They
served in a variety of capacities—nursing, teaching, clerical work, foragers,
porters, and even carrying on agricultural tasks in the camps. One of the
important jobs assigned to women was that of smuggling. Being sent forward to check for "safe places" for the men to stay, as they staged their
reentry into the country, was another task the women carried out. They
mapped and checked for roadblocks that were increasingly set up by the
SADF. Some women engaged in direct combat as well. While Angola was
engaged in civil war, the SADF was supporting UNITA, and MK soldiers
were there fighting UNITA and the SADF. On one occasion, "a woman soldier turned an anti-aircraft gun into an artillery weapon against UNITA,

covering the retreat of her comrades and sacrificing her own life."[152]

On the home front, thousands of women reported to covert operators on bits of information they picked up at work, and especially in the homes of government officials, police, and members of the SADF, who were based in South Africa. Every white family had a maid: an African or, at the Cape, possibly a so-called Coloured woman. Keep in mind that these women were employed because of dire need: some were left behind to support their children while their men were in MK. And yet many courageous members of this underclass served in supporting roles to do their part in bringing about change in the political, economic, and, indeed, social environment.

Not only were women active for change on every front from the mid-1940s until 1994, but many were victims of the struggle as well. There cannot be war without death. Mothers, wives, and children lost their men in the conflicts and to prisons. During South Africa's long war for equality, the townships were hot beds of dissent. At the Cape, for instance, Pan Africanist Congress (PAC) members fought with ANC followers. Traitors existed among those in the black community, especially in the form of paid informants for the SAP. Some members of the ANC were indeed on the police force—again for the money. It is unlikely that anyone will ever be able to recount the losses that occurred within the townships due to these factors and factions, not to mention the psychological issues that developed as a result of living in an almost constant state of turmoil.

Two examples come from women in a township not far from Cape Town—where rivalries between the PAC and ANC were rampant. Jumartha Majola was a schoolteacher before she married. Her husband was a cricket and rugby player of note—he was scouted by a London team and played cricket in Kenya briefly. They were middle class by anyone's measure. In 1976, her three boys were at school, and, they were suddenly "bundled up and put in a van" by the police. No reason was provided—that was part of the unequal system—and the boys were badly beaten.[153] Then in 1980 there was "more trouble." One of her sons went into exile. "The police harassed me," she said, although she had not known that he was involved with any political organization—he was a cricket player. The police took Jumartha to the station and interrogated her until she became ill. Political activity came to characterize her neighborhood. Majola began to intervene on behalf of "youths who had been arrested in demonstrations or other activities." She attempted to find some of them employment: "I would go to the labor bureau where they would tell me they could not give jobs due to the arrests. I would say, 'No. Stop it. Give them a chance.'" The government kept "the kids from working because of their fears. So they were left to their own devices," which came to include marijuana, throwing dice, and general mischief.[154] Incidents like this help explain the growing crime in the townships—combined with the government's dismissive attitude toward black youths.

Ivy Mgcina was directly involved in political activism. She was a member of the ANC Women's League and worked to recruit others, especially in the trade union to which she belonged. By 1983 two of her four sons had joined MK and gone into exile that, along with her ANC activities, resulted in Mgcina being detained while at the white school where she was a servant. The politice took her to the station and locked her up. Later, she was released, only to return home and find that her eleven-year-old son had been beaten. The perpetrators "asked him questions about his brothers," which, of course, the boy could not answer. Another son was harassed for his involvement in the ANC student movement. He left "the country and he died in October '83 in a cross fire with the police in the north."[155]

Her troubles continued. First a petrol bomb was thrown through the window of her house, and almost all of her belongings were destroyed. Then, interorganizational strife began:

> In 1985 when there was this AZAPO [another radical organization] standing around, but the AZAPO was protected by the police when they came to destroy our houses. The police are there—see everybody. It just annoys you, my neighbors always come out when something like this happened. When the police came, they just ask you questions about people who were away [her sons]. Then the AZAPO came and threw tear gas in your house—under the protection of the police. They destroyed everything in sight. . . . When I was in detention in 1988, I heard my third son is dead in Cape Town. He was killed in a cross fire with the police and the informers.[156]

But that was after Mgcina had been detained in 1985 and suffered a broken neck. "We were under assault every day—all of us." In May 1989, she was released and then banned. She went to Lusaka in hopes of meeting with two sons (another, the fourth had joined up) and found that they were in Tanzania. The last time she saw this last son was in October 1990, when the ANC was unbanned. Her youngest son, still out of the country, was the victim of an accident when the tractor he was driving turned over. "So I lost three sons in the struggle." The fourth son carries scars from the beating he received from the SAP before he fled the country.[157]

The emphasis on the ANC in this section is due to the need to condense a major uprising that resulted in the triumph of the all-races election in 1994—and much of the credit for that is due to the ANC. The other two civil rights organizations took a different approach to change. The PAC was anti-white and split with the ANC. The Inkatha Freedom Party (IFP) was mainly based in Natal, and almost all of its membership was Zulu. Its goal was the same as that of the ANC, but its methods were far less militant. By the late 1980s, the IFP leadership was eyeing its place in the New South Africa in opposition to the ANC, leading to a series of confrontations just before and after the transition—from 1990-1994. And some of the whites in the security forces worked covertly to support the IFP in hopes that civil war would pit black and against black. Instead of war, Mandela and others worked out an accord that led South Africa to democracy—at tremendous cost to those women, men, and children who were the victims of not only the war, but the policies toward people of color over the centuries.

CHAPTER EIGHT

On the Road to Freedom and Post-Colonial Issues

The first African country south of the Sahara to gain independence was Sudan in 1956. That country was divided between largely urbanized Muslims in the north and Christian or traditionalist livestock keepers in the south. Sudan provides an example of how the colonial policies of regionalism failed when distinctly incompatible groups were faced with creating their own united polity. In 1955 and before actual independence, a mutiny in Sudan on the part of troops in the south broke out. Conflict continued intermittently until 2011 when the new country, South Sudan, was created.[1]

As for the French colonies, General Charles De Gaulle, as president of France, offered a referendum with certain conditions in 1959, as an outgrowth of the Algerian War. When the colonies voted in 1960, all but Guinea opted for independence, accepting closer ties than Guinea desired. She was immediately cut off, with the French withdrawing almost all movable government property and all support. The country floundered: first turning to the West and, after being rejected, to the Soviet Union. Repression under the one leader was followed by repression on the part of the military when they took power. Guinea remains very poor.

The British colonies that followed Sudan came to independence from 1957 (Ghana) through 1966 (Botswana). Uprisings in the Congo led the Belgian government to cut the ties with that country in 1960, with barely any preparation and few qualified leaders on hand to govern. British and Italian Somaliland were united into a single country in 1960, with the capital located in Mogadishu (former Italian Somaliland). In 1961-1962, Belgium passed the wand of independence to the two small colonies of Burundi and Rwanda. Both had been picked up by League of Nations man-

date following the German defeat in World War I. In Chapter Seven, we witnessed the wars of liberation in Guinea-Bissau, Mozambique, and Angola—with the latter two countries soon involved in civil war. The Cold War played a role especially in Angola, involving South Africa backed by the United States and with the Soviet Union drawing on its dependent, Cuba. South Africa's independence for people of color in 1994 resulted in the first inclusive election, and sent the late Nelson Mandela to the President's Office.

Zimbabwe, as we saw in Chapter Seven, was wracked by war until an accord was reached with the white-led government in 1980, leading to black rule under the increasingly tyrannical Robert Mugabe. In 2000, the former Southwest Africa achieved independence after years of conflict with the South African forces. Ethiopia remained under the watchful eye of Great Britain—to the consternation of Haile Selassie I—until 1944 and the signing of the Anglo-Ethiopian Agreement.[2] The former Italian colony of Eritrea remained in limbo, with the Ethiopian emperor lobbying for its inclusion into his country, which took place in 1962, with Eritrea annexed as a province. Eritrea proclaimed independence in 1993, but in 1998 more conflict developed over borders. This conflict ended in a stalemate but with a signed peace treaty between Eritrea and Ethiopia in 2000.

Regionalism and incompatible religious and indigenous political systems were more marked in the former British colonies than in almost all of the other independent colonies (except for perhaps the Belgian Congo, which had its own problems, including those regarding natural resources). In Nigeria, as we have seen, the Muslim Hausa-Fulani were in the north; the highly stratified political system of the Yoruba people dominated the west; and in the east were the Igbo, where the British had imposed their warrant chiefs, disrupting traditional elder-based polities.[3] We turn now to Nigeria and the civil war that broke out there in 1967.

Biafra: Historical Evidence and the Novel *Half a Yellow Sun*[4]

The indirect rule that worked for the British among the Hausa-Fulani in the north and with the Yoruba in the west was not successfully implemented in the eastern part of the country. As we saw, the British-appointed warrant chiefs were resented. And the British implemented control over the Igbo and the number of other smaller ethnic groups in that area. The Igbos was entrepreneurial; over time many of them had moved around the country and engaged in trade. Some had been employed in the colonial service; and others joined the British military, transitioning in independence to government service or to the Nigerian military forces. Many thousands were located in the north—traders and civil servants predominated among them. A majority of the easterners were Christian, whereas, as we know, Islam dominated in the north.

In dealing with the conflict that rendered devastation and huge loss of life among the easterners—mainly the Igbos—we will draw on Chimamanda Ngozi Adichie's graphic and realistic novel, as well as on Chinua Achebe's memoir, *There Was a Country*, and also on the scholarly work of primarily Jacinta Chiamaka Nwaka and her article "Biafran Women and the Nigerian Civil War: Challenges and Survival Strategies."[5] Regarding the novel, let us turn to a respected senior anthropologist for insights as to historical sources. Sidney W. Mintz begins his "The Anthropological Interview and Life History" with a quote that serves us well: "People think because a novel is invented it isn't true. Exactly the reverse is true. . . .The novelist is more serious than the biographer."[6] The novel, in other words, comes with its own form of truth. So, we may add, does autobiography. In this form of writing, the author's memory is colored by his or her personal experiences or what we may term "selective memory." In regard to Achebe, he referred to his notes and to documents in presenting, sadly, his last testament to his experiences in the Biafran War. These experiences include, to a lesser degree, those of his wife, Christine. In each case, Adichie's novel and Achebe's memoir reflect the historical record.

In May 1986, the eastern region withdrew from the federal government of Nigeria. This was due to the massacre of 30,000 men, women, and children—all located in the north. Those who survived (maybe 2 million) fled to the east, swelling the ranks of residents in towns, villages, hamlets, and rural areas. The approximate population of what became Biafra, before the influx of refugees from the rest of Nigeria, was about 9 million Igbo and approximately 5 million of other ethnic groups, which were similar in culture and polity and, on the whole, supported the move to independence.[7]

Many of the refugees arrived without their husbands. Women were forced to find a place to live and sustenance for themselves and their children. The Biafran government provided a pittance to the widows but hardly enough to provide for basic needs. Further hardships fell on those who lived in the breakaway state, because prosperous relatives from outside had, before, sent back funds to help provide support but no longer did so. Then, too, the multitudes flooded in during the rainy season—when farmers planted their crops. War meant fear of going into the fields, creating further hardships. With few places in which to settle, the refugees began to congregate in camps. By the end of 1968, Nwaka tells us, "650 refugee camps" held approximately "70,000 occupants."[8] As the war gained momentum, air raids and bombs frightened fishermen, who no longer fished in the rivers and streams, resulting in yet another hardship on the population of Biafra.

Among those frightened, harried masses of refugees, "a woman, mute and dazed, arrived in her village with only a bowl on her lap."[9] In the bowl was the severed head of her child—it had been cut off while the mother watched. Adichie's novel presents the same gruesome scene but in a different setting, accurately portraying this event as an outcome of the massacres in the north.

Missing from Achebe and Nwaka's writings but contained in Adichie's novel were some of the characteristics that prompted resentment against the Igbos: the mother who oozed wealth and insensitivity; and the father with a 10 percent take on all contracts and business transactions. These characters, and others like them in real life, exited the country. The hostility toward the Igbo also was introduced into the novel, while Achebe, in his memoir and as a member of the elite, noted that this attitude toward the war lingered in the post-war period as well.[10]

The disingenuous role of Harold Wilson and the British Labour government is covered in the autobiography and in Adichie's novel. In fact, a Biafran woman, Mrs. Oyibo Adinamadu, was sent to London to lobby on behalf of the breakaway nation—along with several men—all unsuccessfully.[11] The British feared that tribal conflict, as they saw it, might spread to other former colonies. Plus, there was oil. The oilfields were located in the east and came under the control of Biafra. Adichie does not dwell on the larger economic factors, although she paints a vivid picture of the hardships experienced among the refugees and those in the east—especially in 1967 after the federal government established a blockade, cutting off supplies to Biafra.

With the British supporting the federal Nigerians and the rest of the West looking the other way (with a few minor exceptions), the early military successes of the Biafrans were reversed, resulting in the loss of territory and an increase in bombing. By 1969, according to Achebe, about 100,000 women and children were dying every six weeks.[12] Relief agencies attempted to provide support. The federal government insisted that they send their supplies to Lagos, where these supplies could be checked. The Biafrans feared that poisoning would be the result. The International Red Cross was involved until 1969, flying in its supplies to Uli, the only open air strip in Biafra, when its plane was bombed. Caritas flew in supplies by night. At some point, a local Caritas official sent a cable to Catholic Relief Services, begging for baby food, because "2000 children die daily."[13] Adichie covers the relief services' attempts to set up feeding stations, with the masses trying to push through the gates to obtain just flour or meal. The pangs of hunger loomed large among the poor as well as the well-to-do who remained. The results, in the novel and in historical perspective, were kwashiorkor and other forms of malnutrition, as well as diseases that penetrated the crowded camps.

As towns fell to bombs or were captured, the populations shifted from one place to another. Both Adichie and Achebe chronicle the displacement and subsequent hardships experienced by those on the move with no safe harbor beckoning them. Achebe's wife, Christine, was forced to relocate while she was pregnant. During her stay Christine Achebe started a school for their own children as well as those of the people with whom they were living.[14] But the family was forced to move in with friends. At one point (the date is not clear in the memoir) Achebe received word that his mother was ill and had requested to see her children. He wrote that, at the time, he was homeless—having left Enugu, their residence at the time, just before what had been their home was bombed. Achebe went to Ogidi, where he was reunited with his siblings and was able to be with his mother before she died. After that, he recalled: "Our people report that her spirit called my family from Enugu to save their lives. I will not challenge that ancient wisdom."[15]

Adichie covers the conscription of any and all available men into the Biafran forces; the change in currency to Biafran notes, presenting another hardship especially for the women who were primarily the traders; the serious undersupply of food, even at the relief centers, leading to kwashi-orkor; and the fear of federal troops, who rampantly killed villagers with no cause except that they were in the breakaway state. While the historical record provides the gruesome testimony that people were so hungry that they ate grass, lizards, and rats—anything and everything they could find in the bush—Adichie's novel complements this with vivid and similar accounts. A journalist photographed a woman "cooking a human leg."[16]

Adichie echoes the reality of the more fortunate women selling their jewelry and household goods in exchange for food; and one of her female characters craved the salt that had actually almost disappeared.[17] Women took to prostitution, both in reality and in the fictional account of the war. One woman was quoted selling her body, not only out of necessity, but as "the easiest route to luxury or scarce goods" and the more useful Nigerian currency.[18]

Markets were easy targets for the federal planes. Thus the markets began to open in the wee hours of the morning or late at night. This, too, was accurately depicted in the novel. In reality Achebe's wife was forced to go to the bush, where many of the markets relocated, in the early morning hours.[19] Trade across borders "was risky business" for the women who attempted to get to the federal side or close enough to conduct business.[20] Toward the novel's conclusion one of Adichie's major female characters, Kainene, disappears from her family and from the story after she sets off on a trading mission to Lagos.

But women were not just victims of the war. They also served in useful capacities. Flora Nwapa, whose novel *Efuru* was the first published by a Nigerian woman, played a role in the Biafran government in several capacities.[21] Jacinta Nwaka noted that women were spies for the armed forces, garnering important information such as troop sizes and locations. Avenging their losses, some women resorted to "eliminating federal troops." And Nwaka specifically singled out one woman who, after the war ended, served former federal soldiers "a soup with a poisonous root."[22]

The entire world was exposed to the plight of Biafran babies and small children—those barely able to stand, or not standing at all, razor thin and starving—or the distended bellies of the children afflicted by severe protein deficiency. When, in January 1969, the Biafran leaders concluded that they could no longer fight—their leader had fled earlier to a neighboring African country—the general estimate of lives lost in the two and one half years of the war exceeded 1million. Of this number, the vast majority were women and children. The reverberations from the war left many of the survivors, and even their descendants such as Adichie, with memories that are still scarred.

As Buchi Emecheta, who was in England during the war, wrote in *Destination Biafra,* "It is time to forgive, though only a fool will forget."[23]

Ethiopia, Somalia, and the Artist Tekleab

In 1974, when Ethiopian Emperor Haile Selassie I was deposed, artist and political refugee Kebedech Tekleab, whose family roots were in Eritrea, was sixteen years old, a student, living at home in Addis Ababa. The period surrounding this event was marked by turmoil. Famine in two provinces had been severe, leading to the deaths of thousands. University students had been in rebellion off and on since the late 1960s. Labor unrest in the capital city led to further disruptions. In the military, junior officers and many of the noncommissioned officers chafed at irregular pay, among other grievances. It all came to a head in a garrison based in Sidamo Province in February 1974, when rebels took a visiting general prisoner and forced him to drink the polluted water and eat the spoiled food that had been their ration for some time.[24] In that same month, lower-level officers and the noncommissioned formed the Coordinating Committee of the Armed Forces, the Police and Territorial Army. Three men were selected from each garrison, from among the police, and from the Territorial Army, bringing together around 110 men who, together, constituted the Derg (Committee). The major figure who emerged from this group was Mengistu Haile Miriam.[25] Soon a wave of terror resulted not only in the arrest and deposition of the emperor, but also in the detention of numbers of people close to him, including highly placed members of the military. With no sign that the Derg was moving toward establishing civilian rule, more protests from students, labor, and even the teachers union resulted. By November 1974, Kiflu Tedasse and others on the left had created the Ethiopian People's Revolutionary Party (EPRP). Other political groups also formed, and among these were the Youth League. Some of these groups were formed in opposition to the EPRP, and all were in opposition to the Derg.

In 1976, then eighteen and in her first year of art school in Addis Ababa, Kebedech joined the EPRP Youth League and the student revolts against the Derg. There were, she said, a lot of women members—each cell was composed of five people who were known to each other but not to the other cells, although "we knew people's political opinions."[26] In the fall of that year, the Derg announced its campaign to eliminate the EPRP through liquidation and intimidation. Torture of those captured was brutal: eyes were torn out and victims were forced to eat their own flesh.[27] Kebedech and many others went into hiding. She spent one and one-half years moving from place to place in Addis Ababa to avoid capture, keeping in touch with her family as she could.

In the fall of 1979, Kebedech and some colleagues formulated plans to depart Ethiopia by moving east to ultimately reach the Red Sea port of Djibouti. All went well when Kebedech and four EPRP men took the bus to Dira Dawa, but "complications" emerged, and they failed to link up with the liaison that was to lead them to Djibouti. At that point, they arranged to accompany some merchants traveling in that direction. But, in a rural area near Harar, they were intercepted by members of the Western Somali Liberation Front (WSLF) and were taken prisoner.[28]

The troubles with Somalia had deep roots reaching back to the early twentieth century. Following World War II, the British, who controlled much of the Somali population, wanted to unite all Somalis into a single state. The result was unification of Italy's former colony with British Somaliland, except for those people located in the disputed area of the Ogaden, on the border between the former Italian Somaliland and Ethiopia, and French-controlled Djibouti. Emperor Haile Selassie I used all means at his disposal to lobby against this, and, finally, the plan was dropped. The border between Somalia and Ethiopia remained roughly defined. In the 1960s, Somalia launched two military campaigns to secure the area, but it was routed by Ethiopian forces on both occasions.

In 1977, a combined force of Somali troops and members of the WSLF (which had been in opposition to the government of Somalia) invaded Ethiopia. Somalia had been heavily armed by the Soviet Union and had one of the largest military forces in Africa. By the end of 1977, the Somalis (WSLF) had reached the edge of Harar and Dira Dawa (and elsewhere in the southern Ethiopian provinces). The Soviet Union, which had by then also begun arming Ethiopia, hoping to have both countries as clients, poured in massive military hardware. This enabled the Ethiopians to push the Somalis (WSLF) out, but guerrillas remained, and, in turn, they recruited Somalis within Ethiopia to their cause.[29] In addition to raiding travelers, the WSLF took many Christians in the Harar area to their camps, where victims "languished for decades."[30]

Upon capture, Kebedech recalled that she was separated from her male companions and was taken by a female soldier to another place where she was alone. In the night, a party of WSLF men came into her quarters, frightening her so that she "rushed out" and into a group of sleeping troops. An officer—hearing her cries—came to her rescue. Kebedech recalled that he spoke "halting English," and once he discovered that she had barely escaped assault, he took her to another safer location. Kebedech was confined by the Somalis in a camp for ten years.[31] She and her colleagues were a drop of water in the vast sea of Ethiopians who either were held as prisoners or had flocked into the Somali-held areas away from the Derg. In 1979, "there were many camps and their inmates were counted in the thousands . . . with refugees from Ethiopia also in the towns nearby."

In an interview with the *Washington Post*, Kebedech recounted some of her experiences during those long years.[32] First, she was selected to serve as part of a medical team, aiding professional doctors and nurses. At some point in her incarceration, she helped establish a school, where she became a teacher.[33] Kebedech recalled "that less fortunate prisoners did backbreaking work in mines and in rice paddies." Meanwhile, she cared for "hundreds of people dying with cholera, malaria and malnutrition." The Somalis placed a prohibition on prisoners writing—especially in Amharic—but Kebedech, denied the opportunity to draw, and seeking a creative outlet to enable her to endure the seemingly endless captivity, plus the daily regimen of illness and death, covertly wrote poetry. Her poem "People from Two Different Worlds"—of epic proportions—was later published. In this poem, Kebedech wrote plaintively about her mother—"struggling to hear her mother's voice."[34]

In fact her family was frantic. They had moved with two of her brothers to the United States. One of her brothers, Kinfa, returned to Ethiopia in search of Kebedech, knowing that she was on the Derg's hit list. Finding no trace of her at all, the family contacted the International Red Cross in the hopes that she was still alive.

Hostilities between Ethiopia and the Somalis were resolved by treaty in 1989.[35] The treaty called for an exchange of prisoners. Not long after this, an official from the Red Cross came to her camp and showed Kebedech her name on the missing persons list. Her family was notified, and they flew her to New York. When the brother saw his twenty-nine year-old sister, he was unable to recognize her. "She looked like an old lady, with gray hair and her face was wrinkled. She couldn't smile."[36] As we will see, Kedebech later established herself as a successful artist and smiled again.

Internal Conflicts: Uganda, Darfur, Rwanda, Congo

The troubles that emerged in these countries were rooted in the historical past and were given impetus by colonialism. In Uganda some authorities claim that the uprisings in the north were an outgrowth of ethnic conflict between Nilotic and Bantu ethnic groups. There was some truth to this in that the Acholi from the north deserted the army when Yoweri Museveni successfully defeated the then current ruler of Uganda in 1985. A large number of them fled back to the north, carrying grievances and with little or no opportunities for employment. At this time, a female prophetess emerged to stir resistance among the disenchanted. She was Alice Auma Lakwena, a former Roman Catholic, who was alleged to have been a prostitute, was said to be barren, and had twice been married. She formed the Holy Spirit Movement, based on a synchronism between Christianity and traditional religions. Lakwena was actually a spirit with whom she communicated and whose name she took.

Lakwena drew a sizable following on the premise that her forces could defeat Museveni's through leading pure lives that accepted the spirit of Lakwena. Furthermore, her army would be able to deflect bullets by rubbing a combination of oil and water on their bodies. Their first encounter with the Ugandan army proved successful, enhancing her power. But within a year (1987), her movement was defeated. It was then supplanted by the Holy Spirit Movement II run by her cousin, Joseph Kony, a former Acholi military commander. Kony changed the name of the organization at least twice before settling on the Lord's Resistance Army in 1992.[37] While Kony was in northern Uganda, he and his forces brought terror to the civilian population. They raped, pillaged, and routed people from their homes. Around 90 percent fled their villages and farms, and "two thirds of those displaced were women and children."[38] Small boys were forcefully conscripted, and there was an aura of fear even among those who took to the bush and relocated. Conflict raged between the government forces and Kony's through the 1990s and into 2006-2007, when peace accords were drawn up, only to be rejected by Kony through his refusal to sign them.

Later Kony took his forces into the Democratic Republic of Congo (DRC) and the Central African Republic, where they continued to plunder and frighten locals. This was especially disruptive in the DRC, which was already caught up in internal chaos. Those Acholi who survived Kony's carnage in northern Uganda began to gradually return to their former homes.[39]

Darfur, in western Sudan, was an ancient kingdom that was swept into Britain's orbit at the outbreak of the First World War as part of the Anglo-Egyptian Sudan. The ruler of Darfur, however, was opposed to subservience. Lacking the resources for yet another conflict, the British worked out an accord whereby the government of Sudan was to be recognized, but local rule was allowed in exchange for a small yearly payment of tribute. This relationship, however, foundered, leading Britain to invade and then annex Darfur in 1916. After that, Darfur settled down while, at independence and following, the major conflicts were fought between the north (Khartoum) and the southern Sudanese. The people of Darfur, like those in the south, were livestock-keeping Nilotic. In published news accounts those Muslims in the north were repeatedly referred to as "Arabs," as were the Muslims who became minions of the Sudanese government when they began their assault on Darfur. Their "Arabness" is problematic in that they were primarily African, with some admixture of Mukluks, the ruling class in Egypt before they were driven out by the Ottoman Turks.

The indigenous people of Darfur had long been neglected. Famine in the 1980s had not been addressed, issues surrounding border claims were ignored, and then the final blow came when government funding from oil revenues reverted to the Muslim "Arabs." Several of the local ethnic groups in Darfur formed the Sudan Liberation Army and the Justice and Equality Movement, leading ultimately to an attack on government military compounds that killed 700 soldiers.[40] The government retaliated by spurring on and supporting the "Arab" Janjaweed militia. Racism on the part of the Janjaweed was a factor in their committing rape, murder, and destruction of crops, livestock, and villages. By 2007, approximately "400,000 people have died as a result of the conflict, of which 300,000 have died due to malnutrition, disease and famine." [41] More than 1 million people sought refuge in camps established in neighboring Chad, carrying devastation to the former French colony, a very poor country with few resources for its own people.

This spillover resulted in acts of violence within Chad. "Halima Ab-delkarim is twenty-one years old. She lives in Chad, just over the border from Darfur, Sudan, and is married with a baby daughter." She is also a black African, making her a "target of the Janjaweed," which was on a "genocidal quest" to control the area by eliminating the African population. In March 2006, the Janjaweed attacked her village, killing men and "kid-napping ten women and girls," with Halima and her ten-year-old sister among them. The next few days witnessed the pregnant Halima and her sister being gang raped. The Janjaweed "beat" Halima "with sticks, and taunted her with racial epithets." Because Halima's sister refused to provide them with her donkey, they killed her.[42] This is an example of the violence women and children experienced in Darfur, and also in Chad, during the years of atrocities that characterized the willful assault on the part of the Janjaweed, as agents of the Sudanese government. As Rebecca Corcoran makes all too clear, "the use of rape as a deliberate military tactic and weapon of war has destroyed Darfur in a way that no other crime could."[43] In fact, rape as a weapon plays a role in all of the inter-African wars that I cover, and it has been prevalent in conflicts throughout history, not just in Africa.

Much of the testimony provided by Human Rights Watch reflects similar conditions: from Joseph Kony's army assaults on women in Uganda's north, to Sierra Leone and Liberia's conflicts that follow. Soldiers rape women who are on their way to the market, to obtain water and grain from the fields. In the case of the Janjaweed, soldiers added the ethnic compo-nents: "dirty black Nuba" and "slaves." One woman testified that, because she had ethnic scarification, the soldiers added more fresh scars, one "for [Sudan President] Omar el Bashir" and another "to do whatever el Bashir wants from you."[44]

In Chad, a young woman refugee revealed her experience in February 2005, and in it we see how violence against women travels: "I went with a group of women searching for firewood at the border, but I was alone . . . when attacked. A man from Chad, not a soldier, caught me, beat me and raped me. . . . When my husband came back some months later and found that I was pregnant, he left me."[45] The stigma of rape is incalculable. It breaks up families, sends girls from their parents, and prevents any positive future for known victims of assault or HIV.

A sixteen-year-old girl was raped in one of the camps. Her family hastily arranged a marriage so as to "protect" the family's honor: "My daughter screams at night. . . . She is [possessed]. . . . I never talk to her about what happened, although she knows that I know. . . . I cleaned her wounds after her return every day, but still talking about it is very difficult."[46] A woman in counseling with Human Rights Watch confessed to being raped by seven Janjaweed: "Now I have a baby, and everyone knows he is a baby from Janjaweed. I did not want this baby, and it is very hard for me."[47]

Those in the camps are susceptible to rape—from Chadian forces, there ostensibly to protect the female residents and male refugees: "It is not safe inside the camp. I have no husband. Many men have forced me to be their wife" was the statement provided by a twenty-six-year old refugee to Human Rights Watch. These traumatic events "have been documented in many other refugee crises," and to repeat each one that occurred is unnecessary—it would even border on sensationalizing these immeasurable hardships.

Down in South Sudan during the struggle for independence, we encounter women who refused to sit on the sidelines. Alual Koch "was 13 when she learnt to kill with a gun, fighting government soldiers as a jungle guerrilla. . . . Now 36, she shows no emotion in recalling how she carried ammunition and treated wounded on the frontlines of the 21-year conflict."[48] But Koch was one of the fortunate; she found work as a prison guard. Other women combatants have had to adopt "high risk survival techniques," such as prostitution. Another stated that she "fought for freedom," but, due to the depth of poverty and the lack of development in South Sudan, she "has no chance of going to school."[49] Several women have experienced "'violent skirmishes' over dowry disputes as the 'ownership' of female ex-combatants." Another woman bemoaned her contributions to the struggle. Having fought, she and others "have no chance of going to school to get education and that cannot be fair." This woman had served as a frontline nurse.

The widow of a fighter noted that she was fortunate in having a job, "but there are many more who have nothing, no support." The United Nations, in 2008, initiated a campaign to help veterans including women adjust, "but critics say it excluded the majority of those who played supporting roles within the combat zones," especially the women.[50] They remained dependent on "male soldiers" with "high rates of sexual violence" from the very troops they were supporting.[51]

The war in South Sudan officially ended, but conflicts have not. Women die at a very high rate in childbirth due to lack of medical facilities and trained personnel. Literacy rates are extremely low, thought to be about 12 percent for girls and women. Seventeen percent of girls are married off before they reach the age of fifteen—remaining commodities for the exchange of livestock and goods. In 2013, women's "post-conflict status is among the lowest of all groups in south [before independence] Sudan, regardless of ethnic or tribal background."[52]

Moving to Rwanda and drawing on Ethel Albert's study of "Women of Burundi" in the 1950s, we can get a slight view of some of the variables that existed within Rwandan social stratification, which roughly parallels the strict lines that were drawn between the ethnic groups and then within the castes of Burundi. A Tutsi man had to marry a woman of the same or higher rank, or he would be "declassed." A poverty-stricken Tutsi could give her daughter "in marriage to a wealthy Hutu," thus combining the two groups. The daughter was, however, disdained by other Tutsi" even if she was likely to "be better treated by a Hutu." Each caste had its stereotypes of body build: "Great height, thinness and an extraordinarily narrow skull are typical of the Tutsi," while a "Hutu five feet tall will not be likely to make a mistake about his inferiority in the presence of the Tutsi of six and one-half or seven feet tall." The Tutsi women are shorter and "much fleshier." (However, Albert notes that there are short Tutsi and tall Hutu.)[53] The Germans, followed by the Belgians, who took over as colonial rulers under the League of Nations mandate, were claimed to have initiated these class-based paradigms that favored the Tutsi. They represented about 15 percent of the population and were the overlords of the Hutu, the majority, in the pre-colonial state.

In the mid-1920s, the Belgians initiated another discriminatory measure by issuing separate identity passes to each group. Education was promoted among the Tutsi, as were the best of the low- paying government jobs. These measures angered the Hutu, who, in the 1950s, still under colonial rule, organized a political party, the Party for the Emancipation of the Hutus. This was followed in 1959 by insurrection against the Belgian government, resulting in violence against the Tutsi, with 150,000 fleeing to Burundi. In Rwanda, Belgium took steps toward independence by allowing local elections in 1960. It was no surprise, then, when the Hutu, the majority, were elected to almost all of the seats.

In 1961-1962, Rwanda and Burundi gained their freedom. Then a Hutu president took over in Rwanda, where fighting was already under way and picked up momentum. By 1963, the Tutsi were being massacred, leading more to seek refuge in Burundi as well as in Uganda. Purges and conflict marred Rwanda from this period until 1975, when General Juvenal Habyarimana, a Hutu, led a coup and established a one-party state with himself as president. Various outsiders—including the French—pressured Habyarimana to make political reforms, including multiparty elections. Although indicating that he would begin reform, Habyarimana sat tight. And by 1986, Tutsi exiles in Uganda formed the Rwandan Patriotic Front (RPF), with Paul Kagame quickly moving to head the RPF army.[54] Also in 1986, and despite his authoritarian rule, Habyarimana was the first leader in Africa to conduct a national survey on AIDS, with the results showing that almost 18 percent of the urban population was infected.[55]

Moving ahead, in 1990 the RPF invaded, and foreign forces, including the French, came in to aid the Rwandan troops. The government fell, and the first cease-fire was in place the following year. The Tutsi who remained in Rwanda suffered retribution, with thousands of them dying. In the fall of 1993, the RPF again invaded, and this time they made it almost all the way to Kigali. The French came in again to attempt a peaceful settlement. Many Hutu fled to the neighboring DRC (called Zaire at the time). Then, in 1994 came a crisis: Habyarimana and the president of Burundi were shot down in the plane carrying them to Kigali. The first reaction came the very next day (April 7) from the Hutu-dominated government forces, blaming the Tutsi, and setting in motion what would later be defined as genocide against them.[56] Outsiders, including the United Nations, failed to intervene. After meetings, discussion, and hand-wringing, a few camps were set up by the UN. UN troops based in Rwanda, whose mission was to protect civilians, were overpowered.

Finally, in July 1994, a new government was established while the slaughter continued. By then both sides were killing each other. The Hutu who fled earlier were, in time, joined by perhaps up to 1 million more in eastern DRC. More consultations, meetings, and advice led finally to trials for those accused of genocide, meaning mainly Hutu. But few Hutu were willing to return—approximately 750,000 stayed on in the DRC, where they began to play havoc internally and in forays conducted against Rwanda.

Paul Kagame took over the presidency of Rwanda. He has been as authoritarian as his predecessor but has been far more successful as president. One of his early mandates was to do away with ethnic designations: everyone is a Rwandan. He also built schools and encouraged equality between the sexes. His cabinet contains three female ministers. The birthrate is high, and Kagame is tackling that problem by educating "women both in school and generally in society to say: 'No.'" Rather than touting condoms for birth control, however, Kagame advises that they seek other pleasures.[57]

A more creative venture under Kagame was his commissioning of a report on "Violence Against Women" in Rwanda. Did those decades of war lead to an increase in domestic violence against women? Carried out under the auspices of Rwanda's Ministry of Gender and Family Promotion and the United States Aid for International Development, the study was conducted in eleven provinces, with the "recommended sample size in each of 857" women between the ages of eighteen and forty-nine. At the conclusion of the study, the "number of respondents obtained was 722 for community violence and 449 for domestic violence."[58]

The findings revealed that "an estimated 32.4% of women were verbally or physically abused in their communities, on at least one occasion" during the years 1997-2003. Of this percentage most of the community violence was verbal in nature (i.e., obscenities). "One in every four women was subject to sexual violence, on at least one occasion," while "psychological and physical violence were both half the rate of sexual violence."[59] Most of the "community violence occurred in 1998. . . . The succeeding years were less violent." This indicated that the further removed from the genocide, the less anger in the communities. The study showed that the "women most affected by community violence are those who are literate, educated and have paid employment. Illiterate women whose sole source of income is farming are less likely to suffer this type of violence.[60] Urban women are more vulnerable.

As to domestic violence "and violence suffered during childhood [during the war years] . . . 47% of respondents recall having witnessed an act of violence between their parents" in childhood. Their findings indicated that, where men were concerned, there was a "strong correlation between current violence and violence suffered by a woman's spouse during childhood." Not surprisingly, "domestic violence was induced by issues such as alcohol consumption, quarrels on how money should be spent, housekeeping and

children." Some of the women—one in ten—"complained of sexual violence in the form of partner imposed sexual intercourse" or forced marital
sex.[61]

The "women . . . are desirous of showing themselves as faithful, available and submissive to their husbands" and "tolerate violence." Half of all
respondents "consider it of the utmost importance to safeguard the appearance of [their] husband's authority in public," with three quarters of the
women reporting that they would not "divulge any violence they experience
in marital relationships unless such violence were very serious." It would
generally be acceptable "for a husband to beat his wife if she committed
adultery," and half of the women agreed that if a "wife refuses sexual intercourse" the husband has the right to beat her—but only 30 percent allowed that it was permissible for a beating to take place for "poor
housekeeping."

The study concluded that "Rwandan men are not more physically violent
than men in other societies (and the researchers had two others—a province
in Uganda and East Timor—for comparison). The men were, however,
"very assertive in their authority." This behavior was due to "the submis-
siveness, availability and willingness to tolerate violence of Rwandan
women." The findings should, it was expected, "lead women as a whole to
adopt a less conciliatory attitude in the face of male 'power and control.'"
Ironically, one of the most criticized facets of Kagame's leadership is his
need to control. Some argue that Kagame's "tidy, up-and-coming little
country . . . is the most straitjacketed in the world."[62]

Devastating civil war broke out in Sierra Leone in 1991 and lasted until
2001. During those years the level of violence against women and children
was all but immeasurable in retrospect and was conducted equally by all
of the sides involved. In April 1992, the legitimate government was routed
by a coup carried out by junior officers. What followed was a tangled web
of events that involved various players, including Charles Taylor, president
of Liberia, who hungered for the Sierra Leone diamond mines, and the Revolutionary United Forces (RUF) and their leader, Fodoy Sankoh, whose
forces were positioned in the east. The RUF rounded up children—boys
and girls— forcing them to fight under the threat of mutilation and making
them high on drugs. The attacks on civilians featured rape, murder, and
bodily mutilations. The Economic Commission of West African States
(ECOMOG) sent observers and later troops. The United Nations attempted

to work out peace agreements, which, in 1995, resulted in an accord signed in Abidjan (Ivory Coast). The RUF refused to take part and did not sign the accord—and in the meantime, the fighting continued. In 1996 the military gave way to a newly elected government, whose president contracted with a South African firm of mercenaries who came in to add their weight. Some of them put aside their contractual obligations in favor of engaging in the illegal diamond trade. The new government fell in May 1997 to yet another military coup. Soon thereafter the RUF joined with the government military in a junta that led to the capture of Freetown (the capital). Yet another faction engaged in the conflict against the preexisting rebel forces, with ECOMOG, UN forces, and British military troops aligned to take back Freetown.

In 1998, the president of Sierra Leone returned from exile in Guinea after the liberation of Freetown. During 1999, the UN sent in even more forces, as did ECOMOG, and attempts were made to rout the rebels, who were dispersed in the countryside, and to restore control over the diamond mines that were mostly back under government control. Peace entreaties continued, with a cease-fire worked out in Lomé (Togo). Still the fighting continued. The combined forces of the British, ECOMOG, and the United Nations finally gained control in 2000, and in 2001 the government began the process of demilitarizing the rebels. It was, however, 2002 before the government forces took over and peace was declared.[63]

The government established a Truth and Reconciliation Commission in order to analyze the brutalities, attempt to assign responsibility for the numbers of war crimes, and provide for healing. Among the findings was the fact that "women were the exclusive targets of rape, sexual abuse and sexual slavery." Citing Amnesty International, Dumbuya reported that "more than 250,000 women and girls" had been subjected to sexual violence and/or sexual slavery.[64] The violence against women was perpetrated by all of the Sierra Leonean forces involved. The number of dead was calculated at more than 50,000. Those who survived included young boys, numbering in the thousands, whose limbs had been forcefully amputated, and most of them had drug-dependence problems. Iyer warned that "one cannot underestimate the damage of the civil war through death, mutilation and displacement in massive numbers."[65] Sierra Leone's government has been slowly rebuilding its economy and focusing, within its limited means, on social transformation. Donor organizations have contributed aid as well as

challenges: "the existence of a multitude of donors points to a variety of
agendas, some overlapping, some contradictory." Peace building is regarded as a goal that all these organizations were to promote while also
dealing with myriad issues pertaining to health—including the spread of
AIDS—and combating malaria. Disarmament, demobilization, and reinte-
gration were still UN goals as of 2011.[66]

The Democratic Republic of Congo achieved independence in 1960,
with a handful of college graduates on hand to replace the Belgian administration. The country fell into chaos almost from the beginning. In 1965
there was a bloodless military coup led by Joseph Mobutu, who promptly
assumed power with the acquiescence, if not the direct support, of the West,
as this was during the Cold War. The country's mineral riches were required
for nuclear weapons, among other things. Mobutu's reign was best characterized as self-indulgence, while the country's infrastructure crumbled and
the economy spiraled into decline. The ailing Mobuto was forced to flee
when Laurent Kabila invaded in 1997. Although Kabila installed himself
and his minions in Kinshasa, the capital, conflict continued in various parts
of the country. When he was killed in 2001, his son Joseph stepped in as
president. That succession in command resulted in changing the country's
name from Zaire to the current DRC—and the deaths of almost 2.7 million
people by 2007.[67]

The Hutu who took refuge in the DRC were and remain a destabilizing
factor in the eastern provinces of North and South Kivu. (See the map of
the Congo.) The sexual violence that occurred in those two provinces has
been the source of a number of studies, which were useful for informational
purposes but have had little or no impact on bringing it to a halt.[68]

One factor seen in the Rwandan study on female subordination also was
present in the DRC. Before the wars and continuing, women were raised
to be submissive. They were married young and culturally bound to their
husbands. Women were victims of domestic violence, including the inability to "require their husbands to use condoms"; thus they were prey to sex-
ually transmitted diseases including HIV/AIDS. AIDS reached alarming
rates, which, beyond the medical issues, created serious economic implications for women and children. Then war in the eastern provinces caused
the virus to spread, bringing more devastation. Again it was the women
and children who paid the heavy toll.[69]

The burden of survival in the eastern Congo falls heavily on women,

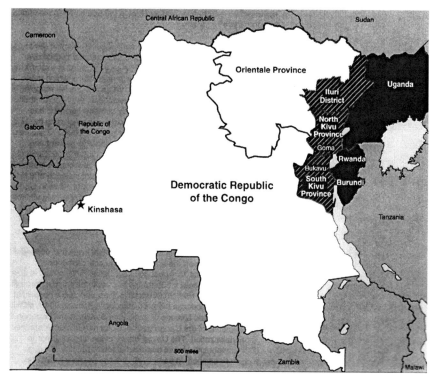

Map of Eastern Congo, Burundi, and Rwanda.
Source: Republic of Rwanda

leading to "survival sex." This is not the rape that is also rampant there, but
it is based on the need to feed and house one's family. In 2001 "Catherine"
was a widow with eight children: "I do not dare to refuse men because I do
not want to leave the children hungry."[70] There is no money for school fees,
if schools are actually operating, and so children engage in sexual relations
with their teachers to stay in school; and employees with their employers.
One non-governmental organization employee opined that the situation in
her part of eastern Congo was so desperate that "families even push their
daughters to prostitution."[71] Human Rights Watch reported on an eighteen-
year-old orphan "who cares for her younger brothers and sisters" living in
a "wrecked automobile on the grounds of a military camp." She "had sex
with men who threatened otherwise to get her expelled from her shelter and
the camp, and has been raped regularly" by a military officer.[72]

Combatants of "most of the forces" in the area—Rwandan Hutu included—use sexual violence "as a weapon of war." As we saw earlier, rape, sexual violence, and war go hand in hand. Soldiers "raped and abused women and girls as a part of their effort to maintain control over civilians and the territory they occupy." But violence is not confined just to the military forces—local boys and men "commit crimes of sexual violence" as do deserters.[73] Whereas the Hutu in the military are the major perpetrators, the Tutsi are not absolved. One fifteen-year-old girl claimed that a Tutsi "kidnapped her sisters" outside Bukavu. The soldiers came to her home, where the family was gathered around the fire. "There were lots of them. . . . They raped my sisters and my mother, but I was able to run. . . . They took away my sisters and we still don't know where they are." They returned and took her mother. She returned after three days. Her father was discouraged from seeking the missing women by neighbors, who "said if he did that the Tutsi would exterminate the whole family."[74] It is this sort of threat that keeps the people under control. Contrary to Kagame's denial, this example also proves that Rwandan forces have been present in the eastern province of the DRC.

But the most graphic if also appalling incidents are the case studies collected in eastern Congo between 2002 and 2006. One young woman, Bupole, was nineteen years old when "the men we so dreaded . . . suddenly appeared." The soldiers circled her village, shooting indiscriminately. Her father was murdered and her mother was also shot. Bupole, in flight, stopped to aid her mother when five men accosted her. "They tied me up and stuffed a gag in my mouth. They they raped me again and again." Bupole was left unaided and unattended until others came along who rescued the survivors and took the dead, including by then her mother, for burial. The outcome of gang rape for Bupole was first severe bleeding followed by an inability to control her urine. At the time she was interviewed, she was waiting for her third surgery in hopes that it would finally correct her incontinence.

Twelve-year-old Byamungu was a hard-working young girl who, for four years, had carried palm wine to the market from her home. While returning from the market one day, she briefly left the group of women accompanying her to relieve herself in the bush. While she was off the path, a group of men arrived, and, as they attacked her, Byamungu's screams sent the others scurrying away. First, she was robbed. Then the men stripped and raped her. "The pain," she recalled, "was like having knives plunged inside my body" as all eight men took their turn in violating her body. Another group of women found Byamungu and took her to the local health center. Her organs were so badly torn that both feces and urine flowed without control. Byamungu was later removed to a hospital where initial surgery corrected the involuntary flow of urine but left her still unable to control her bowels. More surgery followed, and when she was interviewed in 2006, Byamungu had recovered from the physical damage and was undergoing treatment for the severe trauma she had experienced.

Augustine was six years old—the youngest of fourteen children in the family—when she was kidnapped. An interview with her mother provided the setting: "I was preparing the evening meal. Augustine—who loved to play with other children—left the house [when soon thereafter] a neighbor brought the news that our little girl" had been abducted. Fearing that they were about to be assaulted, the other family members hunkered down. "Toward midnight, we heard noises outside and recognized a voice" that they attributed to Augustine. But all were initially too frightened to go out and check. Finally, the father was in such a state of anxiety that he ventured out and found this small child "lying on the ground, abandoned and exposed, naked as a frog." The six-year-old had been repeatedly raped "by grown men." On delivering her to the health center, they found no help available. That forced the family to proceed to a not-very-well-provisioned hospital where it soon became apparent that Augustine's defilement resulted in "tears and complete rupture of the perineum, along with a rectovaginal fistula and severe cachexia." Augustine and various family members spent an entire year in this hospital, but surgeries failed to repair the damage. Finally, she was transferred to Goma, which had better facilities. There she put on weight, received a nutritional diet, and underwent more surgery. This last surgery was successful. Still to be resolved was Augustine's psychological trauma—if ever that could be successfully treated.

Women of all ages were victims of the conflict that enveloped the eastern Congo. Tata Mwasi was sixty-six and the mother of thirteen—some of her children had been "war casualities," as had her husband. In her testimony she recalled that:

> There had been violence and increasing insecurity . . . forcing her to flee to a village . . . where relatives helped her to build a one-room adobe hut. . . .

One morning, four young men, as poorly dressed as she, approached her hut. Two of them forced their way inside while others guarded the entrance. One of those who had entered said, "So she's old, but she's still a woman." They flung her on the ground and raped her in turns. One looked about the same age as her son, and when he finished, he asked if she was satisfied. Her humiliation and bitterness were indescribable.

But worse was to come. As they left, the two who stood guard set fire to the straw roofing of her hut. It burnt like paper and the clothes she was wearing caught fire, burning her flesh before she was rescued by passersby who carried her to the health center. She had severe burns on her trunk, thighs and groin.

Tata Mwasi was eventually cured of third-degree burns that covered twenty-seven percent of her body. But the trauma and humiliation remained as permanent scars.

Pregnant women were victims of vicious attacks as well. Agnes was three months' pregnant when an "armed militia" attacked her and others who were hiding in the bush. "One group began to beat and sodomize her husband; another dragged Agnes away." Hearing gunshots, Agnes worried that her husband had been murdered. In the meantime, her captors forced Agnes "to the ground and brutally raped her until she lost consciousness." Later, when all was quiet, a few women conducted a search of the area. They found Agnes' husband and took him away for burial. She "could not walk" but was carried to the local health center where treatment seemed to save the pregnancy. As she reached full term, and after hours of labor at home, by the time Agnes reached the hospital, the fetus was dead. Then she developed "an uncontrollable and continuous flow of urine" followed by leaking feces. Throughout her pregnancy she had lived with "vesico-vaginal and recto-vaginal fistulas," and, in addition, she was HIV-infected. "Since then she has lived in complete social isolation."

One of the most gruesome of the testimonies was that provided by Giselle. She was married at sixteen (a customary age in eastern Congo). Her first pregnancy resulted in a stillbirth. One night, during these years of conflict, Giselle and her husband were nestled in their home when they heard noises outside. "My husband decided to get me to safety. He did not realize that the group of bandits were already outside" the house. When he opened the door, he was immediately shot. Giselle was taken away "by the leader of the group" who "ordered me to follow him" and his men. They hid out in what was an abandoned Catholic mission. "I was a sex slave to a tyrant for two years, with three other captive co-wives, one of them 15 years old." Then:

> In September 2004, with the process of demobilization un-
> derway, our "chief" was to be transferred. . . . But one morning,
> he summoned me to his presence. I entered the room with fore-
> boding and trembling. Apparently one of his spies had informed
> him that I I had received a greeting from a passerby, and I had
> to be made an example of. But he took an oath . . . saying,
> "You'll soon be free. But I would hate to think of other men
> sleeping with you after me, because I'm jealous. I am going to
> seal your vagina. Then he forced me to take a lamp and burn
> my own genitals, while he stood over me with his rifle cocked
> at my head. Despite my screams to the point of fainting, no one
> could help me.

Following this ordeal her torturer departed. Giselle was left in her room for two weeks with no treatment: the "stench," she said, "was unbearable." When the "chief" returned after those two weeks, he gave her a "medical pass" to the hospital. Following treatment that was only partially successful, Giselle was sent home to her family. It was only then that Giselle realized that her husband still lived. He arrived and took her to a facility where Médecins Sans Frontières (Doctors without Borders) had staff on hand. Surgery in this facility resulted in the successful "removal of sclerotic tissue and dilatation of the vaginal canal. The best outcome for Giselle was that she had her husband for support during the long healing process.[75]

Despite the depressing reports that have emerged, and continue to come from the DRC, some women have become active in peace building. Ac- cording to Marie Godin and Mado Chideka, the DRC "has one of the high- est numbers of women's organizations of any country in Africa." Of course they are not located in the war zones, but they are seeking to mobilize against sexual violence by "raising the awareness" of other women and en- couraging them to commit to help to improve "living conditions." These several local Congolese women's groups also are in contact with members of the diaspora who live in Belgium, who have formed their own organizations. One problem that has presented obstacles is that of perception. The women in the DRC point out that they have different ideas as to what is required to stamp out violence against women than their counterparts in Belgium. In fact, "many say that if they themselves had the chance to migrate they would prefer to start a completely new life, far from what is happening in the DRC."[76] The fact that these organizations exist is, of course, positive despite the futility of peace and change with hostilities continuing.

Post-colonial conflicts have occurred elsewhere in Africa with women and children always involved in one way or another, mostly as victims. In recent years politics often played a part such as occurred in Ivory Coast in the first decade of the twenty-first century. Religion has also served as a motivating factor in the case of Al Shebab in Somalia—spilling over into Kenya where Somali subversives wrecked havoc in a Nairobi shopping center; and with car bombs and other weapons caused deaths and destruction along the Indian Ocean coast. Perhaps the most notorious group, Boko Haram, operated under the pseudo rubic of Islam in northern Nigeria. Boko Haram spread its wave of terror to first towns and villages in the north before moving south to the capital Abuja and elsewhere. In April 2014, Boko Haram militants broke into a girls boarding school in a small village, abducting more than 270 students who were only present on that occasion to take their final examinations—the school had been been closed down due to the increased violence in the area. The Nigerian military were unable to quell the acts of violence—mostly aimed at Christian families—and critics alleged that they were equally guilty of rampant acts of violence against locals in their failed attempts to bring Boko Haram's attacks to a halt. Due to the spillover of refugees and even members of Boko Haram into Cameroon, Chad and Niger, for the first time in post-independence Africa the former French colonies joined Nigeria in a regional effort to suppress Boko Haram's rampant terrorism.

Surveying AIDS and Women in Africa

"AIDS in Africa is about sex."[77] Uganda is where it developed into a recognizable danger to public health in the mid-1970s. By the 1990s, AIDS had spread globally; and by 2003, "38 million HIV-infected persons lived in Africa.[78] As of 2005, when Brooke Schoepf published her study, AIDS had supplanted malaria and measles with the highest death rates for children in black Africa. Its impact has caused severe hardships on women as well: loss of partners/wage earners; orphans to support; the need to care for the sick before they die; and their own capacities to work reduced when they contract the disease. Schoepf's research indicates that AIDS is especially lethal in communities where "poverty, drought, hunger, genocide and war" existed.[79] These factors were present in multiples in so much of Africa south of the Sahara during the 1990s and on, especially during the devastating civil wars that marked Rwanda, Congo, Sierra Leone, and Liberia.

Southern Africa was hit very hard due to the migrations of men into the mines and other industries from states such as Swaziland, Mozambique, Botswana, and Malawi, where there were few opportunities for work. Many of the men left behind wives and families for eleven months a year, but then found "town wives" with whom they co-habited. Not only did these dual families cause economic hardships, they tended to spur the spread of AIDS. African truck drivers—those whose work took them on the road for days or weeks at a time—became infected due to their indiscriminating visits to prostitutes along their routes. Schoepf points out that, although men are responsible for transmitting the disease through patterns of sexual behavior, "many men think of AIDS as a 'disease of women,' that is, a disease spread by women, rather than men.[80] In fact, citing a study on Kigali, Rwanda, she reports that, by 1986, "30 per cent" of the women who delivered babies at the local hospital were found to be positive, and "68 per cent" of them had only one lifetime partner. In fact, "most women continue to be infected by their regular partners," who are obviously not faithful to them.[81]

Once the disease took on epidemic proportions in Uganda, and before any treatment was available, the government launched a campaign devoted to alerting its people to practice safe sex and urged men to use condoms. Pharmaceutical research produced a number of treatments—over time—but these were too expensive for ordinary Africans to afford. Still, non-governmental agencies began to purchase and distribute cocktails of medications, with Uganda benefiting, thus reducing the spread of the disease (keep in mind that those without treatment were already dead) until 2004. Then once again the disease increased to "over fifty percent" between the years 2001 and 2011.[82] This uptick encouraged Beatrice Were, who came forward publicly with her HIV-positive diagnosis and founded the National Community of Women Living with AIDS—a grassroots organization that encompasses more than 40,000 women in Uganda. Were and the community of women living with AIDS suffered a setback by the shift in the Ugandan government's AIDS policy.

The earlier decline in infection rates was due to the aggressive campaign that emphasized prevention in sex education in schools and condom promotion through grassroots women's and religious organizations. The international non-governmental organizations channeled funding from Western donors. USAID played a leading role. In 2003, the U.S. Congress passed the Presidential Emergency Plan for AIDS Relief (PEPFAR), which was sponsored by Christian fundamentalist campaigners. The bill required that two thirds of the funding be devoted to anti-retroviral treatment and the rest be spent educating people on sexual abstinence. The Uganda government was awarded the first PEPFAR grant. President Musevini's wife was on hand during the congressional debates, leaving the impression that condoms were irrelevant to the decline in HIV rates in Uganda. (She credits abstinence.) In 2004, the government stopped the distribution of free condoms in clinics and levied a tax on all sales of condoms in Uganda.[83] Furthermore, the government banned funding to family planning clinics because they conducted abortions.

Beatrice Were received Human Rights Watch's highest award in 2005 for defending "the rights of people living with AIDS against controversial shifts in the country's AIDS policy."[84] This was due to her failure to be intimidated and speaking out regularly on the controversy. PEPFAR policies were responsible for an increase in AIDS, because people were having sex—and not abstaining—with limited access to condoms. Sadly, most of those affected were couples in their most productive years.

Once again Schoepf provides some insights into this reluctance on the part of African men and how it, then, causes such hardship on women. During her fieldwork in Kinshasa (DRC), AIDS researchers advised that "'African men won't use condoms.'" Not only that, but they employed a double standard, "with numerous, often younger sex partners, while wives' sexuality might be strictly controlled."[85] This attitude is not limited to the DRC, but indeed seems to be almost universal across Africa. Condoms reduce sexual pleasure.

Most women are powerless in these sexual encounters. In the case of prostitutes, insisting on using a condom may send the men to other women who do not require protection. For married women, the age-old dominance of the patriarch still holds, not only among traditionalists, but among many modern women as well. Unless a woman is educated, employable, and able to support herself and/or her children, she is powerless. What is especially shocking to Westerners is that, in many societies where families dwell on the local equivalent of one dollar or one dollar and fifty cents a day, some send their daughters into sex work to help earn extra money.[86] These girls may know about AIDS—they probably do—but, again, they lack the power to insist on protection for themselves. If they do not succeed in their work, they are likely to suffer physical abuse at home. In post-independence Africa, prostitutes are found in almost every city. Many rural girls with no education go into urban areas and into sex work as the only means they have to support themselves. The motivating factors are primary, and "this practice has contributed to the spread of AIDS." In Nigeria, "single, unmarried women and divorced . . . women with no support or jobs have engaged in prostitution for decades," and, again, "their partners . . . have been unwilling to use condoms."[87] Yoruba women, however, were often successful in insisting that their partners use condoms, especially those who were economically independent.

As Schoepf also adds, "Sex is often not consensual. . . . The extent of gender violence in Africa is coming to light as more women seek relief from early (and often forced) marriage, spousal battery and forced sex within marriage."[88] Rape—which I will also cover elsewhere—is rampant in some crowded urban areas and especially in South Africa, where it is said that a woman is raped every fifteen minutes. Not only does rape stigmatize a young girl or woman, but it is another way of transferring AIDS from men who are affected to their victim.

The reverse also is possible. A celebrated case in 2005 involved a high official in South Africa's ANC (the ruling party). Jacob Zuma, who practiced polygamy with several known wives, was charged with raping the daughter of a friend whom he knew to be HIV positive. Then, he later testified that he showered after engaging in unprotected sex—alleging that doing so prevented transmission. The woman filed charges against Zuma, with the case going to trial while he was involved in a factional dispute that, ultimately, led to his election as president of South Africa. Drawing on their ethnic background, Zuma claimed that the woman tempted him, and, according to Zulu traditions, he was obliged to "gratify her." She maintained her insistence that she had been raped. The end result was that, due to his power and position, he was able to cast aspersions on her reputation, and he was acquitted. This is just another example of the subordination of women and male domination, and this case played out on an international stage via the press.[89]

John Iliffe has written a comprehensive history of AIDS in Africa. Beyond the scholarly synthesis, Iliffe's work contains moving testimony from the affected. Those who are well educated tended to sink into depression and even contemplated suicide, whereas the uneducated initially failed to comprehend what positive test results conveyed. In one example that Iliffe provides, on receiving his diagnosis a man found himself contemplating suicide. "My 25-year-old wife has been confirmed HIV positive and both and she and one of my daughters have been ill. . . . I do wish my wife had not fallen into this situation" which, of course, was due to his having transmitted the disease to her.[90]

The stigma associated with AIDS compares with that of lepers. In the following quote from Iliffe, comparisons with the leper Saran in Mali are striking:

> Makhale Male found she was HIV-positive in 1993. When she told her husband, he shoved her into a pot of water boiling on the stove, scalding her arm. She went to her job selling shoes "as if everything was okay." But her husband showed up telling her to go back home, get her things and leave him, because how could he live with someone infected with HIV. That was 10.00 in the morning. At 3.00 that afternoon she was fired from her job.[91]

Then there were the charlatans who capitalized on victims of AIDS with phony cures or who attributed the disease to witchcraft—in the latter case, leading to hope and helping reduce the stigma.[92] Opposition from the Catholic Church on the use of condoms was unhelpful, although Catholics in some areas have promoted their use in spite of the church. Then there were the deniers: Thabo Mbeki, as president of South Africa, fell into that category—blaming the disease on poverty. His health minister condemned anti-retroviral treatment for pregnant women despite its being offered free by drug companies. The health minister rejected AIDS drugs as toxic and actively promoted garlic and beetroot as cures. In the early years, these drugs were very expensive and beyond the ability of the huge majority of those afflicted to pay for them. Mbeki embraced the AIDS deniers just when drug companies were being pressed to make drugs more affordable. Policies changed when Mbeki was replaced by none other than Jacob Zuma—with the support of Nelson Mandela.

In 2007, Stephanie Nolen published *28 Stories of AIDS in Africa*, interviews she conducted with victims across the continent (south of the Sahara). Nolen begins her book with a case study from Malawi during a visit she made there as a journalist in 2002.[93] In a small village with people interconnected via familial relationships or as neighbors, Nolen began to realize that "it was hundreds of people. If they weren't sick themselves, they were caring for the sick."[94] The disease impacted the entire community: fewer people to work in the fields, fewer people to teach the children—those children not yet sick themselves, and the orphans of those who had already died and thus had to be cared for. Nolen went to the only hospital in Lilongwe (the capital) and was unable to locate the single doctor. But she did encounter a nurse, whom she described as "stout and slovenly and clearly drunk." After seeing the lines of people "everywhere" waiting and "bone thin and covered in lesions and abscesses," Nolen confessed that she too "felt in desperate need of a stiff drink."[95]

It is to Nolen that we now turn for the life history of Alice Kadzanja from Zomba Central Hospital in southern Malawi.[96]

Alice Kadzanja

It began a couple of years after she graduated from nursing school in 1980. A rumor went around the clinic where she worked that a fellow nursing sister had been diagnosed with AIDS. "People were running away from her," Alice Kadzanja recalled, "saying, 'She's HIV! She's HIV!'" Then another nurse fell ill, not long after, and then so many more. The grim running tally she keeps in her head has reached about two thousand. Two thousand nurses that she worked with or studied with or knew of—all of them killed by AIDS.

"Through the 1990s nurses were disappearing," Alice said, gazing down a crowded hospital hallway through small copper-framed spectacles perched on the end of her nose. "And it got worse and worse. It's not just nurses. Even professors. Or you would ask, 'Where is the cleaner?' They all died. And we are still losing nurses—the government is blaming emigration to rich countries. But in fact, they die."

This goes some way toward explaining the state of the clinic where Alice works today. Zomba Central Hospital, in southern Malawi, is one of the main medical centers in the country. Zomba is the poorest district in the fourth-poorest country in the world, and one of the worst hit by AIDS. Nearly 20 percent of adults have the virus, and three-quarters of admissions to the hospital are HIV related. Zomba Central has three hundred beds, and it runs at 400 percent occupancy: that means two or three skeletal patients in each old iron bed, and many more on the floor. It means sick babies tucked under benches and women in labor left alone in a fly-filled ward. Alice remembers all the niceties of bedside nursing she learned in college, fluffing pillows, wiping sweaty foreheads and offering encouraging words—but there's no time for any of that now: she is one of just six registered nurses in the hospital.

Alice herself came perilously close to being one of Malawi's lost nurses, although the sight of her today—towering, imperious, like a rugby player in a crisp white uniform—makes that hard to believe. "I'm strong like anything," she told me not long after we met at Zomba Central in mid-2005. "You'll never see me reporting sick."

But in June 2002, she was thin and weak, plagued with pneumonia and coughing up blood. Malawi's public hospitals had no ARVs [anti-retrovirals] then, but one could buy the drugs privately, for a hefty fee. Alice, then forty-four, was a research nurse for an international project, and she earned a good salary, $225 a month. So she juggled the family budget and bought the pills. In a matter of weeks, the lung infections were gone and she was back at work, healthy and strong. But all around her, doctors and nurses and technicians kept dying, and it was no mystery what killed them. . . . . I went to Malawi once or twice a year from 2002 onward, and I saw the Herculean efforts being made, and the rare degree of international assistance, and I wanted to know why they were having so little impact on the rate of death. A few days after I met Alice, I went to see Biswick Mwale, a debonair and jovial workaholic doctor who heads Malawi's National AIDS Commission. I put the question to him, and he threw up his hands in frustration. "As much as we want to do scale-up, there are no bodies," he said. "People can't translate money into action when there are no people." The impact of AIDS on Malawi's public system has been crushing. "We have only 10 percent of the physicians we need," Health Minister Hetherwick Ntaba has said, "and only about a third of the nurses." In 2005, this nation of twelve million people had just two thousand nurses and a hundred doctors working in all its public hospitals. It had a total of eleven obstetrician-gynecologists. The vacancy rate for surgeons was 85 percent, for pathologists, 100 percent (that is, the public health service didn't have a single one). The Ministry of Health said that a solid two-thirds of its jobs were unfilled—and that assumes a level of normal staffing so lean as to be unthinkable in a Western Hospital.

So next I went to see Anthony Harries, the government's technical adviser in HIV care and support, in his office in the eerily quiet Health Ministry building on the edge of the capital. He told me the health service had a 2 percent mortality rate. That didn't sound too bad—until he talked me through the math. "With 2 percent mortality, compound it over ten years and you are losing 25 to 30 percent of your health- care workers to death. And before they die, they are sick and can't work."

This critical lack of human resources or "capacity" as it is baldly known in the AIDS world, is not unique to Malawi—it is felt across the continent. When the World Health Organization announced in June 2005 that it would fall badly short of its "3 by 5" target, the primary cause cited was lack of skilled staff. Every single country reported long waiting lists of people desperate to start ARV treatment, but said the health system simply did not have the doctors, nurses, counselors or pharmacists to treat them. . . . A couple of days after I met Alice at Zomba Central, she and I sat down in a patch of sun in the open- air waiting room, finally quiet at four o'clock, and she told me her story. Her husband, Johnny, is a college administrator. Shortly after they were married, she began to suspect him of "going around." In 1994, when she was still breastfeeding their youngest child, she developed a painful case of shingles. Alice knew that healthy people don't just get shingles, and that it was ubiquitous in people with HIV. She stopped breastfeeding that day and went to a private lab to try and get an HIV test. At the lab, staff told her, "But there's no medicine, why does it matter? If we tell you yes, we'll just make you depressed." They sent her away.

So Alice went home and told Johnny that if they were going to have sex again, they would have to use a condom. He flatly rejected that idea, sneering that he would just go to "bar girls" instead—"Why would I bother with an old cockroach like you?" Alice flinched as she recounted his words. She knew, and she will tell anyone who asks, that he had infected her. "I was a virgin when we married, so he couldn't blame me." Johnny didn't get tested for HIV until 2002, after he had twice had tuberculosis. He started ARV's himself, and "soon he was very strong and very fat," she said. "He thought he was healed, and so he started moving all about again. I said to him, 'You know you're HIV-positive and you're going to spray it.' But he went right on spending his salary on bar girls. Alice saw it happening all around her: educated people with jobs like hers kept getting sick—her husband's colleagues at the college, the teachers at her children's schools, her co-workers at the hospital. Her own two brothers and her sister, all of them educated like she was, died of AIDS before the end of the 1990s. The people who ought to know better, she told me take the biggest risks of all. . . . The most urgent matter was to get HIV-infected health-care workers to test for HIV and to start those already ill on ARV's so they could return to health and work. And yet, as Alice explained, that is not as easy as it sounds. "The nurses are reluctant to test," she said with a sigh. "Here in Malawi, women of my age who hear they are HIV-positive, they get so depressed." And the shame of the disease is still so great that many continue to deny any possibility that they could be infected, even as they develop signs they recognize just like Alice did her singles infection. That stigma frustrates her enormously, and she has made it a personal mission to cajole and bully her colleagues into getting tested.

In November 2004, she went to work for Dignitas International, a Canadian humanitarian organization that was setting up shop at Zomba Central Hospital in an effort to try to shore up the collapsing health system. Alice got the job of nurse in charge of the Tisungane Clinic (the name means "coming together to help one another" in Chichewa), which was focused on getting people on to treatment. After a couple of months in the job, she nervously approached the kind, young Canadian doctor running the project and confided that she herself had HIV. She was dreading a negative reaction, but instead he told her she could be their best advertisement, and she took the role to heart.

One crisp spring morning in 2005, I watched her get out of a shared minibus taxi, arriving for work, and lean back through the window, lecturing the driver even as he started to pull away. "There is no reason for you to die, since we've got medicine," she scolded him. "Look at me, I'm also HIV-positive, I'm on ARVs, I'm strong, I can take care of my children!" Smoothing her white skirt as she stepped into the hospital, she shook her head. "These people, they tell me, 'You don't look like one of them. . . .'" Inside the clinic, the low wooden benches were filled with thin, coughing, grim-faced patients. Alice herded one group into a room and, in her deep, gruff voice, began their education. She told them how a person gets HIV: from sex and bold products and mothers passing it to their babies. She told them how the virus works, keeping their body from fighting off the bad germs they catch. And she told them about antiretrovirals: how they must take a pill at six o'clock every morning and six o'clock every evening, every single day, to make them well again." . . . But it snatches the key to your cells out of the virus's hand, so it can't get inside. Your virus stays, but the drugs make it weak so it can't multiply." Surely you know, she pointed out slyly, what it's like to be too weak to have sex? The group laughed, a little shy. Next she told them that they must use condoms when they have sex, and that prompted a ripple of rebellion from the men, who muttered about "eating a sweet with the wrapper on." Alice snorted in frustration: she'd heard *that* many times before. Once again, she explained about spreading the virus, and the risk of getting cross-infected with another strain of HIV.

Then she went back to her office and started calling the names—reading the charts, taking the temperatures, counting out the pills. By midafternoon, her desk was littered with the foil caps of the big drug bottles she had emptied into patients' pill vials. She scolded, joked, teased, hectored: take the tablets at six in the morning, six in the evening, don't come back to see me unless you can't move your arms and legs anymore. "I enjoy working here because I'm able to advise—I know the drugs and the side effects, especially the first two weeks of prickly pain," she confided over a cup of milky tea when the last of the patients were gone. "I reassure them—one day you will pick up. This first-hand experience makes me a better nurse. . . ." Alice earns $430 at the Dignitas clinic, a good monthly salary in Malawi, but even so, she said, "I'm failing to manage." She has a daughter and a son in college, whose tuition she covers by raising chickens; a daughter hunting for odd jobs to pay for college and who dreams of studying in England; it costs $650 a year to keep the youngest two in secondary school; plus she is supporting her sister's two orphans. From the day of her diagnosis, her husband, Johnny, had gone on living with her but contributed nothing to family maintenance; nonetheless, Alice felt she could not divorce him, because divorce is a scandalous thing in Malawi. Then in 2006, he threw her and the children out, installing the bar girl-cum-wife in the family home instead. Alice scrambled, with loans from friends, to rent a small room to house the children. Even the boosted public-sector wages leave staff struggling, and the exodus has not slowed. Although Britain adopted a policy forbidding its public National Health

Service from recruiting staff in developing countries with personnel shortages, private facilities in the U.K. go right on hiring them. Malawian nurses move to London or Birmingham and work for a few months in nursing homes before making the jump to more regular full-time work in the public health service. They can earn fifteen times the salary they had in Malawi; the money they send back is often the only source of income for a vast network of relatives. And the calm, tidy British hospitals, where Malawians join a shift of fifteen or twenty nurses, are another world after Zomba Central.

Alice understands the temptation. She won't leave Malawi now, because she wants to keep a close eye on her children, but when they are finished school she thinks she might try Britain. While Malawi's government pleads with nurses to stay, Alice thinks that unfair. Her colleagues who leave for England have orphaned nieces and nephews to feed and put through school, she said, and they had no choice.[97]

Despite the increasing egregious expenditures—an expensive jet plane for instance—on the part of President Bingu Wa Mutharika, and the lavish lifestyle he led, Mutharika launched a national policy to counteract the rapid spread of AIDS in his country. He appointed officials whose responsibility was to initiate treatment and prevention programs—although resources were severely limited since Malawi was still recovering from the famine of 2002 that presented the worst food crisis in fifty years.[98] In April 2012, Mutharika died of a heart attack, and, despite efforts to conquer HIV, it was still prevalent, especially in the rural areas. Thus, when Joyce Banda, his vice president, succeeded him in office, she faced the challenge not only of AIDS, but of "pulling her troubled South African nation from the brink of economic meltdown."[99]

Banda became the second woman to head an African nation. She was born in Zomba, the southern Malawian town where we met Alice Kadzanja. On assuming office, she decried the spoils of office that marked her predecessors. Indeed, she was so progressive in her policies that, alone among African leaders, Banda advocated changing the laws against homosexuality.[100] Banda reached out to foreign governments and non-governmental organizations for support, and to businesses to invest in her small impoverished country. And she tackled the AIDS problem with considerably more vigor than most of her African counterparts.

In the Central African Republic (CAR), conflict developed between Christians and Muslims (also including along ethnic lines) in late 2013. In January 2014, the National Assembly chose Catherine Samba-Panza as interim president, making her the first woman to lead that troubled nation. Despite ongoing friction, Samba-Panza's appointment was viewed positively. One member of the Central African Women's group expressed the optimism that has not yet been fulfilled, in noting that Samba-Panza was a woman who sympathized with suffering; and a mother who rejected violence. [101] AIDS is secondary to the more pressing needs that have brought forces from outside, including France, to help quell the civil war. Still, CAR, with little in the way of public health facilities, has its share of victims of AIDS as well.

Over in Ghana, in November 2012, the Society for Women and AIDS worked in partnership with the Ghanaian AIDS Commission in organizing a conference on the female condom. This was a practical step in empowering women. If their men were unwilling to protect themselves during sexual intercourse, the women would and will. The head of the Ghanaian AIDS Commission noted that "56 per cent of affected persons in Ghana were women . . . and that women in sub-Saharan African were not only at risk of HIV/AIDS [they] were most affected by the virus. . . . We must all wake up to promote, distribute, educate and use the female condoms."[102] This prescription may be the best possible one for the time being, in warding off this dread disease, which has so devastated a considerable part of Africa.

Female Genital Mutilation/Cutting in Post-Independent Africa

When last we encountered this procedure, we dealt with missionaries and Kikuyu reactions to efforts toward eradicating female circumcision. The term changed to FGM/C, but the practice continued. Among the Kpelle Sande in Sierra Leone and Liberia, initiation into secret societies called for FGM/C and for scarification. Some groups require radical labiadectomies, while others call for clitoridectomies. Those girls who came from educated families or who went to mission schools avoided initiations. But the majority of girls are still subject to both, depending on the requirements of their respective secret society.[103]

One group of people who adopted FGM/C very late, in the mid-twentieth century, was the Jola. The Jola, composed of about 500,000 people, are located in Lower Casamance in Senegal. Due to their proximity to Gambia, the Jola had long established contact with the Muslim Mandinka, who claimed that circumcision was "recommended" for women under the rubric of religion.[104] This is untrue. The Islamic faith does not require FGM for women. During the colonial era, the French induced the Mandinka (and others) to join the cash economy through the production of peanuts. The Jola, as subsistence farmers dependent on rice cultivation, did not earn sufficient profits to meet the taxes that were levied by the French colonial authorities. Thus, many of them turned to growing peanuts and came into closer contact with the Muslim Mandinka, among whom many younger men went to work, crossing the boundary into British Gambia. These young men boarded with Muslim families and soon began to convert to Islam.[105]

Later young women joined the men in Gambia, where they, too, came into contact with the local culture—and Islam is a culture as well as a religion. And, although less reluctant to convert than the men, they found that they could better fit into their new environment by joining female secret societies "associated with Islam and the Mandinka."[106] They not only converted to the religion, but underwent the initiation including FGM. One outcome was that the Jola woman acquired an identity that allowed them to be absorbed into the local social system. They also experienced changes in their economic position that resulted in heavier workloads and loss of economic independence due to factors that included the separation of the sexes under Islam, and the diminished status they enjoyed under their traditional religion as well as Islam.[107]

Some Jola returned to Senegal, as did many of their descendants after conversion to Islam, with the same ill-informed views concerning FGM. As a result, Dellenborg found that the Jola came to view themselves as a separate entity from the rest of the country, with this becoming more pronounced after independence in 1960. The Jola's anti-imperialism pitted them against, first, the French and then the state, creating an even tighter bond among them. The "female circumcision ritual," Dallenborg wrote, "seems to be gaining a particular role in the process." Ironically the Jolla regard this as "part of modernity."[108]

The conflict between those who support and defend FGM and those who oppose it was carried to Europe. After African independence, increasing numbers of former colonials began to stream into urban areas of their former colonial masters, bringing their customs including FGM/C with them. In Europe, although FGM/C was disapproved of, a dilemma developed between the anti-FGM/C group and those who, although not supporters of FGM/C, believed in cultural relativism. The arguments centered on necessity. Almost everyone conceded that FGM/C was not therapeutic. The cultural relativists believed that, by lobbying to outlaw the practice, women's rights were being abused—it was a matter of culture and identity.[109]

Regarding the issue of health, most critics pointed out the possible deleterious effects of even minor scratching of the clitoris. More severe surgeries were dangerous and damaging to women's health. One suggestion was to transfer the surgeries to proper medical facilities—thus making the procedure safer. That, however, failed to satisfy the members of the opposition, who argued that by medicalizing FGM/C more women would see it as legitimate. And, then, there was the issue of sexual pleasure: was it not true that removing parts of the genitalia removes the opportunity for gratification? On the other hand, since this was an age-old practice based on cultural norms (or in some cases erroneous interpretations of scripture), was it fair to the women involved to make these sorts of judgments?[110] In terms of human rights, FGM/C is "condemned" on the basis that women and children have "the right to bodily integrity and that FGM/C is against the spirit . . . of many international instruments" (such as those of the World Health Organization).[111]

In 1985, the United Kingdom passed an act that prohibited FGM/C with some provisions such as the need for cosmetic reconstruction. Then in 1989, FGM "was identified as child abuse."[112] Still the problem persisted, as increasing numbers of Somali and Sudanese refugees came to the UK in significant numbers, with no one able to monitor the practices that occurred covertly. In 1999, a court in France tried twenty-seven women from Mali for "mutilation of minors," which contributed to awareness of the issue there.[113] The Jola, for instance, would have likely migrated to France and would have continued their practice of FGM/C for the religious reasons we have already cited.

Within Africa, legislation was passed against FGM/C by several governments, but the practice has continued. Public health concerns persisted, and awareness of the ill effects was widely publicized in some countries while mostly ignored in others. Agnes Paretic, a Masai from Kenya, underwent FGM in 1965 as a schoolgirl. She tried to resist, but only her father offered support. The women in the family, primarily her mother, insisted. "It . . . spread in my community that I was a coward. So to prove I'm not a coward, I agreed to be cut." It took her three weeks to recover—leaving her with distrust for family members beyond her father. After experiencing FGM, and as an adult, Alice resolved that none of her daughters or "other girls from the Masai community" would be subjected to this procedure. She began involvement with women's organizations in Kenya, with eliminating FGM as her goal. In 1998, Agnes came into contact with a group of girls running away to escape FGM, and that led her to found a home where they could seek respite until they reconciled with their families. In 2000, some women from the United States provided funds to build a "safe house" that would accommodate up to 48 girls, and it is now run by the Tasaru Ntomonok Initiative.[114]

In July 2013, UNICEF released a major study of Female Genital Mutilation/Cutting that covers twenty-five African countries (and Yemen/Iraq). By 2010—the year with the most recent data—twenty-two of the African countries had enacted laws against FGM—and Mali was not among them. The report is statistic laden and includes a wide variety of categories featuring responses from not only women and girls, but in some cases men and boys.[115] It is impossible to provide even a modicum of material from the study, but, in light of the coverage on Kenya and the Kikuyu earlier, some findings relating to them follow.

Some readers may be familiar with Ousmane Sembene's courageous film *Moolade*, which, we are told, stirred debate on the subject.[116] (It seems to have made an impact in Senegal.) In general, girls in wealthiest homes were least likely to be cut or circumcised. In Senegal, only 2 percent of girls from this group experienced FGM/C, compared with 21 percent from less prosperous homes. In Kenya the figures were 2 percent from wealthy homes and 14 percent from other homes.[117] Most surgeries were performed by traditional practitioners: in Senegal, 100 percent; in Kenya, a little over 40 percent, with the balance of the girls' families taking them to health professionals.

Women in about one half of the twenty-seven African countries—based on available data—had the surgery performed on them before they were

Percentage of girls and women aged 15 to 49 years
who have undergone FGM/C, by country.

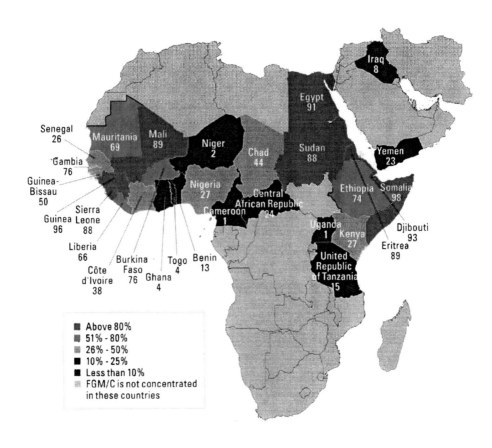

UNICEF map of Africa and FGM/C.
Source: *UNICEF Female Genital Mutilation/Cutting:*
A Statistical Overview and Exploration of the Dynamics of Change, 2013

Percentage of girls and women aged 15 to 49 years
who have undergone FGM/C, by regions within countries.

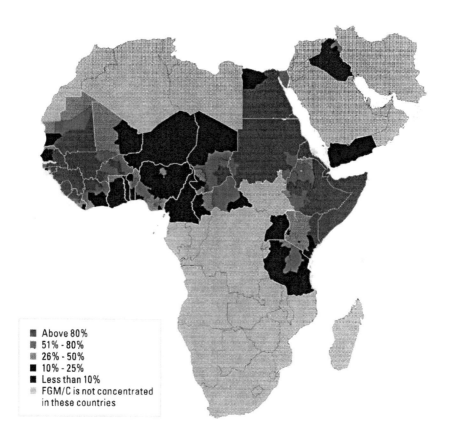

five years of age. In Senegal, however, the data showed that 90 percent were older. In Kenya the numbers varied: approximately 20 percent ages five to nine; approximately 20 percent ages ten to fourteen; and 10 percent at age fifteen or above. In Kenya "mean cutting" ranged from 9 to 16 years, and the figures are defined by ethnic groups that took part in the study. Among the Kikuyu, the mean age was fourteen.[118]

The survey queried girls and women ages fifteen to forty-nine "who had heard about FGM/C" and the issue of whether it should continue. In Kenya the vast majority thought that it should end. Interestingly, in Senegal that figure was more than 80 percent. Among "girls and women with no education," there was more support for FGM/C to continue. In Kenya, among those with no education, the figure was nearly 40 percent. For those with a primary or secondary education, the result was less than 10 percent. In Senegal, among those with no education, the figure was a bit over 20 percent; among those with Muslim controlled or "non-standard" education, the figure was less than 10 percent. (Keep in mind that the Jola are a very small ethnic group and may represent the majority of those who support FGM/C.)[119]

Another chart in the study illustrates that the vast majority of those who support FGM/C by religion are Muslim—another indication of how Islam is being linked with this practice when there is no linkage whatsoever in the religious texts. Among women who underwent the practice and want it to end, in Kenya the figure was around 68 percent; in Senegal it was about 41 percent. Those queried in Kenya reported that FGM has dropped among "some ethnic groups" over three generations. However, the numbers of girls who "were cut before age 10 has increased."[120]

The study also surveyed men and boys for their attitudes. Those findings are not included here, but among the recommendations provided at the conclusion is: "Discussion about FGM/C needs to take place at all levels of society and include boys and men. This is especially important since the data indicate that girls and women tend to consistently underestimate the share of boys and men who want FGM/C to end."[121]

The maps on pages 262 and 263 show the percentage of girls and women aged 15 to 49 years of age who have undergone FGM/C, by country and regions within countries.[122]

Witchcraft and Traditional Medical Practices in Modern Africa

Kikuo Witches Home is in Dagamba territory, near Tamale in northern Ghana. It is one of six existing villages serving women who have been accused of witchcraft. According to informants, camps such as Kikuo, the one featured in Allison Berg's documentary film, have existed for three hundred years. Belief in witchcraft is strong in most African countries, even among those people who are well educated. A male member of Ghana's Human Rights Commission referred to witchcraft as "a delicate subject," even in the twenty-first century. He admitted to being a believer, stating that women "admit it" although it is "contradictory, if hard to deal with."[123] Others surveyed in the capital Accra were equally convinced that witchcraft existed, including a professor of sociology at a university. On the other hand, a female member of Ghana's parliament was quoted as calling for the camps to be shut down. She was sympathetic to the women who were shut away on what she regarded as specious grounds.

The women sentenced to life in the camp revealed various reasons for their incarceration. One said that, if "someone is sick in the family, a witch is suspected and that meant me." Another woman was accused of killing her brother, so "I ran to this place for peace." A third said: "If your people want you back they will ask for you . . . but few do so." Some family members send or bring young girls into the camps to serve as servants of a sort, thus exiling them in the process. One young girl, helping her grandmother, found some outside work so as to buy "things we don't have, like my tobacco." This enterprising girl engaged in trade, buying bananas on credit, and bringing them to the witch's village, where they were sold for a small profit. She said that "Grandmother asked" for her, suggesting that she had no choice, despite her earlier plans to attend school. This desire to attend school may have been unrealistic. The girl, her grandmother, and those women interviewed were poor and illiterate.

The majority of the women—approximately fifty—are Muslim, and Islam is the prevailing religion in the Dagamba area. Despite polygamy being the norm, it is not difficult to suspect that a few of the older women consigned to the camp were wives that were disposable—making it possible for older men to take new young wives. Osman, former husband of one of the central female figures in the film, related that Meimuntu "was my wife. We had six children." His brother became ill and died. Then both Osman and his wife were accused of killing the brother via witchcraft.

Osman was away when retaliation began, and by the time he returned home, "she had been abused." Somehow he was able to avoid persecution, but Meimuntu was sent away to the camp. After her departure, he took another, younger wife. Other men present during the interview noted that Osman "did not want" the original wife. Osman did not answer, but the smirk on his partially bearded face suggested agreement.

The litany of responses encompassed (in the present tense) explanations, such as if a family is unable to protect those accused of practicing witchcraft, "people in the village beat you to death." It was, one of the women allowed, better to be "rescued" and at the camp. Some of the women complained—no doubt quite correctly—that "if you are not liked some will claim that you are a witch." And the claim can result in exile to a camp such as Kikuo. Another respondent spoke of rivalry among wives, the winner staying and the loser being proclaimed a "witch." This older woman said that it was difficult to get money for basic essentials, and thus she began make pots for sale.

Although many of the women in the documentary appeared to be in late middle age or older, the camp also had its younger occupants, and these women were accompanied by their children. In the dialogue between the women and the interlocutor, the consensus was that "it was alright for us now" due to fears of going back. Families had broken down. Troubles might ensue. "Who would want to go back?"[124]

Life is arduous in these camps. The women have to walk through high grass and over impediments of one sort or another (stones/pebbles/climbing rocks) to reach the stream for daily water that they carry back in jugs on their heads. For the older women—and many of them are quite elderly—the trek is exhausting and treacherous. Some carry sticks that they use as canes to aid them in hobbling along. They cut their own firewood. They dwell in small shacks with dirt floors. Relief organizations, at Kikuo at least, provide some funds to help with the diet of mostly gruel.

Contrary to the good intentions by concerned members of parliament in Accra, the editor of the local Tamale paper—who was sympathetic to the plight of the women in Kuku—argued for keeping the camp open. Women, he said, "see it as a sanctuary. They are afraid of being killed" if they are sent back home. An American Catholic priest, John Kirby, succinctly noted that, when it comes to witchcraft in the northern area of Ghana, "one hundred and one percent" are believers. He attributed its continuance to the social insecurity that came as a result of British occupation and the lack of economic development in the north. Poverty, he said, meant that the occult took on special significance among those who could not obtain material goods.

The conclusion—agreed to even among the parliamentarians—was that education is essential to counteract the false beliefs that many Ghanaians hold.[125] Witchcraft has not been confined to Ghana. It is widespread throughout Africa, even among the elite, with roots tied to traditional societies. In South Africa, Johnson reported on "African 'intellectuals' who claimed the 'roots' of modern medicine were African," and therefore they celebrated the traditional healers (*sangomas*). One former ANC MP forsook politics in favor of becoming a *sangoma*.[126] In a wide belt in the southern part of the continent traditional healers are known for stealing and processing body parts for *muti* (medicines). The testicles of small boys are especially desirable for making the healing potions. The *sangomas* sell their medicines in shops and to patrons who call on them for their services. The shops are mainly run by men, but many of the traditional healers in the rural areas are women.

In the early 1990s, in South Africa, two-year-old Nhlanhla Mkwanazi was stolen from his mother. His attackers mutilated his tiny body, cutting off his genitals. Discovered near death, the boy was taken to a local hospital, where, after recovering from slashes to his eyelids and near strangulation, doctors became convinced that the child stood a better chance in adult life as a woman. Repeated skin grafts healed and were followed by three operations that completed the transition from small boy to girl. It was expected that she would be able to enjoy a normal sex life, but she will never know the joy of parenting a biological child.[127]

Whereas the majority of the residents of the witches' villages were Muslim women, the majority of the *sangomas* were traditionalists. Christians were also guilty of being steeped in beliefs that encompass witchcraft, and the treatments were rendered by traditional healers—most of which were specious.

In this chapter, we see that conflict and violence against women has dominated post-independence in several African countries. War rages on in Congo, as do the disputes between Sudan and South Sudan, with Darfur still coming under assault. HIV/AIDS is a scourge that has had an economic and demographic impact in most of these countries, although we touched on but a few of them. The practice of FGM/C is declining, while debate still continues regarding cultural relativism and eradication.

CHAPTER NINE

The March of the Women

Women, Art, and Fashion

Filing the trauma of those years in her archive of memory, Kebedech Tekleab learned to smile again, enrolled at Howard University, and pursued first a bachelor of fine arts degree, followed by a master of fine arts. She joined the faculty at Howard University where, with then renowned Ethiopian artist Askunder Boghossian, she created "Nexus" on commission by the Ethiopian Embassy, which is on permanent display on the Wall of Representation.

In traditional Ethiopia women were relegated to producing handicrafts. The country's long association with Christianity, and the role of the church, meant that most of the murals and paintings centered on religious works, and all these were created by men. After the revolution in 1974, with an emphasis then on equality between the sexes (which did not actually go far or last long), "women as heroines began to appear in posters and paintings.[1] Kebedech was one of the few women who gained admittance to the School of Fine Arts and Design (but not the first), and a small number of women continued to enroll, but only a very few have turned to producing contemporary art. Two of these attended a university in the United States and returned to their home country, where they exhibit. One of these women owns a gallery, where she displays and sells her art, and the other woman works as a studio artist.[2] Several female artists in Ethiopia have broken into the all-male ranks of producing religious art. One of them is a nun; another, self-taught, believes that "her talent came from God" but differs from past stereotypes in that she also now regards God as having given the gift of artistic talent to "both men and women." Among the traditionalists, Yordanos Berhanameskal's father was a recognized artist in Aksum. Although she had no formal training, Yordanos observed and copied her father's

Ama Ata Aidoo
Afua Sutherland

MOROCCO

TUNISIA

ALGERIA

LIBYA

EGYPT

WESTERN
SAHARA

Cerinah Nebanda

MAURITANIA

Tirunesh Dibaba

MALI

NIGER

CHAD

SUDAN

ERITREA

Yordanos Berhanameskal

THE
GAMBIA

SENEGAL

DJIBOUTI

Iman, Waris Dirie

GUINEA
BISSAU

GUINEA

BURKINA

BENIN

SOMALIA

Nadifa Mohamed

SIERRA
LEONE

COTE
D'IVOIRE

TOGO

GHANA

NIGERIA

ETHIOPIA

Yvonne Adhiambo Owuor
Lea Itta Sigei
Vivian Cheruiyot
Kay Makuku

LIBERIA

Chinue Uwatse

CAMEROON

CENTRAL
AFRICAN
REPUBLIC

SOUTH
SUDAN

UGANDA

KENYA

Wangari Maathai

Ngozi Okonjo-Iweala

REP. OF
THE
CONGO

Winnie Ojanga

Buchi Emecheta

GABON

DEMOCRATIC
REPUBLIC
OF THE CONGO

RWANDA

Grace Ogot

Jaiyeola Aduke Alakija
Flora Nwapa

BURUNDI

Magdalene Odundo

TANZANIA

Wambui Waiyaki Otieno

(President) Ellen
Johnson Sirleaf

Gertrude Mongella

Christine Obbo

MALAWI

NoViolet Bulawayo
[Elizabeth Tshele]

Janet and Joy Ngundutse

ANGOLA

ZAMBIA

Bessie Head

Mariama Ba

ZIMBABWE

MOZAMBIQUE

MADAGASCAR

Ntombephi Ntombela and Bev Gibson

NAMIBIA

BOTSWANA

Esther Mahlangu

Nontsielelo Veleko

Caster Semenya

Nadine Gordimer

LESOTHO

SWAZILAND

Mamphela Ramphele

SOUTH
AFRICA

Olive Schreiner

Miriam Tlali

Frene Ginwala

Sindiwe Magona

Miriam Makeba

Helen Suzman

Albertina Sisulu

painting. She produces religious art—paintings and icons—for tourists.[3]

Our attention now shifts to contemporary female artists elsewhere who have mainly remained in their countries, but who have received international attention. According to Constantine Petridis, curator of African art at the Cleveland Museum of Art, traditional creative works by women "such as beadwork" and baskets and ceramics "were not taken seriously by museums or collectors as art." These works were relegated "to culture and when acquired, were seen as ethnological objects, not art. Missionaries, especially Catholic priests, shipped back myriad masks, statues and shrines but not ceramic or beadwork. Women as artists . . . created no interest until the post-colonial period."[4]

Recently women's handiwork has come into its own, from collectors, museums, and tourists as well as from local partisans. Gahaya Links was founded by two Rwandan sisters—Janet and Joy Ngundutse—with the purpose of not only celebrating the art of basket weaving, but also offering local Rwandan rural women with a modicum of economic support. Their craft organization set out to help those who survived the genocide in Rwanda—spreading the message of peace and hope as well as providing useful skills to several thousand women.[5] Here we see art with a purpose, while extending and incorporating the traditional medium.

Down in South Africa, Ntombephi Ntombela and Bev Gibson established Uhuhle Beads with a similar purpose: to empower local women through teaching the art of beading. In Kwa-Zulu-Natal, these skills are taught to several hundred women, who creatively produce pictures from beads as well as jewelry. Their products are sold in local venues, with the profits reinvested for education and community needs.[6] Another South African took a traditional form of art and applied it in a new direction. Esther Mahlangu is a muralist, whose own origins are in the Ndebele community. The Ndebele were famous for bright colorful designs on their small rural homes. Mahlungu, who learned to paint as a child, transitioned from traditional house decoration to "murals to canvas." She has enjoyed an international reputation, having exhibited in South Africa and abroad. Several of her works are now in European museums. Thus we see how early African traditional art can be the basis for works that develop an appreciation in the larger world.[7]

When we think of pottery and Africa, we generally think of function, not creativity. Yet, Kenyan-born Magdalene Odundo has established a major reputation in artistic circles for her original designs. She received her higher education in England, including a Master of Arts degree from the Royal College of Art. Her sculpted designs have been exhibited in museums in North and South America and Europe as well as in Africa. Among her achievements—at a relatively young age, as she was born in 1976, is the award of the Order of the British Empire. Odundo describes her technique as using "coiling, hand building, and sculpting" to create vessels so original that some of them present anthropomorphic interpretations in their design.[8]

In Nigeria, Chinue Uwatse paints. She represents a particular form of art, "uli," that is usually associated with women and Igbo traditions. Uwatse's works have been collected by Westerners and feature in major exhibits of African art.[9] Perhaps as a reminder of the talents of the Igbo, despite their travail, Uwatse has received recognition in her home country for her art, her poetry, and her essays. Uwatse's concept of women bears repeating and absorbing: "The 'average woman' is an anomaly; we are 'superwomen.' We have charm, intellect, but at the same time a certain fragility that can divert our resolved. We be [sic] fixed between worlds; neither old nor new, on the contrary, we can articulate both. We are auspicious women!"[10]

Another form of art that many outsiders identify with Africa is hair design—already noted by Mary Kingsley in her late-nineteenth-century travels in parts of West Africa.[11] That tradition has continued even with more ultra-modern women. The fiber extensions fill out and lengthen hair. In fact this particular form of design has made its way across cultures. Elaborate hairstyles feature interweaving gold, silver pieces, or even bits of wood.[12] Swahili women, borrowing on an Arab tradition, often include strung gold or silver coins around their coiffure. Body tattoos and decorated perforations of the skin are disappearing. The old National Geographic models of this sort of assault on the female body have almost all been relegated to the pre-colonial past. For that we can be grateful to the missionaries.

On the other hand, the missionaries objected to women wearing local tanned leather clothing, especially skirts that were revealing (often displaying their genitals). This clothing was considered unhygienic, as opposed to cotton, which could be easily washed and could be made to cover more of the body. Women were leather workers among the Xauta in southern Ethiopia, producing several types of skirts: each style signified a transitional period in a woman's life, such as marriage and pregnancy. From missionary complaints and then a desire to modernize, the local governor imposed a ban on leather skirts in 1960. This created a hardship on the female artisans, who were forced to make "utilitarian mats and bags," and no doubt for less income.[13] And it failed to take into consideration the cultural norms that "signaled important stages in women's lives" as well as their identity and personal choice of dress. For those who ignored the ban, punishment followed.[14] Here we have an example of the "body" being targeted, and fashion dictated by outsiders and the local government.

The most modern forms of art are now being practiced by African women. For instance, Nontsielelo Veleko, another South African, is a well-respected photographer. Trained in a local photography workshop, Veleko soon outgrew her humble training with works that have been displayed in Europe, the United States, and, of course, in South Africa.[15] Fashion design comes under the rubric of art, and this leads us to another modern creative woman: Kenyan Winnie Ojanga. Starting her career in 2007 with her own creations—those in which she said she hoped to capture "femininity, elegance, class and style"—Ojanga rapidly swept onto the larger stage of fashion design. By 2010 she was nominated for "European Fashion Designer of the Year." Although the prize eluded her, customers and admirers did not. Never losing sight of her home base, she aims to share her designs and her experiences with her Kenyan followers, while her designs are worn by top models in Europe.[16]

Finally, another well-known name in fashion is Iman, whose homeland is Somalia. She, like Kedebech, is a refugee—albeit a very successful one. In 1969, when she was seventeen, Said Barre took power from the then Somali government. Imam's father, a diplomat, was arrested. Upon his release, the family fled to Tanzania. Iman attended university in Kenya, where she was discovered by an American photographer: her height, beauty, and poise attracted his attention. Soon she was modeling and was quickly sought in Europe, where she rose to the very top as a supermodel. Married to singer David Bowie, and an American citizen, Iman has attempted to keep in contact with her Somali roots despite the dangers of traveling to her home country. In 1998, Iman toured refugee camps and visited one of the war-torn villages. This was her first trip back in twenty years and was "full of emotional agony." The purpose was to make a documentary film that "would put a face on pain," where more than "100,000 people had died from drought and warfare." Iman (and her husband) have remained active in promoting human rights and in campaigns to care for children suffering from HIV/AIDS. Of note, Iman's cousin, Waris Dirie, came from a more traditional family background and was circumcised at the age of five. Waris Dirie, also a model, has authored several books and has worked with the United Nations to eradicate FGM.[17]

Woman and Literature

We have drawn on Emecheta's *The Joys of Motherhood* and Adichie's *Half a Yellow Sun* for insights into historical events. We will return to Nigeria and other women writers of fiction, but first we look to South Africa and the first woman novelist to have her work published. Olive Schreiner's *Story of an African Farm* was issued in England in 1883 under the pseudonym Ralph Iron.[18] This daughter of a German LMS missionary and his English wife was born in 1855. Schreiner's early life was hardscrabble—the father was more successful in producing children (twelve children; six lived) than in his missionary work. He was moved from place to place in South Africa, including a brief sojourn in the semi-desert region of the Karoo. Shreiner was forced early on to seek employment which, due to her mother's home schooling, enabled her to secure positions as a governess to several families. By 1881 Schreiner had written two book-length manuscripts, with a third under way, and she had saved enough money to go to England, where she hoped to achieve her goal of becoming a medical doctor.[19] Ill health intervened, and Schreiner was forced to abandon medicine; instead she became acquainted with a varied group of people in England, including Eleanor Marx, Emily Hobhouse, and Havelock Ellis, with whom she formed a lifelong friendship. Involving herself in the British suffrage movement, Schreiner also sought a publisher for her work—finally interesting Chapman and Hall in *The Story of an African Farm*. Soon after the book was published in 1883, Shreiner returned to South Africa as a heroine of sorts, although she was opposed to British colonialism as well as to the attitudes there regarding people of color: "They are victims of a shallow, bigoted religion . . . its easy references to God and authority."[20] While it may seem ironic, considering Boer attitudes toward their darker brethren, Shreiner was sympathetic to their cause during the South African War.

When Emily Hobhouse established the South African Women and Children's Distress Fund, Shreiner became a contributor. Another actual irony is that her novel dealt with the oppression of women—and, as noted, it was written before she went to England or had any awareness of the suffrage movement. Raised in a home where the Bible was paramount, Schreiner had lost her faith in organized religion, and this was before leaving South Africa.

The Story of an African Farm was highly autobiographical. It is set in the Karoo, a desolated area with beautiful vistas of the mountains rising from the nearly barren plateau, and it involves a family of ostrich farmers whose lives are complicated by marriages, intruders, and loss. Lundall, early on a protagonist, goes away from the farm for four years. On her return, she brings with her subversive views such as on the conditions of women, agnosticism, and race. Southern African novelist Doris Lessing wrote that this was "the 'first' real book" that she had read due to the realism in which Schreiner depicted Africa.[21] After her marriage, the South African War, and the birth of the newly united country, Schreiner's second novel, *Women and Labour*, was published. The third and incomplete manuscript that she took to England with her in 1881 remained unfinished at her death in 1920. Schreiner made another journey to England for medical treatment, and she was forced to stay until the end of World War I (which she opposed).[22]

Nadine Gordimer.
Source: Nobel Prize Committee

Nadine Gordimer, who died in 2014, was the most renowned of South Africa's female authors. Her literary output encompassed fifteen full-length novels, several short stories, essays, a play, screenplays, documentaries (one with her husband), and her partial autobiography, *Lifetimes under Apartheid.*[23] She was awarded the Booker Prize for *The Conservationist* in 1974, and the Nobel Prize in Literature in 1991, with myriad other literary prizes falling in between. Born in 1923 in the small mining town of Springs, Gordimer had witnessed profound changes in this country from which she would never seek exile, despite her "sustained literary response" to an ever-oppressive government.[24] Among her many contributions to the genre, as well as to her country, was Gordimer's early call for "a national literature" that included blacks: "My own definition is that African writing is writing done in any language by Africans themselves."[25] Her stance was that, as a Caucasian writer, Gordimer was no less an African. While the major output in her oeuvre was concerned with apartheid and the human effects that it has on all races, after the ANC (which she supported) became the major political party in the country, Gordimer changed course. This was especially the case in *The Pickup*, published in 2002.

The Pickup departs from Gordimer's focus on internal events, once she establishes the themes of isolation and class within South Africa. The male protagonist is an Arab from an undefined, poor, politically conflicted part of the Middle East.[26] The human factors in this work loom large, as does the subordination of women, from the young Julie, who is emotionally abandoned by her wealthy divorced parents, to the women Julie encounters in the Arab world she joins. Julie is a free spirit, whose friends in Cape Town are South Africa's version of white hippies, including a 1960s bearded poet. The Muslim Arab enters into this eccentric crowd of friends, who meet regularly at a table in a nondescript restaurant. Then the mechanic Julie meets when her car breaks down often joins the group at her invitation. Here, Gordimer brings in multiculturalism. "The pickup" becomes her lover. Julie's dysfunctional family gains Gordimer's attention, while Ibrahim (under the pseudonym Abdu) plays foil. He is found to be illegally living in South Africa. He is sent back to his desolate homeland. Julie elects to go along. She finds family and security in this desolate place despite the privations that are alien to her former life. She wins over Ibrahim's mother, the object of Ibrahim's true devotion—only at the end to discover that that he has used her to achieve his end: to escape from the closed world that rejected her earlier. Julie, blanketed in the folds of his family, refuses to leave.

As the story ends, Ibrahim is departing on the money Julie secured from a family member in South Africa. His objectives are achieved. Hers was waiting from him to return. The late Christian Palestinian scholar Edward Said called this novel "a master piece of creative empathy . . . a griping [*sic*] tale of contemporary anguish . . . and it also opens the Arab world to unusually nuanced perception."[27]

Among South Africa's trove of women writers are several who approach the issues of race and apartheid from their perspective as members of the black community. In 1979, Miriam Tlali's *Muriel at the Metropolitan* was banned on publication. The story is set in a furniture store that specializes in exploiting blacks by selling to them overpriced items on credit. The cast of characters include black men, whose job is to repossess these goods and who suffer internally from the consequences, and the white owner and two white clerks plus Muriel, the black typist. This compellingly written story features the details of economic injustices experienced under apartheid.[28] Sindiwe Magona, in *Living, Loving, and Lying Awake at Night*, presents a series of short stories featuring domestics and their relationships with their madams in "Women at Work." Realism is interwoven with irony and coupled with resignation.[29]

Although born in South Africa, the so-called Coloured writer Bessie Head is remembered for her years in Botswana and for the novels and stories she produced during her long years in exile. Head's birth to a white mother and an unknown black father resulted in her mother's incarceration in an institution for the mentally ill, with the baby girl being sent into foster care. Life was difficult from the beginning and, for the most part, remained so until Head's death in 1986. She began her professional life as a journalist, married another, gave birth to her son Howard in 1963, and moved with her family to Port Elizabeth, where her husband became the first African reporter on a progressive local paper. But the Heads had a troubled marriage. Although they each remained active in opposition politics, when the government clamped down on the African Resistance Movement in 1964, Harold Head went to England, and Bessie, with the baby, headed for Bechuanaland (Botswana). She went on a "one-way exit permit," meaning that she was stranded with no citizenship. Due to a series of untoward incidents, some coming from a nervous breakdown, Bessie was unable to secure citizenship in Botswana until 1979, or just seven years before she died.[30]

Her early years in Botswana were fraught with economic hardship and were marked by the support of other white South Africans there who valued her despite her often troublesome antics and outbursts. The negatives, however, did not prevent Head from producing two well-received novels: *When Rain Clouds Gather* (1968) and *Meru* (1971). Soon thereafter the forces of darkness gathered, and, in the wake of the publication of her second novel, Bessie was hospitalized for the madness that had gradually been enveloping her fragile psyche. Despite a diagnosis that had been made years before her release, Bessie bounced back and within six months was back at home with her son. Howard had been in the care of generous friends. She was not entirely well, and the lingering memories associated with her time in the abyss were incorporated in her next, semi-autobiographical novel, *A Question of Power* (1978).

Randolph Vigne, a journalist, antiquarian, and political activist (a founder of the Liberal Party), established a warm friendship with Bessie from her early days as a journalist in Cape Town. In 1964, Vigne fled South Africa to escape arrest. Whereas she tried the patience of many—among them stalwart supporters—Bessie's relations with Randolph rested on an even keel. From exile in England, Vigne helped her immeasurably, from raising money for her support in Botswana to assisting her in her difficulties with publishers and, always, writing her thoughtful and generous letters. After Bessie returned from the mental hospital she wrote him about her experiences and her slow, troubled recovery.

4. Serowe (2)

29 June 1971 – May 1975

[67]

P.O. Box 15, Serowe
29 June 1971

Dear Randolph,

I've just got home. I was locked up in a loony bin for nearly 3 months. Howard is alright.

The truth is I'd lived in a sort of nightmare here for a long time. By end of 1970 I was so broken I could hardly walk. I broke down and poured out the torture in incoherent fashion. I got locked up. At first I just felt relief to seem to have thrown off the horrors that haunted me. But I broke my life here. I am sorting out what to do as the next best thing. I have a little money to keep me going. Howard is alright. Remember I kept on asking you to take care of him? It was that nightmare life. It went on and on and no end and it stemmed from the soul and others were involved. You said not to come to England. I am not sure what to do.

Bessie

[69]

P.O. Box 15, Serowe
13 August 1971

Dear Randolph,

Thanks so much for your letters. I'm not as mad and depressed as the last letter I wrote to you. At least I'm standing up on very shaky legs.

God knows how I wish I could go away somewhere. It's just not that easily done, when you have no travel documents and I have been in touch with United Nations for years, especially while living in Francistown. That song "I have to go away" has been going on for years and years because all the wrong things were happening. Half of it was one man, then another man, then another man and weird versions of love in the air, accompanied by abnormal sights. *Marui* gives a good insight into the situation. I keep on looking back along the road I've travelled and seem to see no alternative to the disaster, as though it were something I had to go through with, and end. I am only crying about the people who got hurt because it was not so bad when I kept silent but once I started speaking, I said both vile and violent things because I could not endure any more torture. It is what I said that so sickens me. You know, very few people understand deep horror, fanatical possessiveness, the extremes of emotion, a kind of battle where evil is used to outwit the enemy, or if not to outwit, then to sever memories. I eventually found myself pulled right down to that level. The terrible thing is that

I did it all by myself when I was ill in health. No standards of nobility remained. You wouldn't understand emotional involvement like that because you refer to your better judgment but now I question love and am deeply afraid of it because its other face is evil. You can come up against a sort of love so vehement and cruel that it is hardly fit for human society. You can find people glued to you like cement and they won't let go and the links were not made now, but centuries ago. The surprise was to pick up those links in a god-forsaken country like Botswana. Everything was here, the past and the future. I was struggling to destroy the past, knowing that it had no place in the future.

Randolph, I deeply value your care and affection and concern for me. Please don't let go of me. There is one thing I can say for myself. I have survived many impossible situations, maybe that is the worst, but I should see my way out of it too because of Howard, for one thing, and because I have learnt so much. It is like saying that really bad experiences create a new perfection. I wouldn't have known the depths of feeling if I had not been dragged down to them and disliked them. I think there is something wrong with superficial goodness and most people are protected by that. I was not allowed that covering and if in the future I say: I can harm no one, I can do no wrong—it is only because of experience, which was real in its way.

I am writing a little and this letter is very much taken from my present themes of thought—that seeing and feeling evil was of value to me, for the future. . . .

I wish like you say that I could leave Botswana. I don't have that much money. I also wanted to say that the war that was going on was not over B. Head, the living woman, but over the soul and its past wealth. B. Head, the living woman, had little opportunity or occasion to create any beauty, such as I saw behind me, where love was a big flare that lit up the skies and piled up great wealth (that is if you take it that the soul has a long history behind it.) I seemed to do little but be swayed this way and that by internal storms and a fierce pull and tug. There was a terrible and persistent theme of obscenity, I think mainly to break me down. I fought it for a long time and what came out over Christmas was the obscenity. What I said then would have made your hair stand on end. It was thought that I was suffering from a form of insanity not yet known on earth but then people know very little about the soul. I knew nothing until I went right through the mill and now I wonder if some years of suffering pay for centuries of hell and that it was well worth it.

Liz Van Rensburg [a friend] told me she had written you an angry letter asking you to do something about my situation as they thought nothing could cure me. I think it was unease at having me around here that caused it. From my side I knew how private was the struggle I was waging and to a certain extent I don't follow the whole process that forced it out into the open. I do nothing drastic unless under pressure that gets too great for me. Years and years of my life went in peaceful solitude, of some kind or the other.

Life is a funny thing. There are no clear warnings along the way, even for the very alert and there is something strange about the soul; it won't get relaxed and free and ungrasping unless suffering is so excruciating as to be a big howl. It is at that point that it widens out and becomes beautiful. I half wish to live a little longer because just now the churning around of thought is much more pleasing to me than it was some time ago.

We were still talking about God and church when I went to the loony bin. You said: "Be still and know that I am God." God is such a vague proposition in the heat of living and so often when I look back on what has been said, God seems to me to be the personality of individuals. I was also just taken aback suddenly about your going to church and mentioning it because we never discussed such a thing before. Also when I say the personality of individuals I mean what they work out for themselves as standards of goodness and some of these standards became universal. God knows I am wild enough to look for the God of the Anglican church: "Be Still." I have a habit of talking to something at night, just to get above myself; but peace of heart, the stirrings of wonder, the things that made the earth and the heavens glow, all came from living people. I wish the unknown God could walk in on me sometime, unexpectedly and say: "Here I am. Now love me." It might have happened to me in some other age and time but I am following through something just at a point where I am down on my knees—how much is personality because it gets you through so much and when you are really broken that's when you ought to see how you will survive.

Please Randolph, whatever else happens, keep a hold on me somewhere and please keep writing.

As ever,
Bessie[31]

NoViolet Bulawayo's first book, *We Need New Names*, was shortlisted for the 2013 Booker Prize.[32] NoViolet was born in Zimbabwe following independence in 1980. Her childhood is marred by racial and political incidents. As Robert Mugabe became increasingly tyrannical, the country spun into economic deprivation for all but his close supporters. The first part of the novel deals with a gang of youths, including Darling (the protagonist), that roam the landscape of the country with empty bellies, which they attempt to satisfy by stealing guava fruit from the whites in "Budapest." They encounter the racism of whites who are dispossessed of their home while they are stealing the guava. "I am ashamed" for the white woman who, in her furor at being taken away, "keeps looking like maybe she wants to pluck us out of the tree with her eyes." Later a member of the gang is murdered. This is "Bornfree," whose name is one of many extraordinary labels NoViolet gives her characters, including "Bastard"; "Paradise" is where they live, and "Budapest" is where the whites dwell with the guava trees. We are given a hint that the scene is going to change when, early on, Darling mentions that she intends to go to America. Her aunt lives in Detroit, where Darling arrives in the second half of the novel. It is cold. Snow is on the ground. Wistfully she looks back to Zimbabwe, but then she remembers the hunger: "then we wouldn't be having enough food, which I will stand being America." However, Darling notes that "I find food does nothing for me, like I am hungry for my country and nothing is going to fix that."[33] This is a mere hint of a touching new novel by a young author.

Kenyan writer Grace Ogot was trained as a nurse in London before turning to journalism and the BBC as a broadcaster in her home country (plus other employment in several fields). In 1984, Ogot was elected to Kenya's parliament, serving for a time as an assistant minister. Earlier, in 1959, she married the historian Bethwell Allan Ogot, by whom she bore four children. Her first published work, a volume of short stories, was followed by five novels. In spite of her professional activities, her growing family, her flow of fiction, Ogot squeezed in a number of essays and articles. But she tells us all of this and more in her autobiography, *Days of My Life*.[34]

Ogot's first novel, *The Strange Bride*, set the pace for her other fiction. She drew on traditional Luo culture and folktales. The daughter of a couple disappears. In time, they conclude that she is dead, and they begin the rituals associated with death, including burying the "fruit of the sausage tree" as representative of the missing body. Then, the child reappears. The family queries the grandmother (the font of traditional wisdom) about what could have happened: "If you have secret knowledge about the disappearance and return of this child, please, don't hide it . . . ." The grandmother advises that they go "and listen to the voice of the divining stones," because the ancestors will "reveal" all of them. After a few failed attempts, one of the stones "danced," and the grandmother is able to read the performance thusly: the mother of the wife of the couple had died a long time ago. She was lonely and had no help for chores. The diviner saw the dead mother, who loved the child "very much; and that's why she came back and took the child to go and keep her company."[35] Will the grandmother return and take her back again? "No, she will not take the girl away again," as it appears to her that the family needs her, and "that is why she allowed her to come back."[36] Here we see the occult, Luo traditions (reading the stones), and a happy ending—to that part of the story at least. Much of Ogot's writing falls into this genre of storytelling, including *The Promised Land* (1966), which drew more heavily on Luo culture.

Another Kenyan woman, Yvonne Adhiambo Owuor, has received critical comment for her 2014 novel, *Dust*. This work is far from the traditional narrative we often associate with African storytellers. One reviewer referred to the "sort of lawless power" in Owuor's text, while "critics may object to the novel's unapologetic density" and perhaps the emotionality is too over powering.[37] Readers will have to determine for themselves, especially regarding the emotionality. *Dust* is both satirical and phantasmagoric (but then perhaps Kenya did have a camel-led "National Library Services caravan?)."[38]

In a more traditional form of the African novel, Somali writer Nadifa Mohamed's *The Orchard of Lost Souls* features Somali women and their trials from the late 1980s until the country disintegrated. Although Nadifa Mohamed was only five years of age when her family left Somalia, she has a keen appreciation for events that occurred as the country became the failed state it is today. Women are depicted as victims with no power who are forced to endure all sorts of violence. But women also are described as providers—in Hargeisa "women are running their families because of the streets have been emptied of men."[39] This young author has created a powerful, and all too accurate, story of her native land.

Shifting to West Africa, we encounter Flora Nwapa, who was an activist in the Biafran War, as well as a writer. Her novel *Efuru* was published in 1966. The story is based on Igbo traditional folktales and includes a goddess who entices Efuru to become a priestess. As such, she can control her own destiny—thus representing an early feminist stance. Her second novel, *Idu* (1970), also draws on folklore and also features strong women characters. When the works were initially published, Nwapa was not recognized beyond a few notices in Nigeria. It was only when scholars began to turn their attention to African women writers that Nwapa's books bore scrutiny in the larger world of literary analysis, especially on the part of feminists.[40]

Buchi Emecheta has enjoyed a long and distinguished writing career. Beyond *The Joys of Motherhood* and *Destination Biafra*, she has almost equaled Nadine Gordimer in literary output—nine novels—and has won several awards. Her early marriage resulted in several children and, soon after the birth of the last, a divorce. Her husband was abusive. His abuse was reinforced when she gave him her first book to read, and he burned the manuscript. In 1966, Emecheta left him and took the children to England, where she published her first novel in 1972. It, like much of her work, is partially autobiographical—describing her own experiences of discrimination in a poor London neighborhood.[41] Her last novel, *The Rape of Shavi* (1983), is referred to as the most critically acclaimed of her works. It "presents an allegory of the encounter between Africa and Western modernity" in a setting that involves a group of Europeans who have fled nuclear war and who end up in the African kingdom of Shavi.[42]

Ghanaian writer Ama Ata Aidoo gave early voice to women's concerns.

Her writings—poetry, short stories, and plays—range from the contrasts associated with urban versus rural life and Westernization; to questions surrounding beauty and what defines it; to husbands who fail to support their wives and families; and to women's oldest profession—prostitution. Farranging in her interests, Aidoo reached into the realm of folk literature in her plays, but she places them within the context of modern theater. Her aim was to extend "the dilemma" folktale into an "extension of the audience's society," making theater relevant to the "theater-goers experience."[43] Like Mary Kingsley, Aidoo saw benefits to polygamy as well as other traditional customs that she believed served a purpose. She relied on history, too, for her work—her portrayal of slavery is brutal and poetic: "I dreamt that I was a big woman. And from my insides were huge holes out of which poured men, women and children." The people were all taken to the sea, where "many giant lobsters" with claws "seized the men and women as they poured out of me, and they tore them apart. . . . Since then, any time there is mention of a slave, I see a woman who is me."[44]

Aidoo was celebrated as a dramatist along with her Ghanaian counterpart, Afua Sutherland. Whereas Aidoo's experiences have been broader and have resulted in academic appointments at major universities, Sutherland pioneered in developing theater in her native country. She and her then American husband established a school in Ghana's up-country, and she also founded the Ghana Drama Studio as a workshop for those who specialized in children's literature. In addition, she was behind the formation of Panafest, a festival celebrating Africans and those in the diaspora coming together to celebrate their cultural heritage (1992). Sutherland also held academic appointments at the University of Ghana, Legon. Producing, organizing, and teaching did not preclude Sutherland from a steady stream of literary outpourings. She, again like Aidoo, drew on traditional folktales and stories, transferring them into modern drama. In *Edufa* (1967), Sutherland drew on traditional belief systems, incorporating them into Western ceremonies, and portraying the lead character as a wealthy modern character highly regarded by his people. But Edufa abandons his moral commitment to his wife in favor of acquisition, while she clings to the moral principles of the past—or tradition.[45]

Mariama Ba's *So Long a Letter (Une si longue lettre)* won the Noma Prize for the best book on African Literature published in 1980, and it was followed in 1981 with *Scarlet Song (Un échant écarlate)*. Unfortunately,

Ba died of cancer before her second book reached print.[46] Whereas Aidoo found benefits to polygamy, Ba was a strong opponent. In this epistolary work, polygamy emerges as a destructive force in the first wife, Ramatoulaye, the model for tradition; meanwhile her best friend, Aissatou (to whom the letter is written), the modern woman, leaves to form a successful career abroad. Both of these women were professional and, in an unusual move, selected their own husbands, despite objections from their respective families (for different reasons). The husbands were their equals in status: one a lawyer and the other a medical doctor.

Ramatoulaye, who bore twelve children, was prostrate when she discovered that her husband had married the teenage friend of one of their daughters—a poor girl whose mother had pretensions and ambitions that resulted in pressuring her to find a wealthy man. He, on the other hand, succumbed to the importunities of an aging swain who deserted his family, but also the modernity he represented. Ramatoulaye's children, representing modernity, urged their mother to divorce. But Ramatoulaye is the bridge between the traditional and the modern, and she elected to stay within the marriage, although her husband provided no support, spending his income on the young wife and her mother. He never returned home. Ramatoulaye is left to guide and care for her large brood alone. One event follows another: a child is injured through careless playing on the street; several of the teenage girls take up smoking; one daughter becomes pregnant, while another marries. All of the girls abandon traditional dress in favor of pants. Yet, Ramatoulaye manages to cope with the sequence of events, finding herself supportive of the pregnant daughter and her student boyfriend. Ramatoulaye transitions again, this time prodded by her daughters and their circumstances.

In the meantime, her husband, Modou, succumbs to the pressures imposed on him by his young demanding wife (and her mother), and he dies of a heart attack. His death places Ramatoulaye in the most compromising of situations: she must share her home with the young second wife during the official Muslim period of mourning. Funds collected from those who call must be shared. Then, the further humiliation is visited on Ramatoulaye in the form of Modou's worthless brother, who comes to claim her as his second wife. Ramatoulaye dusts away the ashes of tradition and refuses. Soon, a former admirer appears, and he, too, wishes to marry Ramatoulaye. It is in her response that Ba allows Ramatoulaye to speak on the negatives of polygamy.

In *Scarlet Song*, polygamy enters when Mireille, the French wife of Ousmane, finds that he has secretly taken as his second wife an ill-educated African woman, to whom he had been committed in youth. Again we see the role of in-laws—his mother resented Mireille because she was white. In this case, race and culture come into play, with the mother-in-law representing the old traditional values, Mireille, colonialism, and Ousmane, the feckless weakling, similar in character to Modou and Assitou's former husband. (Assitou is the friend to whom the long letter is written.) Throughout this turmoil, Mireille, who has given birth to a mixed-race child, tries to hold herself together. But in the end, with Ousmane's second wife pregnant with their second child, Mireille becomes so stressed that she loses control: she kills her child, attacks Ousmane, and goes back to France.

Ba may have been writing of her own life. After giving birth to ten children, she and her husband divorced. It is not clear whether he took a second wife before they parted, but Ba admitted that she shared much in common with Ramatoulaye.[47] And in an interview after winning the Noma Prize, Ba categorically intoned "that all men are basically polygamous."[48] In her public life, Ba was involved with several women's organizations—all of them concerned with bettering the conditions of women. She was furthermore concerned with discrimination against women, which, she believed, lurked everywhere: in the home, in the workplace, "in political institutions," and "in political meetings."[49] She was concerned with identity and with reforming, but not rejecting, African culture.

Legal Pluralism and Gender Equality

Elements of Western legal systems gradually were implanted in the colonies over the course of the late nineteenth and early twentieth century. Basically, in most of the colonies, two types of legal systems developed. Traditional law was left in place where it did not contradict colonial law (the French were more demanding that customary law did not contradict their "notions of French civilization"[50]). Islamic law was relegated to Muslims with criminal and civil matters coming under colonial authority. In the British colonies monogamy was "introduced for educated or Christian 'natives.'" This was important, as it provided "rights of succession to property to spouses and children" that was not usually in place under customary law.[51]

Of importance, too, is that rules regarding death and inheritance remained under traditional law. Thus when independent states adopted new constitutions and passed laws that differed from customary law—such as those applied to death and inheritance, jurists were caught between what had been allowed during the colonial era and what was written, but untried, in the state legal systems.

In Kenya the legal system had been modified, and a new constitution had been adopted. Some of the jurists were, however, white men who stayed on and stayed in place due to their years of legal experience. African men had trained in the law, and several were prominent figures with successful practices in Nairobi. One of these was Silvano Melea Otieno, called SM by everyone. He was married to Wambui Waiyaki Otieno, whom we met during the Mau Mau uprising (in Chapter Seven). In 1986, SM had purchased a small piece of land in Ngong (not far out of Nairobi) on which he raised a few prize bulls. He was proud of his newly acquired property, visiting it often on weekends. He and his wife lived in Nairobi in comfortable circumstances. SM's health had been a concern for some time. He stopped casual drinking, cut down on his smoking, and reduced his hours of work. He was on medications, but nothing seemed untoward until a few days before Christmas (1986), when he alluded to not feeling well but refused to go for medical treatment. Instead, SM paid a visit to his small farmstead with family members. While there he became very ill. The younger men in his party loaded him in his car and drove him to the hospital in Nairobi. SM was pronounced dead on arrival.[52]

What followed his death was a saga that preoccupied most Kenyans for the next five months. SM was taken to the city mortuary, where, before the dramatic events concluded, he was twice embalmed. The "body" became the source of legal wrangling between his widow and one of his brothers, extending to the entire Luo Umira Kager Clan (and other supporters). Wambui, who was a Kikuyu, wished to bury SM in Ngong, claiming that on occasion he had expressed the desire to be laid at rest there. (This claim was backed up by a few others at the trials.) His brother, and increasingly more members of the clan, following Luo traditional law, insisted that the body be returned to his birthplace in Siaya District in western Kenya, home of the Luo people. The details of this struggle are too lengthy to do more than summarize, but what was at stake were several principles that conflicted: ethnic customs versus Kenyan law; individual rights versus tribal ones; and women's rights/modernity versus tradition.

Wambui, as the modern widow, arranged for SM to be buried in Ngong after a funeral at All Saints Cathedral in Nairobi. SM's brother had already announced that the burial would take place at his birthplace in Siaya. Acrimony spread like wildfire, with negotiations between the factions ongoing over several days with no resolution. On December 28 the radio carried an announcement of the burial and funeral as arranged by Mrs. Otieno. And on December 30 she filed suit in the High Court. Justice Shields, the one white judge, heard the case and ruled in her favor.[53] Next, SM's brother filed a counter suit (January 2, 1987) requesting nullification and requesting that Wambui be prevented from removing the body from the mortuary, citing Luo tradition. On January 5 the same judge dismissed the claims on the basis that SM was "metropolitan and cosmopolitan." Drawing on Kenya law, the justice noted that Wambui was the next of kin and therefore entitled to decide the place of internment.[54]

The Luo family and clan then turned to Kenya's highest court, the Court of Appeal. This court initially ruled that Wambui could not remove SM's body from the mortuary until they ruled on Justice Shields's first opinion and the one that followed. In the meantime, while SM's remains moldered in the morgue, the Kenyan press fanned the flames of sensationalism throughout the long ordeal. It took the justices until May 1987 to finally render an opinion: by order of the court, SM was sent to his home village in Siaya District for burial.[55]

As for the widow, she wrote:

> I did not attend my husband's funeral, but my team of video operators and cameramen were there. If Joash Ochieng' [brother] and company think I do not know what happened, they should rest assured that I know all. . . . Umira Kager [the clan] used a mixture of Christian andtraditional burial practices. They had a white cock precede the coffin into the grave; a black cock, a sign of misfortune, had been thrown at Muthiga, my home. . . . However, the black cock was thrown at people who have no traditional beliefs. . . . [This] is an act by an emotional, heathen lot who believe in imaginary things.[56]

Two of the three judges were indigenous Africans, and it is quite likely that they were caught between Kenyan law and their own clans. The Luo burial was against Kenyan law, but this sort of conflict involved in the

case—without the high drama—recurred elsewhere under different circumstances and almost always to the detriment of women.

In Anglo-Cameroon, conflicts over land developed in the post-independence period and again entailed customary law versus statuary law. Anglo-
Cameroon is the western part of the country due to the division, after
Germany lost the colony, between the British and the French, who had been
awarded the rest. Property rights were handed over to lineage groups, but
were viewed as under the control of the chiefs. Under customary law "land
is a highly valuable source of wealth and power . . . with land considered
to be a bridge between the living and the dead."[57] That meant that the spirit
world also was involved and always had men in charge of whatever ritual-
istic purpose was served. Women had no rights, although they did much of
the agricultural labor. Women, even in the colonial era, were "considered
to be property."[58]

Once a new constitution was adopted and after a 1974 land ordinance
was passed, women's rights were, by law, to be respected. But studies revealed that "only a very small percentage of women have access to
landownership." In fact, these studies found that discrimination was widely
practiced. From January 1980 until November 2010, of 12,224 applications
received for land certificates, 10,327 were from men and 1,431 were from
women. The women were allocated only "9.6 percent" of their applications,
whereas the men received "86.6 percent" of theirs.[59] Munge also points out
that women have few in the way of liquid resources with which to purchase
land, as their paid employment is primarily that of domestic servants or
secretaries.[60]

In general a married woman cannot own property even under the new
legal system. What she inherited or acquired before marriage is transferred
to her husband on marriage. However, marriage contracts exist only if they
are agreed on and drawn up prior to the wedding. Conflict is common in
polygamous marriages, in which there is seldom a marriage contract, and
these marriages are in the majority. The only recourse for a woman in a
polygamous marriage is if she buys the property and registers it in her
name. In a monogamous marriage, if land is purchased, it belongs to both
husband and wife. But if one dies without a marriage contract, the rules
can change. For instance, in a dispute over inheritance, or in the case of
divorce, the woman must be able to prove that she has invested in the acquisition. If she cannot, then she will be entitled to "at least one-third" on

the basis of having "worked in the home," sparing her husband from hiring a servant. A woman cannot buy property and register it without her husband's consent—otherwise this could weigh on the husband's pride and cause a divorce. Furthermore, "most men" elect not to marry a woman with resources, because possessing them suggests that a "woman [is] attempting to maintain an independent identity."[61]

These convoluted rules that continue to involve customary attitudes are not unique to Anglo-Cameroon. Polygamous relationships still abound in almost all African societies, particularly in rural areas where the cases involving land acquisition were located. In Senegal, despite the influence of the French in particularly Dakar (the capital), polygamy is enjoying a rebound. In 2012, a café owner in a suburb said that polygamy "is just the way of life." Two years earlier he "inherited" his brother's wife and their six children. Undaunted, he produced a baby with her, bringing the total number of "children under his care to 14."[62] "Rokhaya, a 23-year-old university graduate . . . was forced to marry a 48-year-old rich man," noting that "polygamy is hell and a pack of lies." It is "getting worse" in Senegal, proclaimed a "divorcee who was forced into an 18-year polygamist marriage." She explained that "polygamy violates the principles of equality, promotes gender disparity and compromises women's progress in society."[63] Miriama Ba would agree. A Dakar woman who "secretly counsels and advises" women in these marriages noted that "Polygamy is a form of modern slavery." Yet, Senegal ranks "102 out of 134 countries" in the Global Gender Gap Index, and its girls continue to marry at a young age—most before the age of eighteen. [64]

Da Silva queried young men on whether they would engage in polygamous marriages. Surprisingly, a twenty-two-year-old university student was in favor of it in order to "officialize all of my relationships instead of a string of girlfriends and the rising diseases such as AIDS."[65] Another young man said: "It's like fashion, you follow the trend. Besides, girls outnumber men in Senegal. Polygamy is helping a lot. Almost every man in my area, young or poor is now polygamous. So what?"[66] It is true that there is a gender imbalance, but it is not significant. What is unusual is that the practice is moving into the urban areas "with alarming proportions." And, abuse is said to be "on in the increase, mostly in Dakar, where polygamists are becoming younger and younger." The idea of polygamy as escape from AIDS is, however, one that needs to be studied on a broader scale.

Of note, too, is that Senegal passed a law requiring political parties to "ensure that half their candidates" in elections—local and national—be female. Perhaps female officials will be attentive to seeing that laws on the books protecting women's rights are actually carried out, as opposed to having knowledge of the law and the ongoing hold that traditional customs have over the rule of law.

Migrations: Internal and External

Migration from one place to another is a phenomenon that marks human history. In Africa, during the colonial era, tight lines were drawn between the French, Belgian, Portuguese, British, and Italian colonies. Trade was prohibited, for instance, across borders. Following independence, frontiers tended to open—although not everywhere or entirely. In the 1980s, when Ghana experienced economic difficulties, many Ghanaians sought work in Nigeria. But these were mostly men who left their women behind, like the mine workers in South Africa, who left their women behind in Mozambique, Malawi, and other border states.

An early post-independence study of female migrants in Uganda is found in Christine Obbo's *African Women*. Obbo was the first African woman to earn a Ph.D. degree in anthropology and then to practice in her field. In the early 1970s, she returned to Uganda specifically to study female migrants into what had been the black areas of Kampala. Three main groups attracted her: the Luo who came in from western Kenya; the Nub women (originally from Nubia but long settled in the city); and the Ganda. A preponderance of the Luo and Ganda women were transitioning from small villages in rural areas to the urban capital. Her thesis was expressed in the title page of her study: "'Town Migration Is Not for Women'—This book Is African Women's Reply."[67]

Women, as we have seen earlier, "on occasion used their reproductive abilities to improve their social status." Thus, in a number of case studies Obbo presents examples of women who, soon after arrival in the city, chose to align themselves with men. In each case the small-village girls developed serial relationships with "rich" men, producing several children. Manipulating the births of the children, plus laws in place, allowed them to secure support—they employed a number of devices. Some of the women gained employment through their lovers' interventions. Most of the women refused marriage, because it was, according to one, too restrictive "for sexual freedom."[68]

Not all of these relationships panned out. One woman with serial lovers, and children by several, was insulted when her lover called her a prostitute. Problems sometimes arose with the children raised in homes of these single parents (the lovers were almost all married and not living in). The Nubi emphasized male domination, and, as a result, some boys were abusive to their mothers. Some women sent their children back to the rural areas for the maternal family to raise. Others absorbed their children into their ethnic group to give them an affiliation and identity separate from their fathers.[69]

Political upheaval in Uganda sent fright through many of the Luo migrants in the early 1970s. Many of the men who remained were unemployed, but women were "discouraged" from finding work, as "it would weaken positions of the men." A few of the Luo turned to an independent church, which relied on sorcery and witchcraft as well as drawing from Christian faiths. Among these, many of the women were constrained from going into trade and were in dire straits, with no money on which to live, or, if their husbands earned an income, they were given little support for essential goods. Marital discord resulted, primarily because of the male desire to dominate and control.[70]

Among their "strategies for urban survival," unmarried women who had no wealthy man often pooled their resources. They took rooms close together, worked together, and shared responsibilities for children. Three Ganda women in Obbo's study developed a fictive kinship based on their shared economic and social interests.[71] Despite the overall attempts to be deferential, which Obbo pointed out was "the most effective tool" in dealing with men, she quoted one elderly man who imparted his views on the changes that were occurring in the 1970s: "Today's women are too much. Controlling them is a waste of time. A woman controls and looks after herself." [72]

The above insights into social patterns—all with economic overtones—gave way in Obbo's study to the types of work the rural-to-urban women undertook to survive. For instance, they engaged in unskilled factory work, sewing, and, of course, prostitution. Those who were able to secure a modicum of training went into hairstyling, distilling, brewing, and dressmaking. The major markets in Kampala were attended by the ethnic group of those who ran them, although Obbo noted that most women preferred to shop at the stalls where they "got the best price."[73] Various controversies developed among the different ethnic groups as well. One Luyia (another ethnic group in Kenya) woman tried to open a stall in an area occupied by the Luo. She arrived to find "a skinned rat" and "accused the Luo women" of sorcery.[74]

The last types of income earning for rural–to-urban women were at "the top of the economic ladder" and required capital. Women could parlay their surplus incomes into buying a house, and then rent rooms to boarders. That practice was lucrative, as was keeping a shop, which required money to purchase goods for sale. The sale of maize flour brought good returns. It was the mainstay of most diets, and it also was required for distilling liquor. Furthermore, a woman could begin by cooking porridge, selling it, and then expanding to a small shop.[75]

This section, drawn from Obbo's pioneering work, includes some detail, as it is representative of the experiences of a majority of the women who migrated from rural or small villages to urban areas across Africa. The results of her study reinforce the challenge of women successfully migrating. Another development, although unrelated to rural-to-urban migration, but concerning male domination and the lack of desire to marry, comes from Kenya in 1991. There a contingent of professional but single women declared that they were banning marriage. Kay Makuku, a former teacher and graduate student at the University of Nairobi, proclaimed that she foresaw herself as a "single parent" with a male companion "but not a husband," and in this she was joined by a woman lawyer who advised that "many, many women are not committing themselves to men." These unorthodox views were widely spread in the professional classes and were summed up "in two words: African men." Their grandfathers, they said, looked after their wives. But now, "the average man might contribute to the rent but use the rest for mistresses and beer. They drink a lot."[76]

The consensus was articulated by another female attorney: "Men are ready to be modern outside their homes. . . . Once you are a Mrs., the husband will treat you as though you are bound to him and the home." Another lawyer said, "Most citified African men expect to keep a mistress or two, and for the wife to stay home while he goes out." Some women referred to the intimidation and insecurity men feel when they are married to a successful professional woman. The alternatives posed were to have children by a younger man who is "less likely to boss" them or "to have a child by a married man."[77] The paradox is that by choosing a married man by whom to have children they will be the mistresses they reject if they marry. These women were not migrating, but they may well have been dealing with the types of women Obbo describes in her rural-to-urban migrant study.

External migration brings us back to Kebedech, who was a refugee from Ethiopia. The fall of Haile Selassie I in Ethiopia and the emergence of Mengistu Haile Miriam marked the first exodus; then, in 1991, many tied to the Derg and Mengistu fled from the new regime. Ethiopia's long ties to the United States made it a magnet for the great majority of Ethiopians. This was true, too, of Eritreans—whose government was in conflict with Ethiopia. So the majority of refugees from these two countries took exile in the United States. Thousands of them were women.

In Europe, Africans joined other former colonials for a variety of reasons. The trickle from independent states from the 1960s became nearly a flood in the 21st century. Some were escaping from regimes where their lives were in danger. Others moved for economic reasons. France was compelling to Muslims from Africa south of the Sahara, who joined others from the former North African colonies. The Netherlands attracted former colonials from East Asia, and it soon came to be a refuge for Africans, including Somalis. Hersi Ali, a Somali woman, had no ties to The Netherlands, yet she chose to migrate there to escape an arranged marriage. Settling in, Hersi Ali created a political base, which resulted in her election to parliament. Her rise, however, was offset by political difficulties. The result was that Hersi Ali moved to the United States, where she is a controversial, if attractive, figure. She is outspoken against FGM and for women's rights.

If Obbo's case studies are generally representational of rural-to-urban migrations, this section describes the flow of African people to the United States. I have noted that large numbers of people from Ethiopia and Eritrea came to a single country, as opposed to spreading themselves out in other parts of the West. From 1980 to 2000, the number of people born in Africa who migrated to the United States increased from "just under 200,000 to almost 1.5 million." Compared with other foreign-born people, African immigrants "reported higher levels of English proficiency and educational attainments" and were more likely "to participate in the labor force."[78] Still, a study dealing with African immigrants into the United States reverses this finding in reporting that the "African born were more likely to live in poverty in 2009" than others of foreign birth.[79]

Table 1[80]
Historical Census Statistics on the Foreign-born
Population of the United States

Year	Total Foreign-Born	African-Born	
		Number	Share of Total Foreign-Born
1960	9,738,091	33,355	0.4%
1970	9,619,302	80,143	0.8%
1980	14,079,906	199,723	1.4%
1990	19,797,316	363,819	1.8%
2000	31,107,889	881,3000	2.8%
2009	38,517,104	1,492,785	3.9%

Source: Data from 2000 census; 2009 data from the American Community Survey 2009. Data for earlier decades from Campbell Gibson and Emily Lennon, "Historical Census Statistics on the Foreign-Born Population of the United States: 1850 to 1990" (US Census Bureau Working Paper no. 29, US Government Printing Office, Washington, DC, 1999).

The countries that contributed the most from below the Sahara (beyond Ethiopia and Eritrea) were Nigeria, Ghana, and Kenya. They were followed by South Africa, Liberia, Sudan, Cape Verde (former Portuguese colony), Sierra Leone, and Cameroon. Female migrants were not listed separately by immigration authorities, but the following table reveals the occupations by gender.

Table 2[81]

Occupations of Employed Workers in the Civilian Labor Force Age 16 and Older by Gender and Origin, 2009

	African-Born		Foreign-Born (total)	
	Male	Female	Male	Female
Number of persons age 16 and older employed in the civilian labor force	547,123	369,167	13,143,161	9,377,865
Total (percent)	100.0%	100.0%	100.0%	100.0%
Management, business, finance	12.5%	9.0%	10.7%	10.5%
Information technology	4.4%	1.2%	4.2%	1.9%
Other sciences and engineering	5.1%	1.5%	4.0%	2.2%
Social and legal services	2.9%	4.0%	1.1%	2.0%
Education, training and media, entertainment	5.3%	8.2%	3.5%	7.3%
Physicians	2.6%	1.4%	1.3%	1.0%
Registered nurses	1.4%	8.2%	0.4%	3.6%
Other health care practitioners	3.5%	5.9%	1.1%	3.2%
Healthcare support	3.3%	13.9%	0.7%	5.6%
Services	15.1%	18.7%	18.5%	26.5%
Sales	10.7%	9.0%	7.8%	10.3%
Administrative support	7.4%	13.1%	5.3%	14.2%
Farming, fishing, forestry	*	*	2.7%	1.0%
Construction, extraction, transportation	15.9%	1.8%	24.5%	3.0%
Manufacturing, Installation, repair	9.7%	4.1%	14.2%	7.8%

Source: Data from 2000 census; 2009 data from the American Community Survey 2009. Data for earlier decades from Campbell Gibson and Emily Lennon, "Historical Census Statistics on the Foreign-Born Population of the United States: 1850 to 1990" (US Census Bureau Working Paper no. 29, US Government Printing Office, Washington, DC, 1999).

Aside from working in the field of health care, most people recall the incident in New York back in 2010 when the director of The World Bank was accused of raping a female housekeeper from Guinea. She was one of many African women with few skills who sought immigration to the United States, and who joined a considerable number of other African women in this type of low-paying job. On the other hand, and due to a political coup in Ghana in the 1970s, the poet and author Abena Busia (with her mother) went into exile when her father, the president, was overthrown. Busia was well educated and took a tenured position at Rutgers University. Although more male Africans are on faculties across America, many women—especially from Nigeria—occupy positions on university faculties.

Overall there has been less controversy regarding African immigrants to the United States (and to Canada, which has experienced the "pull factor") than in Europe. Of late, and especially due to the rise of the Islamic militancy, opposition to immigration has increased. The economic situation in some countries—Italy, Portugal, and Spain—has also led to calls to halt the flow from African countries.

Sports

Women were not participants in major sporting events—excluding intramural sports at school—until the past two or three decades. And even then, women from primarily Muslim communities were restrained from participation. In September 2013, *The Economist* devoted part of its International section to "Women in Sport," recognizing that women are now engaging in competition on the world stage. Soccer (football) to the rest of the world has seen women's teams formed and gain international attention. Women tennis players are keenly watched in world-class competitions. But the one sport featuring women that is international in attention and starring African women is track. Ethiopia's Tirunesh Dibaba has won three gold medals, or one more than her fellow countrywoman Kenenisa Bekele. She began her medal run in the Beijing Olympics in 2008. In between she ran successfully in marathons, before another Olympic triumph in London in 2012.[82] Kenya, too, has a stable of female runners: Edna Kiplagat is the current world champion distance runner; and Vivian Cheruiyot is another 2012 Olympic achiever, who won both gold and bronze medals.[83]

Unfortunately, these triumphs were offset by a controversy surrounding the female "body" of Caster Semenya. She hails from the Limpopo area of South Africa, where she participated in track events with seemingly no problem. The controversy began in 2009 when Semenya won a world championship track event in Berlin. Her identity as a woman was questioned before Semenya's medal was awarded, leading the International Association of Athletics Federations (IAAF) to require "gender verification tests." They included, she reported, "unwarranted and invasive scrutiny of the most intimate and private details of my being."[84] In the eight-month hiatus before the IAAF issued its findings—certifying her female identity—Semenya was banned from competition and was the victim of the most blatant sexual gossip in the international press. If there is any positive outcome from this unfortunate incident, it is that the IAAF reviewed its gender policies to ensure that nothing of this nature occurs again. In the meantime, Semenya handily won her gold medal in London and was awarded the medal due from her winning run in Berlin.[85]

Still, African Muslim women are experiencing difficulties competing. In Senegal a *marabout* (Muslim religious figure) raised the issue of female participation in international competition, including the 2012 London Olympics. Although his claims of possible violence were dismissed by the opposition, the Muslim clergy carry consider weight in that country, as they do in other primarily Islamic areas in countries throughout Africa—north as well as south of the Sahara.[86]

Women Achievers

Time and space prevent the coverage that a subject such as this deserves. I begin with Lea Itta Sigei, a Nandi from western Kenya. Born into one of the few Roman Catholic families in Nandi, Lea attended Catholic mission school, where she excelled. On graduation she was accepted at the Royal College in Nairobi, where she majored in history and political science.[87] In 1968 Lea received a scholarship to study for a master's degree at the Harvard School of Education.[88] The next year, even though encouraged by Harvard faculty members to continue on for the advanced degree, Lea married Benjamin Kipkorir, himself engaged in a Ph.D. program at St. John's College, Cambridge. On their return to Kenya, Lea took employment with the government, which, in turn, brought her into an innovative project with outside funding that would study and enhance preschool education.[89] The project sent her and her team to various schools in several parts of the country. They were interested in day care centers in which they could inject educational content. Once the trial steps were taken, the program was extended throughout much of the country. This phenomenon has only begun to be implemented in the United States, although it has been successfully integrated in several European countries. Yet, the foundation for melding day care and early childhood education came from Lea Kipkorir's pioneering work in Kenya in the late 1960s into the early 1980s:

> Work on development of national early childhood education curricula, training teachers and their supervisors was [her] major contribution to her country and to humanity. Many of the ideas that were developed by her and her team found their way elsewhere, both near and far, because they were universal. . . . Books based on the syllabus thereafter were published . . . [containing] poems and proverbs.[90]

A program of this nature, initiated in an African country where resources were limited, may serve as a model to others, even in the West, where programs in early childhood education are so woefully weak.

Jaiyeola Aduke Alakija became a leading figure in Nigeria during the late colonial era. In 1930, as a small child of nine, she went to Wales for her early schooling. With an interest in medicine, she enrolled at Glasgow University in Scotland. Finding medicine not her calling, Alakija transferred to the London School of Economics and completed her diploma in social science "because I wanted to work with people."[91] By 1945, Alakija was back in Lagos, where she founded a social welfare department, working with juvenile delinquents. Being unprepared to defend these juveniles in court, Alakija returned to the United Kingdom and studied law. Home in Nigeria again, Alakija set up practice with another female lawyer, with the two of them following five or six other women into the legal profession in Nigeria. They were the first women to go into private practice. During this time, Alakija accomplished her initial professional goal: that of establishing a juvenile court and becoming the first judge to handle matters pertaining to their special needs.[92]

Moving next into the corporate world, Alakija Aduke was the first legal counsel for Mobil Oil in Nigeria. This was toward the end of the colonial era. After Nigeria's independence, and still with Mobil, Alakija moved into international affairs. For instance, she attended sessions at the United Nations in 1961-1965. At this stage in her career she became active in women's issues, traveling around the United States, elaborating on "what Nigerian women were doing."[93] Next came the ambassadorships: from 1984 to 1987 she represented her country in Sweden, Denmark, Norway, and Finland. Back home, with no respite, Alakija served on a number of community boards and in directorships with multiple companies. In 1964, among her many awards was an honorary degree from Columbia University.[94] Celebrated as "the mother of the Nigerian Bar," Alakija celebrated ninety years of life in 2011 with energy and a mind full of memories.[95]

A younger Nigerian woman emerged from a successful career at the World Bank to take over the challenging (and onerous) job as finance minister. Her higher education all took place in the United States, culminating with a Ph.D. in economic development from the Massachusetts Institute of Technology in 1981. Ngozi Okonjo-Iweala, specializing in economic development in poor countries, climbed the ladder to become the World Bank's managing director. This was the organization's second highest ranking official. From that lofty position in 2006 she returned to Nigeria, first as minister of foreign affairs before agreeing to serve as minister of finance that same year. Her life was fraught with difficulties as she attempted to deal with the financial debacles that marked Nigeria, and with recalcitrant state governors who, at one point, demanded her resignation.[96] Holding on, while confronting the wolves, has marked Okonjo-Iweala's tenure so far.

As an advocate for African women, Gertrude Mongella's life story is inspirational. She started to study at a university, married, and gave birth to her first son in the third year of her studies. Then Mongella transitioned to a teacher-training program. Soon after Tanzania's independence (as Tanganyika until the 1964 merger with Zanzibar), Mongella attended a political meeting at her school. She wrote: "I looked around the room and thought that no one here was qualified to lead, so I stood for the chair and won. In this way I started to know the experienced politicians in my district."[97] In 1975, she won a seat in the East African Legislative Assembly, encouraged by her husband, an archivist. At the time she was breast-feeding her third child. The assembly dissolved in 1977, but by then Mongella was active in the Tanzanian African National Union political party. She worked to establish quotas in local as well as national elections that called for a minimum number of seats for women. In 1982 she was appointed minister for women's affairs, but one of her most significant contributions may have come when Mongella took over the Ministry for Lands, Natural Resources, and Tourism. In that capacity, she banned the ivory trade. "This was not easy. It's a corrupt international system," she wrote.[98]

> When I entered politics, I thought, you will behave like a lady. Men never forgive you if you don't behave like that. But I learned to be prepared to earn enemies or I'd be compromised. Before, most of the women who were in politics were divorcees, so it looked as if only women who had "failed" went into politics. Don't forget the environment in which women are operating. Men don't want to see intelligent women in politics, but I do think it is the less intelligent men who fight you.[99]

Her next crusade was against the spread of AIDS. Active in her own country, Mongella networked with other women worldwide and then moved to the UN. In this important arena, in 1995, she was appointed secretary general of the Fourth World Congress on Women in Beijing. She brought attention to the AIDS crisis and the problems of women in wars, focusing her attention on Africa. Mongella advocated moving women into positions of power and decision making in their countries; creating an international mechanism for the advancement of women; and, of importance where conflict rages, involving women in prevention and resolution of violence.[100]

Whereas the numbers of women in elected offices remain a concern to women such as Mongella, some governments have begun to promote participation. In Nigeria's northern city, Kano, political parties were centered on identity as Muslims and on the north. The Qur'an was the basis for their interpretation, and most of the patriarchal leaders skewed their reading to underline women as dependents. But a few of the imams moved toward a more modern interpretation. Among them were Mallam Aminu Kano, who openly addressed the status of women in the 1950s and 1960s. Mallam Aminu Kano died before he launched his campaign for president, but had he lived he was expected to name a woman, who as his "running mate would have been the first Nigerian woman nominated by any political party for high national office."[101] In the early 1970s, Alhaji Shehu Galadanci, from an important Fulani family, served as an advocate for increased opportunities for women, including in education. He did not address the more important issue of voting rights for women, but in that conservative area one small step was to lead to another. The major political parties were divided on the issue, although women were involved behind the scenes in political activities.[102] They were, however, not politicized to the extent that they advanced their cause beyond education and the right to vote. As time passed, and conservatism marked the north, especially from the 1990s and on, male authority has increased, with increasing restrictions on women's political aspirations.

Uganda, more recently, saw a rise in the number of female elected representatives to parliament, where the speaker is Rebecca Kadaga, the first female to hold that office (2011-2016).[103] Despite a certain number of seats being reserved for women in Uganda, not all of those elected have fared as well as Kadaga. In 2011, the teetotaler Cerinah Nebanda was discovered dead at the home of her "lover." Her death was claimed to be the result of an overdose of heroin. Journalist and health authority Helen Epstein joined others in questioning the local results of the autopsy. One of her informants included General David Sejusa, former coordinator of Ugandan Intelligence who escaped Uganda in 2013. Sejusa claimed that the "lover" was, in fact, a spray "employed by Uganda's Internal Security." In this case (and other unexplained deaths among politicians who called attention to the alleged graft and corruption surrounding President Yowari Musevina and his wife), Nebanda's addiction may have been to her country and the people in her constituency. [104]

Ghana embarked on "increasing women's political participation," beginning in 2010. In 2013, women accounted for a small percentage of positions in parliament (19 of 230), which was regarded as "shockingly low."[105] The report suggests that among the reasons for the lack of female involvement are the lack of resources and the "traditional belief that women are politically inferior." Some men believe that in voting for a woman they will "face the wrath of the gods." Another hindrance is husbands who discourage their wives, and, since political parties select their candidates, the choices remain in the hands of men.[106]

Even in Ethiopia, with the government tightly controlled by one party that prohibits competition, members of the party began to send out signals that changes were under way on issues of gender. New policies were formulated in 2012-2013 to promote "equality between men and women so that women can participate in the political, social and economic life of their country."[107] From the feudalism of Haile Selassie's reign to the end of the Derg, women's interests were immaterial. Lip service from the current government may be preceded by action. But it is too soon to tell.

Senegal introduced a quota system to establish parity between men and women in the legislative body. Hence in 2013, women made up nearly half of that body. For the first time, too, a woman was appointed prime minister.[108] The incongruity is somewhat remarkable: younger middle-class women are being sought for polygamous marriages while their older sisters are serving as leaders in the Senegalese government. The leaders' voices can be expected to be heard on issues such as FGM and polygamy. As we noted earlier, Rwanda's president, Paul Kigame, is controversial: authoritarian on the one hand, yet successful in helping to develop his country in the wake of the genocide that marked the year 1994. Reinforcing this reputation, Kigame "engineered" the election of the "highest proportion of women in the legislature," with 64 percent of the seats.[109]

Down in South Africa, as we saw earlier, women played a significant role in overturning apartheid. Some have been mentioned. Others will have to be celebrated in absentia from these pages. Albertina Sisulu, who died at ninety-two in 2011, was celebrated for her humility and humanity. She trained as a nurse, married her activist husband in 1941, and spent the greater part of her life devoted to him, while he spent twenty-six years of their married life in prison. At their wedding reception, Nelson Mandela forewarned: "Albertina, you have married a man: Walter married politics before he met you."[110] During the years Walter Sisulu was on Robben Island, Albertina was jailed, her children suffered government harassment, and she was banned for ten years. Still, she continued her involvement in politics on behalf of the ANC, in the underground covertly, or openly as a founder of the United Democratic Front (1983). In 1989, Albertina called for sanctions against the South African government in her visits abroad. In her travels to the United States she met with two American presidents: George H. W. Bush and Jimmy Carter.[111] When the political transition came in 1994, Mrs. Sisulu was elected to parliament. She was followed into politics by two of her daughters and one son.[112]

Albertina and Walter Sislulu.
Source: University of Cape Town

Across the color line, Helen Suzman was the only member of the Progressive Party elected to parliament, where she represented the wealthy Houghton district of Johannesburg in 1961. Whereas radical political change was called for by many of the less conservative members of the white community, Suzman touted equal opportunity for all races. Hers was a lonely existence in the government. She was able to survive partly because of her gender: the patriarchal-dominated National Party regarded her as a nuisance more than a threat. Still, Suzman, courageous and outspoken, did not back down when verbal assaults came her way.

In a speech before parliament in 1965 she argued that, if there were skilled labor shortages in the country, blacks should be given the chance for training. "That is all I ask: equal opportunity," she stated. The people of color lack skills "because we do not give them the necessary education. There is no free education for non-Whites, and we do not allow them to enter skilled trades because they are not included in the definition of 'employee.' . . . I am prepared to withdraw the superficial colour bar that protects the White worker, because I believe the White workers will be able to hold their own against non-White workers." Blacks were discriminated against, including their status in South Africa: "I would like to find a country first of all which classified persons born within its borders as 'immigrants' and a country where immigrants who have been living there for one generation or two . . . are still classified as immigrants with no rights."[113] Nothing came of her persuasive arguments. Nevertheless, she remained undaunted in her positions. Suzman was an advocate for political prisoners and those persons who were banned or detained without legitimacy. She was able to make no progress on that front, but she never abandoned her advocacy.

Although many may not be aware of her political activism, the South African singer Miriam Makeba lost her passport in 1960 because of her campaigns against apartheid. When she managed to go into exile, Makeba, like many South African activists, first reached England. From there she moved to the United States, where her career took off. In the early 1960s, Makeba approached the United Nations requesting aid in having her passport returned—she was a citizen without a country. The UN took no action. Several other countries, however, including Guinea, came forward with passports. And it was to Guinea that she and her third husband, Stokeley Carmichael, moved in 1968 following difficulties that arose from their marriage and Carmichael's involvement with what many Americans regarded as radical civil rights activities.[114]

During the fifteen years Makeba lived in Guinea she represented that country as its delegate to the United Nations, winning the Dag Hammarskjold Peace Prize in 1986. Peace had not reigned at home. Makeba and Carmichael separated in 1973. She renewed her friendship, but not her marital ties, with Hugh Masekela, with whom she had performed early in her South African career. They continued to perform on occasion after her 1978 divorce and following her exit from Guinea.[115] Soon after Mandela's release from prison in 1990, Miriam Makeba was able to return home. She continued to perform and produce albums, traveling the world, but her base was in Johannesburg (Gauteng) until her death in Italy, where she was performing, in 2008.

Frene Ginwala was a stalwart supporter of the ANC. When it was banned, and the government began to round up Indian activists along with so-called Coloureds and, of course, Africans, Ginwala went into exile in Da es Salaam. In 1968, and still in exile, she and others launched a campaign to force South Africa to release its political prisoners. Unsuccessful as it was, it helped draw further attention to the oppression that only worsened as the decades passed until the late 1980s. By surreptitious means, communications between Mandela on Robben Island and his lieutenants in the field were carried back and forth. Ginwala was one of those in indirect contact with Mandela. Theirs was a close friendship based on mutual respect. As Mandela assumed the presidency in 1994, and after her election to parliament, he asked this Indian woman to serve as speaker. "I had not wanted to be speaker, but it was very much his decision. . . . Mandela has a tremendous respect for parliament. . . . He advised that you must run parliament in a way that carries on what we have done in negotiations, where we have tried to bring all parties on board. . . . It sounded great in theory but I didn't know what to do, because I had no experience in parliament before then."[116]

Mandela visited parliament often and made regular calls on Ginwala, where she became an effective speaker. She stepped down when Mbeki was elected, and she took on other assignments, such as, in 2007, leader of an "Inquiry" into the persecution of a public official regarding the classification of government documents. Her independence in this inquiry was questioned—how could she, a highly placed member of the ANC serve in a capacity that involved investigating people and/or affairs related to that organization? Ginwala's response was indicative of the political atmosphere that marked South Africa during this period: "There's an assumption that any leader of the ANC is never going to act in the national interest—and on what basis is that allegation made? Why does it? The opposition and white South Africa" was her response.[117]

Yet, things began to change for the ANC in the first decade of the 21st century. Thabo Mbeki was replaced as head of the ANC political party and was followed by Jacob Zuma. Allegations of graft and corruption swelled, even around the president himself. Thus in 2013, Mamphela Ramphele, a much respected doctor, sociologist, educator, author, and lecturer, decided to launch a new political party, Agang (Sesotho for "Let us build"). Ramphele had decided on medical school while still a high school student. She won a scholarship to the segregated Natal Medical School, where she encountered Steve Biko, founder of the Black Consciousness movement. Drawn to the movement before she was attracted to Biko, she threw as much time and energy into the former as she was able. This was in the early 1970s.[118] She went on to a residency in surgery, then became pregnant and gave birth to a daughter. In 1974, while under the care of her maternal grandmother, the child died, leaving Ramphele prostrate. By 1976, Ramphele was again engaged in political activism and was detained in King Williamstown, where she was then living and working after having abandoned surgery.[119]

The relationship with Biko was problematic. His frenetic activities included many other women, plus he had married and sired two children by 1977. Then, Biko vowed to divorce his wife, and the two lovers rekindled their relationship. In September of that year, Biko was detained, taken to jail in Port Elizabeth, and brutally murdered by the police. Ramphele was pregnant again, and this time she gave birth to his son.[120]

Following Biko's death and the birth of the child, Ramphele moved on to many other projects that resulted in numerous publications, and she continued her activism. Earlier, when she was banned, Helen Suzman came to visit and attempted unsuccessfully to have Ramphele's passport restored.[121] Ramphele went back to school, this time obtaining a bachelor of commerce degree, followed by a diploma in tropical hygiene in 1981 and a diploma in public health in 1982.[122] In 1988, now with a passport, she was awarded the Carnegie Distinguished International Fellowship, which took her to Radcliffe College, then aligned with Harvard. By 1991, Ramphele was as renowned as an academic from a series of notable publications and the fellowships abroad—so much so that she was invited to serve as deputy vice chancellor at the University of Cape Town, moving to the vice chancellorship in 1996. She was ushered into the business world as chair of Gold Fields, a mining company, and she served as a managing director of the World Bank.[123]

The ANC remains popular among the masses of black people in South Africa, although support has gradually been slipping—on the left on the part of many of the youths; and in the center from the black middle class. Ramphele hopes to garner support from both groups: "Our society's greatness is being fundamentally undermined by massive failure of governance. . . . Our country has lost the moral authority and international respect it enjoyed when it became a democracy." This comment comes from the woman who aspires to be president of South Africa but has never affiliated with any political party.[124] A few months before the election in May, 2014, Helen Zille, of the Democratic Alliance, who has led that political party in Cape Province briefly aligned her party with Ramphele. But friction soon developed. In the end of the ANC won again but Zille's Democratic Alliance increased its percentage of the vote with several black women running for office on her ticket. As well as having aimed for leadership at the top, women occupy more than 40 percent of the seats in parliament. In fact, women hold a significant number of important positions in the South African government; they run the Home, Defense, and Foreign Affairs ministries, and a woman was governor of the central bank.[125]

The Nobel Prize Winners

Wangari Maathai was born in a rural area of Kikuyu Province (Kenya) in 1940. Her father was a polygamist, and her mother was his second wife. In all, he took four wives and produced ten children. Wangari was her mother's oldest daughter, although two sons preceded her, with two more siblings later.[126] At the time her father took his fourth wife, he sent Wangari's mother and her children back to his ancestral home, where they came

Wangari Maathai.
Source: moralheroes.org

under the supervision of their paternal uncle. This man was a wise and supportive father figure to Wangari. He allowed her to go to a Catholic school (they were not members of the Roman Catholic faith), where she excelled under the tutorship of nuns. Then, she was in one of the first groups of African students who were selected for scholarships under a program initiated by Robert Kennedy and funded by his father's foundation.[127] That scholarship took her to rural Kansas and Mount St. Scholastica, where she proved to be an excellent student. (And she learned something about the complexities of race during her introduction to America.)[128] Her next move up the educational ladder took her to the University of Pittsburgh in 1964, where she earned a master's degree in science the following year.

She noted that, on her return to Kenya, the country had been independent for two years, as she was now embarking on her own independent journey as a professional with a promised appointment at the University of Nairobi. On arrival, however, Wangari discovered that the job had been given to someone else.[129] Ending up with a job at the School of Veterinary Science provided a jolt but also income. Soon she came under the tutelage of a German professor, who sent her to Munich for her Ph.D. Her academic career was marked with a few difficulties that involved discrimination in pay. Nevertheless, and despite her protests, by 1975 Maathai was named senior lecturer in anatomy, followed in 1977 by promotion to associate professor—making her the first woman to hold either of these ranks in the School of Veterinary Science.[130]

Her return to Kenya, however, let Maathai see the toll that modernity exacted on rural people. She was shocked to find farmers' children suffering from malnutrition. Realizing that "many farmers had converted practically all of their land into growing coffee and tea to sell to the international market," Wangari determined that she should work to restore the landscape that dominated her childhood.[131] "Why not plant trees?" They would provide the wood that women could use for fires to provide nutritious food for their families. The farmers would "also have wood for fencing and fodder for cattle and goats," and shade for humans and livestock. Trees "would also heal the land by bringing back birds and small animals" to regenerate the earth. "This is how the Green Belt Movement began. The rest was pure luck, Maathai wrote."[132]

Beginning with this simple idea, Maathai had no foresight regarding the international acclaim that she and the Green Belt Movement would receive, including the Nobel Prize. Nor did she imagine the resistance she would experience from the Kenyan government. For her efforts to promote conservation, and being subjected to harassment by government resistance, Maathai was sent to jail multiple times and threatened repeatedly by President Moi's minions.[133]

She experienced other challenges, including the failure of her marriage and further gender discrimination at her workplace.[134] She unsuccessfully ran for parliament, lost her job, and had to move to smaller quarters that served as the headquarters of the Green Belt Movement for some time. But she managed to overcome these challenges with the security of knowing that she still had the movement and her ties to the National Council of Women of Kenya.[135] These treasures were almost lost through continued machinations on the part of the government. She did win a seat in parliament, which in 1997 led Wangari Maathai to run for president. Moi won again, and, although Maathai was "disappointed," she could hardly have been surprised.[136] Despite the many setbacks, Maathai had a loyal following of women to whom she was devoted. She put her life in danger to support them on several occasions, which meant that she took on the government again and again.

> On the morning of October 8, 2004 . . . my cell phone rang.
> . . . It was the Norwegian ambassador, asking to keep the line
> clear for a call from Oslo. After some time it came. . . . It was
> the chair of the Norwegian Nobel Committee. . . . I was not pre-
> pared to learn that I had been awarded the Nobel Peace Prize.
> I wonder if anybody is?[137]

The Green Belt Movement has spread across the world. At her untimely death from cancer in 2011, Wangari Maathai left a legacy few women in history can match.

Then there is Ellen Johnson Sirleaf, the second black African woman to win the Nobel Peace Prize. She was born in Monrovia, Liberia, in 1938. In her autobiography, *This Child Will Be Great*, Sirleaf went to great lengths to stress that her genealogy was not connected to the old Americo-Liberian ruling class that dominated the country from its founding until the coup in 1980. Nevertheless, Sirleaf began her professional career in Liberia in the Office of Financial Affairs under the presidency of William Tubman, and

Liberian president Ellen Johnson Sirleaf.
Source: "The Hunger Project" website.
(Nobel Prize Committee)

she followed that up by working in William Tolbert's administration. Tolbert was of that privileged group.[138] Her education included matriculation in the College of West Africa in Monrovia (a high school), and after her marriage to James Sirleaf it continued at a business college in Madison, Wisconsin. James Sirleaf was jealous, abusive especially when drinking, and possessive. Her period in Madison was marred by domestic discord, moving her to divorce him soon after her return to Monrovia.[139] In Liberia, where the courts ruled that women had no right to custody of their children after divorce, she found that she would have to relinquish their four children. The children resided for a time with James Sirleaf's family in the rural backwater of the country, although Ellen and her family maintained frequent contact. Taking the job in the Finance Ministry led to contacts with American academics, which, in turn, encouraged Sirleaf to follow up on the degree from the business college with a proper university education. She spent the summer of 1960 at the Economics Institute at the University of Colorado, Boulder, before moving on, with a grant from USAID, to Harvard, from where she received a master's in public administration in 1971.[140]

Back in Monrovia, she joined Tolbert's administration as assistant minister of finance. But in 1980, the bloody coup led by Sergeant Samuel Doe found her working for him—he knew nothing of budgetary matters and she did. Later, she said that she "would be blamed for supporting the coup," but Sirleaf always managed to find a way to survive and move on, albeit with some close calls.[141]

Then it was time to make one of her many moves. Using contacts formed earlier, she found employment with the World Bank. Doe released her and allowed her to depart for Washington. Her recollection was that his action was mitigated by "still trying to be the good boy on the world stage," which must have been viewed askance by many. After the coup, Doe and his troops shot and killed several members of the Tolbert cabinet in full view of the press. Still, she stayed at the World Bank for around a year before rejoining Citibank (where she had had a short appointment before returning to Liberia in 1971) as "the first African woman appointed as a vice president." Her assignment was in Nairobi, but she traveled widely in Africa.[142] As often as she could, she visited Liberia and saw her children.

In 1983, Doe agreed to return the country to civilian control, with elections promised for January 1985. He planned to run, with opposition from another party headed by a distinguished academic. Sirleaf, in contact with politicians at home, decided to return and to affiliate with a new party, the National Democratic Party, making a total of three parties in competition.[143] Ellen would run for the vice-presidency. This was her first taste of presidential politics.

Matters again reached a critical stage during the election campaign, this time with her arrest and brief confinement in jail. Despite being convicted on spurious charges, she was soon released. When the actual election was held in October 1985, Doe won—with "reports of various abuses flooding in." Ellen had, however, won a seat in the Liberian senate, but she refused to take it due to the fraudulent presidential election.[144] Doe survived two coup attempts before Charles Taylor emerged. Sirleaf found Taylor "a young and forceful man, charming and persuasive, with charisma to spare."[145] While in Doe's cabinet, Taylor had been accused of embezzlement, had fled to the United States, and was imprisoned in Boston. Later, Taylor escaped and eventually made his way back to Liberia, where he organized forces in the hinterland. At one point Sirleaf met him there—while she was in the country under the auspices of the Equator Bank, which she had joined.[146]

This period in Liberia's history—the early 1990s—is covered in Sirleaf's autobiography, but with more emphasis on herself than on the tangled web of persons and parties that marked the emergence of Prince Johnson, another opponent whose forces also engaged in civil war. The upshot was eventually that the country was devastated—what infrastructure that had existed in Monrovia and other smaller urban areas was nearly destroyed. Eventually ECOMOG entered. Taylor declared himself president (but the other faction had not given up—meaning that two rival governments existed, but only one, Taylor's, in the capital). The war picked up momentum in 1991, and this is when all of the factions armed child soldiers. The results were maiming, rape, and the same sort of violence we saw in Sierra Leone. There were, according to Sirleaf, between 1990 and 1991, "by some accounts, as many as fifty separate peace talks or peace conferences, producing as many as a dozen distinct peace accords."[147]

In 1992, when she was still with the Equator Bank, the United Nations invited Sirleaf to serve as an administrator to its African Development Program. She was with the UN when Kofi Annan of Ghana became secretary-general.[148] By 1997 peace appeared to have been restored. Ellen Johnson Sirleaf was again approached to come back and to challenge Charles Taylor (who was then regarded as the legitimate president).[149] Taylor won. President Carter, on hand as an election observer, suggested to Sirleaf that she should remain and work for Taylor. She rejected his advice, noting that when Carter submitted his report to the Carter Center, he said, "I was unreasonable."[150] Off again, Sirleaf watched events in Liberia from what became the Open Society Initiative for West Africa.[151]

Finally her opportunity came. Taylor was banished. And Sirleaf was again called back to run for office as president. Running an American-style campaign (with an American advisor), she won. "No one expected me to become president."[152] Her election in 2006 made her the first African woman to assume this high office. Her opposition was a football (soccer) star with considerable name recognition, but poorly educated and inarticulate. (In 2012, with a member of the Tubman family leading the ticket and Weah as vice-presidential candidate, the two faced each other again, with Sirleaf again the victor.)

In 2006, in the wake of her first triumph, one of her first acts was to send Taylor to Nigeria in exile. Later he escaped, was captured, and was tried and convicted in 2012 by the International Court. Beyond that triumph, Sirleaf has had to preside over an economy in shatters, a nation in disarray due to the long period of mayhem and war. Ellen Johnson Sirleaf was selected by the Norwegians for the Nobel Peace Prize in 2011. She has been able to maintain the peace in Liberia but faces many of the same problems that plagued the country when she was first elected. Additionally, the Ebola outbreak that spread from Guinea to Sierra Leone presented a serious challenge to her in 2014.

This chapter has covered a range of subjects pertaining to women in Africa in the post-independence years. The coverage is not as broad as it should be, considering the myriad of events that have taken place and the numbers of women who have emerged to play leading (or even supportive) roles. No survey ever encompasses all, but it was my intention to touch on the few who are representative of the many. I have touched on female artists and writers of fiction. I have touched on legal pluralism and the complexities involved in developing strategies that can weld traditional customary law with that of the state, which continue to exist in all of the countries. I have touched on migration—internal and external—which has created a significant brain drain in Africa while, for those who went elsewhere, opportunities loomed. We saw in Obbo's study how villagers and rural women found opportunities or they created their own.

It was important to feature examples of African women who have achieved—who made a difference in their respective countries. They were and are the role models for younger women who follow in their wake. Although the Hausa women were not united in political advocacy, they made significant progress in education and, in some cases, in organizing as adjuncts to political parties in Kano. The situation in northern Nigeria in the recent past meant that many of these women took cover figuratively (and many, literally) behind the veil. Repressive countries such as Ethiopia post good intentions for public consumption, but little progress has been achieved—even the traditional leather skirt was forcefully outlawed.

Central African Republic, still mired in conflict, has an interim woman president. Malawi had a female president, but, as a poor country, it presented many challenges to Mrs. Banda—including financial scandals that swirled around her and her cabinet. In Liberia, Ellen Johnson Sirleaf has been returned for a second term as president. Her challenges are also innumerable—the wounds of war are still not healed; the economy is far from recovered; and rumbles of discontent are heard, if not acted on. A prominent South African woman has courageously emerged to found a new political party, with the intention of running for president against the odds, and the ANC.

We have encountered lawyers, educators, and civil servants committed to improving the lives of women in their respective countries. Surely the survival in office of the intrepid Ngozi Okonjo-Iweala is desirable, if problematic, considering Nigerian politics. As we end this chapter, we celebrate all of those who have made a difference, although we also know that the road ahead for many is fraught with difficulties. Traditions and customs do not give way easily.

Notes

Chapter One

1. 1 Kings 10:1-11.
2. Quoted in Leeman.
3. Josephus, *Antiquities of the Jews,* quoted in Leeman, *Queen of Sheba,* pp. 68-69.
4. Budge, *Kebra Negast,* pp. 30-35; Leeman, *Queen of Sheba,* pp. 81-82.
5. This story comes mainly from the Kebra Negast, as related in Budge, *Kebra Negast,* pp. 30-35; see also Leeman, *Queen of Sheba,* pp. 87-91.
6. Indicopleutstes, *Christian Topography of Cosmos,* pp. 49-50.
7. Amina is mentioned in the *Kano Chronicle,* a well-regarded and detailed history of the city of Kano, compiled in the late nineteenth century. See also Smith, *Government in ZauZau.*
8. McEwan, *Africa from Early Times,* p. 62. See also Gailey, *Africa from Earliest Times to 1800.*
9. Miller, "Nzinga in a New Perspective," p. 210.
10. "Andrew Battell on the Jaga," in Collins, *Central and South African History,* p. 48.
11. Thornton, "Legitimacy and Political Power," p. 39.
12. Boxer, *Salvador de Sa and the Struggles for Brazil and Angola,* p. 228.
13. Hilton, *The Kingdom of Kongo,* p. 38.
14. Thornton, "Legitimacy and Political Power," p. 40.
15. Becker, "*Efundula*: Women's Initiation, Gender and Sexual Identities in Colonial and Post-Colonial Northern Namibia,"pp. 40, 42.
16. Bay, "Belief, Legitimacy and the Kpijito: An Institutional History of the 'Queen Mother' in Pre-colonial Dahomey," p. 8.
17. Bay, "Belief, Legitimacy and the Kpijito," pp. 12-15. This extract does not contain the numerous sources Bay cited, but they can be found in the article itself: see the bibliography.
18. Shetler, *Telling Our Own Stories,* p. 57.
19. Ibid., p. 64. The story is not quite as simple in outcome as suggested in the final paragraphs, as it entails a large number of names and ethnic groups that detract from the emphasis on Nyakinywa and Sombayo.
20. Kenyatta, *Facing Mount Kenya,* p. 147. All of the founding tradition here comes from Kenyatta's anthropological study of his people that was the outgrowth of his graduate study at the University of London under the supervision of the renowned Professor Malinowski.
21. Ibid., pp. 3-5.
22. Ibid., pp. 6-7.
23. Ibid., p. 8.

Chapter 2

1. Quoted in Van Wyk Smith, "'The Most Wretched of the Human Race': The Iconography of Khoikian (Hottentots)," p. 289.
2. McCrone, *Race Attitudes in South Africa*, pp. 13-14.
3. Ibid., p. 14.
4. Augustin de Beaulieu, quoted in Raven-Hart, ed., *Before van Riebeeck*, p. 100.
5. Padgen, *The Fall of Natural Man*, p. 22.
6. Raven-Hart, *Before van Riebeeck*, passim.
7. Mundy, 1634, quoted in ibid., p. 140.
8. Thomas Best, quoted in ibid., pp. 57-58.
9. Jon Olafsson, 1623, quoted in ibid., p. 111. Actually, nine Englishmen who went into the interior went missing and several of their bodies were later found.
10. Cornelis Claesz and Van Purmerendt, quoted in ibid., p. 44.
11. Pyrard de Laval, 1610, quoted in bid., p. 46.
12. Sir Thomas Roe, 1615, quoted in bid., p. 77.
13. Elphick, *Khoikhoi and the Founding of South Africa*, p. 194.
14. Romero, "Encounter at the Cape: French Huguenots, the Khoi and Other People of Color," p. 12.
15. Thomas Herbert, 1627, quoted in Raven-Hart, *Before van Riebeeck*, p. 119.
16. Nicolaus de Graaf, 1640, quoted in ibid., p. 154.
17. Sir Edward Michelbourne, quoted in ibid., p. 32.
18. Cornelis Matelief, 1608, quoted in ibid., p. 37.
19. John Albrecht van Mandelslo, 1639, quoted in ibid., p. 152.
20. Van Wyck Smith, "The Most Wretched," p. 289.
21. Schutte, in A. J. Boeseken, ed. and trans., *Briefwisseling*, p. 314.
22. Cornelis Claesz, 1609, quoted in Raven-Hart, *Before van Riebeeck*, p. 37.
23. Pyrard de Laval, 1610, quoted in ibid., p. 47.
24. Edward Terry, 1616, quoted in ibid., p. 83.
25. Thomas Hardy, 1627, quoted in ibid., p. 121.
26. Ten Rhyne, "An Account of the Cape of Good Hope," pp. 836-42.
27. Vaillant, *Travels from the Cape of Good Hope*, pp. 250, 299-300.
28. Ibid., pp. 308-9.
29. Ibid., pp. 424-31.
30. Thompson, A History of South Africa, pp. 6-7.
31. At one point the British thought his name was Hadda and thus called him Harry. Seaman Peter Mundy encountered Autshumato in 1632, when he was said to be a clan chief over about 60 "men, women and children" (quoted in Raven-Hart, *Before van Riebeeck*, p. 143). In about 1629, Harry had been taken to Bantam, where he remained a few months and learned some English. By 1632, he was serving as a sort of postman to the British. By 1647, Autshumato was on the mainland, speaking "good English" and defined as a Strandloper (Leendert Janssen, quoted in Raven-Hart, *Before van Riebeeck,* p. 169).
32. Wells, "Eva's Men: Gender and Power in the Establishment of the Cape of Good Hope, 1652-1674," pp. 417-37.
33. Thom, ed., *Journals of Jan van Riebeeck*, vol. 2, p. 238. The narrative regarding Krotoa and her relations with the Company and other Khoe comes from volumes 2 and 3 of the journals, unless otherwise cited.

34. Bhabbha, *Location of Culture*, pp. 32-33.

35. Elphick, *Khoikhoi*, p. 202.

36. Ibid.

37. Ibid.

Chapter 3

1. Shell, *Children of Bondage,* p. 58. See his population pyramid featuring born locally and imported slaves, p. 59.

2. Shell, pp. 78, 108. Shell notes that after the epidemic slaves could be purchased at auction only for cash.

3. Ibid., p. 78.

4. Mentzel, *A Complete Geographical Description of the African Cape of Good Hope,* p. 125.

5. Shell, *Children,* p. 69.

6. Ibid., p. 79.

7. Shell, *Children,* pp. 81-82. Shell presents a partial transcript of Manomia of Bengal's interview with the court and made the point that her three children and twenty-three grandchildren were therefore kept in bondage.

8. Mentzel, *A Complete Geographical Description of the African Cape of Good Hope,* p. 125.

9. Shell, *Children,* p. 78.

10. Mentzel, *A Complete Geographical Description of the African Cape of Good Hope,* p. 126.

11. Ibid., p. 133.

12. Verlinden, "Blacks," pp. 268-70.

13. Hunwick and Powell, *The African Diaspora and Mediterranean,* p. xix.

14. See, for instance, Robertson and Klein, *Women and Slavery.*

15. Alpers, "The Story of Swema: Female Vulnerability in Nineteenth Century East Africa," pp. 185-99. The entire story of Swema comes from the Alpers article and that in turn derived from a French Catholic archive in Paris. Alpers discovered the document in 1978 and obtained permission from Père Bernard Noël, the archivist at the Congrégation du Saint-Esprit to publish the document in French.

16. Ibid., p. 188.

17. Swema's testimony translated by and quoted in Alpers, p. 190. All subsequent translations and quotes derive from Alpers.

18. Ibid., p. 194.

19. Ibid., p. 195.

20. Ibid., pp. 195-96.

21. Ibid., p. 197.

22. Ibid., p. 197.

23. Ibid., p. 198.

24. Ibid. At that time Alpers speculates that Swema was ten years of age. She converted to Catholicism and, in one of the greatest of ironies, in later years dressed the wounds of the very Arab who had been responsible for the death of her mother and who had sent her to her grave (but not death) in Zanzibar.

25. See Semba, *The Vitamin A Story,* passim.

26. Mack, "Hajiya Ma'daki: A Royal Hausa Woman," pp. 14-77. Barbara Callaway, however, in a private communication (September 2012) contends that the emirs do still have concubines of slave lineage.

27. Anon., "The Guinea Coast in the Sixteenth Century," p. 153.

28. Barbot, pp. 369-70.

29. Ibid., p. 370.

30. Ibid.

31. Crow, *The Memoirs of the Late Captain Hugh Crow,* p. 227.

32. Ibid.

33. Kingsley, *Travels in West Africa,* p. 530.

34. Bosman, "Justice and Warfare at Axim," p. 199.

35. Newton, *An Authentic Narrative of Some of the Remarkable and Interesting Particulars in the Life,* pp. 39-43.

36. Ibid., pp. 41-42.

37. Ibid., p. 42.

38. Ibid.

39. Ibid., p. 43.

40. Newton, *Thoughts upon the African Slave Trade,* pp. 101-2.

41. Agiri, "Slavery in Yoruba Society in the 19th Century," p. 130.

42. Kingsley, *Travels in West Africa,* p. 277.

43. Brooks, Jr. "Signares of Saint-Louis and Gorée: Women Entrepreneurs in Eighteenth Century Senegal," pp. 19-44.

44. St. Clair, *The Door of No Return: The History of the Cape Coast Castle and the Atlantic Slave Trade,* p. 1. Special thanks to Professor St. Clair for his many kindnesses during the course of writing this chapter.

45. Ibid., p. 147. All of the narrative and quotes dealing with Cape Castle come from St. Clair.

46. Ibid., p. 148.

47. Ibid., pp. 148-50.

48. Ibid., p. 151.

49. Ibid. St. Clair whimsically commented that the governor's British widow was probably not pleased with this veiled comparison.

50. Ibid., pp. 152-54.

51. Ibid., p. 157.

52. Ibid. Palaver meant, roughly, arrangements and/or discussion.

53. Ibid., pp. 157-58.

54. Vansina, *Being Colonized: The Kuba Experience in Rural Congo 1890-1960,* pp. 24-26.

55. Ibid., p. 31.

Chapter 4

1. Quoted in Sparrman, *Travels in the Cape,* n. 103, p. 207. In the same note, quoting from a journal containing several letters pertaining to this missionary and his conversions, the author said that by 1742 five women had become "sisters in Christ."

2. Randolph Vigne to author, August 18, 2013.

3. Vigne, *South African Letters, Pringle,* p. 131. Regarding attitudes toward the Bush-

man/San, as late as the early 1800s, "some whites could only think of [them] as vermin." Davenport and Saunders, *South Africa*, p. 481.

4. Sparrman, *Travels in the Cape*, p. 284. Sparrman invoked what appeared to be irony in frequently referring to the whites in these passages concerning the Khoe as "Christians" (p. 203).

5. The Duff Mission in the Xhosa area of Eastern Cape was established by the Wesleyan Society in 1827. See Ntantala, *A Life's Mosaic*, p. 1.

6. de Gruchy, *London Missionary Society*, Preface.

7. Elbourne, "Whose Gospel?" in deGruchy, p. 146. In addition to the missionary societies mentioned in the text, the Rhenish Missionary Society established a base in the Cedarberg and in the Cape and gradually moved into what is today's Namibia, where they worked among the Herero and Nama; and after Germany united, this group was active in promoting colonialism.

8. de Gruchy, *London*, p. 4.

9. Horst Kleinschmidt, "A Memorial to Zara Schmelen," p. 1.

10. Ibid.

11. Ibid., p. 2. One letter was dated 1824—thus we know that the project took many years to complete.

12. Ibid., pp. 1-2.

13. Ibid., p. 2.

14. Ibid., p. 1. In southern Namibia, the Schmelens established a school for children and one for adults. These were the first of the formal schools there (p. 3).

15. Achebe, *Things Fall Apart*.

16. Kingsley, *Travels in West Africa*, pp. 473-74. In Buganda, however, twins conferred prestige, especially among the royals. See Nsimbi, *Amanya Amaganda N'enono Zaago*, pp. 96-98. Thanks to Christine Obbo for this citation.

17. Ibid., p. 478.

18. Ajayi, *Christian Missionaries*, p. 59.

19. Burton, *First Footsteps*, p. 93; Appendix 2: "Excision and Infibulation," pp. 285-87.

20. Jahadhmy, *Anthology*, p. 32. A plaque (pictured) at Mwana Kupona's former residence incorrectly states that she wrote the *utendi* in 1830. It was more probably in 1859 or 1860. By 1857-58, when this poem was composed, Hashima was old enough to marry. Girls married just past puberty in those days. Mwana Kupona's husband died between 1851 and 1853.

21. Ibid., pp. 32-37.

22. Kingsley, *Travels in West Africa*, p. 662.

23. Hening, *History of the African Mission*, pp. 29-31. The problem of child brides persists in Africa. Bishop Desmond Tutu announced that he and fellow Nobel Peace Prize winners have committed to ending this practice, the largest numbers of these girls being in Africa. Quoted in *The Washington Post*, October 12, 2012.

24. Romero, ed., *Women's Voices on Africa*, p. 25. See also Ajayi, *Christian Missions*, p. 167.

25. Romero, *Women's Voices*, p. 37; Kingsley, *Travels*, p. 57.

26. Ajayi, *Christian Missions*, p. 15.

27. Ayandele, *The Missionary Impact*, p. 81.

28. Smith, "The Missionary Contribution to Education in Tanganyika," p. 101.

29. Ibid., p. 105.

30. Ibid., pp. 32, 37.

31. Kingsley, *Travels*, pp. 77-78.
32. Ibid., pp. 222-23.
33. Ibid.
34. Henry Francis Fynn, *Diaries*, eds. Stuart and Malcolm, in Collins, *History of Central and South Africa*, pp. 171, 174. It was to Fynn that Shaka called the Zulu woman a dog, comparing her cure to that for "dogs."
35. Ibid., p. 171.
36. Smith, ed., *Encyclopedia of Women in World History*, V. 2, p. 166.
37. Ibid.
38. Ibid., p. 167.
39. Speke, *Journal of the Discovery of the Nile*, pp. 287, 290, 361. Speke repeatedly referred to the Queen Mother as N'yamasore, apparently misunderstanding her title, which was Namasole. See Smith, *Encyclopedia of Women in World History*, V. 3, pp. 281-82, for a biographical sketch of Muganzirwaza. The entry refers to discussions between the Queen Mother and Speke regarding polygamy. Having searched the entire journal, I found no references to the subject, although they did discuss marriage—and that is included in this text. Speke's journal was censored by Blackwood's, his first publisher, before it was published in 1863. The second edition, from which we draw his account in Buganda, was merely reprinted.
40. Ibid., pp. 313-16, 334.
41. Ibid., p. 362.
42. Ibid., pp. 305-7.
43. Ibid., pp. 313-16.
44. Kagwa, *Basekabaka Be Buganda*, pp. 111-12, 121. Thanks to Christine Obbo for this citation.
45. Hanson, "Queen Mothers," p. 222.
46. Ibid., passim.
47. Ibid., pp. 360-61.
48. The fact that no oral traditions, songs, or other forms of remembrance mention Muganzirwaza's drinking habits suggests that she probably engaged in heavy drinking and partying no more than others among the royals at that time. Christine Obbo commented in a private communication (December 12, 2012) that she "seems to have had a long life for an alcoholic! She was given a fantastic funeral . . . in four coffins loaded with the finest imported fabrics and bark cloth."
49. Ibid., pp. 369-73.
50. Ibid., pp. 373, 206.
51. Ibid., pp. 358-59. Speke translated and put in brackets the above pleas.
52. Achebe, *Things Fall Apart*, p. 100.
53. Kingsley, *Travels*, pp. 471-72.
54. Arnot, *Garenganze*, pp. 94, 66.
55. Freeman-Grenville, "The Coast," p. 129.
56. Mtoro bin Mwinyi, *The Customs of the Swahili People*, p. 51.
57. Hasini bin Ismail, pp. 69-70. Lienhardt suggested that this story may have been his excuse for impotence.
58. Interview, Fatuma Abdalla, Mombasa, October 1985.
59. Alpers, "Ordinary Household Chores," p. 588.
60. Reute, *Memoirs*, p. 210.
61. Gqoba, "Tale of Nongquwuse," pp. 211-12. Thanks to Randolph Vigne for providing

the original translation of this document. For a full account see J. B. Peires, *The Dead Will Arise: Nongquwuse and the Great Xhosa Cattle-Killing Movement of 1856-7.*

62. Gqoba, "The Tale of Nongquwuse, pp. 5-9. Thanks to Randolph Vigne for securing this article for me.
63. Ibid., p. 7.
64. Ibid., p. 8.
65. Ibid., p. 9.

Chapter 5

1. The Life and Times of Sara Baartman: The Hottenton Venus." See also Crais and Scully, *Sara Baartman and the Hottenton Venus: A Ghost Story and a Biography.* Sara was also known as Saartjie—the Boer version of Sara.
2. "The Life and Times."
3. Quoted in "The Life and Times."
4. Ibid.
5. Court testimony quoted in ibid.
6. Quoted in ibid.
7. Ibid.
8. Gould, *The Flamingo's Smile*, p. 297. The film version suggests that Cuvier did, finally, convince her to drop the apron.
9. See Crais and Skully for an elaboration of her time in Paris.
10. Quoted in Gould, p. 299.
11. Ibid., p. 294. See also Gilman, *Sexuality*, pp, 292-93.
12. Gilman, "Black Bodies, White Bodies," p. 232. Gilman also noted that in 1829 another Khoe woman was "the prize attraction at a ball given by the Duchess du Barry in Paris."
13. Quoted in Gilman, p. 239.
14. Afrikaners considered themselves as Africans; hence the name they chose rather than the common usage of "Dutch," which, in fact, was inaccurate as they were a mixture of primarily German, Dutch, and French, with more than a smattering of genetic input from Khoe.
15. The Orange Free State adopted the policy of forbidding a black person to own land at independence, and this policy remained in effect until the Act of Union in 1910. See Davenport and Saunders, *History*, pp. 85-86.
16. At the Cape, however, many sophisticated and prosperous Afrikaners got on well with the British, as did some, too, in Natal. They were exempt from the stereotype that marked their brethren in remote areas of the OFS and the Transvaal.
17. Pakenham, *The Boer War*, pp. 190, 433.
18. William, *Sol Plaatje*, p. 193.
19. Pakenham, *Boer War*, p. 431. See also Warwick, *Black People,* p. 36, and a quote from a white woman's diary at the end of 1899 in Mafeking: "the kaffirs dug up dead horses and ate them. They stand and pick at the rubbish heaps. Some of them are starving."
20. Warwick, *Black People,* p. 37.
21. Warwick, *Black People,* p. 148. Warwick noted that these moves were not always approved by the British administration.
22. van Heyningen, "Women and Gender," p. 92.
23. Warwick, *Black People*, pp. 148, 150.

24. Quoted in van Heyningen, "Women and Gender," p. 105.

25. Ibid., p. 95.

26. Ibid., p. 104.

27. Ibid., p. 105.

28. Ibid., p. 104; Stanley, *Mourning Becomes*, pp. 190-91. The other major camp for blacks was Thaba 'Nchu in the OFS, which was established in April 1901.

29. Pakenham, *The Boer War,* p. 340; Stanley, *Mourning Becomes*, p. 185.

30. Gasa, *Women in South Africa,* p. 120.

31. van Heyningen, p. 99.

32. German Colonial Office, *Treatment of Native and Other Populations*, pp. 211-13.

33. Uys, *The Heidelbergers*, p. 168.

34. Ibid., p. 161.

35. van Onselen, *The Seed Is Mine*, p. 11. Van Onselen's biography of Kas Maine is such beautifully composed lyric prose that to paraphrase him is to do injustice to not only his book, but the life of this remarkable family.

36. Ibid., p. 103. The ethnic differences between Kas and his wives are important only in that, when he was forced to move onto the reserves, Kas was able to go to an area reserved for the Batswana people in the northwest Transvaal.

37. Ibid., p. 122.

38. Ibid., passim; Cock, *Maids and Madams,* p. 39.

39. Ibid., p. 128.

40. Ibid., pp. 166-67.

41. Ibid., p. 120.

42. Ibid., p. 239.

43. Ibid., pp. 246-49.

44. Ibid., pp. 478-79.

45. Ibid., p. 337.

46. Ibid.

47. Ibid., pp. 338, 531, 530.

48. Charlotte Manye. Available at http://www.sahistory.org.za. Accessed January 10, 2013.

49. See Romero, *Profiles in Diversity,* p. 194.

50. Charlotte Manye. Available at http://www.sahistory.org.za.

51. Madley, "Patterns of Frontier Genocide," p. 182.

52. Gewald, *Herero Heroes*, p. 32. Other accusations accrued and can be found in Gewald.

53. Madley, "Patterns of Frontier Genocide," p. 183; Hughes, *Germany's Genocide of the Herero*, pp. 107-8.

54. Ibid., p. 183. Madley quoted one German authority as writing that "Racial hatred has become rooted in the very framework of justice."

55. Gewald, *Herero Heroes*, pp. 170-73.

56. Quoted in Madley, "Patterns of Frontier Violence," p. 187.

57. Quoted in Gewald, *Herero Heroes*, p. 190.

58. Ibid.

59. Available at http://africasacountry.com/herero-women-challenge-german-amnesia/. Accessed January 23, 2013.

Chapter 6

1. Portugal ended the slave trade in 1836. The Indian Ocean slave trade was not officially eliminated until 1873, with some Africans being shipped to the Spanish colonies and to Brazil via the Indian Ocean and around the Cape of Good Hope.
2. Higgs, *Cocoa Islands*, p. 47.
3. Quoted in Shillington, *History*, pp. 335-36.
4. Hyam, "Empire and Sexual Opportunity," p. 49.
5. Kourouma, *Monnew*, pp. 44-45.
6. Malcolm, "Colonial Policy and Family Life," pp. 433, 439-49.
7. bid., p. 439.
8. Callaway, *Gender*, p. 48.
9. Quoted in ibid., p. 49.
10. Ibid., p. 50.
11. Ibid.
12. Higgs, *Cocoa Islands*, passim.
13. Ibid., p. 47.
14. Ibid.
15. In Chapter One we dealt with the Ethiopian myth of origin regarding the Queen of Sheba, whose son Menelik I was said to be the son of King Solomon. The King (Ras) of Shewa claimed to be a descendant of the Solomonic line.
16. Prouty, *Empress Taytu*, p. 28. Unless otherwise noted, all of the detail concerning Taytu comes from Prouty.
17. Ibid.
18. Ibid., p. 37.
19. Ibid., p. 40.
20. Ibid., p. 41.
21. Ibid., p. 42.
22. Ibid., p. 53.
23. Ibid., p. 49.
24. Marcus, *Menelik II*, p. 72.
25. Prouty, p. 43. Marcus, ibid., p. 116, states that Antonelli arrived in 1882. Perhaps he did not make an appearance in Menelik's camp until just after the wedding.
26. Marcus, *Menelik II*, p. 117.
27. Prouty, *Empress Taytu*, p. 67.
28. Mondon-Vidailhet quoted in Prouty, p. 137.
29. Menelik's Chronicler quoted in ibid., p. 157.
30. Ibid., p. 159.
31. Quoted in ibid., p. 346.
32. Salme's life and her relationships with her family, the Germans, and the British will be covered in my forthcoming study of "Salme and Her Brothers."
33. Kimambo and Temu, *A History of Tanzania*, p. 98.
34. Coupland, *Exploitation*, p. 437.
35. Ruete, *Memoirs*, p. 287.
36. John Kirk to Colonial Office, quoted in Coupland, *Exploitation*, p. 439.
37. Quoted in Coupland, *Exploitation*, p. 438.
38. Ibid., pp. 439-43; Kimambo and Temu, *A History of Tanzania*, pp. 100-102.
39. Smith, *Baba of Karo*, p. 185.

40. Ofosu-Amaah, "Disease in Sub-Saharan Africa," p. 121.
41. Salmons, "Mask: Ibibo/Amang, Akwa Ibom State Nigeria, " p. 189.
42. Smith, *Baba of Karo*, p. 81.
43. Ibid., p. 190.
44. Zimmer, "Guinea Worm." According to Zimmer, the remaining areas afflicted are Ethiopia, Chad, and South Sudan.
45. Henderson, *Smallpox*, p. 40.
46. Vansina, *Being Colonized,* pp. 140-41.
47. Smith, *Baba of Karo,* p. 46. Smallpox was eradicated in the 1970s.
48. Ibid., p. 218.
49. Ibid., p. 178.
50. McLeod, *The Asante*, p. 162.
51. Ibid., p. 165.
52. Vaughan, *Curing,* p. 69.
53. Ibid., p. 66.
54. Hill, "Infant and Child Mortality," p. 74.
55. For malaria, see Packard, *Malaria*, pp. 22, 46, 90, 103-5, 118-21.
56. Higgs, *Cocoa Islands*, pp. 58, 60.
57. Schweitzer, *On the Edge*, pp. 37-130.
58. Good, *Steamer Parish*, p. 233.
59. Yaws was eliminated in Kenya in the 1920s. John Lonsdale to author, August 8, 2013.
60. Ibid., p. 236.
61. Shepard and Halstead, "Dengue," p. 303.
62. Good, *Steamer Parish,* pp. 245-46. See also Semba, *The Vitamin A Story.*
63. Ibid., p. 225.
64. Vansina, *Being Colonized,* p. 147.
65. Rodrigues, "EPI Target Diseases," pp. 180-81.
66. Ibid., p. 182.
67. Ibid., p. 174.
68. Impey, *Handbook of Leprosy*, p. 2.
69. Ibid., p. 4.
70. Hutchison, "Leprosy in Cape Colony and Natal," *Lepra,* pp. 161-88.
71. Impey, *Handbook,* p. 7.
72. Ibid., pp. 5, 7.
73. Ibid., pp. 13-17.
74. Ibid., p. 26.
75. Vaughan, *Curing,* pp. 82-83.
76. Ibid., p. 83.
77. Ibid., p. 84.
78. Silla, "The Life of Saran Kieta," p. 29. All of the material that follows, including the pages in the extract, comes from Silla's life history of Saran, pp. 28-41. Saran was probably a Muslim, but no inferences to her religion appear in the life history.
79. Silla, "The Life of Saran Keita," pp. 31-35.
80. Ibid., p. 36.
81. Ibid., p. 40.
82. The *New York Times* carried an announcement that brings hope for those who are candidates for leprosy. A new more efficient test has been developed. It will enable medical personnel to detect leprosy in very early stages of incubation. See *New York Times*, Feb-

ruary 10, 2013. As of the late 1980s, there were still approximately three million cases of leprosy in Africa. See Ofosu-Annah, "Disease," p. 121.

83. Vaughan, *Curing*, pp. 129-54.

84. Ibid., p. 132.

85. Quoted in ibid., p. 133.

86. Ibid.

87. Ibid., p. 136.

88. Ibid., p. 137.

89. Ibid., p. 143. In this period, the French military in West Africa encountered severe problems with venereal disease among their African troops. They attempted to stop fraternizing with prostitutes on the grounds that the prostitutes were "carriers of disease." See Thompson, "Colonial Policy and Family Life," p. 433.

90. Ibid., p. 144.

91. Vansina, *Colonialism*, pp. 147-48.

92. Shillington, *History,* p. 371.

93. Quoted in Strobel and Mirza, *Three Swahili Women*, p. 63.

94. Maathai, *Unbowed,* pp. 27-28.

95. Cook quoted in Vaughan, *Curing*, p. 62.

96. Good, *Steamer Parish*, p. 226.

97. Clyde, *History of the Medical Services of Tanganyika*, p. 129.

98. Boahen, *African Perspectives*, p. 106.

99. Callaway, *Gender*, pp. 102, 107.

100. Goonam, "How Do We Fight," pp. 194-95.

101. Dundas, *Beneath*, pp. 104-21.

102. Ibid., p. 105.

103. Ibid., p. 104.

104. Ibid., p. 114.

105. Joshua, "The Church and the 1929," pp. 2, 4. Joshua (p. 3) suggests that the controversy that led to the birth of these independent churches set in motion a series of events among the Kikuyu that produced first the Kikuyu Central Association and later, the Mau Mau. This leap seems too radical, as many other factors entered in. For an expanded treatment of this controversy, see Lonsdale, "Kikuyu Christianities," pp. 157-97.

106. Lonsdale, "Kikuyu Christianities," pp. 18-19.

107. Joshua contended that Kenyatta had both of his daughters circumcised "at a hospital" in Kenya after a contretemps developed between the traditionalists and some of the missionaries.. Ibid., p. 6. John Lonsdale, in private communication to the author (August 8, 2013) suggests that this is unlikely. There was only one hospital in Kenya in 1929, and it is unlikely that, if Kenyatta had requested the surgery, any doctor would have performed it. And one of his daughters was not yet born in 1929. It is possible that the older daughter was circumcised, although no one currently alive knows.

108. Quoted in ibid., p. 6. Despite the law against FGM, many traditionalists in Kenya still practice it. Kenyatta was made prime minister of Kenya in December 1963. The next year in the general election, he was elected president of Kenya.

109. Kanogo, "Women," pp. 73-90.

110. Ibid., p. 74.

111. Kenyatta, *Facing Mount Kenya,* pp. 143-47.

112. See Cohen and Odhiambo, *Siaya*.

113. Bledsoe, *Marriage*, p. 67.
114. Ibid., p. 67.
115. Ibid., p. 73.
116. See Boone, *Radiance in the Water.*
117. Little, "Sierra Leone Protectorate," p. 7.
118. Ibid., p. 8.
119. Ibid., p. 11.
120. Ibid., pp. 13-14.
121. Ibid.
122. Ibid. For further complexities regarding marriage, the law, and colonialism, see Tashjian and Allman, "Marrying and Marriage on a Shifting Terrain," pp. 237-59.
123. Mack, "Hajiya Ma'daki," pp. 64-66.
124. Ibid., pp. 68-69.
125. Vansina, *Colonialism*, pp. 288-89.
126. Ibid., p. 291.
127. Miana, "Colonialism, Education," p. 157.
128. Ibid., p. 291.
129. Ibid., pp. 94-95.
130. Davis, "Charles T. Loram," pp. 88-91.
131. Marks, *Not Either*, p. 105.
132. Ibid., p. 21.
133. Ibid., pp. 2-12.
134. Ibid., p. 106.
135. Ibid., p. 31.
136. Ibid., pp. 31-32.
137. Ibid., p. 34.
138. Ibid.
139. Quoted in Strobel, *Mombasa*, pp. 105-6.
140. Romero, *Lamu*, p. 102.
141. Strobel, p. 113.
142. H. E. Lambert, "The Arab Community of Mombasa: Confidential," pp. 11-12. Typescript courtesy of Edward Rodwell, Mombasa.
143. Ibid., p. 13.
144. Kanogo, *Women*, p. 232.
145. Commire, *Women in World History,* pp. 163-64. See also Snyder and Tadesse, *African Women.*
146. Ibid.
147. Ibid., p. 166.
148. Ibid.
149. Ibid., p. 167.
150. Pillay, "I Always Said," pp. 212-13.
151. Ibid., pp. 213-14.
152. Ibid., p. 217.
153. The *Washington Post*, July 25, 2008.
154. Lydon, "Obtaining Freedom at the Muslim's Tribunal," p. 136.
155. Ibid., p. 149.
156. Ibid., pp. 149-50.
157. Ibid.

158. Ibid., p. 151.

159. Ibid., p. 152.

160. Ibid., p. 156.

161. Charles Steward quoted in ibid.

162. Boahen, *African Perspectives*, p. 110.

Chapter 7

1. Missing, for instance, are most of the civil wars in which women were involved as activists, although to a lesser extent than in the wars of liberation. In Chapter 8, I will touch on some of these civil wars, but mainly with women as victims, not players. The history of post-colonial Africa is dominated by conflict and/or coups in all but a very few of the independent countries.

2. Ibid., p. 113.

3. Awe, *Nigerian Women in Colonial Perspective,* pp. 140-60.

4. Johnson-Odum and Mba, *For Women and the Nation*. Ms. Ransome-Kuti was a celebrated figure who fought for women's rights and was active in politics as a member of the political party headed by Dr. Nmandi Azkiwe. She remained an activist until her death in 1978. The musician Fela (Kuti) was her son. He became radicalized during the late 1960s in Los Angeles, returning to Nigeria with not only fame as a performer, but as an activist, too. In 1978, when General Obasanjo was in power, the military launched a raid against Fela at his music studio and compound. His mother was there at the time of the attack. Fela suffered serious injuries. But his mother, Funmilayo, was thrown out of a second-story window, was severely wounded, and died soon thereafter at age 78. Despite the loss of his music, tapes, and instruments, Fela managed to go into exile in Ghana and continued to perform on the world stage until his death from AIDS in 1997.

5. Achebe, *The Female King of Colonial Nigeria*, pp. 107-22. Due to space limitations Aheba Ugbabe's story is reduced to this limited, if important, appointment. See Achebe for the incredible details regarding the masculinization of gender and Aheba Ugbabe as "king."

6. Van Allen, "'Aba Riots,'" pp. 65-67. See Van Allen for a particularly insightful theoretical construct on politics and power in Igbo society, pp. 68-71.

7 Johnson, "Grass Roots Organizing," pp. 138-39.

8. Ibid., p. 71. See also Rogers, "Anti-Colonial Protest," pp. 22-23; Mba, *Nigerian Women Mobilized,* pp. 60-75.

9. Perham, *Native Administration,* p. 207. Most of this narrative on the "Women's War" is drawn from Perham's account as she compiled it after reviewing the data available to the Two Commissions of Inquiry.

10. Ibid.

11. Van Allen, "'Aba Riots,'" p. 61.

12. Perham, *Native Administration*, p. 207. Perham adds that the second Commission recommended that he be pardoned.

13. Ibid., p. 208.

14. Ibid.

15. Ibid.

16. Rogers, "Anti-Colonial Protest," p. 22.

17. Perham, *Native Administration*, pp. 209-10. For the reference to the Hausa, see Rogers,

"Anti-Colonial Protest," p. 22.

18. That is the women in southeastern Nigeria who engaged in the war. In Abeokuta, a city in the west, Yoruba market women had been taxed from 1918, but after the Women's War in 1929, Pelewura met with the government officials in Lagos and was told that they were not to be taxed. See Johnson, "Grass Roots Organizing," p. 139.

19. Ibid., pp. 213-14. For a discussion and elaboration on Perham's coverage see Bastian, "Vultures in the Marketplace," pp. 260-72.

20. Emecheta, *Joys*, p. 144.

21 Emecheta, *Joys,* pp. 145-46.

22. Ibid., pp 146-82.

23. Oyono, *The Old Man and the Medal,* p. 90.

24. Ibid., p. 95.

25. Ibid., pp. 99-100.

26. Fortes, "The Impact of War on British West Africa," pp. 206-7.

27. Byfield, "Feeding the Troops," pp. 80-83.

28. Fortes, "The Impact of War on British West Africa," pp. 208-11.

29. Byfield, "Feeding the Troops," pp. 78-79.

30. Fortes, "The Impact of War on British West Africa," p. 216. A follow-up on the war in Nigeria led the British, in 1955, to establish the Women's Police force. See the documentary film *Nigeria's First Women's Police*.

31. Romero, *E. Sylvia Pankhurst*, p. 247.

32. Parsons, *African Rank and File*, p. 203.

33. Ibid.

34. Ibid., p. 204.

35. Ibid., pp. 204-5. Parsons made the point that the number of rebels was so large that it was impossible to arrest them all. The result was that many were allowed home leave.

36. Romero, *E. Sylvia Pankhurst*, p. 260.

37. White, "Prostitution, Identity, and Class Consciousness," pp. 265-66.

38. Mandeville, "Poverty, Work and Financing of Single Women in Kampala," p. 43.

39. Worden, *The Making of Modern*, pp. 91-92.

40. Charton, "I am going to be trained," p. 180.

41. Gordon, "The Impact of the Second World War," p. 148.

42. Quoted in ibid., p. 149.

43. Ibid.

44. Ibid., p. 155.

45. Ibid., pp. 154-59.

46. Ibid., p. 159.

47. Ibid.

48. Ibid., and quoted in ibid.

49. Quoted in ibid.

50. Ibid., p. 161.

51. See Cock, *Colonels and Cadres*, p. 216.

52. *New York Times*, June 7, 2013. See also David Anderson's op-ed column, "Atoning for the Sins of Empire," June 13, 2013. David Anderson was one of several historians who lobbied and testified for the compensation that the British agreed to pay to the 5,228 whose claims were part of a long-term suit against the government. See Anderson, *Histories of the Hanged*, a highly respected and thoroughly researched study of the conflict, which became part of the evidence presented in this case.

53. Santilli, "Kikuyu Women," pp. 143-59.

54. Elkins, *Imperial Reckoning.*

55. Santilli, p. 12.

56. Anderson, *Histories,* pp. 63-68.

57. Lonsdale to author, private communication, August 9, 2013.

58. Lonsdale, "Kenyatta's Trials," pp. 10-33.

59. Lonsdale to author, August 9, 2013.

60. Ibid., pp. 55-57.

61. Ibid., pp. 72-73.

62. Ibid., pp. 88-90.

63. Ibid., p. 91.

64. Ibid., pp. 92-93.

65. Ibid., p. 97.

66. Ibid., pp. 126-27.

67. Ibid., p. 130.

68. Ibid.

69. Anderson, "British Abuse and Torture," p. 704.

70. Ibid., p. 705.

71. Ibid., p. 211.

72. Ibid., pp. 700-719.

73. Barnes, *The Ghosts of Happy* Valley, p. 248. I knew Dr. Spoerry, although not well, due to her several trips to Lamu in the 1980s when I was conducting research. She was widely celebrated for her willingness to fly in to the aid of those in need due to injury or serious illness.

74. Ibid., p. 249. The place Barnes met these Kikuyu is called Wanjohi.

75. Ibid.

76. Anderson, "Mau Mau and the High Court," p. 700.

77. Ibid., pp. 705-6.

78. Waciuma, *Daughter.*

79. Otieno, *Mau Mau's Daughter*, pp. 38-39.

80. Ibid., p. 39.

81. Ibid., pp. 39-57, 77.

82. Ibid., p. 79.

83. Ibid., p. 83.

84. Ibid., pp. 87, 88.

85. Clough, *Mau Mau Memoirs*, pp. 135-37.

86. Ibid., pp. 139-40.

87. Ibid., p. 142.

88. Lonsdale, "Authority, Gender, Violence," p. 16.

89. Ibid.

90. Ibid., p. 17.

91. Quoted in Bruce-Lockhard, "It Cannot Be Dealt With," draft paper, p. 3.

92. Ibid., p. 7.

93. Ibid. The saga regarding these camps is derived from new archival material that Bruce-Lockhart has carefully analyzed, and it is forthcoming in published form.

94. Anderson, *Histories of the Hanged*, pp. 273, 277.

95. Ibid., p. 288.

96. Ibid., p. 390.

97. Chabal and Vidal, (eds), *Angola: The Weight of History*, p. 51.
98. Arnfred, private communication, September 1, 2013.
99. Ibid.; Newitt, *A History of Mozambique*, p. 519.
100. Urdang, "Fighting Two Colonialisms," p. 29.
101. Ibid., p. 30.
102. Ibid., p. 31.
103. Ibid., p. 32.
104. Ibid., p. 30.
105. Ibid., p. 31.
106. Ibid.
107. Newitt, "Angola in Historical Context," pp. 63-64.
108. Ibid., p. 75.
109. Campbell, "Angolan Women," pp. 70-76; Ducados, "An All Men's Show?" pp. 11-22.
110. Kukkkuk, "Letters to Gabriella," p. 140.
111. Holness, *Angolan Women Building the Future*, p. 30. How women whose husbands, fathers, brothers, and sons were treated by Angolan members of UNITA, supported by South Africa and the United States (under President Reagan), is a story yet to be revealed.
112. Ducados, "An All Men's Show?" pp. 11-12.
113. Newitt, *A History of Mozambique*, pp. 521-60, provides an in-depth treatment of Frelimo, its leaders, and policies, including those pertaining to women.
114. Arnfred, "Women in Mozambique," pp. 5-6.
115. Quoted in Disney, *Women's Activism*, p. 144. See also Owen, "Lina Magaia."
116. Disney, *Women's Activism*, p. 145.
117. Newitt, *A History of Mozambique*, p. 527; Arnfred, in a private communication, noted that Machel's first wife, Josina, died during the war of liberation.
118. West, "Girls with Guns," p. 186.
119. Quoted in Newitt, *A History of Mozambique*, p. 548.
120. Smith, *Encyclopedia of Women*, Vol. 3, pp. 434-35.
121. Ibid. For Muslim women's activities in the formation of political parties and the role of dance, see Geiger, Women in Nationalist Struggle," in *Tanzania*, pp. 1-26.
122. Arnfred, "Women in Mozambique," pp. 6-7.
123. Deacon, *An Examination of Factors*, p. 8. Arnfred takes issue with the term "sex slavery," stating that women were forced to marry.
124. Perez, *Women and Terrorism, "* pp. 81-82.
125. Kriger, *Zimbabwe's Guerrilla War*, pp. 191-92.
126. Staunton, *Mothers of the Revolution*.
127. Ibid., pp. 112, 116, 121-22, 188, 200, 208-10.
128. Ibid., pp. 149-50.
129. Ibid., p. 192.
130. Ibid., pp. 119-27.
131. Ibid., p. 208.
132. Ibid., p. 176.
133. Ibid., p. 177, and similar sentiments repeated *passim*.
134. Ibid., pp. 225-35.
135. Gasa, "Appendix: Representation and Reality," pp. 256-57.
136. Morris, *Every Step of the Way,* pp. 210-11.

137. Goonam, "We Are Going to Fight This Government," pp. 200-203.

138. Neocosmos, "Remembering Phyllis Naidoo." Available at http://www.dailymaverick. co.za/opinionsta/2013-02-20-remembering. Accessed April 15, 2013. See also Burton, *Brown over Black*, pp. 123-65.

139. Sahistory.org.2a. Accessed June, 2013. The letter bomb was believed to have been sent by the SA security forces.

140. Alexander [Alexandrovitch], "Do You Belong to a Union," pp. 69-76; see also Suttner, (ed.), *All My Life and All My Strength.*

141. Simpson, *Mandela*, pp. 297-301.

142. Ibid., pp. 369-74. See Simpson for extensive information on Winnie Madikezela Mandela, *passim*. Following her divorce, Winnie added Madikezela to her name as she embarked on her own political career.

143. Ibid.

144. Cock, *Colonels and Cadres*, p. 130.

145. Quoted in ibid., p. 130.

146. Ibid., p. 141.

147. Ibid., pp. 142-43. Cock makes the point that both of these women were officially attached to the SAP, although by the 1980s the SAP and the SADF were working closely together.

148. Suttner, "ANC-Led Underground," p. 240.

149. Ibid.

150. Ibid.

151. Ibid., p. 242.

152. Ibid., p. 245.

153. Majola, "1976 Was a Bad Year for Me," p. 128.

154. Ibid., pp. 128-29. Jumartha Majola's son returned home safely at the end of the hostilities.

155. Mgcina, "I Lost Three Sons in the Struggle," pp. 133-34.

156. Ibid., p. 135.

157. Ibid., pp. 136, 131.

Chapter 8

1. Collins, *East African History*, pp. 31-36. The actual civil war took place in 1955-72; war occurred again in 1983-2011.

2. Romero, *E. Sylvia Pankhurst*, pp. 241-45.

3. An anomaly, not discussed earlier in dealing with the Abe Riots, was that the British ultimately appointed a female warrant chief, Abed Urbane. This radical departure is discussed in a recent fascinating study. See Achebe, *The Female King of Colonial Nigeria, passim.*

4. Adichi, *Half a Yellow Sun*. References to the novel run throughout this section, and no attempt is made to tie actual dates to events, as Adichi weaves many of these events into her story, although not necessarily in the sequence in which they took place.

5. Achebe, *There Was a Country;* Nwaka, "Biafran Women," pp. 34-46. See also Emecheta, *Destination Biafra;* Obafemui, *Nigerian Writers on the Nigerian Civil War.*

6. Quoted in Mintz, "The Anthropological Interview," p. 18.

7. Nwaka, "Biafran Women," n. 10.

8. Ibid., p. 37.
9. Ibid., p. 36.
10. Achebe, *There Was,"* p. 228; "Nigeria had not succeeded in crushing the spirit of the Igbo people, but it had left us indigent, stripped bare, and stranded in the wilderness."
11. Ibid., p. 111.
12. Ibid., p. 226.
13. Quoted in Nwaka, "Biafran Women," p. 40.
14. Achebe, *There Was,"* p. 193. She was actually dismissed early from the hospital due to the imminent arrival of federal troops.
15. Ibid., pp. 182-83.
16. Nwaka, "Biafran Women," p. 41.
17. For the facts, see ibid., p. 42.
18. Ibid.
19. Achebe, *There Was*, p. 189.
20. Ibid., p. 44.
21. Ibid., p. 112.
22. Nwaka, "Biafran Women," p. 45.
23. Emecheta, *Destination Biafra*, p. vii.
24. Zewde, *A History*, p. 230.
25. Lafort, *Ethiopia*, p. 276.
26. Interview with Kebedech Tekleab, May 16, 2005, Arlington, Virginia.
27. Tedasse, *The Generation*, Part II, p. 135.
28. Kebedech, interview. Kebedech plans a memoir of her experiences in the Somali camp and reserves the right to discuss the particulars when she does so.
29. Haile-Selassie, *Conflict*, p. 190; Keller, *Revolutionary*, p. 206.
30. Tedasse, *The Generation,* Part II, p. 220.
31. Kebedech, interview.
32. *Washington Post*, September 14, 2005.
33. Phone interview, September 10, 2013.
34. Ibid.
35. Markakis, *National and Class Conflict,* p. xv. Said Barre, president of Somalia when Kebedech was taken prisoner, was overthrown in 1991. Somalia has become a failed state. Mengistu Haile Miriam also was deposed in 1991. A faction led by men from Tigre took over, and despite the façade of elections, remains in power by coercion. Much of the opposition resulted in more refugees pouring out of the country.
36. Kebedech, Interview.
37. Angom, "Women in Peacemaking and Peacebuilding in Northern Uganda," pp. 74-76.
38. Ibid., p. 75.
39. Ibid., p. 77.
40. Singh, "Women, Conflict and Darfur," p. 2.
41. Ibid., pp. 2-3.
42. Corcoran, "Justice for the Forgotten," pp. 203-4.
43. Ibid., p. 210.
44. Human Rights Watch, "Sexual Violence," p. 5.
45. Ibid., p. 8.
46. Ibid., p. 11.
47. Ibid.
48. "Women Fighters in South Sudan." Available at http://www.google.com/hostednews/afp/article.

49. Ibid.

50. Ibid., p. 2.

51. Ibid.

52. Ibid.

53. Albert, "Women of Burundi," p. 185.

54. Many Rwandan men had fought successfully with the Ugandan forces of Yoweri Museveni in overthrowing Ugandan President Milton Obote.

55. Nolan, *28 Stories of AIDS in Africa*, p. 7.

56. Hatzfeld, *A Time for Machetes: The Killers Speak*, p. 27. Hatzfeld's book reveals that, whereas people were reluctant at first to kill, soon after the massacres started they engaged with no remorse.

57. Gettleman, "The Conscience of a Strongman," *The New York Times Magazine*, p. 41.

58. Ministry of Gender and Family Promotion, "Violence against Women," pp. 6-10. Thanks to Jean de Dieu Bizimana for a copy of this report.

59. Ibid., p. 6.

60. Ibid.

61. Ibid.

62. Gettleman, "The Conscience of," p. 40.

63. Pushpa Iyer, "Development *vs.* Peacebuilding," pp. 15, 19, n. 14; United Nations, "Mission in Sierra Leone," pp. 3-4; Dumbuya, "Gender, Violence and Reconstruction," pp. 173-78.

64. Dumbuya, ibid., p. 170.

65. Iyer, ibid., pp. 19-20.

66. Ibid., 21-22.

67. Yager, "Report to Congressional Committees," p. 6.

68. See Yager for various studies, p. 9. See also Human Rights Watch Report 2002; U.S. Commission on Foreign Relations hearing on "The Violent Treatment of Women in Congo and Sudan, 2009.

69. Human Rights Watch, "The War Within the War," p. 21.

70. Ibid., p. 21.

71. Ibid.

72. Ibid., p. 22.

73. Ibid., p. 28.

74. Ibid., pp. 36-37.

75. Longombe, Claude, Ruminjo, "Fistula and Traumatic Genital Injury from Sexual Violence in Conflict Setting," pp. 132-40. Thanks to Jean de Dieu Bizimana for this report.

76. Godin and Chideka, "Congolese Women Activists in DRC and Belgium," p. 34.

77. Schoepf, *"Assessing AIDS Research in Africa,* p. 2. Thanks to Christine Obbo for providing this review essay.

78. Schoepf, "Women and the Politics of AIDS in Africa," p. 1. Here we are discussing HIV-1, which is the most prevalent type in Africa.

79. Ibid., p. 2.

80. Ibid., p. 3.

81. Ibid., p. 4.

82. UNAIDS Global Report, 2012, p. 7.

83. Christine Obbo, personal communication, September 16, 2013.

84. Human Rights Watch/Defending Human Rights Worldwide.

85. Schoepf, "Women and the Politics of AIDS in Africa," p. 6.

86. Ibid., pp. 7-8.
87. Johnson-Bashua, "African Religion and Sexual Exploitation," p. 296.
88. Ibid., p. 8.
89. Johnson, *South Africa's Brave New World*, pp. 146-48.
90. Quoted in Iliffe, *A History of the African AIDS Epidemic*, p. 84.
91. Ibid., p. 85.
92. Ibid., p. 92.
93. Nolen, *28 Stories*, p. 1.
94. Ibid., pp. 1-2.
95. Ibid., p. 2.
96. Ibid., pp. 155-65.
97. Ibid.
98. Available at: http://www.avert.org/aid-Malawi.htm.
99. *The Washington Post*, July 29, 2012.
100. Homosexuals of both genders suffer discrimination or worse in most African countries—although they are protected under law if not always in fact in South Africa. Zamara State in Nigeria introduced a law that targets them as well as prostitutes—calling for gays and lesbians to be stoned to death. This is a radical measure since Nigerian law forbids homosexuality. See Ayuba, Politics and Sexuality in Northern Nigeria," pp. 262-64.
101. *New York Times*, January 21, 2014.
102. Ghanaian Women's Commission, p. 1.
103. Bledsoe, *Women and Marriage,* p. 64; UNICEF, *Female Genital Mutilation/Cutting, "A Statistical Snapshot," p. 3.*
104. Dallenborg, "A Reflection on the Cultural Meanings," pp. 80-81.
105. Ibid., p. 83.
106. Ibid.
107. Ibid., pp. 83-84.
108. Ibid., p. 80.
109. Dustin, "Female Genital Mutilation/Cutting in the UK," pp. 8-9.
110. Ibid., pp. 9-10. Western Feminists had made the clitoris an icon of their liberation, and hence the argument extended to imposing these feminist constructs on those who did not share them. See, for instance, Arnfred, "Rethinking Sexualities in Africa (p. 13), which falls somewhat in this category due to erroneous interpretations of certain practices dealing with female genitalia in Mozambique.
111. Ibid., p. 11.
112. Ibid.
113. Ibid., p. 17.
114. Tasaru Ntomonok Initiative, courtesy of a Swahili female informant, June 2012. A similar organization exists in Moshi Tanzania, "Network Against Female Genital Mutilation."
115. UNICEF, *Female Genital Mutilation/Cutting, passim.* Thanks to Bettina Shell-Duncan and Nicole Petrowski for providing the hard copy of this book-length document.
116. Ibid., p. 12.
117. Ibid., p. 40. The figures do not necessarily reflect all girls in either group but among those who took part in the study. In Senegal only a small number of the overall female population practices FGM/C. In Kenya, more ethnic groups are involved in those who do engage in FGM/C, but many girls from these groups are not represented in the study.

118. Ibid., pp. 40, 44, 50, 51.
119. Ibid., Figure 6.7, p. 69.
120. Ibid., pp. 54, 61, 73, 75, 77, 97.
121. Ibid., pp. 117-18.
122. UNICEF, "Female Genital Mutilation/Cutting: A Statistical Overview and Exploration of the Dynamics of Change."
123. Berg, *Witches in Exile*, documentary filmed in 2004. All references in the following come from this documentary.
124. In 2007, a colleague and I took a group of teachers to another of these camps in the Tamale area while we were in Ghana on a Fulbright-Hays grant. At the camp we visited, younger women dominated in numbers over the old. There were approximately seventy women and children that we observed. Scores of children were very much in evidence. We had no interchange with them, however, beyond our observations that poverty and privation dominated their lives.
125. According to the documentary, the first and only man was sentenced to death in the 1990s.
126. Johnson, *South Africa's Brave*, p. 465.
127. Romero, *Profiles in Diversity*, pp. 21-22.

Chapter 9

1. Makda Teklemichael, "Contemporary Women Artists in Ethiopia," p. 39.
2. Ibid., p. 42. A third contemporary artist trained in Addis Ababa, and she, too, works with a group as a studio artist.
3. Ibid., p. 41.
4. Constantine Petridis, interview.
5. Lowery and King, (eds.), *The Global Africa Project*, pp. 219-20.
6. Ibid., p. 242.
7. Ibid., p. 229. See Lamp, "The Body as Billboard" (pp. 48-51) for the beaded aprons created by Ndebele women.
8. Ibid., p. 235.
9. *New York Times*, August 16, 2013.
10. Uwatse, "What I Have to Say."
11. See Chapter Four.
12. Lamp, *Art of the Baga*, p. 179.
13. Ellison, "The Intimate Violence of Political and Economic Change in Southern Ethiopia," pp. 35-37.
14. Ibid.
15. Lowery and King (eds.), *The Global African Project*, p. 243.
16. "Winnie Ojanga: Kenyan Fashion Designer Nominated for European."
17. "Iman Visits Native Somalia," *Jet*, p. 20; Hasig and Latif, *Somalia*, p. 80.
18. Iron (Schreiner), *Life on an African Farm*.
19. First and Scott, *Olive Schreiner*, p. 84.
20. Ibid., p. 97.
21. Ibid., p. 94.
22. Schoeman, *A Life in South Africa*, pp. 191-99. Schreiner published several other works—short stories and essays plus a book co-authored with her husband.

23. Gordimer, *Lifetimes under Apartheid*.
24. Head, *Nadine Gordimer*, p. 3.
25. Quoted in ibid., p. 5.
26. Perhaps Yemen, based on the description of the architecture, the desolate landscape, and the conflicted politics.
27. Said, quoted on end cover of *Pickup*.
28. Tlali, *Muriel at the Metropolitan*.
29. Magona, *Living, Loving, and Lying Awake at Night*, pp. 3-60. See Cock, *Maids and Madams*.
30. Vigne (ed.), *A Gesture of Belonging*, pp. 3-4, 215, 220. For a full account of Bessie Head's life and works, see Eilersen, *Bessie Head: Thunder Behind Her Ears*.
31. Quoted in Vigne, ibid., pp. 142-48. Vigne, however, notes that Bessie never sent him letter no. 68 (15 July 1971). The copy was in her archive, and it reflected her feelings at the time she wrote it.
32. Noviolet Bulawayo is a pseudonym for Elizabeth Tshele.
33. Bulawayo, *We Need a New Name*, p. 155.
34. Ogot, *Days of My Life*.
35. Ogot, *The Strange Bride*, pp. 23-26.
36. Ibid., p. 27.
37. Selasi, "The Unvanquished," p. 13.
38. Owuor, *Dust*, p. 146.
39. Mohamed, *The Orchard of Lost Souls*, p. 32.
40. Conde, "Three Female Writers in Modern Africa," pp. 132-43.
41. Emecheta, *In the Ditch*.
42. Knowles, "Emecheta, Buchi."
43. Brown, *Women Writers in Black Africa*, p. 86.
44. Quoted in ibid., p. 98.
45. Ibid., pp. 68-69.
46. Ba, *So Long a Letter; Scarlet Song*. See Slaughter, *Sharing the World Stage*, p. 382.
47. Slaughter, p. 385.
48. Quoted in ibid.
49. Ibid.
50. Manuh, "Law and Society in Contemporary Africa," p. 332.
51. Ibid., p. 333.
52. Otieno, *Mau Mau's Daughter*, pp. 136-38.
53. Cohen and Odhiambo, *Burying SM*, p. 7.
54. Ibid., p. 7; Otieno, *Mau Mau's Daughter*, p. 154; Otieno provides her version of the events from the death of SM to the burial in pp. 131-92.
55. Ibid., p. 9.
56. Otieno, *Mau Mau's Daughter*, p. 190.
57. Munge, "Landownership and Gender," pp. 63-64.
58. Ibid., p. 64. Munge cited a case after colonial rule had ended that upheld this concept.
59. Ibid., p. 66.
60. Ibid., p. 64.
61. Ibid., p. 67.
62. Da Silva, "Polygamy Throttles Women in Senegal," p. 1.
63. Ibid.
64. Ibid.

65. Ibid.
66. Ibid.
67. Obbo, *African Women*, pp. 70-161.
68. Ibid., p. 105.
69. Ibid., p. 106.
70. Ibid., p. 113. See Wambui Otieno and her problems with her brother-in-law as an example.
71. Ibid., pp. 114-15.
72. Ibid., p. 120.
73. Ibid., pp. 114-15.
74. Ibid., p. 138.
75. Ibid., p. 140.
76. *New York Times*, March 3, 1991.
77. Ibid.
78. McCabe, "Migration Information Source," p. 1.
79. Ibid., p. 3.
80. McCabe, "African Immigrants in the United States," p. 2.
81. Ibid., p. 3.
82. *New York Times*, August 4, 2012.
83. Ibid.
84. Quoted in *The Guardian*, June 14, 2012.
85. Ibid.
86. Loum, "Sport Femmes Sénégaliaises: Significations Sociales de la Pratique Sportive," pp. 133-47.
87. Kipkorir, *Descent from Cherang'any Hills*, pp. 343-55.
88. Ibid., p. 355.
89. Ibid., p. 372.
90. Ibid., pp. 373-74.
91. Amma and Onyekwere, "Alakija: A Veteran Lawyer," p. 1.
92. Ibid., p. 2.
93. Ibid.
94. Ibid.
95. Ibid.
96. Ojogo, "Nigeria: NGJ to Okonjo-Iweala-Resign Now, You've Mismanaged Our Economy."
97. World Health Organization, "Ambassador Dr. GertrudeIbengwé Mongella," p. 59.
98. Ibid., p. 60.
99. Ibid.
100. Amoako, Annan and Mwaura, "Achieving Gender Equality," p. 90.
101. Callaway, "The Role of Women in Kano City Politics," pp. 148-49.
102. Ibid., pp. 153-55.
103. Jabo, "Women Empowerment Under NRM," p. 1.
104. Helen Epstein, "Murder in Uganda," April 13, 2014, pp. 40-42.
105. Gender Studies and Human Rights Documentation Centre (Ghana), "We Know Politics Project I,I" p. 1.
106. Ibid., p. 6.
107. The Ethiopian Embassy, "National Policy on Ethiopian Women," p. 3.
108. *The Economist*, November 9, 2013, p. 54.

109. Ibid.
110. *New York Times*, June 6, 2011.
111. Ibid.
112. Ibid.
113. Quoted in Collins, *Central and South African History,* pp. 234-35.
114. Makeba and Hall, *My Story*, pp. 30-35.
115. Ibid., pp. 213-14.
116. Nelson Mandela Centre of Memory, "In Conversation with Dr. Frene Ginwala," p. 3.
117. Ibid., p. 5.
118. Ramphele, *Across Boundaries*, pp. 76-85.
119. Ibid., p. 90.
120. Ibid., pp. 117, 133-34.
121. Ibid., p. 146.
122. Ibid., p. 147.
123. *The Guardian*, February 18, 2013.
124. Ibid., p. 2.
125. *The Economist*, November 9, 2013, p. 54.
126. Maathai, *Unbowed*, pp. 16-17.
127. Ibid., pp. 73-75.
128. Ibid., pp. 78-92.
129. Ibid., p. 101.
130. Ibid., pp. 115-118.
131. Ibid., p. 123.
132. Ibid., p. 125.
133. Ibid., p. 145.
134. Ibid., pp. 159-205.
135. Ibid., p. 165.
136. Ibid., p. 259.
137. Ibid., p. 291.
138. Sirleaf, *This Child Will Be Great,* pp. 52-53.
139. Ibid., p. 43.
140. Ibid., pp. 58-64.
141. Ibid., pp. 69-112.
142. Ibid., p. 114.
143. Ibid., p. 120.
144. Ibid., pp. 13-36.
145. Ibid., p. 170.
146. Ibid., pp. 171-75.
147. Ibid., p. 208.
148. Ibid., pp. 195-203.
149. Ibid., p. 211.
150. Ibid., p. 220.
151. Ibid., p. 229.
152. Ibid., p. 244.

Select Bibliography

*All the materials included in the bibliography reflect
actual works read and cited in this book.*

Achebe, Chinua. *Things Fall Apart.* New York: Anchor Books, 1994.

Achebe, Chinua. *There Was a Country.* New York: Penguin Books, 2012.

Achebe, Nwando. *The Female King of Colonial Nigeria.* Bloomington: Indiana University Press, 2011.

Adichie, Chimamanda Ngozi. *Half a Yellow Sun.* New York: Anchor Books, 2007.

Agriri, Babatunde. "Slavery in the Yoruba Society in the 19th Century." In *The Ideology of Slavery in Africa,* edited by Paul E. Lovejoy, 123-48. Beverly Hills, CA: Sage Publications, 1981.

Ajayi, J. F. Ade. *Christian Missions in Nigeria 1841-1891: The Making of a New Elite.* Evanston, IL: Northwestern University Press, 1965.

Alakija, Aduke. "Aduke Alakija." *Palgrave Macmillan Dictionary of Women's Biography.* London, 2005.

Albert, Ethel M. "Women of Burundi: A Study of Social Values." In *Women in Tropical Africa,* edited by Denise Paulme, 179-216. Berkeley: University of California Press, 1971.

Alexander, Ray (Alexdrovitch). "Do You Belong to a Union?" in *Profiles in Diversity: Women in the New South Africa,* edited by Patricia W. Romero, 69-76. East Lansing: Michigan State University Press, 1998.

Allen, J.W.T., ed. *The Customs of the Swahili People.* Berkeley: University of California Press, 1981.

Allman, Jean, Susan Geiger, and Nakanyike Musisi, eds. *Women in Colonial African Histories.* Bloomington: Indiana University Press, 2002.

Alpers, Edward. "The Story of Swema and Female Vulnerability in Nineteenth-Century East Africa." In *Women and Slavery in Africa,* edited by Claire C. Robertson and Martin A. Klein, 185-99. Madison: University of Wisconsin Press, 1983.

Alpers, Edward A. "Ordinary Household Chores: Ritual and Power in a Nineteenth-Century Swahili Women's Spirit Possession Cult." *International Journal of African Historical Studies* 17 (1984): 677-702.

Amnesty International. "Sudan, Darfur: Rape as a Weapon, Sexual Violence and Its Consequences." London: International Secretariat, 2004.

Amoako, Kingsley Y., Kofi A. Anon, and Peter Mawaura. "Achieving Gender Equality." Part II. *Perspectives on Africa's Development, Selected Speeches,* 88-91. Addis Ababa: Economic Commission for Africa, 2000.

Anderson, David. *Histories of the Hanged.* New York: W. W. Norton & Company, Ltd., 2005.

Anderson, David M. "Mau Mau and the High Court and the Lost British Empire Archives:

Colonial Conspiracy or Bureaucratic Bungle?" *The Journal of Imperial and Commonwealth History* 39 (2011): 699-716.

Anderson, David M. "British Abuse and Torture in Kenya's Counter-Insurgency, 1952-1960." *Small Wars and Insurgencies* 23 (2012): 700-19.

Anderson, David. "Atoning for the Sins of Empire." *The New York Times,* June 13, 2013.

Angon, Sidonia. "Women in Peacekeeping and Peacebuilding in Northern Uganda." *Africa Peace and Conflict Journal* 4 (2011): 74-88.

Arnfred, Signe. "Women in Mozambique: Gender Struggles and Gender Politics." *Review of African Political Economy* 41 (1988): 5-16.

Arnfred, Signe, ed. *Rethinking Sexualities in Africa.* Uppsala: Nordiska Afrikainstitutet, 2004.

Arnot, Frederick Stanley. *Garenganze; Or, Seven Years' Pioneer Mission Work in Central Africa.* Edited by Robert I. Rotbery. London: Frank Cass & Co., Ltd., 1969.

Article 19 Africa Programme. "Women's Voices and African Theater: Case Studies from Kenya, Mali, The Democratic Republic of Congo and Zimbabwe." http://www.article.19.org/data/files/pdfs/ publications/gender-women-s-voices. (Accessed January 21, 2013.)

Ayandele, E. A. *The Missionary Impact on Modern Nigeria 1842-1914.* Ibaden: Ibaden History Series, 1967.

Ayuba, J. M. "Politics and Sexuality in Northern Nigeria in the Second Half of the Twentieth Century." In *Gender, Sexuality, and Mothering in Africa,* edited by Toyin Falola and Bessie House-Soremekian, 251- 70. Trenton, NJ: Africa World Press, 2011.

Ba, Mariama. *So Long a Letter.* Translated by Modupé Bode-Thomas. Portsmouth: Heinemann, 1981.

Ba, Mariama. *Scarlet Song.* Translated by Dorothy Blair. London: Heinemann, 1985.

Barbot, John. "An Abstract of a Voyage to Congo River, Or the Zaire, and to Cabinde, in the year 1700." In *A Collection of Voyages and Travels,* edited by Awnsham Churchill and John Churchill, Vol. 5, 170-72. London: Henry Linton and John Osborn, 1746.

Barnes, Juliet. *The Ghosts of Happy Valley.* London: Aurum Press, Ltd., 2013.

Barnes, Teresa. "Virgin Territory? Travel and Migration by African Women in Twentieth-Century Southern Africa." In *Women in Colonial African Histories,* edited by Jean Allman, Susan Geiger, and Nakanyike Musisi, 164-90. Bloomington: Indiana University Press, 2002.

Bastian, Misty L. "'Vultures of the Marketplace': Southeastern Nigerian Women and Discourses of the *Ogu Umunwaanyi* (Women's War) of 1929." In *Women in Colonial African Histories,* edited by Jean Allman, Susan Geiger, and Nakanyike Musisi, 260-72. Bloomington: Indiana University Press, 2002.

Battell, Andrew. "On the Jaga." In *Central and South African History,* edited by Robert O. Collins, 42-52. Princeton, NJ: Markus Wiener Publishers, 1990.

Battuta, Ibn. *Travels in Asia and Africa 1325-1354.* Translation and selections by H.A.R. Gibb. London: Routledge and Kegan Paul, Ltd., 1929.

Bay, Edna. "Belief, Legitimacy and the Kpgito: An Institutional History of the Queen Mother in Precolonial Dahomey." *Journal of African History* 36 (1995): 1-28.

BBC News. "Gambian Women Fleeing Female Genital Mutilation." http://www.bbc.co.uk/news/uk 2393347. (Accessed September 1, 2013.)

Bearak, Barry. "Albertina Sisulu Who Helped Lead Apartheid Fight." Obituary. *New York Times,* June 5, 2011.

Becker, Heike. "Efundula: Women's Initiation, Gender and Sexual Identities in Colonial and Post-Colonial Northern Nambia." In *Rethinking Sexualities in Africa,* edited by

Signe Arnfred, 15-57. Uppsala: Nordiska Afrikainstitutet, 2004.

Berger, Iris, and E. Frances White, eds. *Women in Sub-Saharan Africa*. Bloomington: Indiana University Press, 1999.

Bhabba, Homi. *The Location of Culture*. London: Routledge, 1994.

Boahen, A. Adu. *African Perspectives on Colonialism*. Baltimore, MD: John Hopkins University Press, 1987.

Bosman, William. "Justice and Warfare in Axim." In *Western African History*, edited by Robert D. Collins, 184-90. Princeton: Markus Wiener Publishers, 1990.

Boxer, Charles R. *Salvador de Sa and the Struggle for Brazil and Angola*. London: University of London Press, 1952.

Brian, William. *Sol Plaatje, South African Nationalist 1876-1932*. Berkeley: University of California Press, 1984.

Brooks, George E. Jr. Signores of Saint-Louis and Gorée: Women Entrepreneurs in Eighteenth Century Senegal." In *Women in Africa: Studies in Social and Economic Change*, *e*dited by Nancy J. Hafkin and Edna G. Bay, 19-44. Stanford: Stanford University Press, 1976.

Brown, Lloyd W. *Women Writers in Black Africa*. Westport, CT: Greenwood Press, 1981.

Bruce-Lockhart, Katherine. "'It Cannot Be Dealt with through a Friendly Cup of Tea': Dealing with the Deviance at Kamiti and Gitamayu Detention Camps, 1957-1960." Masterclass Presentation, Struggles Over Emerging State in Africa Conference, Durham University, September 2013.

Bruce-Lockhart, Katherine. "'It Cannot Be Dealt with through Friendly Cups of Tea': Dealing with Deviance at Kamiti Women's Detention Camp, 1954-1960." MSc Dissertation, Oxford University, 2013.

Budge, E.A. Wallis, ed. and trans. *The Kebra Negast*. London: Oxford University Press, 1932.

Bulawayo, NoViolet (Elizabeth Tshele). *We Need New Names*. New York: Little Brown, 2013.

Burton, Antoinette. *Brown Over Black*. Gurgaon (India): Three Essays Collections, 2012.

Burton, Sir Richard. *First Footsteps in East Africa*. Edited by Gordon Waterfield. New York: Frederick Prager, 1966.

Byfield, Judith A. "Feeding the Troops: Abeokuta (Nigeria) and World War II." *African Economic History* 35 (2007): 77-87.

Callaway, Barbara J. "The Role of Women in Kano City Politics." In *Hausa Women in the Twentieth Century*, edited by Katherine M. Coles and Beverly Mack, 178-215. Madison: University of Wisconsin Press, 1991.

Callaway, Helen. *Gender, Culture and Empire*. Oxford: Macmillan Press with St. Anthony's College, 1986.

Callincos, Luli. "Testimonies and Transition: Women Negotiating the Rural and Urban mid-20th Century." In *Women in South African History*, edited by Nomboniso Gasa, 153-84. Cape Town: Human Sciences Research Council, 2007.

Campbell, Horace. "Angolan Women in Search of Peace." *African Journal of Political Science* 3 (1998): 76-78.

Charton, Nancy. "I'm Going to Get Trained." In *Profiles in Diversity: Women in the New South Africa*, edited by Patricia W. Romero, 177-86. East Lansing: Michigan State University Press, 1998.

Churchill, A., and J. Churchill, eds. *A Collection of Voyages and Travels*, Vol. 5. London: Henry Linton and John Osborn, 1764.

Clough, Marshall S. *Mau Mau Memoirs.* Boulder, CO: Lynne Rienner Publishers, Inc., 1998.

Clyde, David F. *History of the Medical Services of Tanganyika.* Dar es Salaam: Government Press, 1962.

Cock, Jacklyn. *Maids and Madams.* 2d ed. London: The Women's Press, 1989.

Cock, Jacklyn. *Colonels and Cadres: War and Gender in South Africa.* Cape Town: Oxford University Press, 1991.

Cohen, David, and E. S. Atieno Odhiambo. *Siaya.* Athens: Ohio University Press, 1989.

Cohen, David William, and E. S. Atieno Odhiambo. *Burying SM: The Politics of Knowledge and Sociology of Power in Africa.* Portsmouth: Heinemann, 1992.

Conde, Maryse. "Three Female Writers in Modern African: Flora Nwapa, Ama Ata Aidoo and Grace Ogot." *Présence Africaine* 2 (1972): 132-43.

Coquery-Vidrovitch, Catherine. *African Women: A Modern History.* Boulder, CO: Westview Press, 1997.

Corcoran, Rebecca. "About Women, War and Darfur: The Continuing Quest for Gender Violence Justice." *Third World Law Journal* (2007): 203-38.

Coupland, R. *The Exploitation of East Africa.* London: Faber and Faber, Ltd., 1939.

Crais, Clifton, and Pamela Scully. *Sara Baartman and the Hottentot Venus: A Ghost Story and a Biography.* Princeton, NJ: Princeton University Press, 2008.

Crow, Hugh. *The Memoirs of the Late Captain Hugh Crow of Liverpool.* London: Longman, Fees, Orme-Brown, and Green, 1830.

Da Silva, Issa Sikili. "Polygamy Throttles Women in Senegal." Inter Press Service, September 9, 2012. Davenport, T.R.H., and Christopher Saunders. *South Africa: A History.* New York: St. Martin's Press, 2000.

Davis, R. Hunt. "Charles T. Loran and the American Model for South African Education in South Africa." *African Studies Review* 19 (1976): 87-99.

De Gruchy, John, ed. *The London Missionary Society in Southern Africa, 1799-1999.* Athens: Ohio University Press, 2000.

Deacon, Zemarie. *An Examination of Factors Influencing Mozambican Women's Attainment of Post-War Well Being.* Ann Arbor: University of Michigan Press, 2008.

Dellenborg, Leiselott. "A Reflection on the Cultural Meanings of Female Circumcision." In *Rethinking Sexualities in Africa,* edited by Signe Arnfred, 79-89. Uppsala: Nordiska Afrikainstitutet, 2004.

Disney, Jennifer Leigh. *Women's Activism and Feminist Agency in Mozambique and Nicaragua.* Philadelphia, PA: Temple University Press, 2008.

Ducados, Henda. "An All Men's Show? Angolan Women's Survival in the 30-Year War." *Agenda* 43 (2000): 11-22.

Dumbuya, Peter. "Gendered Violence and Reconstruction in Post-War Sierra Leone." In *Gender, Sexuality, and Mothering in Africa,* edited by Toyin Falola and Bessie House-Soremekun, 169-98. Trenton, NJ: Africa World Press, 2011.

Dustin, Moira. "Female Genital Mutilation/Cutting in the UK: Challenging Inconsistencies." *European Journal of Women's Studies* 17 (2010): 7-23.

Eilersen, Gillian Stead. *Bessie Head: Thunder behind Her Ears.* Portsmouth: Heinemann, 1995.

Elkins, Caroline. *Imperial Reckoning: The Untold Story of Britain's Gulag in Kenya.* New York: Henry Holt, 2005.

Ellison, James. "The Intimate Violence of Political and Economic Change in Southern Ethiopia." *Comparative Studies in Society and History* 54 (2012): 35-64.

Elphick, Richard. *Khoikhoi and the Founding of White South Africa*. Johannesburg: Raven Press, 1985.

Emecheta, Buchi. *The Joys of Motherhood*. New York: George Braziller, 1979.

Emecheta, Buchi. *Destination Biafra*. London: Allison & Busby, 1982.

Epstein, Helen. "Murder in Uganda." *The New York Review of Books* 21, no. 6 (2014): 40-42.

Ethiopian Embassy. "National Policy on Ethiopian Women." http://www.ethioembassy.org.uk/factfile/a-z/wmen. (Accessed August 20, 2013.)

Falola, Toyin, and Bessie House-Soremekun, eds. *Gender, Sexuality, and Mothering in Africa*. Trenton, NJ: Africa World Press, 2011.

Falola, Toyin, and Nana Akua Amponsab. *Women's Roles in Sub-Saharan Africa*. Santa Barbara: ABC- Clio, LLC, 2012.

Feachen, Richard G., and Dean T. Jamison. *Disease and Mortality in Sub-Saharan Africa*. Oxford: Published for the World Bank by Oxford University Press, 1991.

Federal Information Service (Nigeria). "Nigeria's First Women Police." Documentary film. http://www.colonialfilm.org.uk/1961.

Forbes, Rosita. *From Red Sea to Blue Nile: Abyssinian Adventure*. New York: The Macaulay Company, 1925.

Fortes, M. "The Impact of War on British West Africa." *International Affairs* 21 (1945): 206-20.

Freeman–Greenville, G.S.P. "The Coast, 1498-1840." In *History of East Africa*, Vol. 1, edited by Gervase Mathew, 129-68. London: Oxford University Press, 1963.

Gailey, Harry. *Africa from Early Times to 1800*. New York: Holt, Rinehart and Winston, 1970.

Gasa, Nomboniso, ed. *Women in South African History*. Cape Town: Human Sciences Research Council, 2007.

Gasa, Nomboniso, ed. "Appendix: Cissie Cool." In *Women in South African History*, 256-57. Cape Town: Human Science Research Council, 2007.

Geiger, Susan. "Women in Nationalist Struggle: Tanu Activists in Dar es Salaam." *International Journal of African Historical Studies* 20 (1987): 1-26.

Gender Studies and Human Rights Documentation Centre (Ghana). http://www.gendercentreghana.org/increasing-women-in-political-participation. (Accessed August 21, 2013.)

German Colonial Office. *The Treatment of Native and Other Populations*. Berlin: German Colonial Office, 1909.

Gewald, Joan-Bart. *Herero Heroes*. Oxford: James Currey, 1999.

Gilman, Sander. "Black Bodies, White Bodies: Toward an Iconography of Female Sexuality in Late Nineteenth Century Art, Medicine and Literature." In *Race, Writing, and Difference*, edited by Henry Louis Gates, 233-61. Chicago: Chicago University Press, 1986.

Gilman, Sander L. *Sexuality: An Illustrated History*. New York: John Wiley and Sons, 1989.

Ginwala, Frene. "In Conversation with Dr. Frene Ginwala." http://www.nelsonmandela.org/news- entry-in-conversation-with-dr-frene-ginwala. (Accessed September 20, 2013.)

Glassman, Jonathon. *Feasts and Riots*. Portsmouth: Heinemann, 1999.

Good, Charles M. *The Steamer Parish*. Chicago: University of Chicago Press, 2004.

Gordimer, Nadine. *The Pickup*. New York: Picador, 2001.

Gordon, Robert J. "The Impact of the Second World War on Namibia." *Journal of Southern African Studies* 19 (1993): 147-65.

Gould, Stephen Jay. *The Flamingo Smile*. New York: W. W. Norton and Co., 1985.

Gqoba, William A. "The Tales of Nongqawuse." Translated from the Xhosa by Dr. A. C.

Jordan. *Africa South* 3-4 (July-September 1959): 5-9.

"The Guinea Coast in the Sixteenth Century." In *Europeans in West Africa, 1450-1560,* Vol. 14, edited and translated by William Blake. London: Longman's Green and Co., Ltd., 1937.

Haile-Selassie, Tefarra. *The Ethiopian Revolution 1974-1999.* London: Kegan Paul International, 1997.

Hanson, Holly. *"Queen Mothers and Good Government in Buganda: The Loss of Women's Political Power in Nineteenth Century East Africa."* In *Women in Colonial African Histories,* edited by Jean Allman, Susan Geiger, and Nakanyike Musisi, 219-36. Bloomington: Indiana University Press, 2002.

Hardiman, David, ed. *Healing Bodies and Saving Souls.* New York: Editions Rodopi B.V., 2006.

Hartwig, Gerald W., and David K. Patterson, eds. *Disease in African History.* Durham: Duke University Press, 1978.

Hasani bin, Ismail. *Swifa ya Nguvumali (The Medicine Man).* Edited and translated by Peter Lienhardt. Oxford: Oxford University Press, 1968.

Hassig, Susan M., and Zawiah Abdul Latif. *Somalia.* 2d ed. New York: Marshall Cavendish Benchmark, 2008.

Hatzfield, Jean. *A Time for Machetes: The Killers Speak.* New York: Farrar, Straus and Giroux, 2005.

Head, Bessie. *The Question of Power.* London: Davis Poynter, 1973.

Henderson, D. A. *Smallpox: Death of a Disease.* New York: Prometheus Books, 2009.

Hending, Mrs. E. F. *History of the African Mission of the Protestant Episcopal Church.* New York: Stanford and Swords, 1850.

Higgs, Catherine. *Chocolate Islands.* Athens: Ohio University Press, 2012.

Hill, Aletha. "Infant and Child Mortality: Levels, Trends and Data Deficiencies." In *Disease and Mortality in Sub-Saharan Africa,* 37-74. Oxford: Published for the World Bank by Oxford University Press, 1991.

Hilton, Anne. *The Kingdom of the Kongo.* Cambridge: Cambridge University Press, 1989.

Holness, Marga. *Angolan Women Building the Future.* London: Zed Books, 1984.

Hughes, Jeremy. *Germany's Genocide of the Herero: Kaiser Wilhelm II, His General, His Sisters, His Soldiers.* Cape Town: University of Cape Town Press, 2011.

Hunwick, John, and E. T. Powell. *The African Diaspora and the Mediterranean World of Islam.* Princeton: Markus Wiener Publishers, 2002.

Hutchinson, Jonathan. "Leprosy in Natal and Cape Colony." *Lepra* 85 (1902): 161-88.

Huxley, Elspeth. *Four Guineas.* London: Chatto and Windus, 1954.

Hyam, Ronald. "Empire and Sexual Opportunity." *Journal of Imperial and Commonwealth History* 1 (1986): 34-90.

Iliffe, John. *The African AIDS Epidemic: A History.* Oxford: John Currey, Ltd., 2006.

Imam. "Imam Visits Native Somalia." *Jet,* November 2, 1993.

Impey, S. P. *A Handbook on Leprosy.* London: J and A Churchill, 1896.

Indicopleutses, Cosmos. *Christian Topography of Cosmos, the Egyptian Monk.* London: The Hakluyt Society, 1897.

Iyer, Pushpa. "Development versus Peacebuilding: Overcoming Jargon in Post-War Sierra Leone." *Africa Peace and Conflict Journal* 4 (2011): 15-33.

Jabo, Josepha. "Women Empowerment under NRM." http://www.mediacentre.go.ug/details. Php?catid+leitem=1697. (Accessed August 19, 2013.)

Jahadhmy, Ali A. *Anthology of Swahili Poetry.* London: Heinemann, 1973.

Jamison, Dean T., et al., eds. *Disease Control Priorities in Developing Countries.* Oxford: Published for the World Bank by Oxford University Press, 1993.

Jeppie, Shamil, Ebrahim Moosa, and Richard Roberts, eds. *Muslim Family Law in Sub-Saharan Africa.* Amsterdam: Amsterdam University Press, 2010.

Johnson, Cheryl. "Grass Roots Organizing: Women in Anticolonial Activity in Southwestern Nigeria." *African Studies Review* 25 (1982): 137-57.

Johnson-Bashua, Adepeju Olufemi. "African Religion and Sexual Exploitation of Women." In *Gender, Sexuality, and Mothering in Africa,* edited by Toyin Falola and Bessie House-Soremekun, 289-301. Trenton, NJ: Africa World Press, 2011.

Johnson-Odum, Cheryl, and Nina E. Mba. *For Women and the Nation: Funmilayo Ransome Kuti of Nigeria.* Urbana: University of Illinois Press, 1997.

Jordan, A. C. *Towards an African Literature.* Berkeley: University of California Press, 1973.

Joshua, Stephen Muoki. "The Church and the 1929 Female Genital Mutilation (FGM) Contestation in Kenya, with Special Reference to the Scottish Presbyterian Church and the Kikuyu Community." UNISA. http://uir.unisa.ac.za/bitstream/handle/10500/4517/Joshua-SHEXXXV_1- May%202009.pdf?sequence=1. (Accessed June 11, 2013.)

Kagwa, Apolo. *Mpisa za Baganda.* London: Macmillan, 1952.

The Kano Chronicle. London: Frank Cass, 1908.

Kanogo, Tabitha. *African Womanhood in Colonial Kenya 1900-50.* Oxford: James Currey, Ltd., 2005.

Keller, Edmund J. *Revolutionary Ethiopia: From Empire to People's Republic.* Bloomington: Indiana University Press, 1988.

Kenyatta, Jomo. *Facing Mount Kenya.* London: Secker and Warburg, 1953.

Kingsley, Mary H. *Travels in West Africa.* London: Macmillan and Co., Ltd., 1897.

Kipkorir, B. E. *Descent from Cherang'any Hills.* Nairobi: Macmillan Kenya, 2009.

Kleinschmidt, Horst. "A Memorial to Zara Schmelen." In "In Honour of Women on National Women's Month in South Africa." *Newsletter* 18. Cape Town: Privately printed, August 2013. Thanks to Randolph Vigne.

Knowles, Elizabeth, ed. "Emecheta, Buchi." In *The Oxford Dictionary of Modern Quotations.* http:www.oxfordreference.com/reviews/ENTRY.html. (Accessed June 13, 2012.)

Kourouma, Ahmadou. *Monnew.* Translated by Nidra Poller. San Francisco, CA: Mercury House, 1993.

Kriger, Norma. *Zimbabwe's Guerrilla War: Peasant Voices.* Cambridge: Cambridge University Press, 1992.

Kukkuk, Leon. *Letter to Gabriella.* Sarasota: Florida Literary Foundation, 2003.

Lafort, René. *Ethiopia: An Heretical Revolution.* London: Zed Press, 1981.

Lambert, H. E. "The Arab Commission of Mombasa, Confidential." Typescript. Nairobi: Kenya National Archives, January 1957.

Lamp, Frederick. *Art of the Baga.* Munich: Prestel Verlag, 1996.

Lamp, Frederick, ed. *See the Music, Hear the Dance: Rethinking African Art at the Baltimore Museum of Art,* 48-51. Munich: Prestel Verlag, 2004.

Lebeuf, Annie M. D. *"The Role of Women in the Political Organization of African Societies."* In *Women in Tropical Africa,* edited by Denise Palme, 93-120. Translated by H. M. Wright. Berkeley: University of California Press, 1974.

Leeman, Bernard. *Queen of Sheba and Biblical Scholarship.* Queensland: Queensland Academic Press, 2005.

Little, K. L. "The Changing Position of Women in the Sierra Leone Protectorate." *Africa* 18 (1948): 1-17.

Longombe, Ahuka Ona, Kasereka Masumbuko Claude, and Joseph Ruminjo. "Fistula and Traumatic Genital Injury from Sexual Violence in a Conflict Setting in Eastern Congo: Case Studies." *Reproductive Health Matters* 16 (2008): 132-41. Courtesy of Jean de Dieu Bizimana.

Lonsdale, John. "Kenyatta's Trials: Breaking and Making an African Nationalist." In *The Moral World and the Law,* edited by Peter Cross, 196-239. Cambridge: Cambridge University Press, 2000.

Lonsdale, John. "Kikuyu Christianities: A History of Intimate Diversity." In *Christianity and the African Imagination: Essays in Honour of Adrian Hastings,* edited by David Maxwell and Ingrid Lawrie, 157-97. Leiden: Brill, 2002.

Lonsdale, John. "Authority, Gender and Violence: The War within Mau Mau's Fight for Land and Freedom." In *Mau Mau and Nationhood: Arms, Authority, and Narration,* edited by E. S. Atieno Odhiambo and John Lonsdale, 1-30. Oxford: James Currey, 2003.

Loum, Fatour Dame. "Sport et femmes sénégalaises: significations sociales de la practique sportive." *Présence Africaine* 183 (2012): 133-47.

Lydon, Ghislaine. "Obtaining Freedom at the Muslims' Tribunal: Colonial Kadijustiz and Women's Divorce Litigation in Ndar (Senegal)." In *Muslim Family Law in Sub-Saharan Africa,* edited by Shamil Jeppie, Ebrahim Moosa, and Richard Roberts, 135-64. Amsterdam: Amsterdam University Press, 2010.

Maathai, Wangari. *Unbowed.* New York: Anchor Books, 2007.

Mack, Beverly B. "Hajiya Ma'daki: A Royal Hausa Woman." In *Life Histories of African Women,* edited by Patricia W. Romero, 44-77. London: The Ashfield Press, Ltd., 1988.

Madley, Benjamin. "Patterns of Frontier Genocide 1803-1910: The Aboriginal Tasmanians, the Yuki of California, and the Herero of Namibia." *Journal of Genocide Research* 6 (2004): 167-92.

Magona, Sindiwe. *Living, Loving, and Lying Awake at Night.* Cape Town: David Philip Publishers, Ltd., 1991.

Majola, Jumartha. "1976 Was Bad for Me." In *Profiles in Diversity: Women in the New South Africa,* edited by Patricia W. Romero, 125-30. East Lansing: Michigan State University Press, 1998.

Makeba, Miriam, and James Hall. *Makeba: My Story.* New York: Plume, 1989.

Mandeville, Elizabeth. "Poverty, Work and Financing of Single Women in Kampala." *Africa* 49 (1979): 42-52.

Manuh, Takyiwaa. "Law and Society in Contemporary Africa." In *Africa,* edited by Phyllis M. Martin and Patrick O'Meara, 330-46. Bloomington: Indiana University Press, 1995.

Marcus, Harold G. *The Life and Times of Menelik II: Ethiopia, 1844-1913.* Oxford: Clarendon Press, 1975.

Markakis, John. *National Conflict and Class Conflict in the Horn of Africa.* Cambridge: Cambridge University Press, 1987.

Marks, Shula, ed. *Not Either an Experimental Doll: The Separate World of Three South African Women.* Bloomington: Indiana University Press, 1987.

Martin, Bernard, and Mark Spurrell, eds. *The Journal of a Slave Trader (John Newton), 1750-1754.* London: The Epworth Press, 1962.

Maseko, Zola. *The Life and Times of Sara Baartman: The Hottenton Venus.* VHS. New York: Icarus Films, 1999.

McCabe, K. "African Immigrants in the United States." *Migration Information Source.* http://www.migrationinformation.org/feature/display.cfm?ID=847. (Accessed September 13, 2013.)

McCrone, I. D. *Race Attitudes in South Africa*. Johannesburg: Oxford University Press for the University of Pretoria, 1937.

McEwan, P.G.M. *Africa from Early Times to 1800*. Oxford: Oxford University Press, 1968.

McLeod, M. D. *The Asante*. London: British Museum Publications, Ltd., 1984.

Mentzel, O. F. *A Complete and Authentic Geographical and Topographical Description: African Cape of Good Hope*. Glogau: Christian Friedrich Günther, 1785.

Mentzel, O. F. *African Cape of Good Hope Part II*. Translated by H. L. Mandelbrote. Cape Town: Van Riebeeck Society, 1925.

Mgcina, Ivy. "So I Lost Three Sons in the Struggle." In *Profiles in Diversity: Women in the New South Africa*, edited by Patricia Romero, 131-38. East Lansing: Michigan State University Press, 1998.

Miller, Joseph C. "Nzinga in a New Perspective." *Journal of African History* 16 (1975): 210-32.

Mintz, Sidney W. "The Anthropological Interview and the Life History." *Oval History Review* (1979): 18- 26.

Miranda, Gertrude. "Colonialism, Education, and Gender Relations in the Belgian Congo." In *Women in Colonial African Histories*, edited by Jean Allman, Susan Geiger, and Nakanyike Musisi, 144-63. Bloomington: Indiana University Press, 2002.

Mizra, Sarah, and Margaret Strobel. *Three Swahili Women*. Bloomington: Indiana University Press, 1989.

Mohamed, Nadifa. *The Orchard of Lost Souls*. New York: Farrar, Straus and Giroux, 2014.

Mongella, Gertrude. "Ambassador Dr. Gertrude Ibengwé Mongella." *World Health Organization*. http://www.who.int/pmnch/about/champions/speeches/mongella/en/index.html. (Accessed January 11, 2013.)

Morris, Michael. *Every Step of the Way*. Cape Town: Human Sciences Research Council, 2004.

Moshenberg, Dan. "German Amnesia and Herero Women." http://africasacountry.com/herero-women-challenge-german-amnesia/. (Accessed January 2013.)

Munge, Sone Patience. "Landownership and Gender Conflict in Anglophone Cameroon: A Legal Perspective." *Africa Peace and Conflict Journal* 4 (2011): 62-73.

Murphy, Sam. "London 2012 Olympics: Is Measuring Athletes' 'Femaleness' Ever Acceptable?" *The Guardian*, June 14, 2012. http://www.theguardian.com/2012/jun/14/olympics. (Accessed August 19, 2013.)

Murray, Jocelyn. "The Church Missionary Society and the 'Female Circumcision' Issue in Kenya 1929- 1932." *Journal of Religion in Africa* 8 (1976): 92-104.

Mwakilishi.com. *Kenya Diaspora News Leader* . http://www.mwakilish.com/content/article/2011/04/26. (Accessed January 2013.)

Naidoo, K. Gonaratham. "How Are We Going to Fight This Government?" In *Profiles in Diversity: Women in the New South Africa*, edited by Patricia W. Romero, 193-204. East Lansing: Michigan State University Press, 1998.

Neocosmos, Michael. "Remembering Phyllis Naidoo." *Daily Maverick*. http://www.daily-maverick.co.za/opinionista/2013-02-20-remembering-phyllis-naidoo/. (Accessed April 11, 2013.)

Newitt, Malyn. *A History of Mozambique*. London: Hurst and Company, 1995.

Newitt, Malyn. "Angola in Historical Context." In *Angola: The Weight of History*, edited by Patrick Chabal and Nuno Vidal, 19-92. New York: Columbia University Press, 2008.

Newton, John. *An Authentic Narrative of Some of the Remarkable and Interesting Particulars in the Life of John Newton*. Philadelphia, PA: William Young, 1795.

Newton, John. "Thoughts upon the African Slave Trade." In *The Journal of a Slave Trader (John Newton), 1750-1754*, edited by Bernard Martin and Mark Spurrell, 102-10. London: The Epworth Press, 1962.

"Nigeria in the Middle of Newark." *The New York Times*, August 16, 2013.

"Nigeria's First Women Police." *Colonial Film*. Federal Information Service Film Production Unit, Nigeria. http://www.colonialfilm.org.uk/node/1961. (Accessed September 28, 2013.)

Nolen, Stephanie. *28 Stories of Aids in Africa*. New York: Walker & Company, 2007.

Nsimbi, M. B. *Amanya Amaganda N'enoro Zaago*. Kampala: Longman, 1980.

Nwaka, Jacinta Chiamaka. "Biafran Women and Nigerian Civil War: Challenges and Survival Strategies." *Africa Peace and Conflict Journal* 14 (2011): 36-46.

Nwannekanma, Bertram, and Joseph Onyekwere. "Alakija: A Veteran Lawyer of Many Firsts." http://ngrguardiannews.com/index/php?option=com. (Accessed January 20, 2013.)

Nwapa, Flora. *Efuru*. London: Heinemann, 1966.

Nwapa, Flora. *Idu*. London: Heinemann, 1970.

Obafemi, Olu. *Nigerian Writers on the Nigerian Civil War*. Ilorin: J. Olu Olatiregun Company, 1992.

Obbo, Christine. *African Women: Their Struggle for Economic Independence*. London: Zed Press, 1980.

Obiora, L. Amede. "The Little Foxes That Spoilt the Vine: Revisiting the Feminist Critique of Female Circumcision." In *African Women and Feminism Reflecting on the Politics of Sisterhood*, edited by Oyèrónké Oyĕwūmi, 197-200. Trenton, NJ: Africa World Press, 2003.

Ogot, Grace. *The Promised Land*. Portsmouth: Heinemann, 1966.

Ogot, Grace. *The Strange Bride*. Translated by Okom Okoubo. Nairobi: Heinemann, 1989.

Ogot, Grace. *Days of My Life: An Autobiography*. Kisumyi, Kenya: Anyange Press, Ltd., 2013.

Ojanga, Winnie. "Kenyan Fashion Designer Nominated for European Prize." http://mwashilishi.com/print/articles/2011;kenyanbornfashiondesign. (Accessed September 10, 2013.)

Ojogo, Donald. "Nigeria: NGJ to Okonjo-Iweala Resign Now, You've Mistreated our Economy." http://allafrica.com/stories/201309180183.htm. (Accessed September 20, 2013.)

Oosu-Amaah. "Disease in Sub-Sahran Africa: An Overview." In *Disease and Mortality in Sub-Saharan Africa*, 119-21. Oxford: Published for the World Bank by Oxford University Press, 1991.

Otieno, Wambui Waiyaki. *Mau Mau's Daughter: A Life History*. Boulder, CO: Lynne Rienner Publishers, Inc., 1998.

Owuor, Yvonne Adhiambo. *Dust*. New York: Alfred A. Knopf, 2014.

Oyono, Fernand. *The Old Man and the Medal*. Translated by John Reed. Portsmouth: Heinemann, 1970.

Packard, Randall M. *The Making of a Tropical Disease*. Baltimore, MD: Johns Hopkins University Press, 2007.

Padgen, Anthony. *The Fall of Natural Man: The American Indian and the Origins of Comparative Ethnology*. Cambridge: Cambridge University Press, 1992.

Pakenham, Thomas. *The Boer War*. New York: Avon Books, 1979.

Parsons, Timothy. *The African Rank and File*. Portsmouth: Heinemann, 1999.

Patterson, Donna A. "Women Pharmacists in Twentieth Century Senegal." *Journal of*

Women's History 22 (2012): 111-37.

Peires, J. B. *The Dead Will Arise: Nongqawuse and the Great Xhosa Cattle Killing Movement of 1856-7.* Bloomington: Indiana University Press, 1989.

Perez, Margaret. *Women and Terrorism: Female Activity in Domestic and International Terrorist Groups.* London: Routledge, 2008.

Perham, Margery. *Native Administration in Nigeria.* London: Oxford University Press, 1937.

Petridis, Constantine. Interview. Baltimore Museum of Art, November 4, 2012.

Pillay, Navanethem. "I Always Said I Was Going to Be a Lawyer." In *Profiles in Diversity: Women in the New South Africa,* edited by Patricia W. Romero, 205-20. East Lansing: Michigan State University Press, 1998.

Presley, Cora Ann. *Kikuyu Women, the Mau Mau Rebellion, and Social Change.* Boulder, CO: Westview Press, 1992.

Prouty, Chris. *Empress Taytu and Menelik II: Ethiopia 1883-1910.* Trenton, NJ: The Red Sea Press, 1986.

Ramphele, Mamphela. *Across Boundaries.* New York: The Feminist Press, 1981.

Ramphele, Mamphela. "How Does One Speak of Social Psychology in a Nation in Transition." *Journal of Analytical Psychology* 53 (2008): 157-67.

Raven-Hart, Major R., ed. *Before van Riebeeck.* Cape Town: C. Struik Pty, Ltd., 1957.

Rodrigues, Laura C. "EPI Target Diseases: Measles, Tetanus, Polio, Tuberculosis, Pertussis, and Diphtheria." In *Disease and Mortality in Sub-Saharan Africa,* 174-89. Oxford: Published for the World Bank by Oxford University Press, 1991.

Rogers, Susan G. "Anti-Colonial Protest in Africa: A Female Strategy Reconsidered." *Heresies* 9, no. 3 (1980): 22-25.

Romero, Patricia W. *E. Sylvia Pankhurst: Portrait of a Radical.* New Haven, CT: Yale University Press, 1987.

Romero, Patricia W. "Encounter at the Cape: French Huguenots, the Khoi and Other People of Color." *Journal of Colonialism and Colonial History* (2004). https://muse.jhu.edu/login?auth=0&type=summary&url=/journals/journalofcolonialismandcolonialhistory/v005/5.1romero.html. (Accessed June 16, 2012.)

Romero, Patricia W., ed. *Profiles in Diversity: Women in the New South Africa.* East Lansing: Michigan State University Press, 1998.

Romero, Patricia W., ed. *Women's Voices in Africa.* Princeton, NJ: Markus Wiener Publishers, 1992.

Ruete, Emily. *Memoirs of an Arabian Princess from Zanzibar.* Edited by Patricia Romero. Princeton, NJ: Markus Wiener Publishers, 1989.

"Run First." *South African History Online.* http://sahistory.org.za. (Accessed June 2013.)Salmons, Jill. "Mask: Ibibo/Amang, Akwa Ibon State, Nigeria." In *See the Music, Hear the Dance: Rethinking African Art at the Baltimore Museum of Art,* edited by Fredcrick Lamp, 188-89. Munich: Prestel Verlag, 2004.

Sampson, Anthony. *Mandela.* New York: Vintage Books, 2000.

Santilli, Kathy. "Kikuyu Women in the Mau Mau Revolt: A Closer Look." *Ufahamu: Journal of the African Activist Association* 8 (1977): 143-59.

Schoepf, Brooke G. "Women and the Politics of AIDS in Africa." *Global Dialogue* 6 (2004): 1-2. http://worlddialogue.org/content/php?id=318. (Accessed January 13, 2013.)

Schoepf, Brooke G. "Assessing AIDS in Africa: Twenty-five Years Later." *African Studies Review* 53 (2010): 105-42.

Schreiner, Olive [Ralph Irons]. *Story of an African Farm.* London: Chapman & Hall, 1983.

Schulte, G. J., ed. *Briefwisseling van Hendrik Swellengrebel Jr. oor Kaapse sake 1778-1792*. Kaapstad: A. A. Balkema, 1982.

Selasi, Taiye. "The Unvanquished." *The New York Times Book Review* (March 2, 2014): 13.Semba, R. D. *The Vitamin A Story: Lifting the Shadow of Death*. Basil: Karger, 2012.

Shanker, Shobana. "The Social Dimensions of Christian Leprosy Work among Muslims: American Missionaries and Young Patients in Colonial Nigeria, 1920-1940." In *Healing Bodies and Saving Souls*, 281-305. New York: Editions Rodopi B.V., 2006.

Shell, Robert C. H. *Children of Bondage*. Johannesburg: Witwatersrand University Press, 1994.

Shelter, Jan Bender. *Telling Our Own Stories*. Leiden & Boston: Brill, 2003.

Shepard, D. S., and Scott B. Halstead. "Dengue Fever with Notes on Yellow Fever and Japanese Encephalitis." In *Disease Control Priorities in Developing Countries*, edited by Dean T. Jamison et al., 303-20. Oxford: Published for the World Bank by Oxford University Press, 1993.

Shillington, Kevin. *History of South Africa*. New York: St. Martin's Press, 1989.

Silla, Eric. *People Are Not the Same: Leprosy and Identity in Twentieth-Century Mali*. Portsmouth: Heinemann, 1998.

Sims, Lowery Stokes, and Leslie King Hammond. *The Global Africa Project*. New York: Presful Publications for the Museum of Arts and Design, 2010.

Singh, Anita. "Women, Conflict and Darfur-A Case Study, Critical Concepts in International Security." *Journal of Military and Strategic Studies* 9 (2007): 1-26.

Sirleaf, Ellen Johnson. *This Child Will Be Great*. New York: Harper, 2009.

Slaughter, Jane, Melissa K. Bokovoy, Patricia Risso, Ping Yao, and Patricia W. Romero. *Sharing the World Stage*, Vol 2. Boston: Houghton Mifflin Publishers, 2008.

Smith, Anthony. "The Missionary Contribution to Education in Tanganyika to 1914." *Tanzania Notes and Records* 60 (1963): 91-109.

Smith, Bonnie, G., ed. *The Encyclopedia of Women in World History*, 4 vols. New York: Oxford University Press, 2007.

Smith, David. "Mamphela Ramphele Launches Challenge of South Africa's ANC." http://theguardian.com/world/2013/feb/18. (Accessed September 13, 2013.)

Smith, Mary. *Baba of Karo*. New York: Yale University Press, 1981.

Snyder, M., and M. Tadesse. *African Women and Development*. London: Zed Books, 1995.

Smith, M. G. *Government in Zauzau*. Cambridge: Cambridge University Press, 1966.

Smith, M. Van Wyk. "The Most Wretched of the Human Race: The Iconography of the Khoikhoin (Hottentots) 1500-1800." *History and Anthropology* 5 (1992): 285-330.

Society for Women and AIDS in Africa. *Ghana Annual Conference*. August 2-3, 2011. http://swaagh.org. (Accessed July 2013.)

South African History Online. "The South African Founders of the Women's League." http://www.sahistory.org.za/. (Accessed January 10, 2013.)

Southall, Aidan, ed. *Social Change in Modern Africa*. London: Published for the International African Institute by Oxford University Press, London, 1961.

St. Clair, William. *The Door of No Return: The History of Cape Coast Castle and the Atlantic Slave Trade*. New York: BlueBridge, 2007.

Stanley, Liz. *Mourning Becomes*. Manchester: Manchester University Press, 2006.

Staunton, Irene, ed. *Mothers of the Revolution*. Harare: Baobob Books, 1990.

Sutter, Raymond. "Women in the ANC-Led Underground." In *Women in South African History*, edited by Nomboniso Gasa, 233-58. Cape Town: Human Sciences Research Council, 2007.

Sutter, Raymond, ed. *All My Life and All My Strength.* Newton (South Africa) Publishers: Party, Ltd., 2004.

Suzman, Helen. "Debates of the House of Assembly (Hansard): Fourth Session, Second Parliament, Republic of South Africa, 22nd January to 18th June, 1965." In *Central and South African History,* edited by Robert O. Collins, 233-39. Princeton, NJ: Markus Wiener Publishers, 1990.

Tashjian, Victoria, and Jean Allman. "Marrying and Marriage on a Shifting Terrain: Reconfigurations of Power and Authority in Early Colonial Asante." In *Women in Colonial African Histories,* edited by Jean Allman, Susan Geiger, and Nakanyike Musisi, 237-59. Bloomington: Indiana University Press, 2002.

Ten Rhyne, William. *The Account of the Cape of Good Hope and The Hottentots, The Natives of That Country.* Translated from Latin. Switzerland: Scaffhausen, 1673.

Tekab, Kebedech. Interview by Patricia Romero. Arlington, VA, May 16, 2005.

Tekab, Kebedech. "Creating an Ethiopian Narrative in America." Interview. http://ofnotemagazine.wordpress.com/2009/08/23/748/. (Accessed August 28, 2013.)

Teklemichael, Makda. "Contemporary Women Artists in Ethiopia." *African Arts* 42 (2009): 38-45.

The Economist, November 6, 2013.

The Guardian, June 14, 2012.

The New York Times, March 3, 1991.

The New York Times, February 13, 2013.

The New York Times, June 6, 2013.

The New York Times, June 7, 2013.

The New York Times, August 16, 2013.

The New York Times, January 21, 2014.

The Washington Post, July 25, 2008.

The Washington Post, July 29, 2012.

Thom, H. B., ed. *Journals of Jan van Riebeeck,* Vols. 2 and 3. Cape Town: Van Riebeeck Society, 1952.

Thompson, Leonard. *A History of South Africa.* New Haven, CT: Yale University Press, 1990.

Thornton, John K. "Legitimacy and Political Power: Queen Njinga, 1624-1663." *Journal of African History* 32 (1991): 23-40.

Tlali, Miriam. *Muriel at the Metropolitan.* London: Longman Group, 1987.

United Nations International Children's Emergency Fund. *Female Genital Mutilation/Cutting: A Statistical Overview and Exploration of the Dynamics of Change.* New York: UNICEF, July 2013. (Thanks to Bettina Shell-Duncan and Nicole Petrowski.)

Urdang, Stephanie. *Fighting Two Colonialisms: Women in Guinea-Bissau.* New York: Monthly Review Press, 1979.

Uwatse, Chinue. "What I Have to Say." http://www.africasource.com/house/indcx/php2options=com. (Accessed August 19, 2013.)

Uys, Ian. *Heidelbergers of the Boer War.* Cape Town: Privately printed, 1981.

Vaillant, Monsieur. *Travels from the Cape of Good Hope into the Interior Parts of Africa, I.* Translated from the French. London: William Lane, 1791.

Van Allen, Judith. "'Aba Riots' or Igbo 'Women's War'? Ideology, Stratification, and the Invisibility of Women." In *Women in Africa,* edited by Nancy J. Hafkin and Edna G. Bay, 59-86. Stanford: Stanford University Press, 1976.

Van Heyningen, Elizabeth. "Women and Gender in the South African War, 1899-1902." In

Women in South African History, edited by Nomboniso Gasa, 91-128. Cape Town: Human Sciences Research Council, 2007.

Van Onselen, Charles. *The Seed Is Mine.* Cape Town: David Philip Publishers, 1996.

Vansina, Jan. *Art History in Africa.* New York: Longman, 1984.

Vansina, Jan. *Being Colonized: The Kuba Experience in Rural Congo 1880-1960.* Madison: University of Wisconsin Press, 2010.

Vaughan, Megan. *Curing Their Ills: Colonial Power and African Illness.* Stanford: Stanford University Press, 1991.

Verlinden, Charles. "Blacks." In *Dictionary of the Middle Ages* t. 2, edited by Joseph R. Strager, 38-40. New York: Scribner, 1983.

Vigne, Randolph, ed. *A Gesture of Belonging: Letters from Bessie Head 1965-1979.* Portsmouth: Heinemann, 1991.

Vigne, Randolph, ed. *The South African Letters of Thomas Pringle.* Cape Town: Van Riebeeck Society, 2011.

Warwick, Peter. *Black People and the South African War, 1899-1902.* Cambridge: Cambridge University Press, 1983.

Wells, Julia C. "Eva's Men: Gender and Power in the Establishment of the Cape of Good Hope 1652-74." *Journal of African History* 39 (1998): 417-37.

Were, Beatrice. Human Rights Watch. "Human Rights Watch Honors Ugandan AIDS Activist." http://www.hrw.org/news/2005/10/26/human-rights-watch-honors-ugandan-aids-activist. (Accessed September 13, 2013.)

West, Harry G. "Girls with Guns: Narrating the Experience of Frelimos 'Female Detachment.'" *Anthropological Quarterly* 73 (2009): 180-94.

White, Luise. "Prostitution, Identity and Class Consciousness in Nairobi during WWII." *Signs* 11 (Winter 1986): 255-73.

Witches in Exile. Directed by Allison Berg. VHS. The Soros Documentary Fund for the Open Society and Others. New York: State Council for the Arts, 2003.

"Women Fighters in South Sudan." http://www.google.com/hostednews/afp/article/ALegM5j3UNgriAG-RIOkRAtlanNVsl&F8mw. (Accessed January 20, 2013.)

Worden, Nigel. *The Making of Modern South Africa.* 2d ed. Oxford: Blackwell, 1995.

World Health Organization. "Ambassador Dr. Gertrude Mongella." April 15, 2005. http://www.who.int/pmnch/about/champtions/speeches/mongella/en/index. (Accessed June 30, 2013.)

Zewde, Bahru. *A History of Modern Ethiopia 1855-1991.* Oxford: James Currey, 1991.

Zewde, Bahru. *Pioneers of Change in Ethiopia.* Oxford: James Currey, 2002.

Index

CPSIA information can be obtained at www.ICGtesting.com
Printed in the USA
BVOW05s2217080914

365835BV00001B/3/P